HUNGARY BETWEEN TWO EMPIRES 1526–1711

Top Left: Ferdinand I of Habsburg, Hungarian-Bohemian king (1526–1564), Holy Roman emperor (1558–1564). Unknown painter, after Jan Cornelis Vermeyen, circa 1530 (Hungarian National Museum, Budapest).

Top Right: Sultan Süleyman the Magnificent (1520–1566). Unknown painter, after Titian, sixteenth century (Hungarian National Museum, Budapest).

Left: The Habsburg siege of Buda, 1541. Woodcut by Erhardt Schön, 1541 (Hungarian National Museum, Budapest).

STUDIES IN HUNGARIAN HISTORY

László Borhi, *editor*

HUNGARY BETWEEN TWO EMPIRES
1526–1711

Géza Pálffy
Translated by David Robert Evans

INDIANA UNIVERSITY PRESS

This book is a publication of

Indiana University Press
Office of Scholarly Publishing
Herman B Wells Library 350
1320 East 10th Street
Bloomington, Indiana 47405 USA

iupress.org

This book was produced under the auspices of the Research Center for the Humanities of the Hungarian Academy of Sciences and with the support of the National Bank of Hungary.

© 2021 by Géza Pálffy

All rights reserved

No part of this book may be reproduced or utilized in any form or by any means, electronic or mechanical, including photocopying and recording, or by any information storage and retrieval system, without permission in writing from the publisher. The paper used in this publication meets the minimum requirements of the American National Standard for Information Sciences—Permanence of Paper for Printed Library Materials, ANSI Z39.48-1992.

Manufactured in the United States of America

Cataloging information is available from the Library of Congress.

ISBN 978-0-253-05463-0 (hardback)
ISBN 978-0-253-05465-4 (paperback)
ISBN 978-0-253-05464-7 (ebook)

First printing 2021

CONTENTS

List of Figures ix

List of Maps xi

List of Tables xiii

Acknowledgments xv

Note on Terms and Names xvii

List of Abbreviations xix

Political and Military Chronology, 1526–1711 xxiii

Introduction 1

I. Hungary after Mohács: A Century of Direction Seeking, 1526–1606

1. On the Frontier of Two Empires 7
2. Roads from Istanbul to Vienna: The Ottomans in Hungary 15
3. The Bumpy Road to Vienna: The Habsburgs and the Hungarians 29
4. The Road to Istanbul: The State of King John Szapolyai and His Son 43
5. On a Narrow Path: The Principality of Transylvania 53
6. Society Finds Its Way 61
7. The Economy and Its Roads to Europe 73
8. The Search for a New Home: Ethnic and Demographic Changes 83
9. Finding Faith: Hungary's New Religion 91
10. Seeking a Language: A Cultural Golden Age 101
11. Looking in Vain for a Way Out: The Long Turkish War, 1591–1606 113

II. Decay and Rejuvenation: The Janus-Faced Seventeenth Century, 1606–1711

1. Peace or Civil War on the Border of the Two Empires? *125*
2. New Ottoman Campaigns to Achieve an Old Goal *133*
3. The Rise of the Hungarian Estates and the Break with Vienna *143*
4. Transylvania Flourishes, Then Decays *155*
5. Militarization and Self-Administration: Changes in Society *167*
6. Economic Decline and Reorganization *177*
7. Hungarian Populations Fall—Other Ethnic Groups Rise *187*
8. The Revival of Catholicism—a Prolonged War of Religion *197*
9. Half a Century of Cultural Progress—Half a Century of Military Crisis *207*
10. A Country Liberated but Ravaged: The Long Turkish War, 1683–1699 *219*
11. Independence Movement and Civil War: The Rákóczi Uprising, 1703–1711 *231*

Glossary *241*

List of Rulers and Highest Dignitaries *247*

Select Bibliography (Monographs and Collected Studies) *253*

Names and Nationalities Index *273*

Place Index *279*

FIGURES

Frontispiece:

    Top Left: Ferdinand I of Habsburg, Hungarian-Bohemian king (1526–1564), Holy Roman emperor (1558–1564)

    Top Right: Sultan Süleyman the Magnificent (1520–1566)

    Left: The Habsburg siege of Buda, 1541

Chronology:

    Map of Hungary, after Wolfgang Lazius, 1579, *xxii*

1. Louis II of Jagiello, Hungarian-Bohemian king (1516–1526), *6*
2. The Battle of Mohács, August 29, 1526, *10*
3. Sultan Süleyman the Magnificent (1520–1566), *14*
4. The Ottoman siege of Szigetvár, 1566, *21*
5. Ferdinand I of Habsburg, Hungarian-Bohemian king (1526–1564), Holy Roman emperor (1558–1564), *28*
6. The administration of the Kingdom of Hungary in the last third of the sixteenth century, *33*
7. Pozsony (Pressburg; today Bratislava, Slovakia), the new capital of the Kingdom of Hungary in the sixteenth century, *37*
8. John I Szapolyai, king of Hungary (1526–1540), *42*
9. The Habsburg siege of Buda, 1541, *47*
10. Stephen Báthory, prince of Transylvania (1571–1586), king of Poland (1576–1586), *52*
11. Thaler of Sigismund Báthory, prince of Transylvania, with his portrait and family coat of arms, 1589, *58*
12. Humanist Johannes Sambucus (1531–1584), *60*
13. General Lazarus von Schwendi, border fortress captain György Thury, and Emperor Maximilian II, *67*
14. Figure of Sebestyén Thököly (died 1607), from his charters of ennoblement in 1572, *72*
15. The fortress city of Győr in the sixteenth century, *80*
16. Miklós Zrínyi / Nikola Zrinski (1508–1566), *82*
17. The Kostajnica border fortress on the river Una, *87*
18. István Kis Szegedi (1505–1572), one of the leaders of Hungarian Protestantism, *90*
19. Front page of the Vizsoly Bible, the first complete Bible translation into Hungarian, 1590, *95*
20. Poet Bálint Balassi (1554–1594), *100*

21. Front page of the New Testament as translated by János Sylvester, the first book to be published in Hungary in Hungarian; Sárvár, 1541, *104*
22. Stephen Bocskai, prince of Transylvania and Hungary (1605–1606), *112*
23. The Ottoman siege of Kanizsa, 1600, *117*
24. Matthias of Habsburg, Holy Roman emperor (1612–1619), *124*
25. Ottoman-Hungarian duel in the seventeenth century, *127*
26. Grand Vizier Kara Mustafa (1676–1683), *132*
27. The second Ottoman siege of Vienna, 1683, *138*
28. Miklós Esterházy, palatine of Hungary (1625–1645), *142*
29. The Hungarian coronation of Leopold I in Pozsony on June 27, 1655, *149*
30. Gabriel Bethlen, prince of Transylvania (1613–1629), *154*
31. The city of Kolozsvár in the seventeenth century, *160*
32. Imre Thököly, prince of Hungary (1682–1685), *166*
33. A Hungarian noble and noblewoman in the seventeenth century, *171*
34. Austrian cameralist Johann Joachim Becher (1635–1682), *176*
35. Hungarian soldiers in front of Léka Castle (today Lockenhaus, Austria), *179*
36. Romanian peasants, *186*
37. Ottoman Buda in the seventeenth century, *192*
38. Péter Pázmány, archbishop of Esztergom (1616–1637), one of the leaders of the Catholic revival in Hungary, *196*
39. Front page of the first complete Catholic translation of the Bible into Hungarian by György Káldi, Vienna, 1626, *200*
40. General, politician, and poet Miklós Zrínyi / Nikola Zrinski (1620–1664), *206*
41. Front page of the *Mausoleum* of Hungarian kings by Ferenc Nádasdy, Nuremberg, 1664, *214*
42. Charles of Lorraine (1643–1690), *218*
43. The siege of Buda, 1686, *222*
44. Francis II Rákóczi, leader of the first Hungarian war of independence (1703–1711), *230*
45. Front page of the first Hungarian newspaper, the anti-Habsburg *Mercurius Veridicus ex Hungaria*, January 1710, *238*

MAPS

1. The growth of the Ottoman Empire (sixteenth–seventeenth centuries), *8*
2. Europe, circa 1520, *12*
3. Ottoman campaigns in Hungary, 1521–1552, *16*
4. Ottoman campaigns in Hungary, 1553–1590, *20*
5. The border defense system in Hungary against the Ottomans (after 1580), *23*
6. The composite monarchy of the Habsburgs in Central Europe in the second half of the sixteenth century, *30*
7. Development of the Principality of Transylvania between 1541 and 1570, *49*
8. Foreign trade in the Carpathian Basin in the second half of the sixteenth century, *75*
9. The Long Turkish War, 1591–1606, and the Bocskai uprising, 1604–1606, *114*
10. The campaigns of the princes of Transylvania in Hungary, 1619–1645, *129*
11. The Turkish war in Hungary and Transylvania, 1658–1664, *134*
12. Hungary in four parts, 1682–1685, *163*
13. Administration in the mid-seventeenth century, *173*
14. The Long Turkish War, 1683–1699, *220*
15. The war of independence of Francis Rákóczi, 1703–1711, *233*

TABLES

1. Change of court and loss of position in the decades after Mohács: the key characteristics of the late medieval court in Buda and the common Habsburg court, 33
2. Key characteristics of the institutions of the late medieval and the early modern Kingdom of Hungary, 36
3. The annual costs of the border defense system against the Ottomans stretching from the Adriatic to Transylvania, and the income of Hungary and of the Habsburg Monarchy in the 1570s and 1580s, 38

In loving memory of Katalin Péter
(1937–2020)

ACKNOWLEDGMENTS

This work is the fusion of my own research over the last quarter of a century in various archives in Central Europe, on the one hand, and, on the other hand, of the findings of the most important new research from Hungarian and international historiography—from Oxford to Vienna and Budapest to Cluj-Napoca. I do not have the space to list the many dozen American, Canadian, British, French, Dutch, Belgian, Spanish, German, Austrian, Czech, Slovak, Croatian, Slovenian, Romanian, Polish, Turkish, Russian, and Hungarian historians and archivists who supported my work and with whom I could do so much thinking about the history of early modern Hungary and of the Habsburg Monarchy and the Ottoman Empire. So I would express my heartfelt thanks to all of them at once. I would, however, like to thank Professor Pál Fodor, director general of the Research Center for the Humanities, without whose persistent encouragement I would not have completed this task. I am also indebted to David Robert Evans for his excellent and constructive work on the translation of the book. Most of all, I would like to thank my wife, Magdolna, for tranquil family surroundings and support at so many levels, providing the ideal opportunity for creative work even in the hubbub of today's world.

Budapest,
January 2020

NOTE ON TERMS AND NAMES

At the first occurrence of major Hungarian positions or ranks and after their English translations, I provide in parentheses their Latin or German versions as well as their Hungarian ones to assist the reader as fully as possible. A glossary of specialist (Hungarian, German, Latin, Ottoman, etc.) terms is also provided at the end of the book. For people's names, I use the original Hungarian name and order, except, of course, for rulers. As regards the latter (German emperors, Ottoman sultans, Hungarian kings, and Transylvanian princes), as well as the most important Hungarian and Croatian dignitaries (royal governor, palatine, chief justice, ban, and archbishop of Esztergom, etc.), the reader is pointed toward the list of rulers and highest dignitaries at the end of the volume.

As regards place names, and despite the considerable border alterations of the twentieth century, I use not the present designations but rather the historical ones (Hungarian, German, Croatian, and so on). To do otherwise would lead to ahistorical and anachronistic usage. So, for example, I do not write Bratislava for Pozsony (Pressburg) or Cluj-Napoca for Kolozsvár (Klausenburg), as these names did not exist before the twentieth century. Likewise, I never refer to the Hungarian royal capital (Buda) as Budapest, which was established only in 1873. Of course, if a Central European place name has an agreed English form, as is true for Vienna or Nuremberg, then of course this is used.

Finally, following Robert J. W. Evans's 1979 classic work, *The Making of the Habsburg Monarchy 1550–1700*, I refer to the Central European composite state of the Austrian branch of the Habsburg dynasty as the Habsburg Monarchy, and I use the term *Habsburg Empire* only for the enormous conglomeration of states of Emperor Charles V. In this way the German, Holy Roman, or Old Empire can clearly be distinguished from the Habsburg Monarchy, made up as it was of German, Austrian, Hungarian, and Bohemian lands.

Assistance with the more precise identification of place names is given in a detailed gazetteer at my home page: https://tti.academia.edu/G%C3%A9zaP%C3%A1lffy/Books.

ABBREVIATIONS

AEP	Academic Electronic Press (Bratislava)
BFL	Budapest Főváros Levéltára [Archives of Capital City Budapest] (Budapest)
BHM	Budapest Historical Museum (Budapest)
BTK TTI	Bölcsészettudományi Kutatóközpont, Történettudományi Intézet [Research Center for the Humanities, Institute of History] (Budapest)
CEU	Central European University (Budapest)
Columbia UP	Columbia University Press (New York)
DE	Debreceni Egyetem [University of Debrecen] (Debrecen)
ELTE	Eötvös Loránd Tudományegyetemen [Loránd Eötvös University] (Budapest)
ELTE BTK	Eötvös Loránd Tudományegyetemen, Bölcsészettudományi Kar [Loránd Eötvös University, Philological Faculty] (Budapest)
EME	Erdélyi-Múzeum Egyesület [Transylvanian Museum Society] (Kolozsvár/Cluj-Napoca)
EOM	Evangélikus Országos Múzeum [Lutheran National Museum] (Budapest)
GyVL	Győr Város Levéltára [Győr City Archives] (Győr)
HAS	Hungarian Academy of Sciences (Budapest)
HNM	Hungarian National Museum (Budapest)
HÚ SAV	Historický ústav Slovenskej akadémie vied [Institute of History of the Slovak Academy of Sciences] (Bratislava)
ISP	Hrvatski institut za povijest [Croatian Institute of History] (Zagreb)
JATE	József Attila Tudományegyetem [Attila József University] (Szeged)
JU HÚ	Jihočeská univerzita v Českých Budějovicích, Historický ústav [Institute of History of the South-Czech University in České Budějovice] (České Budějovice)
KGRE	Károli Gáspár Református Egyetem [Gáspár Károli Calvinist University] (Budapest)
KLTE	Kossuth Lajos Tudományegyetem [Lajos Kossuth University] (Debrecen)
KSH	Központi Statisztikai Hivatal [Hungarian Central Statistical Office] (Budapest)
METEM	Magyar Egyháztörténeti Enciklopédia Munkaközösség [Society for Encyclopedia of Church History of Hungary] (Budapest–Pannonhalma–Szeged)
MNG	Magyar Nemzeti Galéria [Hungarian National Gallery] (Budapest)
MNL	Magyar Nemzeti Levéltár [Hungarian National Archives] (Budapest)
MNL OL	Magyar Nemzeti Levéltár Országos Levéltára [Hungarian National Archives, State Archives] (Budapest)
MOL	Magyar Országos Levéltár [Hungarian State Archives] (Budapest)
MTA	Magyar Tudományos Akadémia [Hungarian Academy of Sciences] (Budapest)

MTA BTK	Magyar Tudományos Akadémia, Bölcsészettudományi Kutatóközpont [Hungarian Academy of Sciences, Research Center for the Humanities] (Budapest)
MTA BTK TTI	Magyar Tudományos Akadémia, Bölcsészettudományi Kutatóközpont, Történettudományi Intézet [Hungarian Academy of Sciences, Research Center for the Humanities, Institute of History] (Budapest)
MTA ITI	Magyar Tudományos Akadémia, Irodalomtudományi Intézet [Hungarian Academy of Sciences, Institute of Literature] (Budapest)
MTA TTI	Magyar Tudományos Akadémia, Történettudományi Intézet [Hungarian Academy of Sciences, Institute of History] (Budapest)
MTT	Magyar Történelmi Társulat [Hungarian Historical Society] (Budapest)
ÖStA	Österreichisches Staatsarchiv (Vienna)
OSZK	Országos Széchényi Könyvtár [Széchényi National Library] (Budapest)
Oxford UP	Oxford University Press (Oxford)
PPKE	Pázmány Péter Katolikus Egyetem [Péter Pázmány Catholic University] (Budapest–Piliscsaba)
PUF	Presses universitaires de France (Paris)
RCH	Research Center for the Humanities (Budapest)
SZIT	Szent István Társulat [Saint Stephen Society] (Budapest)
VML	Vas Megyei Levéltár [Archives of Vas County] (Szombathely)
VÖAW	Verlag der Österreichischen Akademie der Wissenschaften (Vienna)
VPU	Vydavateľstvo Prešovskej univerzity [Publisher of Prešov University] (Prešov)
VSAV	Vydavateľstvo Slovenskej akadémia vied [Publisher of the Slovak Academy of Sciences] (Bratislava)
VWGÖ	Verband der wissenschaftlichen Gesellschaften Österreichs (Vienna)

Map of Hungary, after Wolfgang Lazius, 1579. Engraving by Franz Hogenberg (Hungarian National Museum, Budapest).

POLITICAL AND MILITARY CHRONOLOGY, 1526–1711

August 29, 1526: The Battle of Mohács; the death of Louis II of Jagiello, Hungarian-Bohemian king.

November 10, 1526: István Podmaniczky, bishop of Nyitra and the country's most senior prelate, crowns John I Szapolyai king of Hungary with the Holy Crown at the Hungarian diet of Székesfehérvár; his rule lasts until his death in 1540.

December 16, 1526: The Pozsony diet elects Ferdinand of Habsburg, king of Bohemia and archduke of Austria, to be king of Hungary.

November 3, 1527: After his successful military campaign in Hungary, Ferdinand is crowned king of Hungary by István Podmaniczky, bishop of Nyitra and the country's most senior prelate, also at Székesfehérvár and also with the Holy Crown; he rules until his death in 1564.

January 8, 1528: Ferdinand I establishes his first new Hungarian government body, the Hungarian Chamber, which, on account of the Ottoman campaign of 1529, fled and continued its operation in Pozsony from 1531.

February 28, 1528: King John I signs a treaty with Süleyman the Magnificent in Istanbul, becoming his vassal. The sultan recognizes Szapolyai as king of Hungary and promises him his assistance.

March 8, 1528: After the defeat at the Battle of Szina (Abaúj county), John Szapolyai flees to Tarnów, Poland; his forced exile lasts until November.

September 26–October 15, 1529: The troops of Sultan Süleyman unsuccessfully lay siege to Vienna.

February 1530: John Szapolyai's diet at Buda appoints Lodovico Gritti, confidant to the sultan and treasurer to King John, as governor.

April 25–August 31, 1532: A new Ottoman campaign against Vienna. Led by Miklós Jurisics, the small castle of Kőszeg (Güns)—as well as the considerable army of Emperor Charles V and Ferdinand I stationed at Wiener Neustadt—forced the Ottomans to retreat.

1533: In Krakow, Benedek Komjáti publishes the Hungarian translation of the Epistles of Saint Paul; this is the first printed book in Hungarian.

August 11, 1534: Lodovico Gritti arrives in Transylvania, where he has Imre Czibak, who is discontented with his governorship, killed; in response, on September 29 in Medgyes, the Transylvanian nobles dismembered the Venetian-born governor, along with his entourage.

September 1, 1537: Hans Katzianer, commander in chief to Ferdinand I, instigates a campaign against the Ottomans to retake Eszék, on the Drava; on October 9 he suffers a terrible defeat at Gorjani (Hungarian *Gara*).

February 24, 1538: The Treaty of Várad—a secret agreement is signed at Várad between Ferdinand I and John I.

March 2, 1539: John I takes Isabella, daughter of Sigismund I of Jagiello, king of Poland (1506–1548), to be his wife.

July 7, 1540: Queen Isabella gives John I a son, John Sigismund.

July 21 or 22, 1540: John Szapolyai's death; his successor is the baby John Sigismund (1540–1571), who is elected king on September 13 by the diet of Rákos, near Pest.

August 29, 1541: On the fifteenth anniversary of the Battle of Mohács, the Ottomans lay siege to Buda in underhand fashion. With her one-year-old son, John Sigismund, Queen Isabella moves to Transylvania.

December 29, 1541: In Gyalu Castle, Transylvania, Friar George Martinuzzi signs an agreement with envoys of Ferdinand I on passing Transylvania into Habsburg hands.

1541: In Sárvár, Benedek Abádi publishes the first book to be published in Hungary in Hungarian, the New Testament as translated by János Sylvester.

1542–1551: George Martinuzzi is governor during John Sigismund's childhood.

September–October 1542: With troops kept with Holy Roman imperial aid, Ferdinand I tries to retake Buda after it has been lost, but to no avail.

1543–1544: The Ottomans broaden the territory of the vilayet of Buda by occupying first Siklós, Pécs, Esztergom, Tata, and Székesfehérvár, then Visegrád, Vác, Hatvan, and Nógrád. Pál Várday, archbishop of Esztergom, and his chapter flee to Nagyszombat (today Trnava, Slovakia); the archbishopric would remain there right up to the eighteenth century.

June 19, 1547: The Ottoman Empire and the Habsburgs sign a peace treaty for five years in Edirne.

September 8, 1549: Representing Queen Isabella, George Martinuzzi signs the Treaty of Nyírbátor with Ferdinand I on the transfer of Transylvania to the Habsburgs.

December 17, 1551: The soldiers of General Gianbattista Castaldo kill George Martinuzzi in Transylvania.

June–October 1552: Another Ottoman campaign against Hungary begins, led by second vizier Kara Ahmed, in the course of which the area of the Maros, Temes, and Tisza Rivers falls under Ottoman control; of the larger fortresses, Temesvár, Lippa, and Szolnok are lost.

September 9–October 18, 1552: Led by Captain István Dobó, the defenders of Eger fortress stop the besieging forces of Kara Ahmed and Hadim Ali, pasha of Buda.

March 1554: The Pozsony diet elects Tamás Nádasdy as palatine; he remains in this office until his death in 1562.

September 1554: The fortress of Fülek falls, becoming the Ottomans' northernmost administrative center in Hungary.

July 15, 1556: With the siege of Babócsa Castle, Szigetvár, under siege from the Ottomans, is liberated by the forces of Archduke Ferdinand of Tyrol, chief military commissioner Sforza Pallavicini, and palatine Tamás Nádasdy.

October 22, 1556: Queen Isabella and John Sigismund, who left Transylvania in 1552, make a triumphant entrance into Kolozsvár after their return from Poland.

November 1556: The Transylvanian estate assembly in Kolozsvár swears allegiance to Queen Isabella and to king-elect John Sigismund.

November 17, 1556: In Vienna, Ferdinand I creates the Aulic War Council to organize the defense system against the Ottomans and to direct military affairs.

March 14, 1558: At the imperial diet in Frankfurt, Ferdinand I becomes ruler of the Holy Roman Empire; he rules until his death in 1564.

September 15, 1559: Queen Isabella dies; John Sigismund, who was elected king at birth (1540), becomes prince of Transylvania (1559–1571).

September 25, 1562: Ferdinand I appoints Miklós Oláh, archbishop of Esztergom, to be royal governor; he remains in this office until his death in 1568.

September 8, 1563: Archduke Maximilian, king of Bohemia, is crowned king of Hungary in Pozsony within his father's lifetime—the first coronation of a ruler in the city.

July 25, 1564: Ferdinand I dies. He is succeeded by Emperor Maximilian II; as king of Hungary, he is Maximilian I. He rules until 1576.

August–September 1566: The country's two key fortresses, Szigetvár (after the demise of Sultan Süleyman and the heroic death of Miklós Zrínyi / Nikola Zrinski) and Gyula, fall into Ottoman hands.

April 1, 1567: The Szepes Chamber, with jurisdiction over Upper Hungary, is founded in Kassa.

February 17, 1568: After negotiations conducted in Edirne and Istanbul, Emperor Maximilian II and Sultan Selim II sign a peace treaty valid for eight years; this ends the period of the fortress wars that began in 1541.

August 16, 1570: Emperor Maximilian II and prince of Transylvania John Sigismund sign the Treaty of Speyer.

May 25, 1571: The diet of Gyulafehérvár elects Stephen Báthory of Somlyó as prince of Transylvania; he rules until 1586.

September 25, 1572: At the diet of Pozsony, Archduke Rudolf is crowned heir to the Hungarian throne.

July 8, 1575: At the Battle of Kerelőszentpál (Küküllő county), Stephen Báthory is victorious against the forces of Gáspár Bekes, a pretender to the throne who is supported by the Habsburgs.

Summer 1575: Despite the peace, the Ottomans occupy the castle of Fonyód by Lake Balaton in Transdanubia and those of Kékkő, Divény, and Somoskő in the frontier region defending the mining towns. With this occupation, the Ottoman conquest reaches its farthest point in Hungary in a northerly direction.

December 14, 1575: At the diet of Krakow, the Polish estates elect Stephen Báthory king of Poland; his coronation is on May 1, 1576, in Krakow. He rules until his death in 1586.

October 12, 1576: King of Hungary Maximilian I dies. His successor is Emperor Rudolf II, who as king of Hungary is Rudolf I; he rules Hungary until 1608.

1583: The court of the Habsburg Monarchy is relocated from Vienna to Prague.

December 13, 1586: Stephen Báthory dies in Grodno, Poland; in Transylvania, his successor is Sigismund Báthory, and on the Polish throne, it is the Swedish-born Sigismund (III) Wasa (1587–1632).

1590: The Vizsoly Bible, the first complete Bible translation by Protestant pastor Gáspár Károli of Gönc, is published.

1591–1606: The Long Turkish War between the Habsburg Monarchy and the Ottoman Empire. Initially confined to the Croatian-Slavonian borderlands, the war is broadened by the attacks of Hasan Pasha, beylerbey of Bosnia.

April 1592: The Ottomans occupy Bihać, the key to the Croatian frontier region.

June 22, 1593: A crucial Habsburg victory at Sziszek (Croatian *Sisak*) over Hasan, pasha of Bosnia, who lay siege to the fortress.

October 1593: Grand Vizier Sinan occupies Veszprém (October 6) and Várpalota (October 10); with this, the war spreads to the whole of Hungary.

November 1593–March 1594: Under the leadership of Miklós Pálffy and Christoph von Teuffenbach, the royal forces secure victories in Pákozd, Transdanubia (November 3), and in Romhány in the north (November 11), then retake the fortresses of Divény, Fülek, Szécsény, Buják, Somoskő, Hollókő, Drégely, and Ajnácskő (November–December 1593), then that of Nógrád (March 1594).

May–June 1594: Led by Archduke Matthias, the Habsburg forces besiege Ottoman Esztergom, but without success; the poet Bálint Balassi dies a hero's death during the siege (May 30).

July–September 1594: Grand Vizier Sinan occupies first Tata (July 13) and then, after a long siege, Győr (September 29); the whole of northern Transdanubia comes under Ottoman control.

October 29, 1595: Transylvanian and Wallachian troops defeat Grand Vizier Sinan at Giurgiu on the Danube in Wallachia.

September 20–October 13, 1596: Sultan Mehmed III occupies Eger fortress.

October 26–28, 1596: At the Battle of Mezőkeresztes, Mehmed III succeeds in defeating the forces led by Archduke Maximilian.

March 29, 1598: With a surprise maneuver, the troops of Adolf of Schwarzenberg and Miklós Pálffy retake Győr.

November 3, 1599: After suffering defeat at Sellenberk at the hands of Michael the Brave, voivode of Wallachia, Andrew Báthory, the new prince of Transylvania, is killed as he tries to flee. Voivode Michael's rule over Transylvania begins.

September 10, 1600: Giorgio Basta, captain general of Upper Hungary, enters Transylvania with his forces.

September 18, 1600: The Battle of Miriszló (Fehér county)—the imperial-royal and Transylvanian forces defeat those of voivode Michael the Brave.

October 20, 1600: The Ottomans take Kanizsa fortress.

August 3, 1601: The Battle of Goroszló (Kraszna county)—the combined forces of Giorgio Basta and Michael the Brave defeat the troops of Sigismund Báthory.

August 19, 1601: Giorgio Basta has Michael the Brave killed.

September 9–20, 1601: The imperial and royal army recaptures Székesfehérvár, which had fallen in 1543; on August 29, 1602, however, the Ottomans retake it again.

January 20, 1602: Emperor Rudolf II appoints General Basta to be governor of Transylvania; he remains in this office until 1604.

July 17, 1603: Near Brassó, the voivode of Wallachia, Radu Şerban, easily defeats the army of the new prince of Transylvania, Moses Székely, who himself falls in the battle.

January 6, 1604: The troops of Giacomo Barbiano Belgiojoso, captain general of Upper Hungary, forcibly occupy the Lutheran church (the former Church of Saint Elisabeth) in Kassa and hand it over to the Catholics.

October 15, 1604: The hajduk soldiers of Stephen Bocskai defeat a considerable royal detachment at Álmosd (Bihar county).

November 1604: Bocskai's defeats at Osgyán (November 17) then at Edelény (November 25–28) at the hands of General Basta's troops.

February 21, 1605: At the Transylvanian diet of Marosszereda, the Szeklers and the gentry of the noble counties elect Stephen Bocskai as prince; he is officially inaugurated at the diet of Medgyes on September 14.

April 20, 1605: At the diet of Szerencs, the insurgent Hungarian estates elect Bocskai as prince of Hungary.

November 11, 1605: In the fields by Rákos, near Pest, Grand Vizier Lala Mehmed hands Stephen Bocskai the sultan's *ahdname* that makes him king of Hungary and places on his head the Ottoman crown brought from Istanbul.

December 12, 1605: Stephen Bocskai settles almost ten thousand hajduks in Szabolcs county.

June 23, 1606: The Treaty of Vienna between Prince Stephen Bocskai and Hungarian king Rudolf I (as Emperor Rudolf II).

November 11, 1606: The Treaty of Zsitvatorok is signed between the Habsburg Monarchy and the Ottoman Empire with Bocskai's mediation.

December 29, 1606: Stephen Bocskai, prince of Transylvania, dies in Kassa; his successors are Sigismund Rákóczi in 1607–1608 and Gabriel Báthory in 1608–1613.

June 25, 1608: In the Treaty of Libeň, Emperor Rudolf II, while keeping the imperial title and Bohemia, relinquishes the throne of Hungary (and the Holy Crown) and the Austrian hereditary lands to Archduke Matthias of Habsburg.

September 9–November 19, 1608: At the diet of Pozsony, Matthias II is crowned (he rules until 1619), while István Illésházy is elected to the office of palatine that has been unoccupied since 1562. The first compromise between Vienna and the estates in the seventeenth century.

October 23, 1613: The diet convened at Kolozsvár elects Gabriel Bethlen, who enjoys the support of the Ottoman forces, as prince of Transylvania.

October 27, 1613: Prince Gabriel Báthory is murdered in Várad.

June 1616: In return for the Ottomans' help in bringing him to power, Gabriel Bethlen relinquishes the fortress of Lippa to them.

September 28, 1616: King Matthias II appoints Jesuit Péter Pázmány as archbishop of Esztergom; he remains in this office until his death in 1637.

May 1618: The uprising of the Bohemian estates in Prague marks the onset of the Thirty Years' War (1618–1648).

March 20, 1619: King Matthias II dies, and Ferdinand II of Habsburg ascends to the throne; he rules until 1637.

September–October 1619: Together with his army, Gabriel Bethlen joins the anti-Habsburg uprising of the Bohemian estates and begins a military campaign in Hungary. He occupies Kassa, Érsekújvár, and Pozsony; the northern areas of the kingdom come into his hands.

January 8, 1620: Prince Gabriel Bethlen rejects the title of king of Hungary as offered to him by the diet of Pozsony controlled by him.

August 25, 1620: The diet of Besztercebánya elects Bethlen as king, but he does not have himself crowned, even though the Holy Crown is in his possession after he took Pozsony in October 1619.

December 31, 1621: The Peace of Nikolsburg is signed between Ferdinand II and Gabriel Bethlen.

July–August 1622: The diet of Sopron—the second compromise of the seventeenth century between Vienna and the Hungarian estates.

August–November 1623: Prince Gabriel Bethlen's second campaign in Hungary against the Habsburgs.

May 8, 1624: The Treaty of Vienna is signed by Ferdinand II and Gabriel Bethlen; the Treaty of Nikolsburg is renewed.

October 25, 1625: Miklós Esterházy is elected palatine at the diet of Sopron; he remains in the office until his death in 1645.

August–October 1626: Prince Gabriel Bethlen's third anti-Habsburg campaign occurs in Hungary—the troops of Albrecht von Wallenstein and of Bethlen mutually avoid a decisive confrontation.

1626: The first complete Catholic translation of the Bible into Hungarian is published in Vienna; it is the work of Jesuit György Káldi.

November 15, 1629: Gabriel Bethlen dies in Gyulafehérvár; his successor is Catherine of Brandenburg until 1630, followed by George I Rákóczi (1630–1648).

1629–1637: Construction of the Jesuit church in Nagyszombat, marking the beginning of the Baroque in Hungary.

July–October 1631: Peasant uprisings occur in Gömör, Borsod, Abaúj, and Torna counties, led by Péter Császár; after he is captured and charged, he is executed in Kassa on March 4, 1632.

May 12, 1635: Péter Pázmány, archbishop of Esztergom, founds a university in Nagyszombat.

February 15, 1637: Ferdinand II dies; his successor is King Ferdinand III of Habsburg, who rules until 1657, thereby outliving Ferdinand IV, who is crowned in Pozsony on June 16, 1647, but dies in 1654.

March–April 1644: George I Rákóczi's first anti-Habsburg campaign in Hungary; he occupies Kassa (March 12) and Upper Hungary, then advances as far as the Vág valley. By October, however, he is squeezed back into the northeastern part of the country.

May 28, 1645: George I Rákóczi's second campaign against Ferdinand III in Hungary; his troops take Nagyszombat.

July 18, 1645: The Transylvanian prince's forces unite with the Swedish below Brünn.

December 16, 1645: Ferdinand III and George I Rákóczi sign the Treaty of Linz.

September 1646–June 1647: The diet of Pozsony. The third compromise of the seventeenth century between Vienna and the Hungarian estates.

October 11, 1648: George I Rákóczi dies at Gyulafehérvár; he is succeeded by his elder son, George II Rákóczi (1648–1660).

March 24, 1649: At the diet of Pozsony, Pál Pálffy is elected palatine; he remains in this office until his death in 1653.

January 6, 1657: Without gaining permission from the Ottoman Porte, Prince George II Rákóczi begins an attack on Poland; after its successes in the spring and summer, the entire Transylvanian army is now held captive by the Crimean Tatars.

May–October 1658: The campaign of Grand Vizier Köprülü Mehmed Pasha against Transylvania to punish George Rákóczi. Transylvania is utterly devastated. As of September 14, Ákos Barcsay is the new prince (1658–1660).

November 1659: Seydi Ahmed, pasha of Buda, repeatedly defeats the army of George II Rákóczi.

1659: Civil war between princes George II Rákóczi and Ákos Barcsay in Transylvania.

May 22, 1660: Seydi Ahmed, pasha of Buda, defeats George II Rákóczi at Szászfenes (Kolozs county); the injured prince dies of his wounds in Várad on June 7.

August 27, 1660: After a prolonged siege, the army of Serdar Köse Ali Pasha captures Várad, the gateway to the Principality of Transylvania.

January 1, 1661: The Transylvanian diet of Szászrégen elects John Kemény as prince; he rules until 1662. Meanwhile, in July, he has his rival, Ákos Barcsay, assassinated.

June 1661: Miklós Zrínyi, Croatian-Slavonian ban, begins the construction of the fortress of New Zrínyi Castle in Ottoman territory, near Kanizsa, provoking an outcry from the Ottoman Porte.

June–September 1661: General Raimondo Montecuccoli's unsuccessful campaign into Transylvania. Meanwhile, the diet of Marosvásárhely, under the military auspices of Serdar Köse Ali Pasha, elects Michael Apafi as prince; he rules until 1690.

January 22, 1662: John Kemény falls at Nagyszőllős in the battle against Küçük Mehmed, beylerbey of Temesvár and Jenő, who arrived to offer support to Michael Apafi.

September 25, 1663: Following their victory at Párkány, on the Danube (August 7), the forces of Grand Vizier Köprülü Ahmed take Érsekújvár, which will be the Ottomans' last new administrative center for a vilayet in Hungary.

January–February 1664: The winter campaign of Ban Miklós Zrínyi and Julius Wolfgang Count of Hohenlohe generates a significant diversion in Ottoman Hungary; its greatest achievement is the burning of the bridge at Eszék, on the Drava (February 2).

May–August 1664: The campaign of Grand Vizier Köprülü Ahmed into Hungary. He liberates Kanizsa, which was besieged by the Habsburg side, and he occupies and then destroys the New Zrínyi Castle. In the Battle of Szentgotthárd–Mogersdorf (August 1), however, he is defeated by the allied forces led by Raimondo Montecuccoli.

August 10, 1664: The Treaty of Vasvár (Vas county) between the Ottoman Empire and the Habsburg Monarchy.

1664: The *Mausoleum* of Hungarian kings is published in Nuremberg, paid for by Ferenc Nádasdy.

August 27, 1666: Palatine Ferenc Wesselényi sends envoys from his castle at Murány to the Porte—in return for guarantees of estate privileges and the free election of kings, he is willing to accept the authority of the sultan.

April–September 1670: The leaders of the so-called Wesselényi movement (conspiracy) are taken into custody; a considerable imperial and royal army is marched into Upper Hungary. In Pozsony, a special court is established to hear the cases of those suspected of participation in the uprising.

April 30, 1671: Condemned to decapitation and forfeiture, Péter Zrínyi / Petar Zrinski and Ferenc Kristóf Frangepán / Franjo Krsto Frankopan are executed in Wiener Neustadt, Ferenc Nádasdy in Vienna, and Ferenc Bónis in Pozsony.

1672: The movement made up of the *bujdosók* (exiles) who fled from Upper Hungary to Transylvania and the Partium is established.

February 27, 1673: Leopold I creates a six-member council of governors (Gubernium) to lead Hungary.

April 4, 1674: An exceptional court in Pozsony sentences almost four hundred Protestant preachers and teachers; finally, in March 1675, more than forty ministers who never renounce their faith are sold in Naples and Buccari as galley slaves.

February–May 1676: Netherlandish admiral Michiel de Ruyter (February 12) and John George II, elector of Saxony (May 2), buy the freedom of the Hungarian galley slave priests sold in Naples and Buccari.

1678: Led by Imre Thököly, the troops of the *bujdosók* occupy Upper Hungary; on November 1, however, they are defeated at Barsszentkereszt.

Summer 1680: Thököly's forces make raids into the Vág valley and break into Moravia.

April–December 1681: Leopold I comes to agreement with the Hungarian estates at the diet of Sopron—they disband the Gubernium and strengthen estate privileges. On June 13, the diet elects Pál Esterházy as palatine; he remains in the office until his death in 1713. This is the fourth compromise between Vienna and the Hungarian estates in the seventeenth century.

August–September 1682: The forces of Imre Thököly capture Kassa (August 14), then Fülek (September 10); this is where, on September 16, the pasha of Buda appoints Thököly to be ruler of Hungary. With this, Hungary breaks into four parts, establishing Thököly's principality in northern Hungary.

March–October 1683: Grand Vizier Kara Mustafa's unsuccessful campaign to occupy Vienna. An allied victory occurs on September 12 at Kahlenberg, near Vienna, as Charles of Lorraine and John III Sobieski, king of Poland, defeat the besieging forces.

October 27, 1683: Esztergom falls into anti-Ottoman hands.

March 1684: Nurtured by Pope Innocent XI, the Holy Alliance, the anti-Ottoman diplomatic coalition, is formed. Its members are the Habsburg Monarchy, Poland, Venice, and, from 1686, Russia.

July 7–August 19, 1685: Érsekújvár is retaken from the Ottomans.

September–October 1685: The advancing Habsburg troops liquidate Imre Thököly's principality in northern Hungary; Thököly is taken prisoner by the pasha of Várad.

June 18–September 2, 1686: Buda is recaptured.

August 12, 1687: Significant allied victory at Nagyharsány, at the so-called second Battle of Mohács, over the forces of Grand Vizier Süleyman.

October 27, 1687: Agreement at Balázsfalva between commander in chief Charles of Lorraine and prince of Transylvania Michael I Apafi.

December 1687: Eger fortress is liberated; at the diet of Pozsony, the Hungarian estates relinquish the right to the free election of kings.

1687: The blood-soaked executive court of General Antonio Caraffa at Eperjes.

May 9–10, 1688: The Treaty of Fogaras between Antonio Caraffa and prince of Transylvania Michael I Apafi.

1688: Székesfehérvár (May 19) and Belgrade (September 6) fall into allied hands; in the Rhine region, however, Louis XIV attacks the strengthening Habsburg Monarchy.

October 16, 1690: Leopold I passes the so-called *Diploma Leopoldinum*, regulating the situation in Transylvania; after some smaller amendments, its final publication is on December 4, 1691.

1690: Kanizsa is liberated from Turkish rule (April 13); meanwhile, Belgrade is retaken by the Ottomans (October 8).

August 19, 1691: Louis of Baden's victory in the Battle of Szalánkemén (Serbian *Slankamen*).

September 21, 1695: The last Ottoman victory in Hungary, over the forces of Transylvanian commander in chief Friedrich Veterani at Lugos.

June–August 1697: The Hegyalja uprising.

September 11, 1697: The grand triumph of Prince Eugene of Savoy over the troops of Sultan Mustafa II at Zenta.

January 24, 1699: The Treaty of Karlóca (German *Karlowitz*) between the members of the Holy Alliance and the Ottoman Porte; with the exception of the Banat, Hungary is liberated from Ottoman rule.

April 9, 1701: Leopold I prohibits Protestant worship in the areas regained from the Ottomans.

May 6, 1703: Francis II Rákóczi's proclamation of Brezan.

May 21, 1703: The Tiszahát uprising; the beginning of the Rákóczi revolt.

July 8, 1704: The diet of Gyulafehérvár elects Rákóczi as prince of Transylvania; he is officially inaugurated at the diet of Marosvásárhely on April 5, 1707.

May 5, 1705: Leopold I dies; he is succeeded by Joseph I (1705–1711).

May 30, 1705: The first issue of the first Hungarian newspaper, the anti-Habsburg *Mercurius Hungaricus*, is published.

September 12–October 2, 1705: The *kuruc* assembly of Szécsény—the foundation of an independent state entity, of Rákóczi as the leading prince, and of the Senate and the Economic Council.

June 12, 1707: The kuruc assembly of Ónod declares it will dethrone the house of Habsburg.

Autumn 1707: The kuruc fighters lose Transylvania.

September 15, 1707: The Treaty of Warsaw between Francis II Rákóczi and Peter the Great, Russian tsar.

February 29, 1708: For the first time since 1687, a Hungarian diet begins in Pozsony (until 1712/15).

August 3, 1708: Rákóczi's troops are defeated at the Battle of Trencsén.

November 28–December 20, 1708: The kuruc assembly in Sárospatak.

Late 1709: The kuruc fighters lose Transdanubia and the Szepes region for good.

April 17, 1711: Joseph I dies; he is succeeded by Charles III (as emperor, Charles VI; 1711–1740).

May 1, 1711: The Treaty of Szatmár. The fifth compromise of the long seventeenth century (1606–1711) between Vienna and the Hungarian estates.

HUNGARY BETWEEN TWO EMPIRES 1526–1711

INTRODUCTION

The Battle of Mohács in 1526 was a genuine turning point in the history both of the Kingdom of Hungary and of Central Europe as a whole. From the eleventh to the fifteenth centuries, the Hungarian state was consistently the defining middle power of the region, and Europe's eminent dynasties (the Anjous, Luxembourgers, Habsburgs, and Jagiellonians) competed for its throne, but after the rout at Mohács this role was fundamentally changed. Hungary stepped into one of the most difficult periods of its history. It faced serious choices and challenges, while it had to experience on a daily basis the terribly destructive consequences of constant military engagement. In a quarter of a century, its territory was broken into three parts: its central regions fell under Ottoman Turkish occupation, while what remained of the kingdom became part of the nascent Habsburg Monarchy in Central Europe, and its eastern territories became the Ottoman vassal state of Transylvania. What is more, these were by no means temporary phenomena.

After 1526, for almost two centuries, Hungary became the periphery and battleground of two empires, the Ottoman Empire and the Habsburg Monarchy. For the former, it remained merely the most northern inland frontier region, but for the latter, in the space of fifty years, it became one of the most important and cherished areas—and for this reason one that was under considerable scrutiny. All of this left a lasting mark on the country's network of settlements and institutions, fundamentally altering its ethnic composition and crucially influencing the development of its economy and society. Indeed, these changes led to Transylvania's long-term breaking away from Hungary. For centuries, these same changes would also restrict the sovereignty of the Kingdom of Hungary, which enjoyed special status within the Habsburg Monarchy, even if its only means of survival was integration into the monarchy. The leading Hungarian politicians of the day had to bitterly recognize that the fate of the three parts of their previously unified country would principally be determined in Istanbul, Vienna, and Gyulafehérvár in Transylvania, and, on occasion, even at the royal Polish court.

Amid the entirely new circumstances in the "short" sixteenth century after Mohács (1526–1606), everyone tried to find new directions. This was true not only in a political and social sense but also in terms of religion, language, and education. This search for new directions, despite the difficulties, brought significant results; the first part of this book deals with these in detail. Thanks to its particular union with the Habsburg Monarchy, the Kingdom of Hungary, fast becoming the "bulwark of Central Europe," was in political and military terms more closely connected to its Western neighbors than it had been in the last decades of the Middle Ages. Nevertheless, given the beneficial opportunities of the age, the parts of the territorially split country would in economic terms continue to be closely connected to one another; indeed, the country played a crucial role in Europe's commercial mechanism. And, thanks to humanism, the Renaissance, and the Reformation, Hungary and Transylvania played a defining role in the intellectual system of the "old continent." Indeed, the turn of the century would prove a golden age for Hungarian culture. The Hungarian language blossomed for the first time, making continual inroads both in literacy and in publishing, thereby producing the first treasures of Hungarian poetry and prose.

However, the Long Turkish War of 1591–1606 heralded a period of long-lasting destruction. Chances for recovery in the first half of the seventeenth century were then marred by the repeated military campaigns of the princes of Transylvania against the Habsburgs in Hungary, which were instigated as part of the Thirty Years' War and without exception turned into civil wars. In the kingdom ravaged by Turkish-Crimean Tatar, Transylvanian, Hungarian, and imperial-royal German forces, from 1619 onward and for the best part of a century, more and more people would be uprooted from normal everyday existence. This brought about a widespread ruination of society and the economy, while cultural and intellectual life also suffered monumental damage. These processes are explored in the second part of the book. At the time of the uprising led by Imre Thököly, if for the briefest of periods (1682–1685), Hungary had now been split into four parts. This represented the nadir of early modern Hungarian history.

The desire for renewal was nevertheless constantly present in the people of the seventeenth century (1606–1711)—a century described, because of its swings between decay and rebirth, as two-faced or Janus-like. Hungarian estate politics was rejuvenated, while the noble counties enjoyed their first flourish; every social class desired privileges and autonomy, and a revived Catholic Church regained a good part of its late medieval authority. In addition, the Hungarian language became further unified, and its literature developed new genres while the education system accrued new institutions. Book publishing and communication underwent radical transformation, and art and culture would blossom anew, albeit briefly. Yet these tendencies toward renewal would be severely constrained by a permanent war footing often akin to a war of religion, by a decay in public life, and by the large-scale militarization of society.

In the light of all these developments, it is less than apt to label the era from the Battle of Mohács in 1526 to the Treaty of Szatmár in 1711 simply as the "Ottoman period" or the first part of "Habsburg rule" in Hungary and even less so to refer to it as the period lived in the grip of the "two pagans," as has so often been done until now in Hungarian historiography. It is also worth disposing with the interpretation that has achieved mythical status in Hungary, according to which the seventeenth century brought a series of Hungarian national independence or national unity movements instigated from Transylvania. For all the achievements of Hungarian culture, no national unity movement can have been set into motion from Transylvania, which was under the constant watch of the Ottoman Porte, but neither were the areas of the royal kingdom individually capable of this. New research findings reveal that the expulsion of the Ottomans and the reintegration of the three parts of Hungary were possible only with the financial and military assistance of the Habsburg Monarchy and within the framework of that monarchy, even if there was a high price to pay for this. That the Kingdom of Hungary would remain in the eighteenth-century Habsburg Monarchy with such special status was ensured by the dogged persistence of its estates and by the various armed movements they employed. And although, after the liberation from the Ottomans in 1699, a small part of the Hungarian political élite led by Francis II Rákóczi attempted to pursue the path of independence from 1703 to 1711—with the assistance of the masses downtrodden by the wars of the seventeenth century—there was no realistic opportunity for this in the given domestic and international circumstances.

It makes more sense to investigate the history of the three parts of Hungary from 1526 to 1711 less with the lens of the various national and romantic narratives of the nineteenth and twentieth centuries and more within the framework of and along the boundaries of the two empires of the period, the Ottoman Empire and the Habsburg Monarchy, combined with a knowledge of the international processes at work and the aforementioned basic challenges, inevitabilities, and positive and negative changes. It is only in this fashion that we can comprehend and judge one of the most critical periods in Hungarian history more realistically than our predecessors have. This volume is an attempt to present a summary of these processes.

* * *

This book covers two centuries of history of the Hungary, a middling power, half a millennium old, that the crushing defeat of the Battle of Mohács in 1526 had broken into three parts. The writing of this book was primarily necessitated by the lack of any comprehensive work in English on the realm of St. Stephen in the sixteenth and seventeenth centuries. Thus, this volume deliberately follows on from Pál Engel's 2005 monograph, *The Realm of St. Stephen: A History of Medieval Hungary, 895–1526*. My first objective in this enterprise was to provide, in a single volume, a wide-ranging survey of events in the Carpathian Basin between 1526 and 1711, with university students and those less au fait with the history of the region especially in mind. For this reason, footnotes accompany only quotations, less well-known concepts, and most recent research achievements and debated subjects. The reader is pointed toward further study, however, by a select bibliography (circa 470 items—monographs and collected studies).

I

HUNGARY AFTER MOHÁCS: A CENTURY OF DIRECTION SEEKING, 1526–1606

Fig. 1. Louis II of Jagiello, Hungarian-Bohemian king (1516–1526). Unknown painter, sixteenth century (Hungarian National Museum, Budapest).

1

ON THE FRONTIER OF TWO EMPIRES

In the summer of 1532, six years after the Battle of Mohács, a great encounter almost took place. The rulers of two empires both approaching their zeniths, Sultan Süleyman I of the Ottoman Empire and Holy Roman emperor Charles V of the Habsburg Empire (along with his brother, Ferdinand I, king of Hungary), had their troops stationed in Kőszeg (Güns) and Wiener Neustadt, awaiting the military clash between the two most powerful men in the world. But the battle did not ensue. The unusual standoff was nevertheless symbolic. It was the final sign that the medieval Kingdom of Hungary, which had covered the whole area of the Carpathian Basin, was a thing of the past and that Hungary had been conclusively pushed to the frontier of two empires. For both great powers, the road leading to this series of conflicts in the Danube basin had been a long one.

The empire of the Ottoman dynasty, founded by Sultan Osman I (c. 1280–1324/26), was one of the fastest-growing states in world history and also one of the longest lasting (surviving until shortly after the First World War). Tradition holds that the Ottoman Turkish principality was born in the 1280s to the southeast of Bursa, in what is today northwest Turkey, from a mere four hundred tents of a Turkmen tribe fleeing the Mongol invaders in Central Asia. Over the space of a century, the small principality grew into a more significant state, and within two centuries it would become a major power. Finally, by the early sixteenth century, it became one of the world's greatest empires (see map 1).

The Ottomans primarily had their clever flexibility and marriage policy to thank for their quick rise to such heights, though they were assisted by good luck and sometimes cruel innovations guaranteeing the dominance of the ruling family and state power, such as fratricide. A military and bureaucratic elite emerged, drawn from the slave (Turkish *kul*) class, the institution of the janissaries, the promotion of Muslim religious leaders to official government posts, and other sources. In addition, they were highly effective in adopting and further refining elements of the state apparatus (tax system, public administration, etc.) of their enemies, particularly the Seljuk Turks and Byzantium, which helped the Ottoman state thrive. They also recognized that it would be more advantageous to expand into the divided Balkan peninsula, which they first set foot on in 1354, than into Asia Minor. By 1369, Osman's descendants were already in charge of Edirne (in today's northwest Turkey), and as auxiliary troops of the Bulgarian and Serbian princes, they soon found themselves embattled with the armies of the Hungarian kings Louis I of Anjou and Sigismund of Luxembourg, who intervened in the conflicts of the South Slav states.

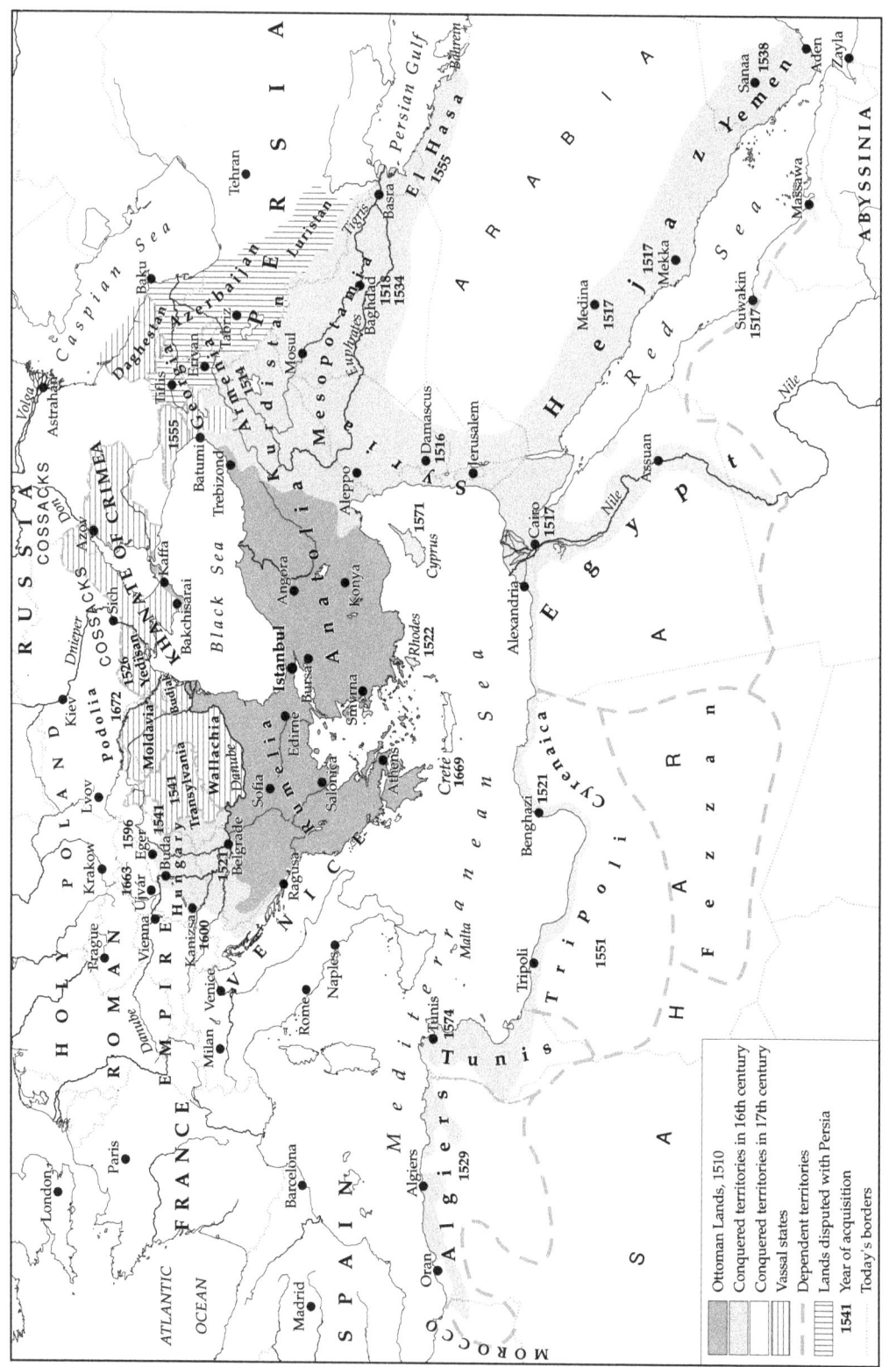

Map 1. The growth of the Ottoman Empire (sixteenth–seventeenth centuries).

After the battle for the throne in the early fifteenth century (1402–1413), the burgeoning state became a local great power—or southeastern European middling power—by occupying Constantinople in 1453. From here, after the acquisition of the Balkans (Serbia in 1459 and part of Bosnia in 1464), there was but a single last step to world power status. Sultan Selim I took this step in the 1510s by occupying the lion's share of the Middle Eastern Islamic world (Iran in 1514, Syria in 1516, and Egypt in 1517). Thus, in 1520, his son, Süleyman I (the Magnificent), inherited an empire of 1.5 million km² with a population of 12–13 million, an annual income of 4–5 million florins, and the world's only standing army (of about 100,000–120,000 men). Indeed, unlike other armies in Europe at the time, this army had reserve divisions. In addition, the sultan had a growing Mediterranean fleet at his disposal. By this time, the Ottoman Empire had become a decisive factor in European politics.

In 1521, those at the Istanbul court proposing war in Asia and at sea were overruled by those demanding campaigns in Europe; thus, it soon transpired that the Kingdom of Hungary, lying in the line of northern expansion, would be the next enemy to be defeated. The kingdom's territory (including Croatia, which it had been in a union with since 1102) was a mere 325,000 km², its population was 3.3 million, and its income was just 400,000–500,000 florins a year. The fall of Nándorfehérvár (known today as Belgrade) and the southern system of border defense built in the fifteenth century was now just a question of time. Hungary's opportunities to resist the Ottoman Empire—which was five times its size and four times its population and had enormous economic and military superiority—were very limited indeed. Furthermore, Sultan Süleyman's army was qualitatively different from the armed forces of Hungarian-Bohemian king Louis II of Jagiello (see fig. 1), as a permanent, well-trained, and fully employed mercenary force facing an army that was quite numerous but difficult to muster. The telling saying of a later grand vizier was pertinent for the Hungary of the 1520s, too: "A fly cannot harm an elephant."[1]

A defeat such as that at Mohács in 1526 was inevitable in the long term (see fig. 2). After this, Hungary's fate would be largely at the mercy of external factors: primarily the decisions of the Ottoman leadership but also, to a lesser extent, Hungarian domestic circumstances and the steps taken by the political and military leadership of the Kingdom of Hungary's western neighbor, Austrian archduke Ferdinand of Habsburg.

In this crisis situation, Hungary was nevertheless distinctly lucky that it would soon be on the border of two empires. After 1521, Archduke Ferdinand was already providing significant financial and military aid to his brother-in-law, Louis II, to help defend the Croatian and Slavonian territories—not out of charity but rather from carefully considered interests, namely the defense of his southern territories (Carniola, Styria, etc.). This assistance was, of course, in line with the Habsburg dynasty's old intention to obtain the Hungarian throne. Ever since the start of their ambitions to build a Central European empire, the Habsburgs had paid great attention to the Hungarian areas to the east of the Leitha (Hungarian *Lajta*) River.

Like that of the Ottomans, the empire of the Habsburgs, originating at Habichtsburg in the later Swiss canton of Aargau, was one of the fastest to grow and longest to survive (right

Fig. 2. The Battle of Mohács, August 29, 1526. Gyula Tury's copy (1896) of an Ottoman miniature from 1575 (Hungarian National Museum, Budapest).

until 1918) in world history. Although they had already lost their Swiss territories in the early fourteenth century (the battle of Morgarten in 1315), they had meanwhile, with Hungarian help (the battle of Dürnkrut in the Marchfeld in 1278), acquired the legacy of the extinct Babenberg dynasty: Austria and Styria. Although their continued rise could often be put down to good fortune, their territories gradually increased (Carinthia and Carniola in 1335; Tyrol, Friuli, and Gorizia in 1363) and circumscribed what was by now a Central European middle power.

This finally came about in 1437, when German king Albert II came to power—the first Habsburg to come to the Hungarian throne, as Albert I (1437–1439). From this time until 1806, with one brief interruption (1742–1745), the Habsburgs ran the Holy Roman Empire, governing their growing number of territories. Within a century, with the rise to the imperial throne of Charles V (1519), they would be in control of one of the world's most prestigious empires—one on which, as the saying goes, the sun never set. Even when Emperor Charles abdicated in 1556 and the world power was split into its Spanish and Austrian parts, the Habsburgs' Central European monarchy, which included Hungary, remained a crucial force on the European political scene.

First and foremost, it was emperors Frederick III and Maximilian I who played a key role in establishing a superpower. While the former distinguished himself with hard politicking, miserliness, and surviving his every opponent, the latter, alongside his military reforms (the organization of the landsknecht army and the construction of arsenals), began the series of fantastic Habsburg marriages that brought many territories to the dynasty. It was no accident that the following dictum was immortalized: *Bella gerant alii; tu, felix Austria, nube!* ("Let others wage war; you, happy Austria, marry!") The marriage of Maximilian to Mary, the daughter of Charles the Brave, prince of Burgundy, had in 1477 provided the Habsburgs with the inheritance of a good part of one of Europe's most economically advanced provinces, the principality of Burgundy (including the Netherlands). An even bigger dowry was brought by the marriage in 1496 of Maximilian's son, Philip of Castile (called the Fair), to Johanna, the daughter of Isabella of Castile and Ferdinand of Aragon. After the death of the Spanish heirs to the throne, this marriage would bring Spain, Sardinia, Sicily, and the kingdom of Naples under the control of the Habsburg dynasty, not to mention their enormous colonies brought by the discovery of the New World (see map 2).

After a number of unsuccessful attempts to acquire the Hungarian throne (in 1463, 1491, and 1506), it was ultimately the marriage contract signed in Vienna in the summer of 1515 that laid the foundation for what would be realized in 1521–1522. On this occasion, Archduke Ferdinand married Anna of Jagiello, daughter of Hungarian king Władysław (Vladislav) II, while Władysław's son Louis would marry Maximilian's granddaughter, Mary of Habsburg. So, after the death of Louis II in the Battle of Mohács in 1526, Ferdinand could submit his demand for the Hungarian throne. Hungarian custom decreed that the throne could be granted only by an election, however, which eventually took place on December 16, 1526, in Pozsony. His ascension to the throne was finally established by a legally fully binding coronation ceremony in Székesfehérvár on November 3, 1527. The road to this point was a long one, as we detail in a separate chapter (part 1, chap. 3).

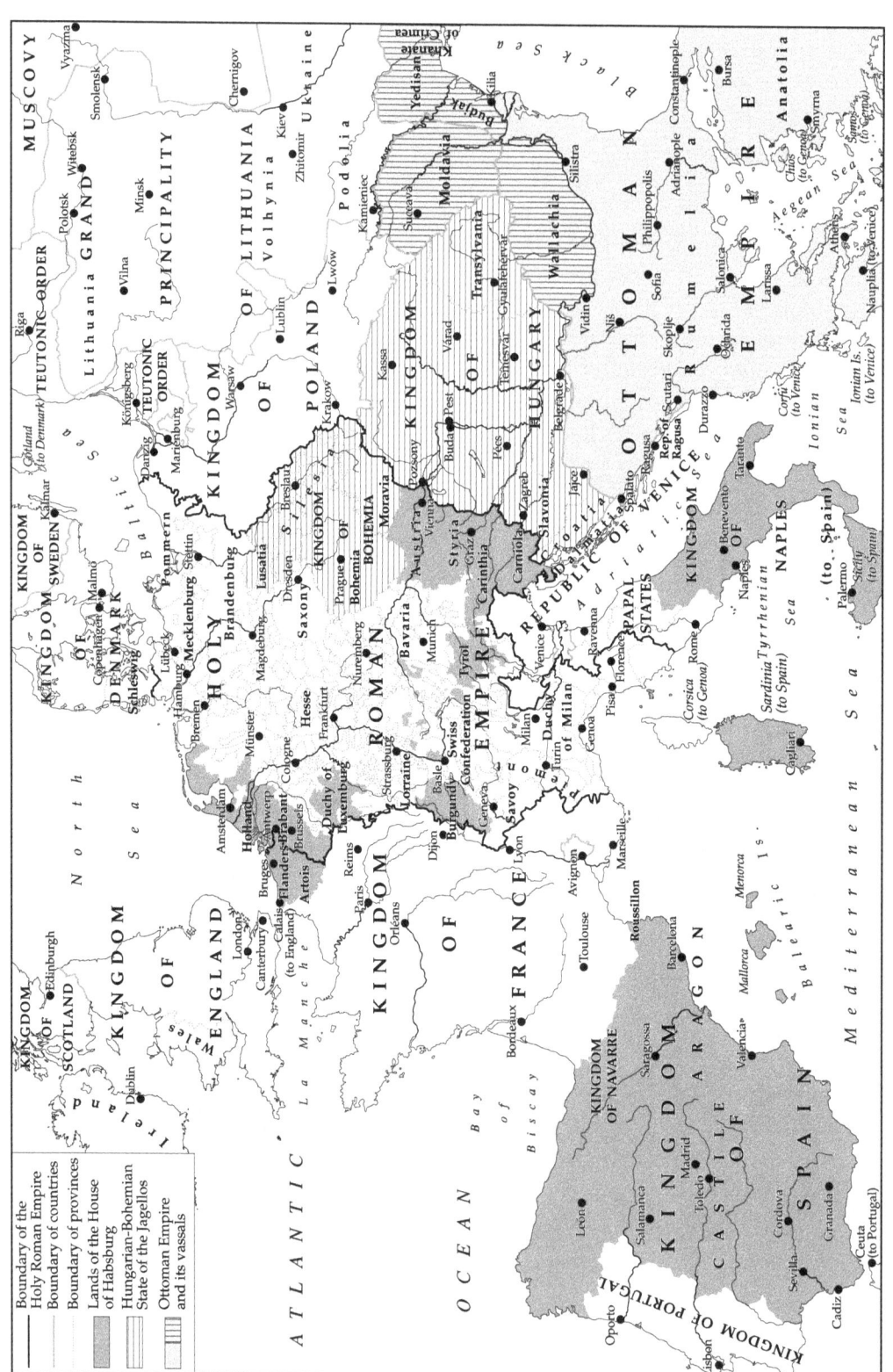

Map 2. Europe, circa 1520.

Although it did not affect the course of events, it is worth noting that if Maximilian of Habsburg had acquired the Hungarian throne in 1490/91 or in 1506, the history of early modern Hungary would probably have developed very differently—that is, much more beneficially. For in this instance a Habsburg Monarchy centered on Buda—as had very briefly existed under the rule of Albert of Habsburg in 1437–1439—might have come into being. But at the end of 1526, it was only amid the greatest of difficulties that Archduke Ferdinand set about the task of establishing order in Hungary while also having to deal with serious problems in his Austrian territories. That the Kingdom of Hungary did not all fall victim to the Ottoman conquest, by which it was distinctly imperiled, was due in part to errors made by the sultan's military high command and in part to Central Europe's difficult but ultimately successful cooperation.

Note

1. Josip Žontar, "Michael Černović, Geheimagent Ferdinands I. und Maximilians II., und seine Berichterstattung," *Mitteilungen des Österreichischen Staatsarchivs* 24 (1971): 210.

Fig. 3. Sultan Süleyman the Magnificent (1520–1566). Engraving by Agostino Veneziano, 1535 (Hungarian National Museum, Budapest).

2

ROADS FROM ISTANBUL TO VIENNA

The Ottomans in Hungary

The Ottomans used the same techniques of conquest against Hungary as they had employed in Asia Minor and in the Balkans in general. In line with this strategy, their first step was to largely occupy the Serbian and Bosnian buffer states that had previously acted as a defense for Hungary, which they accomplished by the 1460s. Next, they weakened Hungary's border defenses with constant incursions into southern Hungary and into the Croatian and Slavonian territories, fully quashing these defenses in the years after 1521. While it may well have been the domestic state of affairs in and the political leadership of his empire that forced the young Süleyman (see fig. 3) to attack Hungary again in 1526, the Battle of Mohács was a resounding defeat for the army of the Kingdom of Hungary. Despite this significant victory, the sultan was only briefly able to occupy the Hungarian capital, Buda, and at the end of 1526, he left occupying forces only in the Syrmium region between the Drava and Sava Rivers (see map 3). For his main objective was to occupy not a region but the whole of Hungary!

One movement in Hungarian and international military historiography—one not adequately aware of international interdependencies—holds that the sultan wished not to conquer Hungary but rather to turn it into a vassal state merely with a sultan's promise, as he had rationally concluded that it was beyond the operational radius of his army;[1] recent research work into Ottoman studies has convincingly contradicted this view.[2] From 1521 onward, the real objective of Süleyman, who entertained plans for world domination and a revival of the ancient Roman Empire as "the new Alexander the Great," was always the complete annexation of the Kingdom of Hungary, if possible. This is neatly revealed in the fact that the sultan led seven of his thirteen campaigns (in 1521, 1526, 1529, 1532, 1541, 1543, and 1566) into Hungary.

From 1527 onward, the Ottomans' real opponent would no longer be Hungary but rather the Habsburg dynasty that had taken her throne. The previous Hungarian-Ottoman conflict would, that is, turn into a clash between two empires: the nascent Central European Habsburg Monarchy and the Ottoman Empire. In the century and a half that followed, the Hungarian areas of the Danube Valley would be turned into the inland theater of war. The Ottoman military leadership wished to annex all of these areas at once, however—as it had annexed Serbia in 1459, for example—and it hoped to achieve this by delivering a lethal strike against Süleyman's great rival, Ferdinand of Habsburg, with the new target of occupying his headquarters of Vienna (known as the Golden Apple[3]).

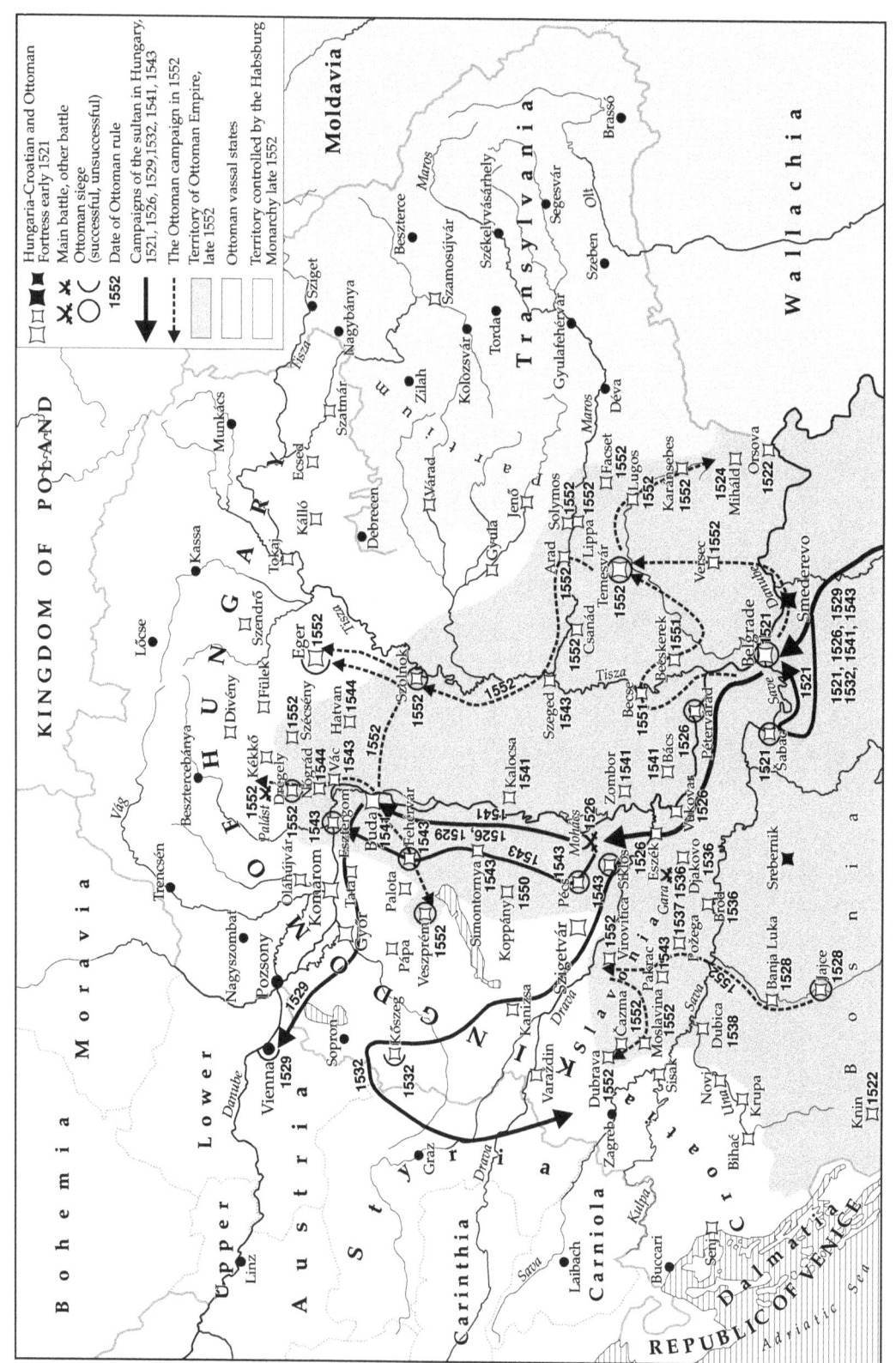

Map 3. Ottoman campaigns in Hungary, 1521–1552.

To achieve this goal, Süleyman soon found a significant sympathizer within Hungary. As we discuss separately (part 1, chap. 4), in autumn 1527, John Szapolyai, the first Hungarian king crowned after the Battle of Mohács, turned in desperation to the sultan for assistance; he then, like it or not, soon became a vassal and an author of the tragic fate that befell his rule over Hungary. The sultan's attempts at world domination were crushed under the fortresses of Vienna in 1529 and then little Kőszeg (Güns) in 1532. Had the Ottomans been triumphant, the large part of Hungary would probably have succumbed to fast military occupation and would have become a permanent part of the empire. In this instance, Hungary's history would have been connected to the history of the Balkan countries for a very long period.

Although the paths of the Ottomans would, during the sixteenth and seventeenth centuries, again lead in the direction of Vienna, the defeats near the residence of Ferdinand of Habsburg introduced for the sultan a new strategy of conquest for Hungary, too. There were, of course, other international and Hungarian factors at work in this. The Ottoman military command had to wake up to the fact that, despite its significant military superiority, it would not be able to bring the Habsburgs—a far tougher opponent than its previous adversaries—to their knees in a single stroke. But in Istanbul they were not even fully aware that, north of the Balkans, they would have to face states with different social systems and cultures—states that, thanks to centuries of historical development, their previous positions of power, and, most of all, their social durability, would collapse much less easily and would, in fact, fight to the bitter end to remain within the Christian civilization of Europe. Finally, the change to the European overland attack concept was reinforced by the Ottoman Empire's obligations to the East in the 1530s (Persia in 1534–1535 and South Arabia in 1538). The Mediterranean front opened by Emperor Charles V in the 1530s was also decisive in restricting Ottoman military room for maneuver in Hungary—a fact that even international historiography would often forget.[4] Thus, indirectly, the emperor greatly helped his brother, King Ferdinand, to hold his positions in Hungary.

By the mid-1530s, it was clear that the complete occupation not only of Central Europe but even of Hungary alone would be too difficult a task for Süleyman's empire. For all these reasons, the Ottomans thereafter reversed the course of the acquisition of the Habsburg capital and the annexation of Hungary. Although they tried to acquire the Kingdom of Hungary via Vienna on two occasions after Mohács (in 1529 and 1532), they were forced to recognize that it would be more expedient if their path were through the occupation of Buda and thus advanced gradually to the Austrian capital. Yet in the end, it was a particular event that pushed the sultan to take Buda: the attempt in autumn 1540 by the armies of King Ferdinand to take the seat of John Szapolyai, who had died in July. With this attempt, the Habsburg troops sought to enforce the decisions of the Treaty of Várad signed between the two kings in 1538, which was favorable to Ferdinand.

The conquest of Buda, completed with intrigue on August 29 (the Ottomans' lucky day[5]), brought with it not only the permanent occupation of the central areas of the Kingdom of Hungary, and thus the final separation of Hungary into three parts, but also the end of John Szapolyai's reign as an Ottoman vassal king. After some deliberation, the sultan decided that the role of his Hungarian "quartermaster" had expired, and the baby son of King John (John Sigismund) would in the future be no more than a pawn in the political game fought vis-à-vis the Habsburgs. For this reason, Süleyman made John Sigismund the *sanjak-bey* of Transylvania, while the Banat (Hungarian *Temesköz*, German *Banat*) was placed under the *ispán* of Temes (Latin *comes Temesiensis*, Hungarian *temesi ispán*), Péter Petrovics/Petrović, and the rest of the Transtibiscan (Trans-Tisza) area was put into the hands of the bishop of Várad, Friar George Martinuzzi. In the Ottomans' minds, this meant that from here on King John's former territories in central and eastern Hungary were now part of the Ottoman Empire. Even though these areas were in fact only virtual parts of the global empire, in the summer of 1541 Süleyman pulled hard on the vassal's reins: the young prince and his followers were obliged to pay ten thousand florins in annual tax to Istanbul.

By occupying Buda, the sultan laid the foundation for his rule in Hungary. In the autumn of 1542, the army of almost fifty thousand men from the Holy Roman Empire and the Austrian lands was unable to retake the fortress; it was then clear to their contemporaries that the Ottomans had settled in Hungary for good. The Turkish part of Hungary, still only a wedge into its territory in 1541, then expanded in the years that followed in the direction of the ultimate goal of the Habsburg capital (see map 3). In 1543 it was the sultan's main army itself that moved westward, and in enormous strides, taking the bishopric of Pécs, the coronation and royal burial city of Székesfehérvár, and the center of Hungarian Catholicism, Esztergom on the Danube. All of these conquests were expanded in every direction by 1544–1545 by invading armies of considerable size (Esztergom and Székesfehérvár, for example, each had three thousand Ottoman soldiers serving in them): to the north and east, they occupied Visegrád, Nógrád, and Hatvan, while in the border area of Transdanubia they occupied Simontornya, Ozora, and Tamási. In the 1540s, it proved possible to surround Buda with a defensive ring strong enough to confirm the stability of Ottoman power. Hungary now fell conclusively into three parts: Ottoman Hungary, the areas occupied by the Turks (Hungarian *hódoltság*); the ever-smaller Kingdom of Hungary; and the three virtual sanjaks of eastern Hungary and Transylvania, as yet with an uncertain future.

By establishing the first genuine Ottoman province in Hungary, the vilayet of Buda, Süleyman had embarked on a new strategy. We can rightly call the quarter century that followed the era of the fortress wars, as the Turks' castle battles continued almost relentlessly until 1566. The only periods that offered any respite from this were when the Porte again had military obligations in the East (Yemen conflict of 1547; new war of Persia, 1548–1550)—that is, a crisis erupting in the eastern part of the Ottoman Empire would again be to Hungary's advantage. In 1547 the sultan even signed a five-year peace treaty in Edirne with Emperor Charles V, head of the House of Habsburg, a treaty that also applied to Hungary. For all this, he had not given up on his plans to attack Vienna but had to acknowledge that he was not in a position to undertake a fast and complete occupation of Hungary. King Ferdinand, meanwhile, had no choice but to accept the division of the country and even an obligation to pay an annual thirty thousand florins in compensation for the "peaceful" ownership of the Hungarian territories under his control. Later incarnations of this tax, called the "respectful gift" (Latin *honorarium munus*, German *Ehrengeschenk*), would be paid to the Porte until as late as 1606.

The five-year treaty of 1547 had not even run its course when Sokollu Mehmed, beylerbey of Rumelia, again led his troops against Hungary. This latest Ottoman campaign was precipitated by a secret agreement (Nyírbátor, 1549) between the double-dealing governor of Transylvania, Friar George Martinuzzi, and Ferdinand I, directed at unifying the territories of the Turkish vassal John Sigismund with the Kingdom of Hungary. Naturally, the sultan would not allow his recalcitrant vassal to endanger the Hungarian conquests he had made to that point. In September 1551, the beylerbey occupied the fortresses of Becse, Becskerek, and Csanád; in the next year, those of Lugos, Karánsebes, Temesvár, Lippa, and Szolnok also fell (see map 3). Thus in 1552 the formerly nominal Turkish province of Banat became the Ottomans' second vilayet in Hungary, with Temesvár as its center. And although, in the autumn of that year, the defenders of the fortress of Eger gave Hungarians munition with their heroism for many years to come, the retention of this key to the Upper Hungarian borderlands actually did little to weaken the Ottomans' positions. For even before the attack on Eger, in the summer of 1552, Ali Pasha of Buda had further expanded through Transdanubia by taking Veszprém and Várpalota in the vicinity of Lake Balaton. In the north, he would annex the fortresses of Drégely, Szécsény, Hollókő, Buják, Ság, and Gyarmat for the sultan's empire; it was also in this period that a large part of the area between the Drava and Sava Rivers came under Ottoman authority.

These acquisitions of territory contributed greatly to Transylvania's avoiding inclusion in the Ottoman Empire, though it had originally been marked for occupation. Nevertheless, the conquest of Banat essentially decided Transylvania's fate as a Turkish vassal state, as from here it would be straightforward for the Ottomans to supervise these areas over the century and a half that followed. In the central part of Hungary, meanwhile, the region occupied by Turks and surrounded by border fortresses was established by the end of 1552. Finally, on August 9, at the Battle of Palást (in Hont county), Ali Pasha of Buda defeated the Hungarian and German troops marching against him, thereby further increasing the number of victories the Ottomans had achieved in open battle.

After 1552, the Ottoman troops in Hungary—despite the sultan's main forces again being occupied in the east and south (in the Persian war, 1553–1555; the conquest of Libya, 1556; and the failed siege of Malta, 1565)—further wormed their way toward their chief goal of occupying Vienna with a series of new fortress battles. In autumn 1554, Toygun Pasha of Buda occupied Fülek fortress, establishing there the northernmost Hungarian sanjak center in the Ottoman Empire. And just a year later, he had grabbed the fortresses of Kaposvár, Korotna, and Babócsa, thus bringing the main fortress, Szigetvár, into a vulnerable position (see map 4). The only slight comfort for the Hungarian side was that in 1556 it was possible to remove Ali Pasha of Buda from the besieged Szigetvár. Indeed—as fresh Hungarian research has recently drawn to the attention of international historiography—after 1526 it was the Austrian-Hungarian-Bohemian troops (under the nominal leadership of Ferdinand of Habsburg, archduke of Tyrol, and the real leadership of palatine Tamás Nádasdy together with military commissary general Sforza Pallavicini) that first won a victory over the pasha of Buda alongside the Rinya River in Somogy county.[6]

The period of the fortress wars (1541–1566) finally came to a close with the sultan's campaign of 1566. With his last Hungarian campaign, Süleyman would end his days with his reputation as a successful invader intact, despite never having achieved his great goal of conquering Vienna. By occupying Gyula fortress and Szigetvár (see fig. 4), defended to the

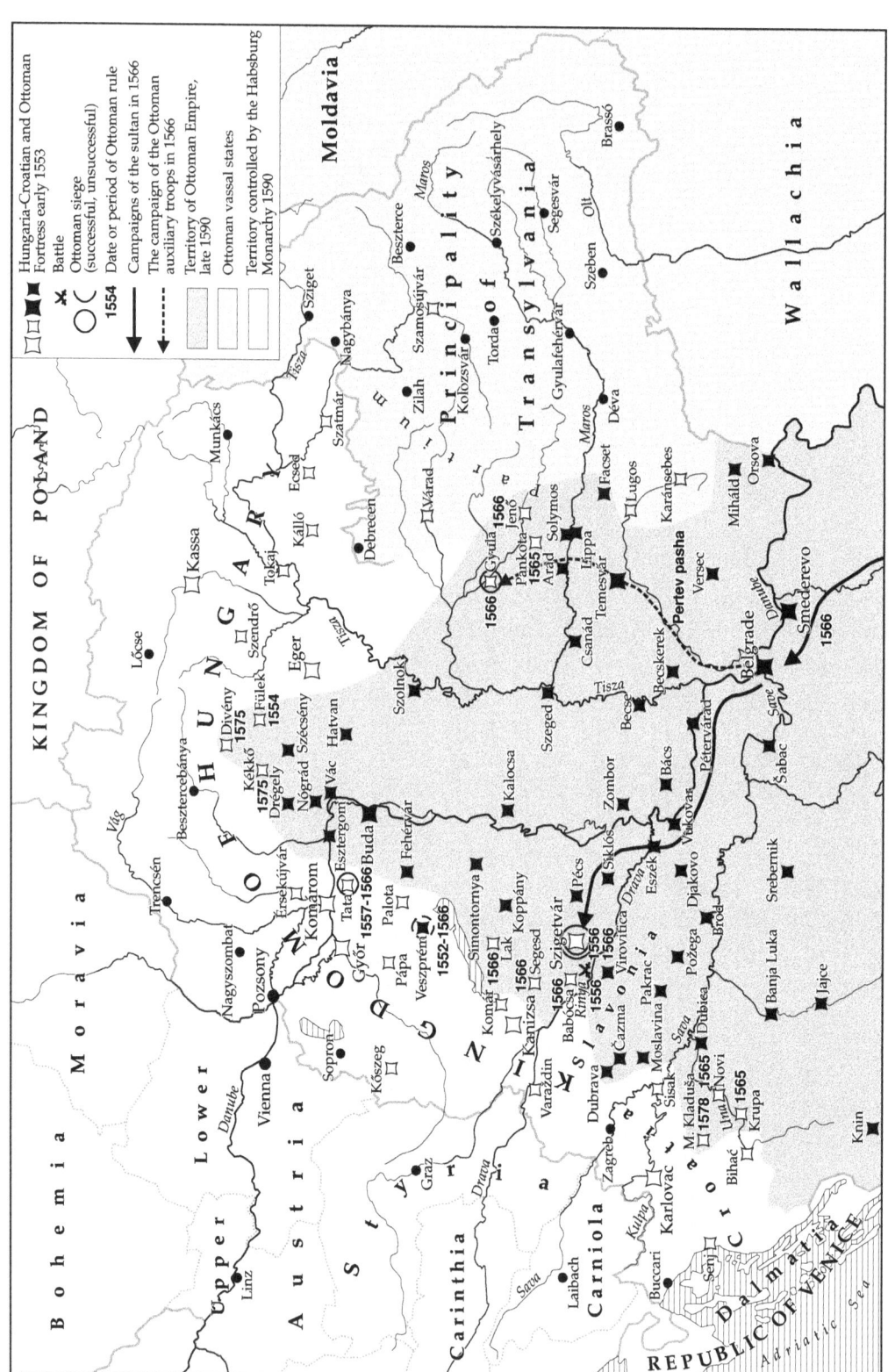

Map 4. Ottoman campaigns in Hungary, 1553–1590.

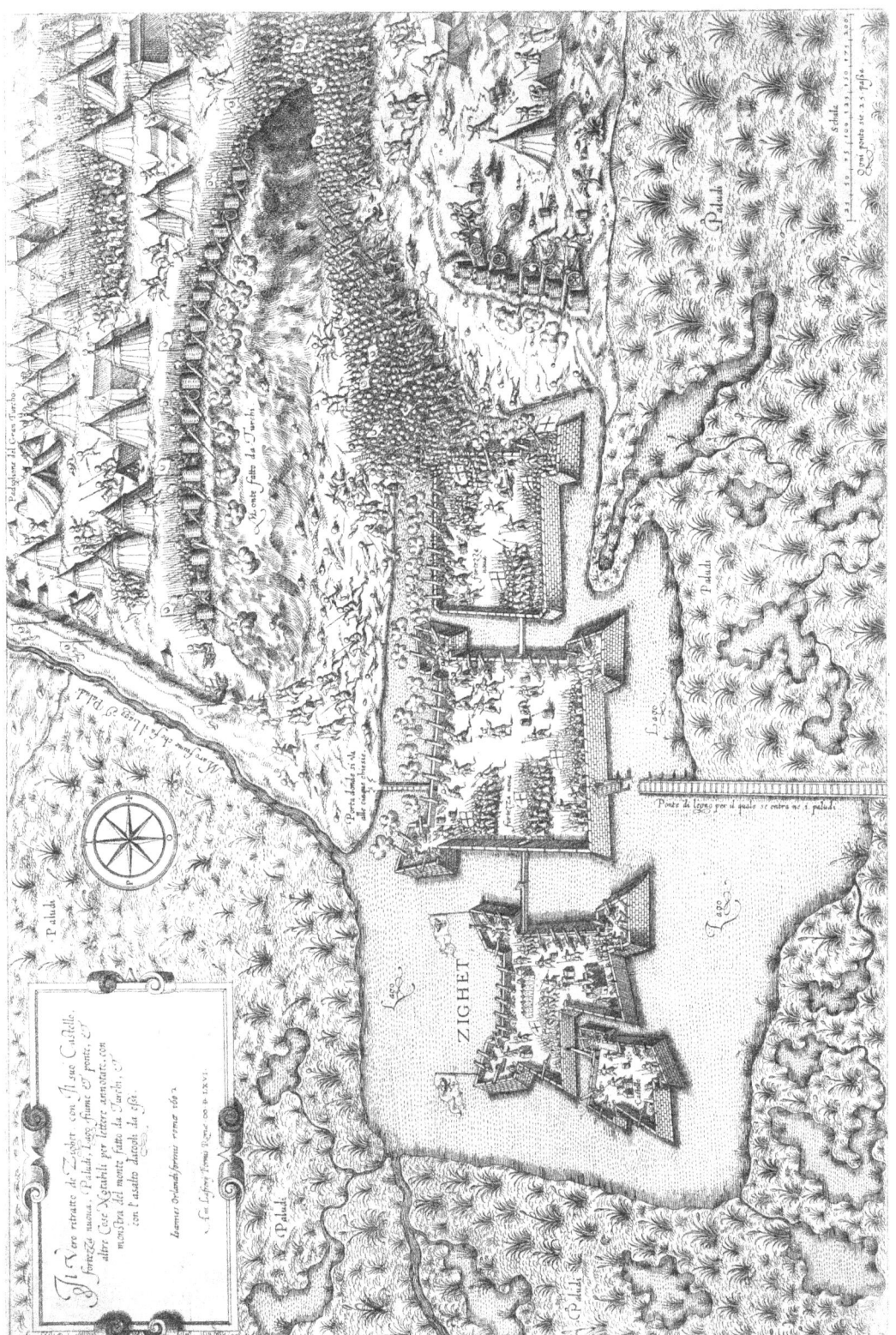

Fig. 4. The Ottoman siege of Szigetvár, 1566. Engraving by Antonio Lafreri, 1566 (Hungarian National Museum, Budapest).

last by Captain General Miklós Zrínyi (Croatian Nikola Zrinski), Süleyman now had some 40 percent of St. Stephen's realm in his possession; what is more, these were the most important central areas, which could henceforth act as a base for the Ottoman high command's further attempts on Vienna.[7] The Treaty of Edirne between Sultan Selim II and Emperor Maximilian II in 1568 would nevertheless put a prolonged stop to the Turkish acquisition of territory in Hungary. During the Ottomans' continued wars in the east and at sea (the capture of Tunis, 1570; occupation of Cyprus, 1570–1571; defeat at Lepanto, 1571; Persian war, 1578–1590; and invasion of Azerbaijan, 1585), there were almost twenty-five years of what was supposed to be peace on the borders of the two empires, peace that was more akin to "wartime peace years" (German *Kleinkriege*), full of incursions.

For the Ottomans, this more peaceful period provided an opportunity to organize their arrangements in Hungary. In contrast to their original objectives, these arrangements would also be only half-baked at best. Although the Turkish provinces in Hungary were without question bastions of the Ottoman Empire thrust forward, they failed to become intrinsic to the global power in the way the vilayets in the Balkans or in Anatolia were. This unusual state of affairs was perfectly characterized by the Hungarian magnate János Balassi in 1555: "The Turks might have occupied particular parts of our country, but have left them behind more than conquered them. For they have not managed to bring in their own institutions and laws, and they are forced to accept that these areas remain with their own organization and with their own statutes."[8] For a century and a half, this situation would not change very much in the northern part of the territories of Ottoman Hungary.

Of the methods of the system that was entrenched and working in the Balkans, the Ottomans were unable to apply many in practice in Hungary. The military occupation was of course successful, as a significant part of the empire's armed forces was permanently stationed along the Hungarian borderlands. In the second half of the sixteenth century, the military of the Buda and the Temesvár vilayets alone numbered at least twenty-five thousand men (eighteen thousand mercenaries guarding fortresses and patrolling rivers, and seven thousand spahis). It is worth noting that at this same time there were a "mere" seventeen thousand soldiers stationed along the royal series of border fortresses on the other side. Throughout the sixteenth century, the Hungarian border region remained the most important European inland front for the Ottomans (see map 5).

During the military conquest, the Ottomans gradually established their own system of fortresses, from the Adriatic Sea to the Temesvár borderlands. This system had a number of duties to perform. Its key fortresses provided protection for Buda and the Danube military line, and they served as a base for attacks to acquire more western territory. Finally, they became centers for the civil and military administration that was being developed. They were intersections from which the surrounding areas could be supervised militarily and also administered and taxed. This new line of Ottoman castles was made up of some 100–130 fortresses in all; the military command in Vienna had a similar number at its disposal, as we see in the next chapter (part 1, chap. 3). The pillar of this multilayered chain of castles was made up of a few more significant fortresses (Buda, Pest, Esztergom, Székesfehérvár, and Temesvár) in which one to two thousand soldiers served. As well as these key fortresses, the border was protected by other larger castles (Szigetvár, Fülek, Hatvan, Jenő, and Lippa), each

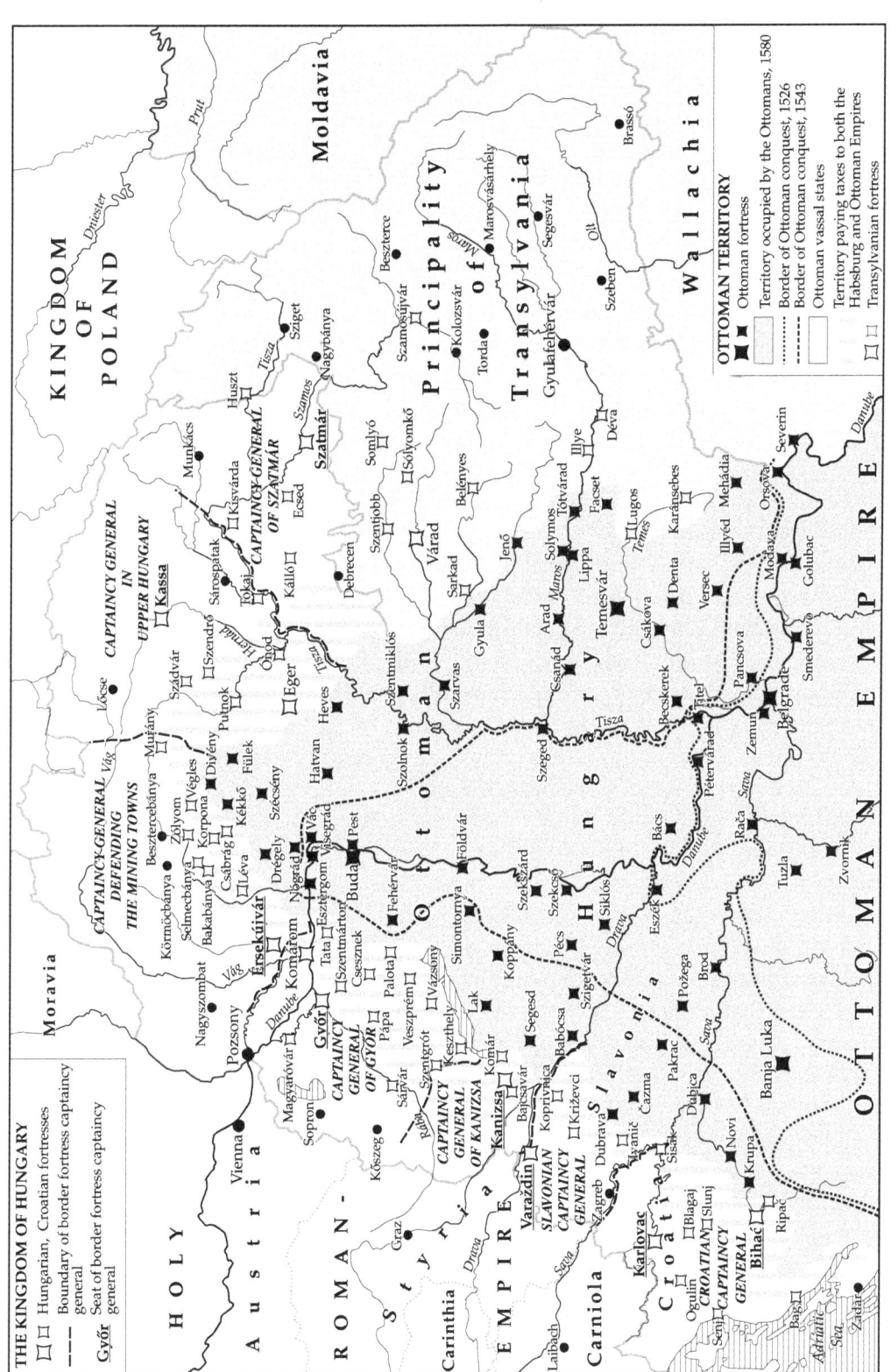

Map 5. The border defense system in Hungary against the Ottomans (after 1580).

with four to six hundred soldiers. The third level of the system of fortresses were the smaller border posts defended by one to three hundred soldiers, while the fourth level consisted of ridges, partly newly built and fortified by palisades (Turkish *parkan*).

The Ottomans arranged the vilayets (and the sanjaks that they were divided into) around the larger fortresses. Alongside the vilayets established in Buda in 1541 and Temesvár in 1552, a further four would be created during the Long Turkish War at the end of the sixteenth century (see part 1, chap. 11). Three of these were in Transdanubia, brought into being so they could be even better filled with soldiers and used to prepare further expansion to the west. In 1594 the vilayets of Pápa and Győr were established, but they remained only until the fortresses were recaptured (in 1597 and 1598). The province of Eger, founded in 1596, and that of Kanizsa, created in 1600, would survive until the end of the seventeenth century. In the important area to the south of the latter lay the vilayet of Bosnia, founded in 1580.

The leaders of the vilayets and the sanjaks (the beylerbeys and *sanjak-beys*) were at once the military, administrative, and financial leaders and the keepers of the peace. Also under their authority were the paid equestrian spahis with official estates (Turkish *timar* estates) and their armed escorts paid from the income from those estates. Alongside their military functions, the *sanjak-beys* rigorously collected taxes, coordinated the administration of estates, and supervised the judiciary. On the economic front, they ensured that taxes were properly levied, determined on the basis of a thorough survey of the population and agricultural output. It was strongly in their interest to protect the productive capacity of the occupied territories, as this was the guarantee of the financial viability of their occupation. This means that the previous view, which held that the Ottomans pursued an exploitation economy in Hungary, does not stand up to scrutiny. In fact, their system of taxation run by the defterdars would in many respects be harmonized with circumstances in Habsburg Hungary, and its operation was distinctly efficient.[9]

The areas occupied by the Turks varied greatly, depending on their distance from the front and the composition of their population. Yet the general statement can be made that the remaining Hungarian population of Ottoman Hungary sensed less change in its everyday life than the residents of Serbia did after the Turks' annexation of the country in 1459. Unlike in the Serbian case, the Ottomans were unable to fully conquer Hungary, so after they established themselves they could not liquidate the political elite. The Hungarian nobility had, after all, found shelter in the kingdom led by the Habsburg rulers, and it thought (or rather it hoped) that Turkish rule would be only temporary. To this end it strove to maintain all the previous connections it had with the territories of Ottoman Hungary, primarily the estates near the border, which it continued to consider as its own. Indeed, where it maintained its ownership rights, the nobility continued to extract taxes from its subjects. The Ottomans divided and taxed the areas of the Kingdom of Hungary along the border, in similar fashion. As a result, a broad area of the chain of castles of the opposing sides fell under double ownership and dual taxation, an area we call *condominium*.[10] These areas also played a key role in the provision of food supplies to the larger royal border fortresses (Szigetvár and Gyula, until 1566, and afterward principally Eger). This explains why, even though it would have been justified in military terms, scorched-earth tactics were almost never used in the areas the Turks occupied.

One advantage of the preservation of estates in Ottoman Hungary was that it allowed former institutions to keep operating in the Turkish areas. The administrative centers of the occupied noble counties (Latin *comitatus*, German *Komitate*, Hungarian *megyék/vármegyék*) might have been transferred to a particular royal fortress in each case, but, through their noble judges and jurors, they continued to perform their functions in their same jurisdictions. Of the so-called fugitive counties (Hungarian *menekült vármegyék*), it was first and foremost the activity of Pest–Pilis–Solt county and of Heves–Outer Szolnok that was significant. The Transdanubian and Slavonian counties, on the other hand, could hardly muster any influence on the Turkish areas. The Hungarian rulers residing in Vienna or Prague, well aware of the significance of all of this, would bestow the estates falling into treasury hands on border fortress officers, even in the area of Ottoman Hungary; these officers would then come and go and do their duties in enemy territory with considerable gusto. And neither did the institutions of the Catholic Church disappear entirely from the Ottoman areas. Albeit nominally, the bishop's cathedra was filled on a continuous basis, a good sign that, like the secular landlords, the church still laid claim to its former estates.

Ultimately, the roots that the various Protestant confessions managed to lay in Ottoman Hungary, and the establishment of their church institutions, could only mean that the Turks did not seek to build the civic institution in full. In this it was through their key figures in local administration, the kadis, that they had an opportunity to spread their control. In addition to their judicial functions in their jurisdictions (Turkish *kaza*), the kadis would in principle have been local factotums for the state administration. In Hungary, however, they had much less influence on the day-to-day lives of the masses than they did in the Balkans—at least in areas with Hungarian population. Only in part did they become competitors to long-established local governments and to the apparatus of the fugitive counties. Indeed, the market towns (e.g., Kecskemét, Nagykőrös, and Kiskunhalas) fought aggressively—with pleas and even bribes, if necessary—to maintain their autonomy. And as the army enforcing the occupation and the civil population it brought with it were not particularly significant in size, this new class was unable to do much to weaken Hungarian society with its centuries-old roots, let alone to disband it.

Thus, Ottoman Hungary would, for the Porte, always remain a western defense bastion for the empire, one in which the right time for the installation of everyday civic institutions would never really arrive. The only exceptions to this were a few larger military centers (Buda, Temesvár, and Pécs) and the southern regions that would lose their Hungarian populations forever. The civic life of the new, mostly Serbian, Vlach and Bosnian populations of the south territories of the Ottoman Hungary (the Syrmium, Banat, and the southern half of the area between the Danube and the Tisza) would by the second half of the sixteenth century differ little from that seen elsewhere on the Balkan Peninsula. In other words, to some extent the Ottoman conquest drove the Balkans up into Hungary. One lively piece of evidence for this is how the Hungarian Catholic Church almost completely lost its hold on these southern areas. From the 1570s onward, its place was taken first by apostolic visitations of the Holy See launched from the Balkans (primarily Bosnian Franciscans, as well as Benedictines, Franciscans, and Dominicans from Ragusa) and then, from the second decade of the seventeenth century, by Jesuit missions, who were to have the greatest success, as we discuss separately (part 2, chap. 8).

Notes

1. Géza Perjés, *The Fall of the Medieval Kingdom of Hungary: Mohács 1526–Buda 1541* (Boulder, CO: Social Sciences Monographs, 1989), 83–170.

2. Pál Fodor, *The Unbearable Weight of Empire: The Ottomans in Central Europe—a Failed Attempt at Universal Monarchy (1390–1566)* (Budapest: Research Center for the Humanities, Hungarian Academy of Sciences, 2015), 48–133.

3. Pál Fodor, *In Quest of the Golden Apple: Imperial Ideology, Politics, and Military Administration in the Ottoman Empire* (Istanbul: Isis, 2000).

4. Zoltán Korpás, *V. Károly és Magyarország (1526–1538)* [Emperor Charles V and Hungary, 1526–1538] (Budapest: Századvég Kiadó, 2008).

5. It was on this day that Belgrade was occupied in 1521, that the Ottomans were triumphant on the fields of Mohács in 1526, and that they acquired Buda in 1541.

6. Pál Fodor, ed., *Remembering a Forgotten Siege, Szigetvár 1556*, comp. Péter Kasza (Budapest: Research Center for the Humanities, Hungarian Academy of Sciences, 2016).

7. Pál Fodor, ed., *The Battle for Central Europe: The Siege of Szigetvár and the Death of Süleyman the Magnificent and Nicholas Zrínyi (1566)* (Leiden: Brill, 2019).

8. Ferenc Szakály, *Magyar intézmények a török hódoltságban* [Hungarian institutions in Ottoman Hungary] (Budapest: MTA TTI, 1997), 7.

9. Cf. Géza Dávid, *Studies in Demographic and Administrative History of Ottoman Hungary* (Istanbul: Isis, 1997), 103–117, 173–179, 205–213, etc.

10. Ferenc Szakály, *Magyar adóztatás a török hódoltságban* [Hungarian taxation in Ottoman Hungary] (Budapest: Akadémiai Kiadó, 1981); Szakály, *Magyar intézmények a török hódoltságban*. Cf. recently Markus Koller, *Eine Gesellschaft im Wandel: Die osmanische Herrschaft in Ungarn im 17. Jahrhundert (1606–1683)* (Stuttgart: Franz Steiner, 2010); Éva Sz. Simon, *A hódoltságon kívüli "hódoltság". Oszmán terjeszkedés a Délnyugat-Dunántúlon a 16. század második felében* [Ottoman advance in southern Transdanubia in the second half of the sixteenth century] (Budapest: MTA BTK TTI, 2014); Antal Molnár, *Magyar hódoltság, horvát hódoltság: Magyar és horvát katolikus egyházi intézmények az oszmán uralom alatt* [Ottoman Hungary, Ottoman Croatia: Hungarian and Croatian church institutions under Ottoman rule] (Budapest: BTK TTI, 2019).

Fig. 5. Ferdinand I of Habsburg, Hungarian-Bohemian king (1526–1564), Holy Roman emperor (1558–1564). Engraving by Hans Sebald Lautensack, 1556 (Hungarian National Museum, Budapest).

3

THE BUMPY ROAD TO VIENNA

The Habsburgs and the Hungarians

THROUGHOUT THE SIXTEENTH AND SEVENTEENTH CENTURIES, THE MAIN objective of the Ottomans was the capture of Vienna, but the Hungarian estates (German *Stände*) were less keen on visiting it. Yet in the wake of 1526, one of the greatest questions of the age was how they could best see their interests served at the Vienna court of their new ruler, Ferdinand of Habsburg, Hungarian and Bohemian king, and from 1556/58 also Holy Roman emperor (see fig. 5), a court that—crucially—he held beyond Hungary's borders. In other words, in what form would the Kingdom of Hungary, its territory shrunk by Ottoman advance, become part of the nascent Central European Habsburg Monarchy (see map 6), this new monarchy made up of various countries and provinces, one we would refer to as a composite state (German *zusammengesetzte Habsburgermonarchie*)?[1]

In this situation, one that was extraordinary for the new ruler and the Hungarian political elite in equal measure, there were huge challenges to the establishment of suitable relations. It is customary, however, to emphasize that Ferdinand I, like John Szapolyai before him, became ruler of Hungary amid entirely legitimate circumstances—that is, not through the aforementioned nuptial agreement in Vienna of 1515. He was elected king (in Pozsony on December 16, 1526) and then crowned (in Székesfehérvár on November 3, 1527) by the free will of the Hungarian estates. As this had taken place in similar fashion in early November 1526 in the case of John Szapolyai, from this point on—and in a way unparalleled throughout Hungarian history—there were, for almost a decade and a half, two legitimate rulers of the country. For Ferdinand, however, the second to ascend to the throne, there was no other option but to retake the country by means of force from King John, who had meanwhile become an ally of the Turks. This resulted in a destructive civil war, the clearest beneficiary of which was the Ottoman Porte itself.

Though King Ferdinand—even in the shadow of his older brother, Emperor Charles V—had greater military financial resources at his disposal than did Szapolyai, who in and of himself would not have been a very serious opponent, Ferdinand's room for maneuver against a King John enjoying the support of global conqueror Süleyman was distinctly limited. Emperor Charles, on account of his military obligations in the Mediterranean, could assist him with one or two thousand Spanish and Italian mercenaries annually in these decades, which was a great help for Hungary. Seen from Madrid or Toledo, the Hungarian front would, understandably, have ranked as only a third theater of war after North Africa

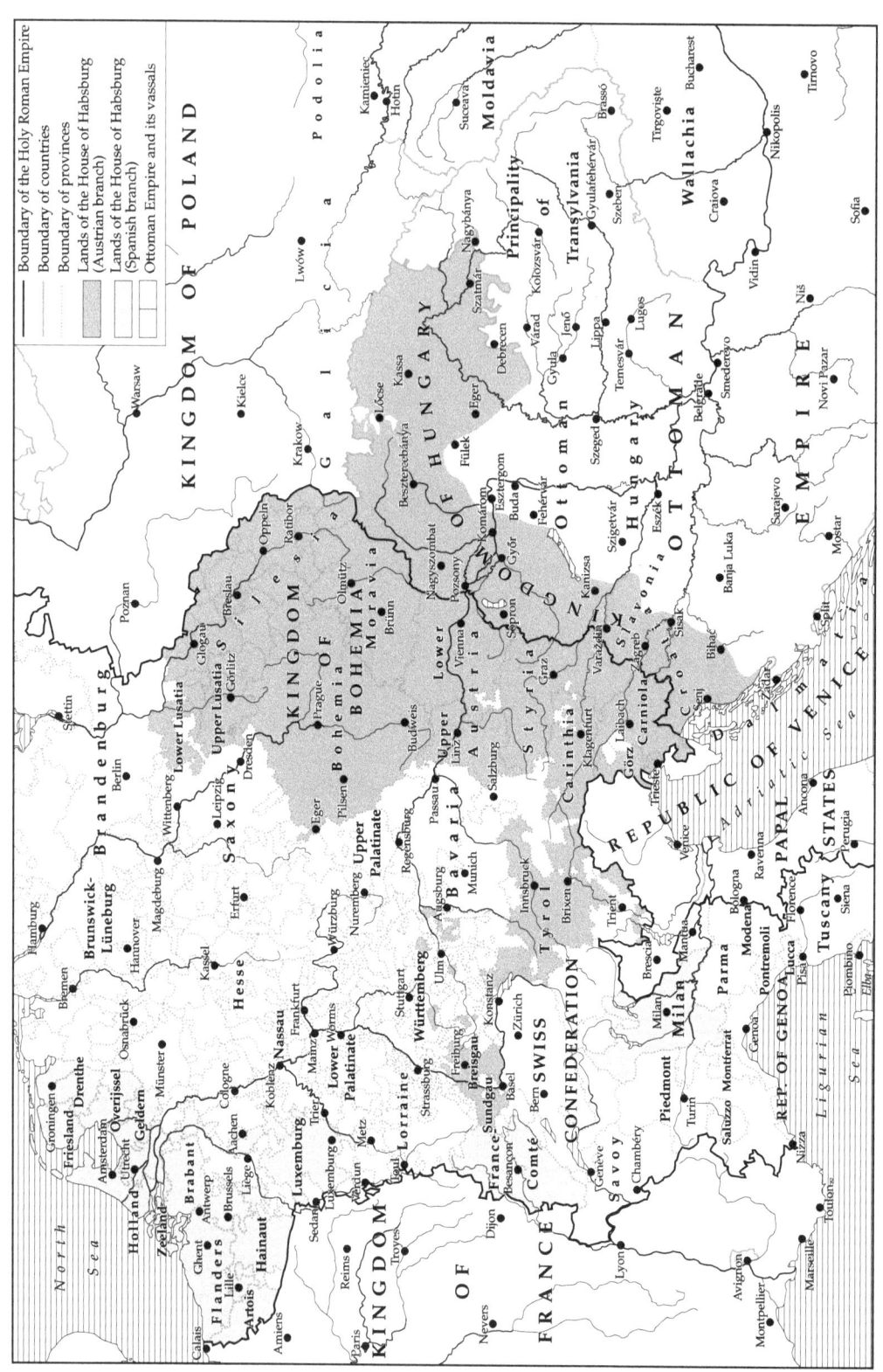

Map 6. The composite monarchy of the Habsburgs in Central Europe in the second half of the sixteenth century.

and the Habsburg part of Italy. Before the fall of Buda in 1541, however, even the Austrian estates had failed to recognize the real threat the Ottomans posed, busy as they were resisting their ruler's unstoppable attempts at centralization. In 1525 the situation was further complicated by a great peasant revolt stretching all over Austria, as well as by the fast spread of the Reformation.

All of these factors fundamentally restricted Ferdinand of Habsburg's military room for maneuver in Hungary. And yet, after he was declared king, his hand was forced: either he would have to employ military means to acquire and arrange his new country, or he would have to forsake it, settling on the Austrian borders in opposition to Szapolyai and the Ottomans—though this latter option was probably not even considered. Ferdinand continued the tradition of medieval Hungarian rulers protecting their country over prolonged periods of time with the use of buffer states directly before their borders. So, to protect his Austrian territories, he first attempted to gain as large an amount as possible of what remained of the Kingdom of Hungary, and then here, as if on a defense bastion thrust forward, intended to construct a new series of border defenses. The difference was that he saw Hungary not as a buffer state but as a bulwark. His medieval predecessors, such as Sigismund of Luxembourg or Matthias Corvinus, were only nominally kings of Bosnia, for example, while Ferdinand was Hungary's genuine crowned ruler.

In a country turned into a war zone, however, the conditions were far from right for governing and the making of a bulwark. Ferdinand initially had limited political support, even though the most important Hungarian politicians were quick to join his camp—the likes of Palatine (Latin *palatinus*, Hungarian *nádor*) István Báthory of Ecsed, Chancellor Tamás Szalaházy, Chief Justice (Latin *judex curiae regiae*, Hungarian. *országbíró*) Elek Thurzó, and later Pál Várday (archbishop of Esztergom) and Tamás Nádasdy. His political leadership in Vienna, however, did not have adequate local knowledge of Hungary or have diplomats aware of Ottoman customs; in fact—apart from a few top officers visiting the Croatian borderlands before 1526—it did not even have the apparatus needed to construct a new defense system to protect against the Turks. Hungary's geographical characteristics did not favor the attainment of his goals, either: it was not possible to build a new system of fortresses on the flat expanse of the Great Plain. In light of all this, modern historiography considers as hasty the view that criticizes Ferdinand for a series of negligent decisions, if only because, in the second half of the fifteenth century and in much more advantageous circumstances, it also took Matthias Corvinus a long time to organize an efficient border defense system in the area of the Lower Danube and Sava.

Neither can the kingdom's lords and estates correctly be ascribed the dismissive epithets (such as opportunist and slothful) used by Hungarian romantic historiography in the nineteenth and twentieth centuries. For they decided on the bumpy road to Vienna, even if, for them, this meant serious sacrifices regarding the running of the country. A growing number of them appreciated that Hungary's survival was possible only with the assistance of Ferdinand's Austrian and Bohemian provinces in Central Europe. As ban of Croatia and Slavonia, Tamás Nádasdy, appropriately put it in the summer of 1539, "If Your Holy Majesty does not support this country with your other provinces it will certainly happen that, due to the loss of this country, the other provinces of Your Holy Majesty will be lost."[2]

Despite constantly having to make pleas for assistance, the Hungarian estates understandably did not wish to relinquish anything of the key role they had previously played in the leadership of the country. The leaders of the Austrian provinces, however, who were providing increasingly significant military and financial support, wished for a say in the running of the armies that guaranteed their security as well as Hungary's in return for their assistance. All this led to increasingly jurisdictional conflicts between the commanders in chief of the foreign troops in Hungary (German *Oberstfeldhauptmann*) and the top leaders of the Hungarian estates—first the palatine (István Báthory, 1526–1530) and then the royal governor, a new official representing the absent Ferdinand (Latin *locumtenens regius*, Hungarian *királyi helytartó*; Elek Thurzó, 1532–1542; Pál Várday, 1542–1549). Similar difficulties surfaced in financial and foreign affairs, which were undergoing modernization. With Ferdinand's ascent to the throne, with the common governance of the Austrian, Bohemian, and Hungarian lands, and with an increase in the Ottoman threat, these issues were no longer just Hungarian ones but the most pressing issues facing the new Habsburg state. In the terminology of the time, they had become mixed issues—*negotia mixta*.

For the Hungarian estates, there really was no way out of this vicious circle. In vain did they press for Ferdinand to live in Hungary, as, given the Ottoman advance, there was no realistic hope for this: the Kingdom of Hungary had quickly become a dangerous frontier country. Similarly in vain did they request that "in Hungarian matters and affairs His Majesty be pleased to act on Hungarian advice,"[3] as, in the composite state—apart from domestic politics and the justice system—there were no purely Hungarian matters (see fig. 6). Yet all of this was far from being unique for the region. In the Hungarian-Croatian joint state in existence since 1102, there were no separate Croatian (foreign) affairs; in the same way, when Ferdinand came to the throne, Bohemian and Austrian aristocrats had to face similar problems. Indeed, the Bohemian magnates had faced a similar situation between 1490 and 1526, when the Hungarian-Bohemian rulers held court mostly in Buda and not in Prague. The people in the most privileged position were always those whose country the ruler resided in. In the case of Ferdinand I, this was the nobles of Lower Austria, as from the 1530s Ferdinand's court was permanently based in Vienna.

This unusual situation confronted the Hungarian estates with one of the greatest challenges in their history. Although in medieval times there had on rare occasions been similar experiences, when Ferdinand left Hungary in spring 1528, the independent Hungarian royal court ceased to exist. As a result of the joint administration of the Habsburg Monarchy and the Kingdom of Hungary, the court of the Hungarian king was merged with the court of the Austrian territories and of the Bohemian king; from 1556/58, it would be made part of the emperor's court held in Vienna, meaning that a common Habsburg court was established. This was, in practice, a state of affairs distinctly similar to that of the union of the Hungarian and Croatian kingdoms in the Middle Ages, where there was no separate Croatian royal court, only the common royal court in Buda. All in all, however, in the decades of transition after Mohács, the obligatory change of court and the rather slow integration into Vienna life meant that the Hungarian political elite suffered a significant decline in its position, as table 1—comparing the ruling court before and after 1526, based on the most recent research findings—shows us.[4]

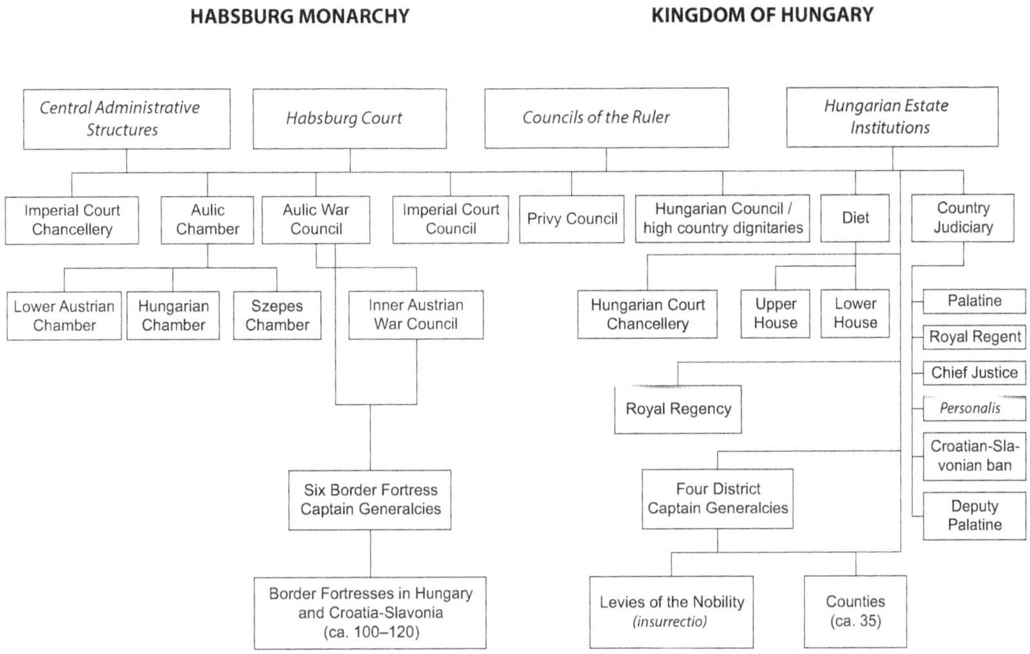

```
                    HABSBURG MONARCHY                                    KINGDOM OF HUNGARY

    ┌─────────────────────┐   ┌─────────────────┐           ┌─────────────────────┐   ┌─────────────────────┐
    │Central Administrative│   │ Habsburg Court  │           │ Councils of the Ruler│   │ Hungarian Estate    │
    │     Structures       │   │                 │           │                     │   │    Institutions     │
    └──────────┬──────────┘   └────────┬────────┘           └──────────┬──────────┘   └──────────┬──────────┘
               │                       │                                │                         │
    ┌──────────┼──────────┬─────────┬──┴────────┐         ┌──────────┬──┴──────────┐   ┌─────────┼─────────┐
    │          │          │         │           │         │          │             │   │         │         │
 Imperial   Aulic      Aulic War  Imperial   Privy      Hungarian Council /       Diet        Country
 Court      Chamber    Council    Court      Council    high country dignitaries              Judiciary
 Chancellery                      Council
```

Fig. 6. The administration of the Kingdom of Hungary in the last third of the sixteenth century.

Sub-structures under Habsburg Court: Lower Austrian Chamber, Hungarian Chamber, Szepes Chamber, Inner Austrian War Council → Six Border Fortress Captain Generalcies → Border Fortresses in Hungary and Croatia-Slavonia (ca. 100–120).

Sub-structures under Hungarian Council: Hungarian Court Chancellery → Royal Regency → Four District Captain Generalcies → Levies of the Nobility (insurrectio), Counties (ca. 35). Upper House, Lower House.

Under Country Judiciary: Palatine, Royal Regent, Chief Justice, *Personalis*, Croatian-Slavonian ban, Deputy Palatine.

Table 1: Change of court and loss of position in the decades after Mohács: the key characteristics of the late medieval court in Buda and the common Habsburg court

The late medieval Hungarian royal court	The common court of the Habsburg Monarchy
Center: Buda.	Center: Vienna; from 1583, Prague.
Members: about four to five hundred.	Members: under Ferdinand I, about five hundred; later, it would increase slightly in size.
At once the court of the Hungarian, Bohemian, and Croatian kings.	At once the court of the archduke of Austria and the Bohemian and Hungarian kings; after 1556/58, it was also the court of the Holy Roman emperor.
The Hungarian presence was crucial at all levels of the court—more than 50 percent.	The Hungarian presence was modest relative to the role of the Kingdom of Hungary: until the 1550s, Hungarians were present only rarely; in the rest of the century, there were usually twelve to twenty of them, which was a mere 3–4 percent of the total.
The highest court dignitaries (the country's high dignitaries) were almost all Hungarian. The royal lord steward was also the president of the royal council, with enormous political power.	In the whole of the sixteenth century, there were only two Hungarians among the high dignitaries of the Habsburg court: Ferenc Thurzó, president of the Aulic Chamber from 1556, and Miklós Pálffy, so-called *Oberstsilberkämmerer* in 1576–1578; there were no Hungarians among the councilors of the central government organizations.

The delay in the Hungarian integration in Vienna was due not to some special resistance on the part of the Hungarians but simply to the extraordinary difficulties of the age. A smoother path of adjustment to the Vienna court for Hungarian nobles was impeded by constant conflicts with the Ottomans and with Szapolyai. During these conflicts, their lands were in considerable danger, and so they were keener to stay at home and protect them. The Hungarian lords had at best only modest connections to the leaders of Ferdinand's court in Vienna. The ability of the Hungarians to acclimatize was also limited by the foreign milieu, the courtiers being mostly of foreign origin (Austrian, German, Spanish, and Netherlandish), as well as by difficulties in language and communication and by different court customs. None of this was helped by the anti-German sentiment that was still alive after the aforementioned inheritance and marriage agreements signed with the Habsburgs (in 1463, 1491, and 1506). In addition, life in Vienna, developing as it was into a residence, became more and more expensive, and, because of Szapolyai and the Ottomans, Hungarians faced a certain, not insignificant distrust. All this was only further encumbered by the Hungarian language being so difficult to understand and the Hungarians' dress customs being rather Eastern in style. Austrian and German nobles, quick as they were to lay their hands on the key roles at the court, had little interest in handing their positions on to others. Finally, from 1528 to 1542, King Ferdinand himself did not enter the territory of the Kingdom of Hungary a single time, making any improvement in his relations with his Hungarian followers very difficult.

As a result of all this, in the decades after 1526, the broader strata of the Hungarian political elite were unable—could never really have been able—to effectively adapt to the Habsburg court in Vienna. Clutching on to their positions at the court of Ferdinand and his successors, first in Vienna and then in Prague, was thus an exhausting and expensive enterprise, and at first only a few recognized the real returns on this investment. But those who saw the value of this opportunity and who were capable of availing themselves of it (like, in the sixteenth century, the members of the Balassi, Báthory of Ecsed, Batthyány, Draskovics/Drašković, Erdődy, Drugeth de Homonna, Mérey, Nyáry, Perényi, Révay, Thurzó, and Zrínyi families) would later see splendid returns on their "Vienna investment." The career of a young nobleman would be determined by an upbringing at court and the advantages of good contacts and acquaintances.

This is clearly borne out by the fact that almost all Hungarian lords and their sons who served in the Vienna court would sooner or later achieve high office (as high dignitary, captain general, or councilor) in Hungary. Indeed, some—such as Miklós Pálffy, György Thurzó, and György Zrínyi, all raised in the court—would be able to use their former Viennese connections to attain the very highest Hungarian military and political office, anchoring or reinforcing their families' positions in the highest echelons of the Hungarian aristocracy. All in all, this meant that, from the very outset, integration into court life was one of the best opportunities for the prospects in Hungary for the Hungarian high nobility. After the Habsburg court moved to Prague in 1583, the very great geographical distances would further limit their ability to be fully involved, and so by the end of the sixteenth century the Hungarian lords (for example, the Dobó, Dóczy, Forgách, Liszthy, Pethő, Révay, and Thurzó families) had come up with a new strategy: they would send their sons not to the court of

Emperor Rudolf II in Prague but rather to that of archdukes Ernest and Matthias, based in Vienna.

Although the public sense of history in Hungary—projecting nineteenth-century Austro-Hungarian animosities back onto the period after Mohács—still often holds that the Habsburgs used Hungary as no more than a simple buffer state and did little to improve its defense or its development, new research findings have done much to modulate this view.[5] From the 1530s, the Kingdom of Hungary was given a more prominent place in Ferdinand I's centralization and modernization program than the Bohemian or Styria areas were. As a country, Hungary was of great importance both militarily and economically, but it remained dangerous throughout on account of the Ottoman advance. So, paradoxically, its significance was a result precisely of its dangerous state. All this would have serious consequences by the second half of the century. These consequences would fundamentally alter the administration of the Kingdom of Hungary and would bring inevitable privations for the Hungarian estates, just as the advent of the joint Habsburg court had done. Table 2 illustrates the long-term effects of these changes.

For all the centralizing reforms (primarily the establishment of new central specialist offices, as listed in the table, regularly meeting at an existing site) of Ferdinand and his successors, we cannot speak of "Habsburg domination" with regard to the Kingdom of Hungary. Thanks to its close connection with the Habsburg Monarchy, Hungary did indeed lose its previous role as a middle power in Central Europe in the half century after 1526; there was no other option for the survival of its western and northern regions. The only realistic possibility for the Kingdom of Hungary to be defended, lying as it did in the main line of attack for the Ottoman conquest, and for the Hungarian people to remain within European civilization was integration into the monarchy. This led to a restriction of sovereignty in precisely the most important areas of public administration (foreign, military, and financial affairs). Thus, right until 1848, the most important questions facing Hungary would be decided in the new government bodies (Privy Council, Aulic War Council, and the chambers) established by Ferdinand (see fig. 6). These would only very rarely have Hungarian members, such as Ferenc Thurzó, who, with his excellent contacts at court and Austrian-Bohemian family connections, was from 1556 the president of the Viennese Aulic Chamber—effectively the monarchy's finance minister—for a few years.

As a consequence of all this, there is no case for talking of independent Hungarian military affairs or a Hungarian national army, for example, in the sixteenth and seventeenth centuries after the establishment in 1556 of the Aulic War Council (German *Wiener Hofkriegsrat*). Any such notions, despite often appearing in literature—even when of the life and times of the general, politician, poet, and writer Miklós Zrínyi (1620–1664)—are ahistorical and anachronistic. A country whose central military issues were settled by top foreign officers in the court of a "foreign" ruler could not have its own independent military affairs and army. Neither did it, until as late as 1918. That is to say, the changes after 1526 quite literally decided the administration of the Kingdom of Hungary for several centuries.

Although the eminent border fortress captain general Simon Forgách, whose wife happened to be Austrian, complained in 1588 that "it is against the state of things that a country is governed by the advice of foreigners,"[6] and despite the country's new type of

Table 2: Key characteristics of the institutions of the late medieval and the early modern Kingdom of Hungary

Late medieval Kingdom of Hungary	Early modern Kingdom of Hungary
Center of power: the Hungarian royal court and the royal council, Buda.	(1) Center of power: the joint Habsburg court and (by the standards of the time) modern central government bodies, Vienna, and, in the late sixteenth century, Prague. (2) Local centers of power: Pozsony (see fig. 7; "domestic capital" and, from 1563, coronation city) and, in part, Kassa and Zagreb.
All affairs were Hungarian (Hungarian Croatian).	A good part of affairs were common affairs: foreign affairs, military affairs, and financial affairs. Only domestic affairs and the justice system remained entirely Hungarian.
On all national questions, the royal council and the high dignitaries decided at both a national and a local level. On financial matters, the role of the treasurer was increasingly significant.	*At a national level*: Military affairs: Aulic War Council (from 1556) and the Aulic War Council of Inner Austria (1578). Foreign affairs: Privy and Aulic War Council (initially made up of Hungarian and South Slav diplomats, then mostly Austrian and German ones). Financial affairs: Aulic Chamber (1527) and, under its auspices, the Lower Austrian Chamber (1527), Hungarian Chamber (1528), and Szepes Chamber (1567); the Hungarian Chamber had a German chancellor. There was a very high level of centralization in all three areas, but at the local level, the role of the Hungarian high dignitaries and estates was significant, even indispensable.
Role as a middle power in Central Europe, with complete state (administrative) sovereignty.	The Kingdom of Hungary was a key part of a new composite state, the Central European Habsburg Monarchy—more precisely, its defense bastion and larder (breadbasket); its common administration was in Vienna, but limited sovereignty was granted in certain fields of public administration. It was carefully overseen part of the monarchy, on account of its significance, and one that became a cornerstone of the Central European economy.
The Hungarian political elite had national influence and dominated the court.	This denoted a significant loss of power both at the new joint Habsburg court and in the modernized public administration—and, to some extent, at a national and regional level.

administration, the state sovereignty of the Kingdom of Hungary was never brought into doubt. In fact, as regards sovereignty, its situation was much more favorable than that of the Austrian hereditary lands (German *Erbländer*) or the Bohemian kingdom. For in the sixteenth and seventeenth centuries, the political leadership in Vienna almost never wished to force Hungary to join the hereditary lands and to transform what it regarded as foreign Hungarian institutions in line with the Austrian model. Neither did it have any hope of doing so, what with the strength of the Hungarian estates and the country's local, linguistic, and judicial limitations and special features. That is to say, Hungary could be successfully governed only by involving the Hungarian elite, even if, in a number of areas, the country's sovereignty was unquestionably limited by its central administration.

For all these disadvantages, in joining the Habsburg Monarchy, the Kingdom of Hungary became a key part of Central Europe's strongest military alliance and of the region's

Fig. 7. Pozsony (Pressburg; today Bratislava, Slovakia), the new capital of the Kingdom of Hungary in the sixteenth century. Engraving by Georg Hoefnagel, 1588 (Hungarian National Museum, Budapest).

Table 3: The annual costs of the border defense system against the Ottomans stretching from the Adriatic to Transylvania, and the income of Hungary and of the Habsburg Monarchy in the 1570s and 1580s

Pay required for the border fortress army	Other planned military expenditure	The income of the Kingdom of Hungary	Estimated income of the Habsburg Monarchy
1,400,000–1,600,000 R.f. *Total cost of border defense*	400,000–500,000 R.f.	800,000 R.f. *Percentage of the total cost of soldiers' pay and the cost of border defense*	2,000,000–2,400,000 R.f. *Percentage of the total cost of border defense*
1,800,000–2,100,000 R.f.		c. 50%–c. 40% In the case of real military expenditure of 400,000 R.f.: c. 25%–c. 20%	c. 90–100%

Abbreviation: R.f. = Rhenish florin (*Rheinischer Gulden*)

economy. With the country on a constant war footing, this was an enormous achievement—it was only in this fashion that complete Ottoman occupation could be avoided. Hungary thus played its role as the bastion of Central Europe, but there were also great sacrifices made by the monarchy's Austrian and Bohemian territories and indeed by the subjects of the Holy Roman Empire. The 1539 statement from Tamás Nádasdy fitted the facts: Hungary was in need of Central Europe's financial and military assistance, as table 3 shows.

Hungary was thus in a position to cover only a small part of the cost of the border defense system completed by the 1570s (border soldiers' wages and the expenditures on munitions, construction of fortresses under supervision of military architects from Spanish territories of Italy, the military fleet, intelligence, and military administration) from its own finances—even in the most favorable instance, this part was 25–30 percent. The Kingdom of Hungary therefore depended on regular annual financial assistance from the Central European provinces, while the Habsburg Monarchy essentially depended on Hungary for its own defenses. So the very considerable Hungarian shortfall was for many decades covered by the so-called *Türkenhilfe* (Turkish taxes and monetary aids) paid by the estates of Carinthia, Carniola, Styria, Lower Austria, Moravia, and the Holy Roman Empire. The mutual interdependence meant that all sides had great sacrifices to make.

Hungary's crucial significance in the sixteenth century is borne out by the other important proportion seen in the table. Although 40 percent of its medieval territory had been occupied by the Ottomans by 1566, and at its eastern edge the Principality of Transylvania had come into being (see part 1, chap. 5), even with its reduced size the Kingdom of Hungary represented an enormous financial and economic force in the Habsburg Monarchy as a whole. The incomes from the war-ravaged areas were invaluable not just for protection against the Turks but also for the financial system of all of the monarchy. Even from the second half of the 1550s, and for decades, these came to some 750,000–850,000 Rhenish florins. This means that, over the second half of the sixteenth century, the Habsburg's Hungarian frontier territory provided around 30–40 percent of the monarchy's income. Although taxation remained the business of the estates, the great reforms in financial administration (chambers, restructuring of the customs system, and the introduction of an accounting system) brought considerable returns.

The reorganization of the Hungarian military would bring similarly impressive results. By the 1570s, Hungary was home to one of Europe's longest and most effective border defense systems. This was the joint success of the (not always straightforward) cooperation between the Aulic War Council and the Hungarian estates. A sign of the vital role played by the latter, as recent research tells us,[7] is that even the Hofburg had to accept that a small and not very significant aspect of the administration of border defense, the institution of the so-called district captain general, had to remain in the hands of the estates throughout. As a result, the Hungarian border system—in line with the dualist nature of the government—become two-faced. The pillars of the border defense system (see map 5, in chap. 2) were the border fortress captaincies general in charge of the individual areas (borderlands) of the 100–120 border fortresses. From the Adriatic Sea to the Transylvania border, these were (1) the first to be created, the Croatian and Adriatic coastal region based in Bihać, then later in Karlstadt; (2) the Slavonian or Wendish Captaincy General, based in Varasd; (3) the Kanizsa Captaincy General; (4) the Győr Captaincy General; (5) the so-called Captaincy General Defending the Mining Towns, centered on the newly constructed Érsekújvár fortress; and (6) the Captaincy General for Upper Hungary, based in Kassa. These were directed centrally by the Aulic War Council in Vienna, except the Croatian and the Slavonian Captaincies General, which after 1578 fell under the auspices of the Inner Austrian Aulic War Council in Graz.

The additional parts of border defense, the district captaincies general in charge of the military affairs of the counties and the uprising of the nobles (Latin *insurrectio*), were arranged in similar regions: (1) Croatia and Slavonia; (2) Transdanubia; (3) the so-called Cis-Danubian area,[8] stretching from Pozsony to Gömör county; and (4) Upper Hungary. These were operated by the estates, and so their offices could be filled only by Hungarian lords.

The role of the Hungarian estates in the new administrative structure of the Habsburg Monarchy had sunk from the pre-1526 level of central governance to the local level and to military and financial affairs. At this level, though, the estates would remain crucial, indeed vital (see fig. 6). While Hungary was dependent on foreign aid, Vienna was also evidently dependent on the constant counsel of the Hungarian and Croatian lords with large estates near the border and considerable influence, not to mention experience of the struggle against the Ottomans. These aulic lords and prelates, especially the latter, were the disciples of the influential Miklós Oláh, archbishop of Esztergom (1553–1568), controlling Hungarian domestic politics and the justice system while limiting the centralizing attempts of the court in Vienna. In short, they were the leading protectors of the integration into the monarchy of what remained of the Kingdom of Hungary.

Cooperation with and resistance to the Habsburg court during the sixteenth century could be reconciled, even if Hungarian historiography has, rather unimaginatively, instead tended to present this as an irresolvable dichotomy. What mattered was to find the right balance, and all too often it was the activities of the various and opposing groups of Hungarian lords and prelates and court lobbies, rather than the national interest, that played the greater role in establishing this balance. Another sign of the clout of the Hungarian political elite was that the role of the diets (Latin *diaeta, comitia*, German *Landtag/Reichstag*, Hungarian *országgyűlés*) remained very significant. Hungarian aristocrats retained their standing not only in the country's judicial system but also in local administration and in the life of the counties. Indeed, as we have seen in the previous chapter (part 1, chap. 2), it was primarily thanks to the country's nobility that the northern and middle part of the country, occupied by the Ottomans but with a local Hungarian population, was retained as part of Hungary. In addition—as we discuss later (part 1, chaps. 9–10, and part 2, chap. 8)—the aristocracy and nobility made an enormous contribution to the blossoming of Hungarian language and literature and of Protestantism, and indeed to the rejuvenation of Catholicism.

Notes

1. R[obert] J[ohn] W[eston] Evans, *The Making of the Habsburg Monarchy 1550–1700: An Interpretation* (Oxford: Oxford UP, 1979); J[ohn] H[uxtable] Elliott, "A Europe of Composite Monarchies," *Past and Present* 117 (1992): 48–71; Thomas Winkelbauer, *Ständefreiheit und Fürstenmacht: Länder und Untertanen des Hauses Habsburg im konfessionellen Zeitalter, 1522–1699*, vol. 1 (Vienna: Ueberreuter, 2003).

2. ÖStA, Haus-, Hof- und Staatsarchiv, Ungarische Akten (Hungarica), Allgemeine Akten, fasc. 39, Konv. F, 1539 Juni–Juli, fol. 36–37.

3. *Magyar törvénytár. (Corpus Juris Hungarici) 1526–1608. törvényczikkek* [Acts of 1526–1608], with explanatory notes by Dezső Márkus (Budapest: Franklin-Társulat, 1899), 502–503 (act 35 of 1563).

4. Géza Pálffy. *The Kingdom of Hungary and the Habsburg Monarchy in the Sixteenth Century* (New York: Columbia UP, 2009), 71–88.

5. Ibid., 89–138.

6. Sándor Takáts, *Szegény magyarok* [Wretched Hungarians] (Budapest: Genius Kiadás, 1927), 32.

7. Géza Pálffy, "The Origins and Development of the Border Defence System against the Ottoman Empire in Hungary (Up to the Early Eighteenth Century)," in *Ottomans, Hungarians, and Habsburgs in Central Europe: The Military Confines in the Era of the Ottoman Conquest*, ed. Géza Dávid and Pál Fodor (Leiden: Brill, 2000), 3–69; Géza Pálffy, "The Habsburg Defense System in Hungary against the Ottomans in Sixteenth Century: A Catalyst of Military Development in Central Europe," in *Warfare in Eastern Europe, 1500–1800*, ed. Brian J. Davies (Leiden: Brill, 2012), 35–61.

8. Cf. Borbála Bak, *Magyarország történeti topográfiája. A honfoglalástól 1950-ig* [The historical topography of Hungary from the conquest to 1950] (Budapest: MTA TTI, 1997), 33, 77–78.

Fig. 8. John I Szapolyai, king of Hungary (1526–1540). Woodcut by Erhardt Schön, circa 1539 (archive photo of a graphic work that has been out of sight since 1958, Hungarian National Museum, Budapest).

4

THE ROAD TO ISTANBUL

The State of King John Szapolyai and His Son

Hungarian historiography of the nineteenth and twentieth centuries—depending on the prevailing political winds—saw the kingdom of John Szapolyai (see fig. 8) as in most ways a continuation of the medieval Hungarian state, even sometimes as a "Hungarian national kingdom." Recent research has significantly tempered this view.[1] Today we know that in the Europe of the sixteenth century there were no "national kingdoms," only dynastic states,[2] while the independent Hungarian state of King John ceased to exist when the Holy Crown was placed on the head of Austrian archduke Ferdinand in autumn 1527. Although, within a month of his coronation on November 11, 1526, Szapolyai had acquired almost absolute power, the election of Ferdinand to the throne in mid-December must have made it clear to Szapolyai that, whether by negotiation or through force, he must fight his stronger rival king for the country. He hoped it would be the former of these.

King John chased after illusions on almost every front. He trusted that the Italian wars with the French and the internal problems facing the Austrian lands would prevent his Habsburg rival from sending troops against him to Hungary. He also hoped that his kingdom would be recognized throughout Europe, that he could establish international alliances, and that he could then, once on firmer ground, manage to sign a peace both with Ferdinand and with the sultan. Instead, his position would decline substantially from early 1527, just months after assuming the throne. An attempt at peaceful negotiation with Ferdinand in June 1527 at Olmütz—with the mediation of the Polish ruler, Sigismund I of Jagiello (1506–1548), a relative of both kings—was unproductive. For, as we have seen (part 1, chap. 3), Ferdinand had no option but to restrain his opponent by military means. Neither did the attempt to achieve international recognition end with success.

The enemies of the Habsburg dynasty, most of all Francis I, king of France (1515–1547), had the same plans for King John as did Sultan Süleyman: as a pawn to use against their great European rival, the Habsburgs. King Sigismund of Poland attempted to remain neutral vis-à-vis his relative, however, and no particular help was forthcoming from Henry VIII, king of England (1509–1547), either. In short, Szapolyai was isolated internationally, his Hungarian support was ever weaker, and from July 1527 Ferdinand's hardened troops were pushing him further and further back, culminating in a decisive victory over him next to Tokaj in eastern Hungary on September 27. As such, by the autumn, his reign was threatened with complete collapse.

None of these difficulties gave Szapolyai, driven as he had been for decades by his ambition to rule, pause as to whether he should abdicate. We cannot know how this eventuality would have affected his country's fate; what is sure is that his decision, looking for a way out of a difficult spot, ultimately had catastrophic consequences. On October 18, before the coronation of Ferdinand of Habsburg as king (November 3), he sent an envoy, the Pole Hieronim Łaski, to plead at the Ottoman Porte for help. By doing this, he accepted the sultan's offer of an alliance and decided on a Turkish orientation to his policy. The Istanbul treaty that would ultimately be signed on February 28, 1528, meant that the Hungarian ruler had become a vassal of the sultan, even if the bond of dependency was still rather loose at this stage. It would soon transpire, however, that the path King John had taken could not be reversed. For there could be no tracing back of steps from the Ottoman "alliance," either for the independent Kingdom of Hungary he desired or for a united Hungary. An independent Hungarian principality did not appear in Süleyman's long-term political plans. He had simply sought a Hungarian stooge, according to the well-oiled choreography of conquest as previously detailed (part 1, chap. 2), one who would split Ferdinand's strength and who could support the sultan's army during the campaigns against the Habsburgs. With this treaty, King John had inadvertently stepped into the role of Hungarian "quartermaster" for the Ottomans.

John's decision was even more transformational in terms of Hungary's development. With the road to Istanbul, King John had expanded in a new political direction. For until 1526, Hungarian politicians—John included—had decisively rejected any kind of cooperation with the Ottomans. With Szapolyai's search for an ally, this anti-Turkish unity collapsed. In fact, more and more politicians would follow suit, people who thought—perhaps fired by anti-German sentiment, perhaps out of conviction, perhaps out of self-interest—that an acceptance of dependence on the Ottomans would bring the desired remedy; this despite the fact that the Balkan states provided plentiful evidence that, in the shadow of the Ottoman superpower, there was not the remotest chance for independent statehood across the line of military attack along the Danube. They were generally headed for disappointment, as it would soon transpire that the main force driving events, the sultan's military command, would not waste a great amount of time on the "Turkophile" Hungarians.

Szapolyai would hear the news of the Istanbul treaty not in Hungary but in forced exile in Poland (Tarnów). Ferdinand's latest campaign had shunted him out of the country. The army, led by Commander in Chief Hans Katzianer, would again bring victory for the Habsburg ruler on March 8, 1528, near Szina (Abaúj county). This meant that by May, King John was forced to flee for good, and he was able to return only once everyone both in Vienna and in Buda knew that Sultan Süleyman was starting a new great campaign against the Habsburgs. In August 1529, Szapolyai wasted no time rushing to visit the sultan. At the battlefield at Mohács, he had shown his respect by kissing his ally's hand. The sultan did not fail to show his gratitude. By mid-September, King John again had Buda, taken from Ferdinand's troops, where the sultan left a Turkish army of a few thousand men to make sure of his vassal's loyalty. These troops meant that Szapolyai's independent Hungarian kingdom would never be more than an illusion. There was no turning back.

Squeezed into a corner, Szapolyai nevertheless continued the process of building the government that he had begun at the end of 1526. By the more peaceful mid-1530s, this would bring real results. In the old pre-Mohács tradition, King John arranged his royal court, which in this period was held partly in Várad and partly in Buda. Relying on the nobility, on his good number of private supporters, and on a handful of eminent if often self-interested and unscrupulous lords (in particular Péter Perényi and Bálint Török) and preserving the structures of the Middle Ages, he succeeded in establishing state and public administration as well as the justice system. Thanks to being on a war footing, his power was very centralized; that is to say, Szapolyai recognized the need for centralization. At his diets he did not have to worry about any real resistance from the estates—all their participants had him to thank for their rise to prominence.

For this reason, King John had unprecedented, almost exclusive power, which would be inherited by the princes of Transylvania (see part 1, chap. 5). He alone decided on all matters of importance, involving his chancellor, István Werbőczy, author of the famous *Tripartitum* (Hungarian *Hármaskönyv*), only in the execution of affairs of state. He did less to modernize financial affairs; these continued to be directed primarily by his treasurers (Jakab Tornallyai and then Friar George Martinuzzi). Further eminent posts and offices were largely handed to his acolytes who had recently risen to prominence. His government apparatus—as much in terms of its structure and personnel as of its actual operation—was overall a direct if simplified continuation of that of the Jagiellonian period. The only exception to this was presented by his diplomatic corps, staffed as it was by polyglots, often of humanist erudition, if mostly foreign (Hieronim Łaski, Tranquillus Andronicus, and Giovanni Statileo).

This overly strong power invested in the king had a huge drawback, however: if someone had a hold over the ruler, they would essentially take over the running of the entire country. The two decades after 1530 provided ample evidence of this. This role was played first by Venetian adventurer Lodovico Gritti, hung around King John's shoulders by the sultan, and then by Friar George Martinuzzi, the cleverest double-dealer of the age, capable even of deceiving the Porte. While Gritti, from 1530 to his assassination in 1534, was Szapolyai's governor, Martinuzzi was both treasurer (1534–1551) and governor (1541–1551) to King John's son, the infant John Sigismund—this meant that he was the almost entirely unchecked arbiter of domestic and economic policy in the "eastern" Hungarian state. Martinuzzi would also, for a decade and a half from the mid-1530s, play a crucial role in seeing that the country of King John—who would lead Isabella of Jagiello, the daughter of the Polish king, to the altar in early 1539—and then of his son would not disappear. Indeed, though initially neither Sultan Süleyman, King Ferdinand, nor Martinuzzi wished to establish a new country in Transylvania, ultimately they would all play a key part in the birth of the Ottomans' unique vassal state, the Principality of Transylvania, from Szapolyai's kingdom.

The governance of Friar George Martinuzzi was in many ways similar to that of Gritti. But while the Venetian rogue was essentially interested in serving his own ends, Martinuzzi was motivated by loftier goals. He put the financial affairs of the vassal kingdom in order, reinforced the ruler's authority, and then, with the sultan's troops often away, began to take the first steps toward rapprochement with the Habsburgs. He knew from Gritti's case, however, that any incautious step might surrender the country to the Ottomans. This explains how he used a series of refined diplomatic maneuvers that it was hard to keep pace with in order to implement his attempts to unite the country. The first important step in this was the secret treaty of Várad, signed on February 24, 1538. In this treaty, the two rulers agreed that Szapolyai and Ferdinand could keep their existing territories and that they would help one another against the Ottomans. After King John's death, however—even in the event of his having a son—his part of the country would fall to the House of Habsburg. Szapolyai's heir would receive the principality of Szepes (German *Zips*), to be established in Upper Hungary, in exchange.

Nothing would become of the peace treaty, as after King John's death in July 1540 Friar George himself shrank from putting it into practice. He did not think the time had yet come for the country to be unified. His retraction sped up the course of events. In two unsuccessful campaigns (in 1540 and 1541), Ferdinand attempted to take Buda (see fig. 9), which, in the revenge campaign of 1541, would in the end be occupied by janissaries, with an unusual ruse, and without a single cannon being fired. On this occasion Sultan Süleyman managed to outwit even Martinuzzi. It is no accident that the governor himself considered the event to be one of the greatest errors of his life: "Thus far I have not erred in my acts, except perhaps in handing Buda over to the Turks, for which I was not the only culprit."[3]

After taking control of Buda, the sultan would, as we have mentioned (part 1, chap. 2), disband the kingdom of Szapolyai and divide its territory into three virtual sanjaks. While this showed that in the long term he did not wish for this region to be independent, his decision nevertheless represented a step in the direction of the foundation of the later principality. The development of the area beyond the Tisza River, known as the Partium—and which in medieval times was not at all connected to the Transylvanian voivodship—would henceforth be ever more closely tied to Transylvania. The leaders of the counties in the area beyond the Tisza were quick to realize that it would be increasingly hard to retain their connections with Ferdinand of Habsburg from within Friar George's "sanjak." The Torda diet of 1544 was a key point in this process: here the deputies of the Partium counties declared that they would accept the rule of John Sigismund and thereafter would participate in meetings of the Transylvanian estates, not the royal ones. Meanwhile, Friar George made further attempts at unification.

Despite the Ottoman occupation of Buda, the royal and Transylvanian nobility, the Habsburg political elite, and Friar George all believed that a unified Kingdom of Hungary could be established. It seemed that the shock of the fall of the Hungarian capital could have brought these forces together again. The treaty signed on December 29, 1541, at Gyalu Castle (Kolozs county), which renewed the treaty of Várad, was evidence of this. Queen Isabella promised to give her son's part of the country (as well as the Holy Crown, which was in her possession) to Ferdinand, in return for the estates in the Szepes region. After the defeat of Ferdinand's troops under Buda in September 1542, however, Friar George, quite understandably, called a retreat. In response, the Transylvanian estates annulled the Gyalu treaty at the Torda diet at the end of the year and recognized the elected Hungarian king, John Sigismund, as their ruler. To the suspicious Ottoman Porte, meanwhile, they sent ten thousand florins in tax in the middle of 1543 as a sign of their loyalty, making it clear that the vassalage of the eastern territories had in practice become greater. For all this, it is probable that Martinuzzi's repeat volte-face in late 1542 saved John Sigismund's country from complete Turkish occupation. At this stage the sultan's military command was at least as strongly opposed to the creation of an "eastern" Hungarian state as was its Habsburg rival.

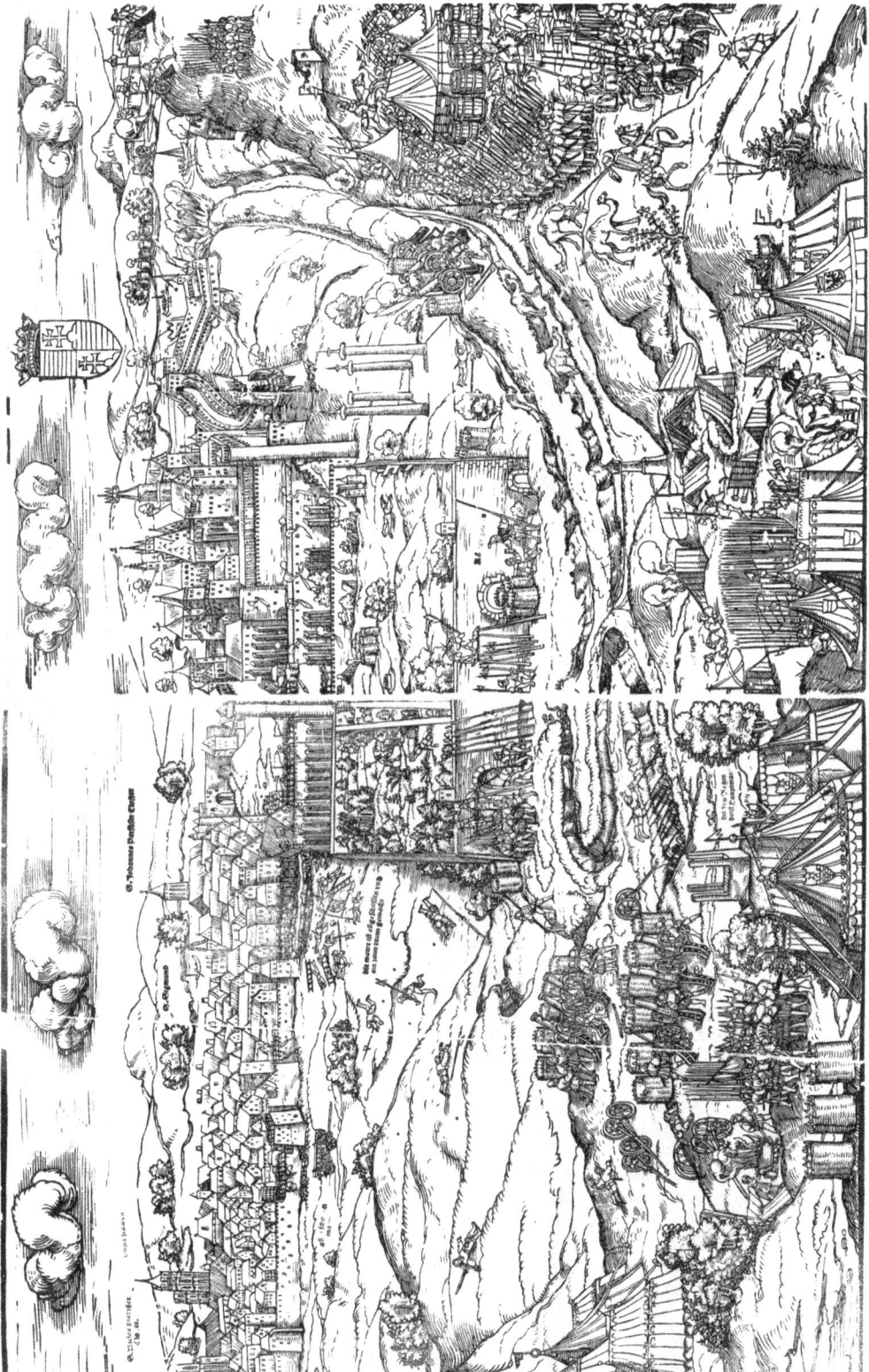

Fig. 9. The Habsburg siege of Buda, 1541. Woodcut by Erhardt Schön, 1541 (Hungarian National Museum, Budapest).

The Porte's indecision thus allowed the question of unification to remain on the agenda: as legitimate Hungarian king, Ferdinand considered himself to be the ruler of the whole of Hungary de jure, while his greatest enemy, Sultan Süleyman, thought exactly the same way. The opportunity for another attempt would finally come after the Ottoman-Habsburg peace of 1547 and Emperor Charles V's victory over the Schmalkalden alliance at Mühlberg (April 24, 1547). Friar George tried again. The Turks already settled in Buda meant he had to be highly cautious. He continued his secret negotiations with Ferdinand's envoys while also trying to convince the pasha of Buda of his loyalty. The final upshot of this would be the Nyírbátor treaty of September 1549. This stated that John Sigismund and his mother would revoke their claims to their country in return for one hundred thousand florins in compensation and the Silesian principalities of Oppeln and Ratibor.

Friar George thus managed to sustain his astonishing if dangerous diplomatic chess game. He was threatened, however, by Queen Isabella's resistance and her revealing the truth of the treaty in Istanbul. This political game, one that many found hard to follow, was increasingly at Süleyman's expense. For this reason, in August 1550 Süleyman asked the Transylvanian estates to "cut off his head or supply him alive to the king's son [viz. John Sigismund], so that the country not be lost for the sake of such a rogue."[4] Although the governor managed to resist those wanting to carry out the sultan's order (Péter Petrovics, voivodes Elias [Ilie] II of Moldavia and Mircea IV of Wallachia, and Pasha Kasim of Buda), he would soon be fated for defeat. His double-dealing scheme would not be understood in Vienna, either. On the night of December 17, 1551, he was murdered by the soldiers of Commander in Chief Gianbattista Castaldo, who was attempting to occupy Transylvania. The troops of Ferdinand I were not able to unify the country, either, though in early 1552 they managed to persuade Isabella and her son, who had returned the Holy Crown to the Habsburg ruler in late summer 1551, to leave Hungary for good. The ultimate course of events would again be determined by the Ottoman troops. They decided the fate of the eastern Hungarian areas during their campaign of 1551–1552: when they occupied the area of Banat and Szolnok, on the banks of the Tisza, Transylvania and the Partium were geographically irrevocably separated from the kingdom and became a province that the Ottomans could easily supervise.

Learning from the efforts of the royal troops in Transylvania from 1551 to 1556, the sultan's military leadership would also recognize that it would better divide the Habsburgs' forces in Hungary if it gave up on the occupation of Transylvania and instead retained it as a vassal. After the return to Transylvania of Isabella and John Sigismund in October 1556, this is how a part of the country that previously no one wanted became the Principality of Transylvania (see map 7), an Ottoman vassal with independent domestic policy, later known by the Turks as "the work of Sultan Süleyman."[5] But no one at the time thought that Friar George's plan to unify the country would only be accomplished three centuries later, in 1867 by the Settlement/Compromise. And by a particularly unjust quirk of fate, the Ottomans and the Habsburgs would expunge Friar George, who had fought by brazen means but for a noble cause, from the history of Hungary, in the same way that they did for many unscrupulous dilettante lords who had craved royal power. For example, this was true of Péter Perényi, who used his own son as a hostage for the sultan, and the opportunist lord Bálint Török. Perényi was imprisoned by Ferdinand I during the royal campaign in autumn 1542; Török

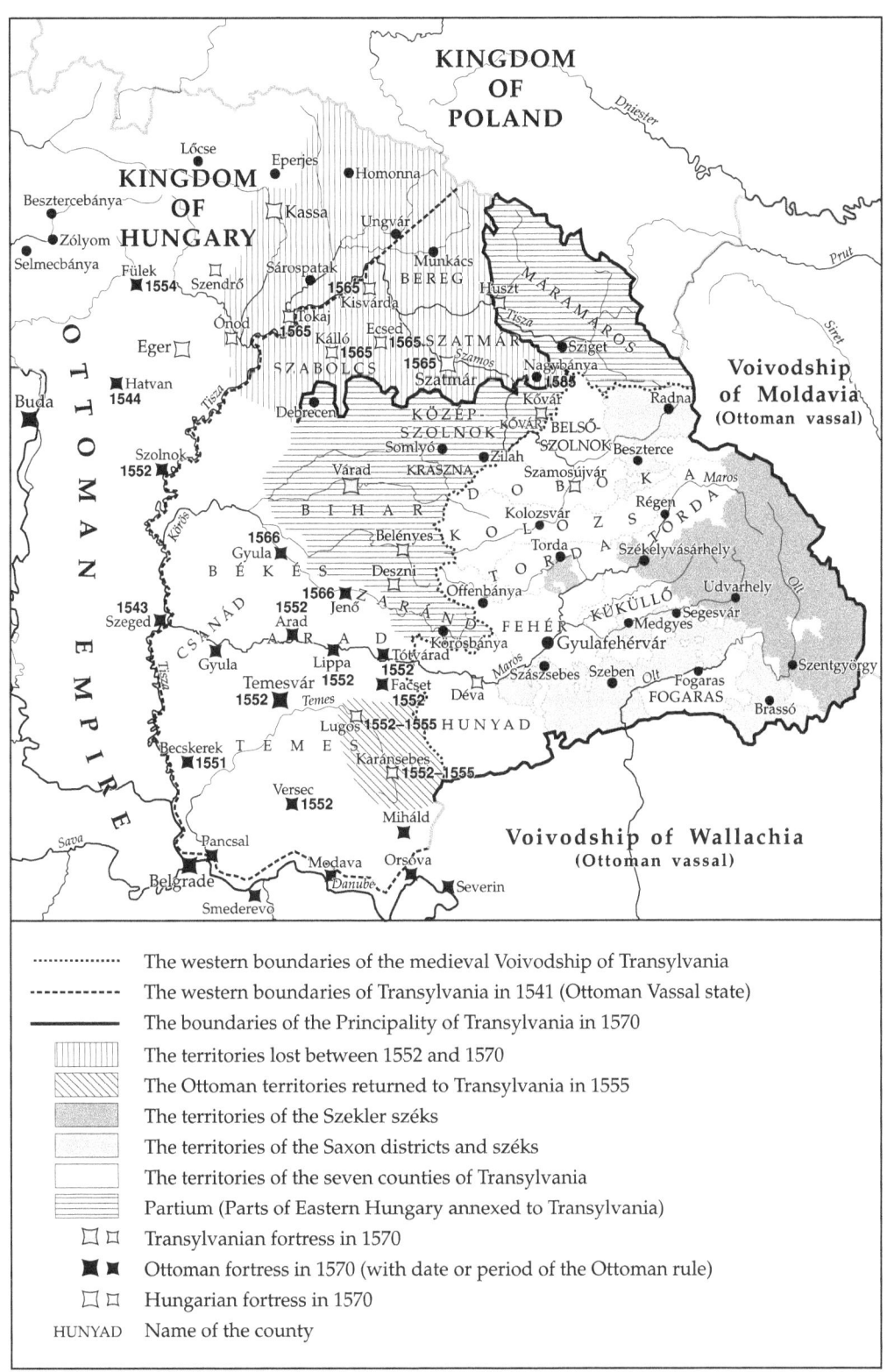

Map 7. Development of the Principality of Transylvania between 1541 and 1570.

was jailed for life by Süleyman when he took Buda and would end his days in the Yedikule prison in Istanbul.

The decisions brought by the Ottoman Porte in the 1550s would seal the fate of the most eastern and also least developed province of the Kingdom of Hungary, the voivodship of Transylvania, for a great many years to come. With the return of the Holy Crown, the constant strengthening of Turkish vassalage, and then the loss of the royal title, the legal continuity of the Kingdom of Hungary as preserved by John Szapolyai would also become a thing of the past. From this point on, Transylvania was no longer legally the heir to the former Hungarian state, even if it understandably retained a great many traditions from it in terms of administration and culture. Transylvania came to have a life of its own—under Ottoman tutelage.

Notes

1. Gábor Barta, *La route qui mène à Istanbul 1526–1528* (Budapest: Akadémiai Kiadó, 1994); *A Forgotten Hungarian Royal Dynasty: The Szapolyais,* ed. Pál Fodor and Szabolcs Varga (Budapest: RCH, 2020).

2. Cf. Richard Bonney, *The European Dynastic States, 1494–1660* (Oxford: Oxford UP, 1991).

3. Gábor Barta, *Vajon kié az ország?* [Whose is the country?] (Budapest: Helikon Kiadó, 1988), 100; cf. recently Teréz Oborni. *Az ördöngős Barát. Fráter György (1482–1551)* [The devilish monk: Friar Georg, 1482–1551] (Pécs: Kronosz Kiadó, 2017), 89–109.

4. Sándor Szilágyi, ed., *Monumenta comitialia regni Transylvaniae/Erdélyi Országgyűlési Emlékek* [Documents from the Transylvanian diets], vol. 1, *1540–1556* (Budapest: MTA, 1875), 310.

5. Fodor, *Unbearable Weight of Empire,* 129–130; Teréz Oborni, "The Country Nobody Wanted: Some Aspects of the History of Transylvanian Principality," *Specimina nova dissertationum ex Instituto Historico Universitatis Quinqueecclesiensis* [Pécs], Pars prima: Sectio mediaevalis no. 2 (2003): 101–107.

Fig. 10. Stephen Báthory, prince of Transylvania (1571–1586), king of Poland (1576–1586). Engraving by Jost Amman, 1576 (Hungarian National Museum, Budapest).

5

ON A NARROW PATH

The Principality of Transylvania

In the two decades after 1556, the province of Transylvania, previously intended for unification, would, on account of its Ottoman jurisdiction, go so far as to become an enemy of the Habsburg Monarchy and the dynasty-governed Kingdom of Hungary, in a political and military sense. From this time, the interests of the kingdom and of Transylvania would by necessity diverge for the most part and for a prolonged period. Transylvania was squeezed to the periphery of two great powers, often becoming a tool for their struggles against each other, forcing its princes to pursue politics amid enormous difficulties, or, in other words, on a narrow path. As Pál Gyulay, councilor to Prince Sigismund Báthory, fittingly put it in 1585, Transylvania and its key western bastion of Várad "are between Turks and Germans. One of these is a huge nation, the other a very practical-minded one. To learn to behave in a way that there be trouble from neither side is no small feat."[1]

The "practical-minded" nation, the Habsburgs, never gave up on unifying the kingdom and the principality, and yet they would soon prepare to defend themselves from it. In military terms it was impossible to retain Transylvania—as the failed attempt to do so in the 1550s showed—and so the Viennese court were forced to put their illusory hopes to one side. The Habsburg Monarchy's financial and military resources had rather to be expended on constructing the border defense system against the Ottomans—as had been explicitly recommended in 1555 to the military leadership in Vienna by András Báthory, the chief justice of Hungary, a lord who lived close to Transylvania. He saw that in the absence of this defense system there would never be a chance to unite the kingdom and the principality, as the fate of the Ottoman vassal state of Transylvania would depend first and foremost not on the Hungarian rulers but on the decisions of the Ottoman Porte.

In the next few decades, Transylvania would enjoy a different status in the politics of the court in Vienna. That the Turkish ally had now become an enemy was clearly shown by a line of border defense being built from the end of the 1550s in the northeastern part of the kingdom, similar to the one defending against the Ottomans. After Szatmár fortress was taken from John Sigismund in 1565, this brought about the birth of the captaincy general of Szatmár (see map 5 in chap. 2) within the Upper Hungarian captaincy general, led by General Lazarus von Schwendi, a military leader and military theorist known throughout Europe. The castles here were dedicated to halting the advance not of the "eternal enemies of Christianity" but rather of the troops of the Hungarian princes who were their vassals.

But we should immediately add that John Sigismund, the first prince of the new state of Transylvania (*princeps Transilvaniae Partiumque regni Hungariae*), was also constructing his own series of castles against the kingdom. In fact, there would soon be a list of border customs between the two Hungarian states that had been forced to follow separate paths and had become constitutionally distinct. Despite this, Transylvania would remain part of the European system of states (see map 7 in chap. 4).

This was borne out by the Agreement of Speyer in 1570, the failure of which further worsened the situation. In vain did the envoys of John Sigismund and Emperor Maximilian II agree in the German imperial city that at the former's death Transylvania would pass to the Habsburgs. After the death of the young ruler on May 25, 1571, the Transylvanian estates chose Stephen Báthory of Somlyó to be their prince (see fig. 10); Báthory would soon succeed in breaking away from the narrow path—and in quite extraordinary fashion. Between 1571 and 1575, the military command in Vienna, by supporting Gáspár Bekes, also attempted to weaken, even depose, Báthory by means of force. But Bekes's defeat at Kerelőszentpál (Küküllő county) on July 9, 1575, put a final end to such efforts. Báthory's power was consolidated by the execution of the almost forty lords who had supported his rival. Meanwhile, Sultan Murad III expressed his appreciation by raising his annual taxes from ten thousand to fifteen thousand florins.

The Porte would soon agree to Báthory's kingdom of Poland, principally because the prince had won the Polish throne from Archduke Ernest of Habsburg. At the time of the Porte's wars in the Mediterranean and Persia, it suited Istanbul all too well that the principality, reinforced in this way, could tie up the Habsburgs' significant financial and military resources. The numbers tell the story best: in 1576, the total pay of the roughly 6,100-strong army serving the thirteen fortresses of the captaincy general of Upper Hungary (see map 5 in chap. 2) amounted to about 70 percent of the annual income of the Kingdom of Hungary. Vienna was forced to spend more on the defense of these territories than on the border region near Győr that protected the imperial capital itself. Süleyman's calculation had proved right: by putting the principality on its own path, he had succeeded in dividing the Hungarian forces and using Transylvania in the battle against the Habsburgs. What is more, Báthory's dual rule over both Transylvania and Poland meant that some members of the Hungarian high nobility were forced to waver in their loyalties. In the northeast parts of the country, they had started to believe in a new illusion: that, by establishing an eastern Hungarian kingdom (a Turkish vassal, if need be) from Transylvania or Poland, they could unite the principality and the kingdom or a part of it. But any reprieve from the narrow path set by the Ottomans could be only a brief one.

Obligations elsewhere prevented the Ottomans from opposing Báthory's rule of Poland. Indeed, they considered a Transylvanian state strengthened by this Polish support as an even more useful trump to assist their conquests in the direction of Vienna. As they themselves emphasized at the time, Báthory "owes it to the Turks, in return for assistance to Transylvania and Poland, to assist in the occupation of the rest of Hungary."[2] For the residents of Transylvania, the looser status of vassal state was adequate for this purpose. This meant, more specifically, that the princes could pursue an independent foreign policy only with the sultan's approval but that in domestic policy they would be given a free hand. To prove their loyalty, they paid taxes to the Porte, which would rise from the amount of ten thousand florins paid in the first year (1543) to twenty thousand by the end of the century. All in all—and together with various other obligatory gifts—this was a considerable drain on the country's resources, representing about 10 percent of its annual income. The prince was elected by the estates, but he would ascend to the throne for certain only once he had received the sultan's celebratory letter of agreement (*ahdname*) appointing him, as well as the symbols of his inauguration (flag and baton).

Despite all these forms of bondage to the Ottomans, it should be emphasized that Transylvania's vassalage was the most favorable of all the relationships enjoyed with the Porte by its vassal states.[3] In the neighboring two Romanian voivodships, Wallachia and Moldavia, domestic policy as well as foreign policy followed the wishes of the sultan's court, the voivodes were appointed by the Porte, the taxes they paid were much higher than those paid by the Transylvanians, and to all intents and purposes their role was to provide meat for Istanbul and to guarantee passage along the Danube. Turkish vassalage left much less of a mark on the political and everyday life of Transylvania. It was only with the arrival of carpets, blankets, embroidered pillows, and decorated weapons that the Ottomans had any particular influence on crafts and the arts.

While the princes' room for maneuver on foreign policy was severely limited, they had more or less complete control over domestic policy. In contrast to the Kingdom of Hungary, the influence of the estates in Transylvania was modest. It was only really in time of war, and with the support of either the Ottomans or the Habsburgs, that a lord could challenge the authority of the prince and be a pretender to his throne. The economic strength of the princes, on the other hand, was guaranteed by the "state" domains (e.g., Szamosújvár, Somlyó, Várad, Déva, Gyulafehérvár, and Kővár), which by Transylvanian standards were quite considerable, as well as their lands in the Partium and sometimes even in the Kingdom of Hungary. One special feature of Transylvania was that a good few of its rulers (e.g., John Sigismund, Stephen Bocskai, and the Rákóczi dynasty) were originally from the Kingdom of Hungary.

The outcome of all this was that the princes had almost unchecked power over domestic policy. This meant that, together with a few influential advisers, they would decide on all matters of importance, whether home, financial, or military affairs. In the sixteenth century, it was only during the Long Turkish War (1591–1606) that the ruling authorities could be threatened by a significant pretender with the support of the Ottoman Porte (such as Moses Székely in 1603). The prince was even in a position to confiscate the lands of those defying his will or to execute his top advisers. This is what Sigismund Báthory did to Councilor Pál Gyulay in 1592, to Lord Steward János Gálffy in the following year, and then in 1594 to almost the entire opposition camp. István Jósika, a descendant of Chancellor Farkas Kovacsóczy, one of those executed, would similarly end his life on the scaffold four years later. Events such as these were almost unimaginable in the Kingdom of Hungary; all this was a consequence of the unique institutional structure of the principality.

After the government of the Transylvanian state was established in the middle of the century, John Sigismund and his closest advisers had two traditions to fall back on. They could build in part on the centralized power structure of the kingdom of John Szapolyai and in part on the executive of the late medieval Transylvanian voivodship. As the institutions of central government were never established, in its defining attributes the operation and administration of the principality remained medieval. Of King John's court, only the positions of chancellor and treasurer survived, together with the toothless sovereign council. No other high office (such as palatine, or chief justice) existed in Transylvania, as these could not operate after the legal continuity as a kingdom was lost. Although the ruler's propaganda often attempted to present the principality as the legitimate heir to the medieval Kingdom of Hungary (even appealing to the fact that the Habsburg rulers regarded Transylvania as part of the realm of St. Stephen), not even "independent" statehood, numerous traditions held over from the Middle Ages, and the considerable advance of Hungarian culture could mask the fact that this was an illusion. The profundity of the change was summarized with finesse by the famed French traveler Pierre Lescalopier in 1574: "Everyone speaks Hungarian, the original language of the country—for Transylvania was previously a province of Hungary."[4]

The most important administrative and executive body of the principality would ultimately become the chancellery, as organized by Mihály Csáky, councilor to Queen Isabella, in the 1560s. As his foundation, he looked not to the chancellery of the Transylvanian voivodships before 1526 but rather to that of King John, which had mostly preserved the traits of the medieval royal chancellery. So did this government body become trustee to the whole state public administration. Of its two sections, the larger chancellery attended to foreign issues, with the approval of the Porte, and directed domestic affairs with its own orders. The smaller chancellery was primarily concerned with judicial matters, keeping a written record of the judgments of the court of justice. A few official posts in financial and military administration (treasurer, chief tax collector, general of field troops, and court chief captain) remained or were reintroduced, but these did not restrict the key role the chancellery played in financial and military affairs, as the holders of these posts tended to be either relatives of or on familiar terms with the ruler. As such, these offices tended to reinforce central power rather than weaken it, particularly if the members of the council had the right only to give an opinion.

Neither did the Transylvanian diet present a significant restraining force on the prince. This probably had its roots not in the Hungarian diet of King John but rather in the provincial assembly of the voivodship of Transylvania—that is, over time it took on the functions of a diet (such as levying taxes and legislation). While the Transylvanian diet may have met a number of times a year, it would restrict the prince's power only on rare occasions. There was no upper house—that is, there was no class of secular or church magnates with political and economic power to obstruct the actions of the princes. In addition, the princes could exploit the often opposing interests of the three nations with estate representation, namely the Hungarians, Szeklers, and (Transylvanian) Saxons that had made up the estates of Transylvania since the union of Kápolna of 1437 and that sat in the same chamber. But considering that in the sixteenth and seventeenth centuries there was no estate system at all in the Romanian voivodships, the construction of the Transylvanian estate state amid Ottoman vassalage can be seen as a considerable achievement.

The economic and social structure of Transylvania in the sixteenth century also remained basic. It was hard to alter the heritage from before 1526, as the voivodship—despite its rich natural advantages—was one of the medieval kingdom's least developed provinces. The new statehood that grew out of being squeezed between great powers can have done little to improve this situation. In this sense, the rule of Stephen Báthory (1571–1586) was an unusually positive era. In this period, in more peaceful circumstances, Transylvania would on the one hand—thanks to traders from Kolozsvár, Várad, Nagyszeben, and Brassó—become more closely involved in long-distance trade to Central Europe and to the Ottoman Empire, and on the other hand it would be able to significantly increase its incomes (c. 220,000 florins per year) by reviving rich sites for noble metals (Abrudbánya, Offenbánya, Körösbánya, Zalatna, and Nagybánya) and for salt (Dés, Torda, Kolozs, Szék, and Vízakna).

The weakness of the estate system and problems facing the economy were in no small measure connected to the specificities of the society built on the three nations (Hungarian, Szekler, and Saxon), to its divisions, and to the transformation it was currently undergoing. Within the Hungarian nobility, the absence of a class of magnates presented a problem throughout. Great numbers of Szeklers fought a desperate struggle to maintain the various privileges (first and foremost, exemption from tax) they had earned for themselves on the battlefield. Their uprisings were repeatedly defeated by the prince's troops (in 1562 and 1595–1596), thrusting the country into a serious domestic political crisis. In early November 1599, during the Long Turkish War, it was none other than the Szeklers who finished with Prince Andrew Báthory, after just half a year of his rule. Their situation was finally be resolved by Prince Sigismund Báthory (see fig. 11) at the end of 1601, when he newly granted their ancient freedoms and restored their government.

Despite Ottoman vassalage and a deficit in its development, there were many advantages to Transylvania being its own state. These did not, of course, include the anachronistic portrayal of the sixteenth century in Hungarian historiography and public knowledge, according to which the principality meant the continuance of the "national kingdom" or the "Hungarian national state." For one thing, there were no nation-states in Europe at this time; for another, as we have seen (part 1, chap. 3), the Kingdom of Hungary, not the principality, would be a legitimate legal successor to the medieval Hungarian state. The greatest achievement can be seen as the relatively peaceful development of Transylvania and the flourishing Hungarian culture, which in many ways was favored by their forcible disengagement and isolation. Although most of these tendencies—as we see in part 1, chapter 10—could also be discerned in the Kingdom of Hungary, in the latter, with the ruling court moving to Vienna, support for Hungarian culture, language, and literature was provided mostly by the Hungarian aristocratic courts and the literary and artistic societies of prelates. In Transylvania, on the other hand, this task could continue to be undertaken by the princely court, which from the rule of John Sigismund to the governance of Sigismund Báthory could do much for Hungarian literature and culture. Indeed, the son of King John would achieve renown not just for creating his Renaissance court but also as a supporter of Protestantism.

A crucial role was played in all of this by Transylvania, which, like the Kingdom of Hungary, "changed religions" during the sixteenth century, so to speak—a phenomenon we discuss in a separate chapter (part 1, chap. 9). Indeed, in the principality, even more radical trends would find a foothold. For all this, there was as yet no decision at the 1568 diet of Torda on the institutionalization and acceptance of the four free confessions (Catholic, Lutheran,

Fig. 11. Thaler of Sigismund Báthory, prince of Transylvania, with his portrait and family coat of arms, 1589 (Hungarian National Museum, Budapest).

Calvinist, and Unitarian), as previous research has suggested; there was merely a decision on the right to preach the scriptures freely. At this time, these religions did not have established church institutions based on finalized dogmatic principles—as recent church history investigations have found.[5] They were, however, listed individually and as established churches at the Gyulafehérvár diet in April 1595: "We saw to it that the received religions, *catholica sive romana, lutherana, calvinistica et ariana* [Catholic or Roman, Lutheran, Calvinist, and Unitarian], all be observed throughout the country."[6] Hungarian and international Protestant church history can rightly be proud of this, as it is one of the first examples of its kind in the whole of Europe.

For all these undeniably favorable aspects, the independence as appointed by the Ottomans would in the long term have a number of damaging consequences. Even the Hungary of this period struggled to accept that a province of such considerable size was continuing its existence in separation. This separation also meant that this part of the country, which had already been backward in its development, would now make progress in an uneven, largely medieval fashion. Although in the sixteenth century Stephen Báthory was the one who steered the cleverest political course along this narrow path between the "huge" and the "practical-minded" nations, considerably expanding his room for maneuver even in foreign affairs, none of this did much to change the fact that Transylvania's economic, social, and administrative deficit after 1526 would only grow relative to that of the Kingdom of Hungary. And yet, squeezed between two empires, there was no other course of action. As such, it was quite an achievement in and of itself that, despite Turkish vassalage, Transylvania remained part of the European system of states. For Ottoman control was unavoidable; it was simply reality itself. In the early seventeenth century, Péter Pázmány, archbishop of Esztergom, was right in saying, "Cursed be the man who would encourage you [Transylvanians] to break away from the Turks, to kick back at them, until God takes mercy on Christendom, for you live in their throats."[7] And yet the seventeenth century would bring Transylvania a real golden age (see part 2, chap. 4).

Notes

1. György Szabó, *Abafáji Gyulay Pál* [Pál Gyulay de Abafa] (Budapest: Akadémiai Kiadó, 1974), 92.

2. Lajos Szádeczky, *Báthory István lengyel királlyá választása, 1574–1576* [The election of Stephen Báthory as king of Poland, 1574–1576] (Budapest: MTA, 1887), 355.

3. Gábor Kármán, and Lovro Kunčević, eds., *The European Tributary States of the Ottoman Empire in the Sixteenth and Seventeenth Centuries* (Leiden: Brill, 2013).

4. Kálmán Benda and Lajos Tardy, eds., *Pierre Lescalopier utazása Erdélybe (1574)* [The voyage of Pierre Lescalopier to Transylvania (1574)] (Budapest: Európa Könyvkiadó, 1982), 71.

5. The new summary work on this issue is Mihály Balázs, "Tolerant Country—Misunderstood Laws: Interpreting Sixteenth-Century Transylvanian Legislation Concerning Religion," *Hungarian Historical Review* 2 (2013): 85–108.

6. Sándor Szilágyi, ed., *Monumenta comitialia regni Transylvaniae/Erdélyi Országgyűlési Emlékek* [Documents from the Transylvanian diets], vol. 3, *1576–1596* (Budapest: MTA, 1877), 472.

7. Éva V. Windisch, ed., *Kemény János és Bethlen Miklós művei* [Works of János Kemény and Miklós Bethlen] (Budapest: Szépirodalmi Könyvkiadó, 1980), 100.

Fig. 12. Humanist Johannes Sambucus (1531–1584). Engraving by Theodor de Bry, 1597 (Hungarian National Museum, Budapest).

6

SOCIETY FINDS ITS WAY

Half a century of deep-rooted changes had forced all classes of Hungarian society to face very real challenges. The dual election of kings, the Ottomans' occupation, and an almost permanent war footing had taken their toll on everyday life. Much depended on whether people could acclimatize to these new circumstances. Hungarian society would, however, until the end of the sixteenth century, prove its capacity to revitalize itself and to survive. It would get back on its feet from adversity again and again, until the Long Turkish War took it down the road to ruin. But a number of distinct changes would take place before then: it survived one of the largest emigrations in the history of the nobility, while becoming more diverse; its aristocracy underwent great transformation, and in the meantime a new social group came into being.

After 1526, the most influential echelon of Hungarian society remained the nobility, which ran the country's internal political life. Indeed, as interpreted at the time, it was only the nobles and the residents of free royal cities who counted as gentlemen of the realm (Latin *regnicolae*, Hungarian *országlakók*), citizens, or citizens with full rights. The nobility represented about 2.5–3 percent of the population—in the Kingdom of Hungary, its number in the middle of the century was almost ten thousand, or as many as sixteen thousand together with Slavonia and Transylvania. If we include family members, we estimate the size of the nobility in the area of the former medieval kingdom to be eighty to one hundred thousand. Relative to a total population of about 3.3 million, this represents a significant proportion, even by European standards. From the last quarter of the century, indeed, ennoblement was becoming ever more frequent; a few decades later, it would be happening en masse, a phenomenon we term *noble inflation*.[1] Thanks to the good services of the Hungarian rulers resident in Vienna or Prague, more and more border soldiers or city burghers enriched by trade were being accepted to the ranks of the nobility. The backing of a magnate could also see their acquaintances or educated peasants be raised up into privilege. But in this period it was also not unknown for people to purchase certificates of nobility for money.

Despite its constant expansion and the preservation of its key role in the running of the country, in the sixteenth century the Hungarian nobility nevertheless lived through one of its most difficult periods. From the 1540s onward, it was forced to flee the territory occupied by the Ottomans—which by 1566 would represent 40 percent of the country—and remained in larger numbers only in areas close to the border of this territory and in some larger market towns. From the inner parts of Ottoman Hungary, it was forced to flee in very large numbers (and in tragic conditions) either to the Kingdom of Hungary or to Transylvania.

For example, after the fall of Buda in 1541, there was a considerable emigration from the areas to the south of the capital to the northern parts of the country; when Szigetvár and Gyula fell in 1566, there was a similar move from the provincial counties of Baranya, Somogy, and Tisza-Maros to the western and northern areas of the country. Meanwhile, in the 1540s, Croatian nobles had migrated in great numbers to Transdanubia and even to Austrian and Moravian territories. In the north, on the other hand, Abaúj and Nógrád counties were overrun by a large number of gentry who had lost their lands in Ottoman Hungary. Yet it was evidence of an unusual social self-organization that the displaced nobility attempted to retain its property rights from the Kingdom of Hungary or the Partium, even within Ottoman Hungary.

The exodus of the Hungarian and Croatian nobility in the mid-sixteenth century can be seen as extraordinary, even by the standards of Central Europe. Its scope and significance are exemplified by the case of the world-renowned humanist polymath Johannes Sambucus (Hungarian János Zsámboky) (see fig. 12). His father had fled the market town of Zsámbék (archaic form: Zsámbok), thirty kilometers to the west of Buda, to royal Nagyszombat—hence his surname. His mother, meanwhile, was from Croatia, or at least her surname, Horváth, suggests as much. He was thus descended from refugees on both sides and then pursued a fine career at the Habsburg court in Vienna.[2]

The forced emigration of Hungarian nobles and noble inflation meant that it was the poorest echelon of the nobility that flourished most. In Sopron county in western Hungary, for example, this class grew four- or fivefold from the middle of the century to its end. The largest group in the nobility, the gentry, with middling and small domains (one to one hundred plots or Latin *porta*), was best defined by its diversity. While in principle the privileges described by István Werbőczy in his *Tripartitum* meant that all nobles "were among equals" (*una eademque nobilitas*), the strata of the gentry were distinctly separate. Which group one was in depended principally on the amount of his wealth, the role he had played in administering the counties, his connections to magnates, and his relatives.

Of the great many members of the gentry, only 2,500–3,000 were nobles with estates; the rest were all in the "poor" category. The former were led by the (few hundred) wealthy nobles with middling estates (*bene possessionati*), who had a number of villages (fifty to one hundred plots) and who would often enter the service of a magnate as a *familiaris* (i.e., noble retainer). As in Hungary the feudal hierarchy had not been established, the system of familiarity was of great significance in the Middle Ages. This meant that some middling and small landowners belonged to the family (hence the term) of a magnate; more precisely, they served their lords according to the contract signed with them. Wealthier nobles would be court subordinates to magnates, acting as their representatives in various offices, or their office-bearers performing military, economic, and administrative tasks, or officers in their private armies. Any one magnate could have a hundred such subordinates, but even the archbishops of Esztergom had almost a hundred court "familiars." As a well-to-do middling landowner could have a few servants, the system grew into a hierarchical network. The institution of familiarity much aided the magnates' political and military influence on a given region. It was partly this wealthier middling landowner class that would provide the elite of the counties, their top leaders and deputies at the diet.

The lion's share (90%) of the landowning nobility was made up of the small landowners, however. And within this the largest group was of those whose estate did not even reach ten plots. Some of these nobles undertook familiar roles in manorial castles and domains. Thanks to this, and to connections made by marriage, even those with meager estates could take up office in the county apparatus (deputy of the county's *ispán* [Latin *vicecomes*, Hungarian *alispán*], noble judge, juror, notary, or delegate at the diet). By the early modern period, that is, the distribution of roles in the political life of a given county was decided not only by the sizes of estates but also by one's network of familiars and relatives or even by one's education. Thus could it happen that, by the end of the sixteenth century, members of the poorest families or families with no lands could become noble judges or, thanks to their studies, lawyers.

This lowest echelon of the gentry was made up of nobles with a single plot of land and of so-called curialists and armalists. This many-thousand-strong group would often spend its days living the lives that serfs did, distinguished from the serfs merely by their noble lands or houses with noble status (Latin *curia*, Hungarian *kúria*) and by their charters of ennoblement (Latin *litterae armales*, Hungarian *nemeslevél*) and the privileges these brought. Such nobles often lived in separate settlements, so-called noble villages (for example, in Zala, Vas, Sopron, and Pozsony counties, or, in the north, in Borsod, Abaúj, Zemplén, Szabolcs, Szatmár, Ung, and Bereg counties). They did, however, have the chance to better themselves, if to a smaller degree than their middling landowner peers. For them, too, the best escape routes from poverty were provided by soldiering on the borders or by serving alongside a magnate in his army or in administering his domain. In the sixteenth century, another important method of self-advancement would be an intellectual or administrative career. The Sopron county small landowner Mózes Cziráky, for example—primarily thanks to his excellent work as a lawyer and then as a judge—rose in two decades from being an ordinary county noble judge to the protonotary office of chief justice (Latin *prothonotarius judicis curiae*), one of the country's highest judicial positions. Then, as the so-called Personal (Latin *personalis*, Hungarian *személynök*), he went on to become president of the lower house of the Hungarian diet.

For all its diversity, the Hungarian gentry was more or less united on one point. In terms of native tongue and ethnicity, the nobility was, until the second half of the sixteenth century, predominantly Magyar. Exceptions to this were in the Croatian and Slavonian territories and a few northern border provinces. In Trencsén county, for example, there were a good few Slovak small landowners; the Slovak and Hungarian nobility were also mixed in Zólyom, Árva, Turóc, and Liptó counties. In these areas the aristocratic class was often Slavic in origin, though most groups were Magyarized (e.g., the Podmaniczky family, the Osztrosics/Ostrošić family, and later, the Szvatojánszky, rechristened Szentiványi, family). In Máramaros county in the northeast, Orthodox Romanian small landowners were numerous, while in the southern provinces it was South Slav (Serbian and Croatian) dignitaries who took the place of the Hungarian nobles who had left. This would be connected to changes in the ethnic map of the country, as we see in part 1, chapter 8.

The most important class of nobles, despite its small size (about thirty families), was made up of the secular and church large landowners with more than three hundred plots and the nobles (c. fifty families) with middling to large domains between one hundred and three hundred plots. Although the country's ruling class suffered terrible loss of life at the Battle of Mohács (where a dozen magnates and seven prelates fell), only one family (the Pálóczy one) was to die out completely. In terms of the number of families within it, the highest echelon of society remained unchanged through the sixteenth century (with some fifty to eighty families). But especially in a political and military sense, it was really the new era after 1526 that brought fundamental change to the high nobility. Most of the magnate families of the turn of the sixteenth century would, by the 1570s, have been replaced or have lost much of their former influence.

In the two decades after 1526, another four eminent families followed in the footsteps of the Pálóczy family (the Kanizsai, Ernuszt, Szentgyörgyi-Bazini, and Korlátkövy families), while the most powerful lord of the Jagiellonian period, John Szapolyai—trapped in the eastern part of the country, having lost his castles—quickly disappeared from among the largest landowning families. Then, by the 1560s, the Bebek, Országh, Losonczy, and Drágffy families were all lost, with no male heir. But the defunct families were in no time replaced by others (the Nádasdy and Serédy families and the foreign Salm, Nyáry, and Choron ones, as well as the Draskovics/Drašković, Erdődy, and Zrínyi/Zrinski families in Croatia). They all had King Ferdinand to thank for their rise, as through marriage, talent, connections, military service, or just pushiness, they had all acquired lands in the safer areas of the kingdom.

To take the example of Tamás Nádasdy, the former royal secretary founded his fortune on one of the most opportune marriages of the first half of the sixteenth century. By taking the hand of Orsolya Kanizsai in 1535, able through the institution of so-called prefection ("turning into a son," Latin *prefectio in filium, in haeredem masculinum*, Hungarian *fiúsítás*) to inherit,[3] he came into an enormous estate (comprising Kanizsa, Kapuvár, Sárvár, and Léka), one that was in well-defended Transdanubia. The most influential betrothal of the second half of the century was that of Miklós Pálffy to Maria Fugger, daughter of a prestigious German banking family, in 1583, with which he reinforced the value of his connections in the Holy Roman Empire and at the Vienna court. Both Nádasdy and Pálffy laid the foundations for the financial well-being of their families for many centuries to come, as did Miklós Zrínyi, the hero of Szigetvár in 1566, who, through his own marriage and those of his sons, even penetrated the supranational aristocracy of the Habsburg Monarchy. They would also set an example for their descendants in the world of politics and military leadership.

István Dobó (the hero of Eger in 1552) and Simon Forgách rose to prominence for their invaluable service to running the new system of border defenses. Meanwhile, Ferenc Révay, Mihály Mérey, and the historiographer Miklós Istvánffy had their intellectual and administrative careers to thank for their rise from ordinary bureaucrats to the country's chief judges. Of the old families, it was the Perényi, Bánffy, Báthory, Batthyány, Thurzó, and Drugeth de Homonna families and the Frankopans with their estates in Croatia that were able to maintain their positions, mainly thanks to their lands being in areas more protected from Ottoman incursions and because of their eminent national positions.

Of course, not all the families that improved their standing in the first half of the century succeeded in clinging to their place in the elite. The significance of certain less eminent families lasted but a single generation; that of the Choron, Dobó, Mágochy, and Serédy families lasted for only two, mostly because they died out so quickly. The power of the Draskovics, Erdődy, Nádasdy, Nyáry, and Zrínyi families, on the other hand, would last for centuries. Alongside them, in the third generation after 1526, new families would again appear (the Alaghy, Illésházy, Istvánffy, Pálffy, Rákóczi, and Thököly families), similarly by acquiring the estates of the defunct families. By this stage, however, there were fewer opportunities for the acquisition of grand estates than there had been in the years after the Battle of Mohács, and these were mostly through marriage. Of these, the Illésházy, Rákóczi, Pálffy, and Thököly would retain long-term significance.

Accession to the Habsburg Monarchy and in particular the establishment of a joint Austro-Hungarian military left a deep impression on the Hungarian high nobility. While Hungarian aristocrats had to build new connections at the court in Vienna, as we have seen (part 1, chap. 3), a new noble class of foreign extraction appeared in Hungary, one that initially acquired its lands through marriage and in return for military service. Some were granted Hungarian nobility (Latin *indigenatus*),[4] especially the nobles from Lower Austria who in this period played a crucial role in the management of the monarchy as a whole. Just a few more important examples were Erasmus Teufel, cavalry captain, in 1542; Eck Count of Salm und Neuburg, captain general of Győr, in 1563, together with his brothers (Niklas and Julius); Leonhard von Harrach and Adam von Dietrichstein, lord stewards of Vienna, in 1563 and 1583, respectively; and Hans Rueber, captain general of Kassa, in 1572. Jiří Pruskovský (1563) and Ladislav Popel z Lobkovic (1572) were the first of those arriving from the Bohemian lands, through their connections established along the northwest border. In this period, however, only a few established roots and acquired significant lands in Hungary, even provisionally, as the elite of the monarchy considered it a dangerous frontier country because of the Ottoman wars.

Concurrently, Hungarian aristocrats could also attain "citizenship" abroad. However, on account of difficulties in integration, as detailed above, this was slightly less prevalent than the headway made by foreigners in Hungary. We currently know of only eight Hungarians who joined the *Herrenstand*, the highest echelon of the estates of Lower Austria, in the sixteenth century: Bernát Thurzó (1550), Simon Forgách (1568), and András Dóczy (1593), principally thanks to their Austrian relatives; János Pethő (1563), who had a house in Vienna, for his services against the Ottomans and because of his second wife, the Austrian Elisabeth von Sinzendorf; Gábor Majláth (1567), son of Transylvanian voivode István, and the much-mentioned Miklós Pálffy (1589), mostly for their service to the court; and finally, János and István Liszthy (1599), on account of the successful activities in Vienna of their relative János Liszthy, Hungarian court chancellor, and his similarly foreign relatives. But in this century only one Hungarian aristocrat had both Austrian and Bohemian nobility: Miklós Pálffy, the brilliant soldier raised at the Habsburg court.

Overall, for all its transformation and the appearance of new arrivals, the Hungarian high aristocracy was not watered down. The fifty-odd aristocratic families and a handful of rich prelates owned about 40–50 percent of all the tax-paying plots (*porta*). For this reason, the high nobles and the prelates would continue to determine the direction of the domestic political life of the country. They would fill the highest national offices, and they would sit on the Hungarian Council and preside over the high courts. They also made up the upper house of the diet, to which, along with the county's *ispán*s (Latin *comes*, Hungarian *ispán*, i.e., sheriff), they would receive personal invitations from the ruler. And, thanks to their fortresses, great estates, and private armies, in some parts of the country they had so much power (e.g., the Zrínyi family in the Muraköz region or the Nádasdy and Batthyány families in Transdanubia) that many Austrian, Bohemian, and German aristocrats would have been envious. As we will see, they were capable of acclimatizing to favorable economic developments, and as such they controlled both domestic political and economic power, as well as being the greatest supporters of Hungarian arts and culture (see part 1, chaps. 7 and 10).

Along with changes to the nobility, one of the most distinctive aspects of social history after 1526 was the development of the border defense army serving the royal fortresses. This new social class would exist only temporarily, for a century and a half from its birth in the mid-sixteenth century, but for this period its privileges (such as not being subject to feudal authority, freedom from taxation, an independent military justice system, and freedom of religion) made it a so-called in-between class between the nobility and serfdom, and much closer to the former. Soldiering on the border was thus for many a springboard with which to use the bearing of arms to rise up from the subjugated class to that of the privileged—that is, of the nobles. As the number of border soldiers was about twenty to twenty-two thousand men overall (some one hundred thousand together with their families), this social class, called *vitézlő nép* ("valiant people") in contemporary Hungarian sources, formed almost 5 percent of the population of the Kingdom of Hungary. Its existence had an effect on all other echelons of society, on the aristocracy and gentry as much as on the serfs, and on the urban bourgeoisie.

The fragmentation of the military population according to ethnic background played a key role in its becoming a separate social class, even Hungarians far outnumbered Germans, Croats, and Serbs. Its rank and file were mostly made up of serfs and small landowners who had lost their lands, and its junior officer corps by small landowners; its more senior posts (castle captains and their deputies) were normally filled by middling landowners, while either Hungarian or foreign aristocrats were elected to the chief captaincies and captains general. Confusion with the nobility can significantly have helped in the most influential class in society, after a certain initial resistance, accepting the special and privileged status of the new social group. Although it proved possible to block a law of the diet that would have reinforced the independent military legal code for the border defense soldiers, this code did come into being, one for the cavalry hussars and one for the infantry. Lazarus von Schwendi, captain general of Upper Hungary (1565–1568) (see fig. 13), played a key role in their elaboration: following the Hungarian example, he later prepared the military code for the German cavalry and infantry, which was put into law by the German estates at the imperial assembly of 1570 in Speyer. Thanks to their collective rights, the Hungarian border fortress soldiers also grew more united in spirit and thus became an independent and influential class in Hungarian society.

The least among the privileged classes in sixteenth-century Hungarian society was made up of the citizens of free royal and mining towns. In the second half of the century, they may have numbered a good fifty thousand, though this must have been boosted to quite a

Fig. 13. General Lazarus von Schwendi, border fortress captain György Thury, and Emperor Maximilian II. Engraving by an unknown German master, sixteenth century (Széchenyi National Library, Budapest).

degree by those fleeing the areas under Turkish occupation, as the aforementioned example of Johannes Sambucus shows. The Ottoman conquest forced most of the respectable German burghers in Pest and Buda to flee to Vienna and Pozsony, while larger groups of them (especially Hungarians) arrived in Nagyszombat, Kassa, and Várad and even in the Transylvanian Kolozsvár. The formerly significant urban centers of the territory of Ottoman Hungary gradually lost their importance and their Hungarian-German population over the century.

The nobility moving into the cities also presented a great challenge to the urban bourgeoisie. It was mostly high nobles and high office holders who moved to the administrative and religious centers further away from the Ottoman front line (e.g., Pozsony and Nagyszombat), and mostly soldiering nobles who moved to free royal cities (e.g., Kassa) and market towns (e.g., Győr and Komárom) that were part of border defense. A significant garrison would be sent to these latter towns, one that would also influence the progress and lifestyle of the bourgeoisie. The nobility and the military limited the existing positions of burghers, as they did not pay taxes, something that would often lead to considerable friction. Both social groups tried to make use of the favorable economic opportunities provided by the town; that is, both wished to take their cut of the benefits of trade. The less wealthy class of nobles soon began to blend with the elite of the bourgeoisie through marriage, while in Kassa, German infantrymen became related to German bourgeois families. The lifestyle of the nobility moving to the cities thus increasingly became a model for the top class of the bourgeoisie. As the Lutheran preacher István Magyari wrote, "Bourgeois order has affected noble dress, and nobility has had its influence on that of the aristocrats, and the aristocrats have cultivated the princes, such that you can hardly tell the difference between them."[5] One of the key objectives of the members of the urban bourgeois elite for a prolonged period was the acquisition of land and certificates of nobility. This was a tendency observed all over Europe, and it had a great influence on Hungarian bourgeois development.

The history of Hungarian towns and cities tends to group Hungarian settlements on the basis of the legal system—that is, it sees as "real" urban citizens the residents of the free royal cities (in the second half of the sixteenth century, Pozsony, Nagyszombat, Sopron, Kassa, Eperjes, Bártfa, Szakolca, and Trencsén, as well as Lőcse and Kisszeben) associated with the royal master of the treasury (*tavernicorum regalium magister*, Hungarian *tárnokmester*) and the so-called Personal (*personalis*, Hungarian *személynök*), or those cities in which they could take their trial cases by appeal to the office of the royal treasurer or that of the Personal. Despite this, in the sixteenth century a few more important manorial market towns had considerable privileges (such as customs and tax relief, the right to stop goods, and the right to supply wine). Thus, in terms of their economic role and urban activity, they occupied a more important position in the country's economic life and its system of cities than did a less developed free royal city or mining town. Indeed, the residents of the market towns would often outdo the "real" burghers in terms of wealth and standard of living. Good examples of this are Győr, the fortress and trading city on the Rába River, and the civic city of Debrecen, excelling in cattle breeding and animal trade. Despite the proximity of the front line, these privileged market towns were able to increase their privileges, thereby taking the first steps to acquiring the rank of free royal city that had finally been won after the Ottomans had been driven out.

Despite the Hungarian nobility's impressive size, the broadest echelon of the country's society was made up of the serfs (peasants) with no privileges. Although there were attempts throughout the century and in all parts of the country to implement the rooting of serfs to the soil, as announced after the 1514 peasant uprising led by György Dózsa, hardly anywhere was this successful. The Turkish wars, the border army, and the need of the grand estates for manpower, as well as the uncertain future of the Ottoman frontier zone, all helped the mobility of the serfs. The serfs did not, of course, present a united front. Where the lord's power was greater, the serfs working on the estate had countless tax and labor burdens.

The peasant burghers or occasional rich peasants of the market towns of Ottoman Hungary could consider themselves prosperous. Thanks to their role in the breeding and trade of cattle, the better-to-do part of this group, the merchant farmers, generally had a better standard of living than did nobles with a single estate in the noble villages. But even the less well-off serfs who survived purely on breeding animals would often employ day laborers and maidservants. Their increasing prosperity brought them a significant role in local administrative bodies.

Participation in vine growing also favored the enrichment of the serfs. The viticulturists employing day laborers even had their own local government: they united in hillside communities (Hungarian *hegyközség*), holding hillside assemblies many times a year, where they themselves would select the person to lead their vineyard slopes, the hill master, and the six to twelve men to assist him, sworn by oath. It was also here that the so-called hillside laws (statutes) that regulated the lives of the hillside communities were decided on.

This exceptional diversity was also found in what at least appeared to be the poorest class of society, the *zsellér* (Latin *inquilinus*), or landless peasant (cotter). Compared to the end of medieval times, in the sixteenth century, this diversity was found particularly in the outlying areas of Ottoman Hungary. Countrywide there were about twenty-five to thirty *zsellér* per hundred serfs. While a good proportion of them lived in very modest circumstances, some of them, even without a serf plot, were not in fact poor. Those who engaged in animal breeding or vine growing on rented grazing land, clearings, and vineyards were often more prosperous and led a better life than serfs who had their own plots. The poorest of them, though, did not even have a house to live in—hence their name, unhoused *zsellérek* (Latin *subinquilini*)—and so would live next to rich peasants, working for them as day laborers. The number of *zsellérek* was increased by the presence in the tax records of so-called paupers, whose worldly goods were so scarce that they did not reach the tax threshold of six florins and so were exempt from paying tax. Their numbers grew the most in areas most affected by Ottoman incursions.

The greatest sacrifice in the sixteenth century had to be made by the largest and poorest class of society. Enemy attacks damaged them the most: it was in their ranks that destruction brought by the sultan's or royal troops took the most victims, and they were the most affected by the arson, starvation, and epidemics these troops brought in their wake. The serfs also had to provide unpaid work (Latin *gratuitus labor*) to reinforce defense bastions, which also drained the strength of their animals and wore down their implements. Meanwhile, alongside a state war tax to be paid to the ruler and the ninth (Latin *nona*) they owed their lord, they had to pay a tithe to the church (Latin *decima*). They were also the ones most affected by the disintegration of the network of settlements. For all these reasons, their impoverishment only continued as the century progressed. Yet for many years, they would also display an extraordinary ability to regenerate, as after any given destructive incursion they would return to their burned-out and looted villages and start working the land again. This would only really end with the Long Turkish War at the turn of the seventeenth century (see part 1, chap. 11).

Notes

1. F[erenc] Maksay, "Le pays de la noblesse nombreuse," in *Études historiques hongroises 1980 publiées à l'occasion de XVe Congrès International des Sciences Historiques par la Commission Nationale des Historiens Hongrois*, ed. D[ezső] Nemes et al., vol. 1 (Budapest: Akadémiai Kiadó, 1980), 167–191.

2. Recently, cf. Christian Gastgeber and Elisabeth Klecker, eds., *Johannes Sambucus / János Zsámboki / Ján Sambucus (1531–1584): Philologe, Sammler und Historiograph am Habsburgerhof* (Vienna: Praesens, 2018).

3. This meant that Orsolya, daughter of the late László Kanizsai, who left no male heir, could, with the special privilege of the ruler, inherit her father's estate as if she were a man.

4. Recently, cf. István M. Szijártó, ed., *Az indigenák* [The "Indigenae"] (Budapest: ELTE Eötvös Kiadó, 2017).

5. István Magyari, *Az országban való sok romlásnak okairól* [On the reasons for much ruin in the country], ed. Tamás Katona (Budapest: Magyar Helikon, 1979), 83.

Fig. 14. Figure of Sebestyén Thököly (died 1607), from his charters of ennoblement in 1572. Calligraphy by György Bocskay and his Viennese circle, 1573 (Hungarian National Archives, Budapest).

7

THE ECONOMY AND ITS ROADS TO EUROPE

The sultan's campaigns after 1526, followed by the fortress wars and never-ending Ottoman-Hungarian incursions, brought immeasurable destruction to Hungary. Agricultural activity and material goods incurred enormous damage, while the division of the country into three parts threatened to send Hungary's economy into decline. Yet the following decades brought quite the opposite. In spite of political disintegration and regular military conflict, economic life underwent a very real revival. The early modern transformation of the European economy brought distinctly favorable opportunities for growth. And this would be exploited by residents of the kingdom, the principality, and even the Ottoman territories.

In the sixteenth century, the population of the areas most crucial to the Hungarian economy (namely, the Austrian, German, Italian, Bohemian, and Polish ones) increased by some 20–25 percent, in line with broader European trends. The population of the German imperial cities grew in particular, but Vienna, which became the residence and imperial city, along with the expanding army, required more and more food supplies. As a result, the provision of food to these areas became increasingly difficult. The demand for agricultural produce quickly lifted prices, and the resulting agricultural boom was an enormous opportunity for Hungary and Poland. For the former, indeed, it was an advantage that its western and northern regions had become part of the Habsburg Monarchy. It soon transpired that the monarchy was dependent on the Hungarian territories not just in military terms but also in economic ones: by the second half of the sixteenth century, Hungary had become not just defense bastion but also breadbasket or larder to the Central European great power.[1]

In contrast to previous claims that this represented the "Habsburg colonization" of the country, in fact it established the Hungarian economy as playing a key role in Europe. One district of Vienna (the area between Stubentor and Rotenturmstraße) had from medieval times been a center for the storage facilities of German and Italian trading houses, where from this time Hungarian traders could establish even closer ties. The Vienna aulic quartering registry (German *Hofquartierbuch*) of 1563 reveals Hungarian traders having permanent residences near the houses of the most prestigious merchants from Vienna, Nuremberg, Augsburg, and Regensburg and from Italy.

More than anything else, the markets of Central Europe needed livestock, cereals, and agricultural raw materials. As a result, by the second half of the sixteenth century, Poland and Hungary had between themselves divided up the provision of the Bohemian, German, Austrian, and Italian territories. While Poland supplied the Bohemian-German areas to the north of Prague with its key goods in bulk (such as cattle, cereals, and furs) and other export items (such as wood, potash, and hemp), Hungary delivered to the German, Austrian, and north Italian provinces to the south. The largest export items from Hungary were cattle, sheep, and horses, alongside leather, suet, and honey. Horned cattle were the top export, as in the second half of the century one hundred thousand were sold to the Austrian-German territories every year and forty thousand to Italy, though many tens of thousands of sheep were also sold to the west. Miklós Oláh, later archbishop of Esztergom, could write with understandable enthusiasm in his 1536 work *Hungaria*, "There are so many herds of cattle, goats, and sheep and there is such a wealth of game of all kinds that not only Hungary is fully supplied but the neighboring countries partake of them as well. Cattle are supplied to the entire Venetian area of Italy, to Austria, Moravia, Bavaria, the Swabian principality, and all of Germany to the Rhine."[2] This made Hungary one of the largest exporters of meat and leather in Europe. Whenever the cattle exports were disrupted, Vienna and the German provinces experienced serious shortages.

With only minor alterations, the most important trading routes followed the medieval system (see map 8). In a northwesterly direction, to Silesia, to the Bohemian and Moravian territories, and even toward Nuremberg, the itinerary was via the town of Hustopeče (German *Auspitz*); toward Vienna and the southern German cities, it was along the Danube, through either Pozsony or Magyaróvár. But while in medieval times the former of these two routes was the more important, from the 1540s the Tata–Győr–Magyaróvár–Vienna line would become dominant. As far as trade with the south was concerned, the most important route was via Kanizsa and Légrád in the direction of Venice and Italy. After the customs (one-thirtieth) stop at Nedelic in Muraköz (Međimurje), the road split three ways. The most northerly reached Venice via Pettau (Ptuj) and Laibach (Ljubljana). The middle one went through Zagreb to Fiume (Rijeka) and Trieste. The most southerly also went through the Croatian capital, then Modrus, and out to the coast at Zengg (Senj). Meanwhile, traders would take their wares from the northern provinces of the kingdom through Kassa, toward Krakow.

Of the routes leading to the Ottoman Empire, the one along the Danube, via Eszék and Belgrade, would become more significant than the other, via Szeged and Temesvár, on account of goods from the Levant. In the sixteenth century, it was mostly Ragusan, Serbian, and Jewish merchants who traded on these routes. Transylvanian merchants were also part of international trade, for, despite occasional embargos made by the Porte, they would take their goods from Kolozsvár to Wallachia via Nagyszeben and Brassó, to Moldavia via Beszterce, and to Poland and the German-Austrian territories via Várad and Debrecen.

As well as cattle, Hungarian wine, which was easy to transport and thereby export, played a major role in long-distance trade. Wine production was subject to a greater change since the late medieval period. Before 1526, the best Hungarian wine had been produced in the Syrmium region between the Sava and Danube Rivers. After repeated destructive attacks by Sultan Süleyman's troops, however, the Syrmium wine region was first overshadowed by the Somogy-Baranya-Tolna region in Transdanubia, then from the second half of the sixteenth century increasingly by the Tokaj-Hegyalja region. By the end of the century, considerable quantities of wine were transported on the traders' carriages heading toward

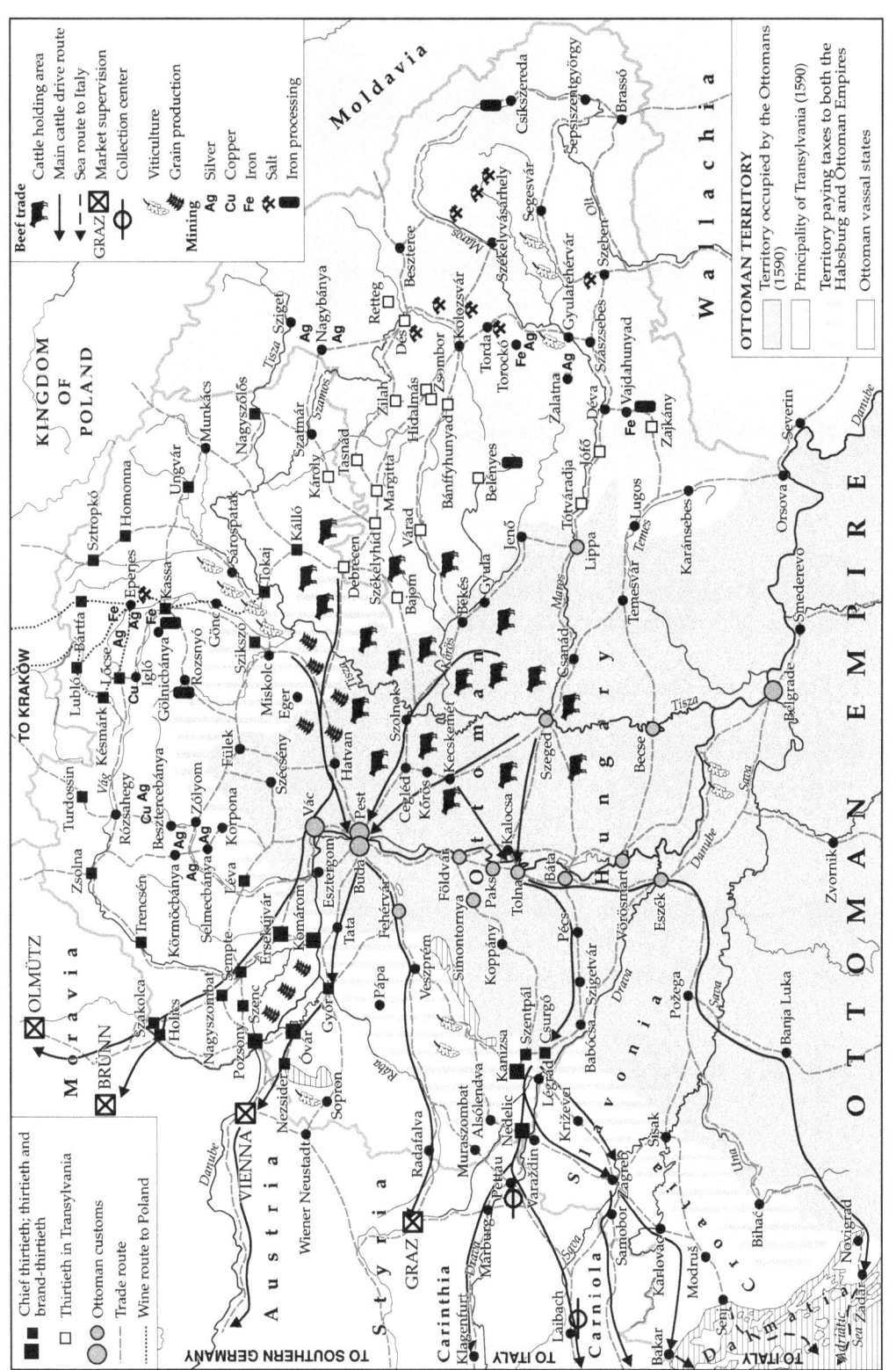

Map 8. Foreign trade in the Carpathian Basin in the second half of the sixteenth century.

Krakow; a century later, Tokaj wines would establish a grand reputation all over Europe (*rex vinorum*). Cereals, meanwhile, were transported mainly from the Csallóköz region, along the Danube, to Austrian areas.

The raw copper extracted from mines in the valley of the river Garam (today Hron, Slovakia) also retained its prestige as an export, as run from the 1530s by the Thurzó–Fugger company founded in 1495. The copper mined around Besztercebánya, rich as it was in silver, reached Venice in the south and Gdańsk (German *Danzig*) in the north; from the latter, by sea, it would even reach Antwerp in the Netherlands and Spain (namely, circa 30% of the annual production in Hungary). Although the extraction from ever-deeper shafts, which were damp and hard to ventilate, became increasingly costly, copper mining remained one of the most important economic sectors. A sign of the profitability of Hungarian mining, invaluable for the weapons industry and for coinage, as well as providing a good part of Europe's silver output, was that in the second half of the century the more prominent copper mines were rented by such eminent merchant bankers as the Manlich family of Augsburg until 1569, then the consortium of the Paler, Weiß, Wagner, and Herbst families, then the Paler-Castell group, and finally from 1602 the Paler family and Lazarus Henckel Sr., one of the key financiers of the Long Turkish War.

The composition of the goods imported to Hungary hardly changed during the sixteenth century. All kinds of textiles (cloth, canvas, silk, etc.) continued to flood into the country, as did various industrial and luxury goods (such as knives, scythes, tin plates, tools, small metal items from Nuremberg, fur caps, Venetian glass items, and clocks, as well as oranges, figs, and lemons) and spices (saffron, pepper, and ginger). All of these items found their way to aristocratic courts, to the bourgeois homes of the cities, and to the more impoverished homes of the border soldiery and of the peasantry.

All of this meant that after 1526, not even the unfavorable political and military circumstances could prevent economic connections from blossoming. And thanks to this burgeoning trade, in the sixteenth century a large part of Hungary remained in Europe's economic bloodstream. The country was also more or less able to preserve itself as a single economic unit, despite breaking up into three parts. Strange as it may seem, wartime conditions helped this favorable situation come about. Because conditions were so dangerous—and in contrast to their custom in medieval times—German and Italian merchants no longer entered the battlefield that Hungary had become. This meant that the role of their Hungarian partners grew, as they now had to operate as their agents, overseers, and suppliers. So, like the military command in Vienna, foreign traders were dependent on the Hungarians. Meanwhile, these connections would represent great help for Hungarians, as their enterprises were supported with credits for goods by their foreign partners who had more significant capital. So it was long-distance commerce, jointly run by foreign and Hungarian merchants, and mining that were the key sectors of the country's economy. Despite contemporary sources being full of references to cattle and weapons smuggling, more than 60 percent of the "state" income of the Kingdom of Hungary was from income from the thirtieth customs levy and from mining taxes.

The residents of the different parts of the disintegrated Hungary—despite being in an inimical relationship with each other—were quick to recognize that the maintenance of economic relations would be not merely advantageous but a key shared interest. There was urgent need in the Habsburg Monarchy for the cattle and sheep bred in Ottoman Hungary, which had to be transported via the Kingdom of Hungary. The same was true of the so-called Turkish goods from the Ottoman Empire (wool and cotton fabric, fine canvas, carpets, cushions, leather goods, etc.), for which there was increasing demand in the west. Meanwhile, the residents of the kingdom, the Turks, and the subjects of the Transylvanian prince were all equally desirous of European industrial and luxury goods—that is, the opposing sides had an interest in maintaining trade connections, as dropping them would cause serious financial losses.

The 1589 case of the designation of the markets in the small Ottoman border town of Kakat (also known as Párkány) on the Danube is a good example of this. In spring of that year, Memi Sokolović, *sanjak-bey* of Esztergom, turned to his enemy, Miklós Pálffy, captain general of the Komárom fortress, with the following request, hoping to guarantee the future of the lucrative markets:

> Your Excellency should consider which days would be suitable throughout the year and also which day of the week would be appropriate for the weekly market. If Your Excellency decides and lets me know, we will accept it on our honor, honesty, and humanity and all multitudes and individuals may come and go to the market here at Kakat, whether they are believers or not. They will suffer no harm from anyone, neither while traveling nor at the market, whether they come from Léva, Érsekújvár, Komárom, Nagyszombat, Pozsony, Vienna, Prague, or anywhere else. They should have no fear but come and go confidently with their cattle and buy and sell as they please.[3]

In the light of all this, Hungarian economic historiography is justified in beginning to refer to the calmer quarter century after the peace of Edirne of 1568 as one of the early modern golden ages for Hungarian enterprise.[4] A broad swath of society was involved in the highly lucrative breeding of livestock. The bulk of this commercial class was made up of the so-called peasant citizen residents of market towns in Ottoman Hungary and the areas around it. Their poorer echelons played an important role in breeding, and their richer ones in the trade itself. More fortunate merchants accrued ever-greater wealth, and the most prosperous moved to the cities of the kingdom or principality (Nagyszombat and Kassa, as well as Várad, Kolozsvár, and Debrecen), where they would soon rise to prominence. In the early 1560s, for example, one of the best-known trading companies was that of Máté Szabó from Debrecen, who had around fifty thousand Hungarian florins in cash and goods. For the sake of comparison, this was five times the annual taxes paid to the Ottoman Porte by the Principality of Transylvania and some 6–7 percent of the kingdom's yearly income.

Of the successful Hungarian traders in the second half of the century, Sebestyén Thököly (ancestor of the later prince Imre [see part 2, chap. 3]) and János Trombitás were the most prominent (see fig. 14). The former, thanks to the connections he had established in Ottoman territories, had gone from merchant on the Great Plain to one of the richest entrepreneurs in the country, doing more than ten thousand florins' worth of cattle trade a year, as well as overseeing deliveries of manufactured goods and even, on occasion, of forbidden arms. He would finally be given the title of magnate—be welcomed, that is, into the Hungarian aristocracy—in 1593. János Trombitás, meanwhile, combined his work as a merchant with the profession of spying that often accompanied it. He did this too well, if anything, acting as an agent for both sides, and so had a close relationship with Pasha Mustafa Sokollu of Buda. As a result, in 1574–1575 he went as far as to intervene in high politics—namely, in the struggle between Stephen Báthory, prince of Transylvania, and his Habsburg rival Gáspár Bekes. Trombitás, who later settled in Nagyszombat in the Kingdom of Hungary, would ultimately be brought down by this secret craft, ending up on the scaffold in 1592. His career is nevertheless an excellent example of the great opportunities that trade offered, even to those from a modest background, in the economic golden age of the second half of the century.

Yet it is important to stress that although older Hungarian historiography paints the nobles as among those resisting economic enterprises, a statement from an unbiased Austrian contemporary, Wolfgang Puchheim, in 1550, dismisses any such doubts: "The Hungarian gentlemen practice commerce, accept traders at their side, and trade in cattle, cloth, lead, copper and all kinds of other things."[5] Hungarian aristocrats (e.g., members of the Nádasdy, Perényi, Zrínyi, Thurzó, Dobó, Forgách, Drugeth de Homonna, Erdődy, and Mágochy families) played a key role in trade, both domestic and long distance. The same was true of the captains general and castle captains of this period, whether Hungarian or from elsewhere. For example, István Dobó, the hero of Eger in 1552, and Ferenc Zay, the captain general of Kassa, were part of the same group cooperating in order to make considerable profit.

Hungary's breakup into three parts and the increasing role of trade left a deep imprint on the development of the network of cities. At the end of the Middle Ages, Hungary (including Transylvania) was home to 30 royal towns and 150 significant privileged towns or market towns with city obligations. Some 8 percent of the country's total population lived in these towns, already well behind the figure of 10–15 percent for Germany. This lag would only increase in the sixteenth century. Of the seven regional centers in medieval times (Buda/Pest, Pozsony/Sopron, Körmöcbánya, Kassa, Várad, Szeged, and Pécs), three (Buda, Pécs, and Szeged) would come under Ottoman rule, while Várad would become the key fortress of the Principality of Transylvania. This led to a transformation of the former structure of towns.

Pozsony and Kassa, both more peripheral in geographical terms, were now tasked with much more important functions than before. The former, now the country's capital (see fig. 7 in part 1, chap. 3), and the latter, now center of Upper Hungary, performed these well. The development of both was favored by their becoming political and financial centers, and their citizens could partake in this blossoming commerce. Indeed, for Kassa and its four neighbors (Eperjes, Lőcse, Bártfa, and Kisszeben), the so-called Pentapolis,[6] merely supplying the extensive Kassa garrison and the soldiers at the border fortresses presented a great commercial opportunity. All this led to Pozsony becoming the capital and coronation city, while Kassa came to play a greater, national role. Sopron and Lőcse lost something of their former significance during the sixteenth century, while the free royal cities and mining towns along the Garam River (Körmöcbánya, Besztercebánya, Selmecbánya, Újbánya, Bakabánya, Libetbánya, and Bélabánya) continued down the path of urbanization. This showed itself, for example, in the steps they took in health, public hygiene, and fire safety.

While the free royal cities that fell under Ottoman control saw their significance decline, the unusual military and economic situation meant that the roles of other cities would increase. In this regard, the free royal city of Nagyszombat and the privileged prebendal market town of Győr are particularly worthy of note. The development of Nagyszombat was helped by the fall of Esztergom in 1543, after which the archbishops and chapter settled there. While the political residence of the archbishops was Pozsony, as evidenced by their palace there being the upper house of the Hungarian diet, Nagyszombat emerged as a center of culture and of ecclesiastical government. All along, the town's Hungarian citizenry was quick to respond to the opportunities afforded by the cattle trade and thus would constantly thrive.

Győr, likewise, had the most profitable sector of the period to thank for its progress (see fig. 15). After the fall of Buda in 1541, the prebendal market town became the key bastion shielding Vienna, and so, like the imperial city, by the 1560s, it was built into a modern fortress or fortress city (German *Festungsstadt*) under supervision of Italian military architects.[7] This meant that it was fortified with enormous bastions, its streets were formed into a regular network, and it was served by a Hungarian and German army of at least a thousand. Military objectives were a far greater priority than the interests of the citizenry, and so foreign captains general would limit the privileges and economic activity of citizens in a number of areas. For all this, the proximity of the front line brought real advantages to the residents of the city. First, supplying the soldiers was a market for local traders and craftsmen. Second, Győr merchants could make use of the most important cattle-driving routes passing right past their city. They became active middlemen in long-distance commerce, which made them very prosperous. The citizens of Győr expanded their privileges in line with this. Thus, the fortress city became not just a cornerstone of the border defense system but a key arena for Hungarian economic life.

The period after 1541 brought a similar flourish to some of the market towns of Ottoman Hungary. Though unquestionably subjects of the Porte, they retained a crucial role in breeding cattle, sheep, and horses and in driving them to the west. Particularly significant were Nagykőrös, Cegléd, and Kecskemét. But other market towns (e.g., Kálmáncsehi, Mezőtúr, Nagymaros, Ráckeve, Tolna, Simánd, and Nyírbátor), where previous activity is hardly recorded, would achieve economic significance. While the peasant bourgeois residents of Nagykőrös, Cegléd, and Kecskemét worked intensively on cattle breeding on fields rented at the edge of their cities, those of these other towns played a decisive role as trading intermediaries. As both the breeding and the driving of animals took place with herds of a few hundred, this gave tens of thousands of peasant farms an interest in breeding and sale and in turn provided them material wealth. Debrecen's merchants also made the best of the giant grazing lands next to the city. A number of market towns in the kingdom (e.g., Komárom, Pápa, Nyírbátor, and Sárospatak), and even in Transylvania (e.g., Nagyenyed) were also fortified by commerce.

The peculiar opportunities afforded by the Hungarian economy in the sixteenth century were less favorable for the development of the industrial guilds that were already lagging behind. Burghers would usually turn profit from trade not to industrial enterprise but rather to buying up vineyards and land, for it was the latter that could help them rise into the noble class. Thus, urban industry remained within the existing framework of the guilds. Another obstacle to the development of craftsmanship were the cheap manufactured goods flooding in from the west. This all led to industry become increasingly backward relative to that of

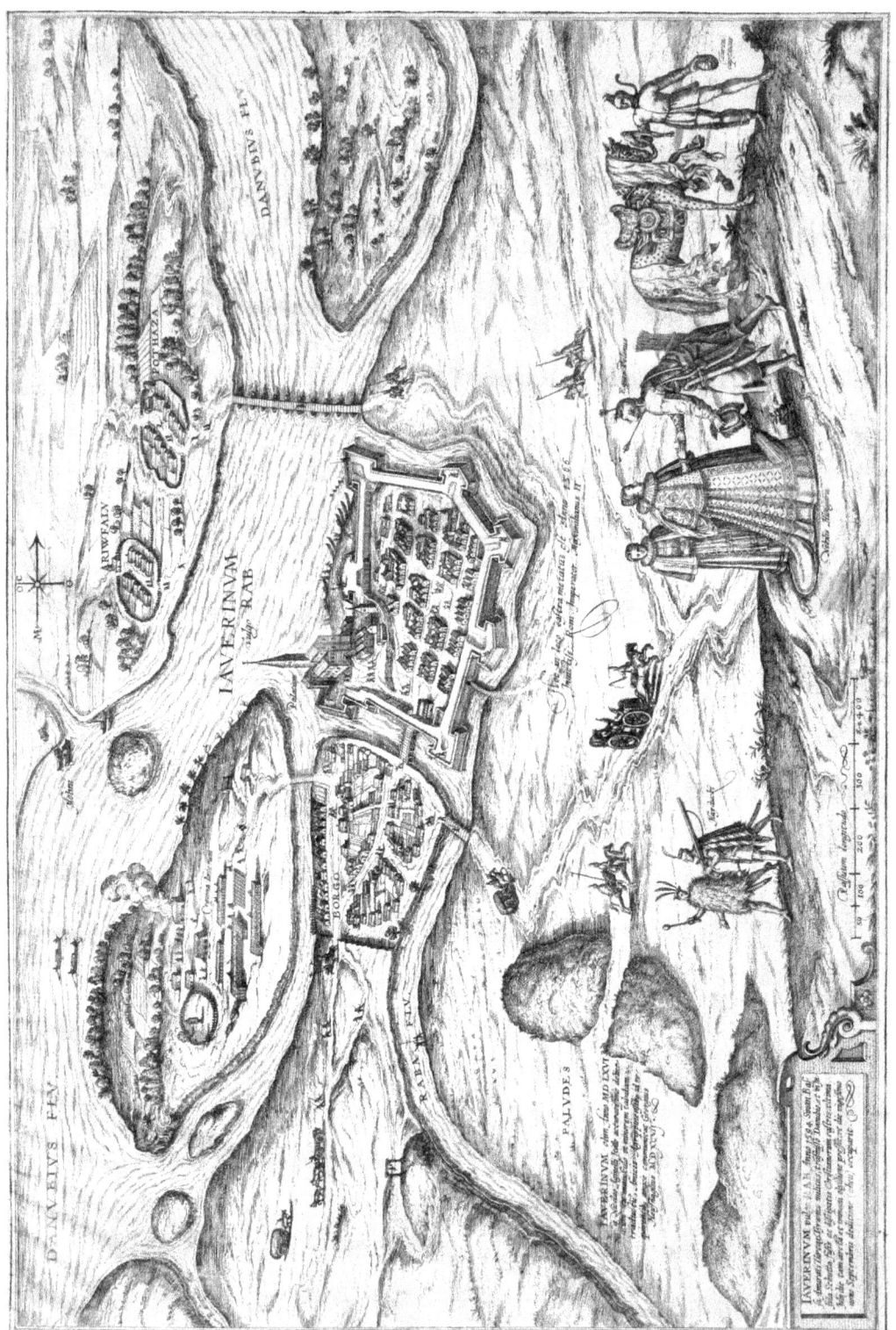

Fig. 15. The fortress city of Győr in the sixteenth century. Engraving by Georg Hoefnagel, 1597 (Hungarian National Museum, Budapest).

Western Europe. The tailoring trade did better business, as the number of its guilds grew as a result of cheap western cloth. The jewelry sector also performed impressively well, especially in Transylvania, rich as it was in mineral treasures. Its craftsmen came from the wealthier class of Hungarian and Saxon citizens; the market for more expensive items were the princes and the Hungarian nobility, while for more ordinary items it would include more or less all classes of society. In a century full of military campaigns, people were keener to invest their money in possessions that could easily be hidden or moved.

It would, of course, be a mistake to replace the negative picture in the public imagination of the sixteenth-century Hungarian economy during the Ottoman conquest with one that is too rose-tinted. Yet it is important to emphasize that the people of this time, despite the terrible destruction wrought by wars, did not live in misery. In fact, sniffing out the economic opportunities of the age, they did their best to enjoy them—whether as an eminent Hungarian landowner, as the German captain of a border fortress, as a subject of the prince of Transylvania, as a free royal citizen in the kingdom, or as the resident of one of the market towns of Ottoman Hungary.

Notes

1. Géza Pálffy, "The Bulwark and Larder of Central Europe (1526–1711)," in *On the Stage of Europe: The Millennial Contribution of Hungary to the Idea of European Community*, ed. Ernő Marosi (Budapest: Research Institute for Art History of the Hungarian Academy of Sciences, 2009), 100–124.

2. Nicolaus Olahus, *Hungaria—Athila*, ed. Colomannus Eperjessy and Ladislaus Juhász (Budapest: K. M. Egyetemi Nyomda, 1938), 30–33.

3. Pál Jedlicska, "XVI. századi török-magyar levelek Pálffy Miklóshoz (A gr. Pálffy-család levéltárából)" [Sixteenth-century Turkish and Hungarian letters to Miklós Pálffy (from the archives of the Count Pálffy family], *Történelmi Tár* [Historical magazine] (1881): 693.

4. Ferenc Szakály, *Gazdasági és társadalmi változások a török hódítás árnyékában* [Economic and social changes in the shadow of the Ottoman conquest] (Budapest: MTA TTI, 1994), 11–13.

5. Takáts, *Szegény magyarok*, 143.

6. István H. Németh, *Várospolitika és gazdaságpolitika a 16–17. századi Magyarországon (A felső-magyarországi városszövetség)* [Urban and economic policies in sixteenth and seventeenth century Hungary (the city alliance of Upper Hungary)] (Budapest: Gondolat Könyvkiadó, 2004).

7. Lajos Gecsényi, "Ungarische Städte im Vorfeld der Türkenabwehr Österreichs: Zur Problematik der ungarischen Städteentwicklung," in *Archiv und Forschung: Das Haus-, Hof- und Staatsarchiv in seiner Bedeutung für die Geschichte Österreichs und Europas*, ed. Elisabeth Springer and Leopold Kammerhofer (Vienna: Verlag für Geschichte und Politik, 1993), 57–77; Lajos Gecsényi, *Grund- und Hausverzeichnisse der Festungsstadt Győr / Raab 1564–1602* (Győr: GyVL, 2003).

Fig. 16. Miklós Zrínyi / Nikola Zrinski (1508–1566). Engraving by Nicolo Nelli, 1567 (Hungarian National Museum, Budapest).

8

THE SEARCH FOR A NEW HOME

Ethnic and Demographic Changes

As the first comprehensive census in Hungary was held under the rule of Joseph II (1780–1790), we can only estimate the population size in the sixteenth century, primarily on the basis of surviving Hungarian and Ottoman tax records and urbarial records (*urbarium*) that kept tabs on the services provided by serfs. This explains the wide variance of calculations in the last century as to the total population of the late medieval Kingdom of Hungary: from 2.3 million to 4.5 million. Current scholarly consensus puts the figure at 3.3 million,[1] rising to about 3.5–3.7 million in the early seventeenth century. This all means that in the first century of Ottoman occupation, and in contrast with most previous claims, the total population did not fall; in fact, it increased slightly. There were a number of factors behind this.

After the breakup of the country, the largest part of the 3.5 million population lived in the Kingdom of Hungary, which was the most densely populated (15 inhabitants per km^2). Records from 1598 tell us that around 1.8 million people lived there. In Ottoman Hungary, which was of similar size, the population density was much lower, around 7 inhabitants per km^2, and so its population may have been around 900,000. Finally, the population of Transylvania, including the Partium, may have been about 800,000 (13 inhabitants per km^2), the majority of whom were Hungarian and Romanian (around 550,000 in total), alongside Szeklers (150,000) and Saxons. Everywhere the great majority of the population lived in small villages of some 20–25 houses. In Ottoman Hungary, about 140 people lived in an average village—which were also further apart from one another—while in the more densely populated Kingdom of Hungary, a village would usually house about 150–170. Even here, Hungarian population density was much lower than that in Italy (50–120 inhabitants per km^2) or in Holland (40), and lower even than in Austria (18).

The perceived population growth of 6–10 percent over a century was misleading, however: in the Europe of this period there was very significant population growth (15–80%). Neither did this demographic explosion escape Central Europe. In Austria and the Bohemian lands growth was about 20 percent, and in Poland the figure was 36 percent, while the population of the Holy Roman Empire increased by 75 percent. This population explosion was also present in Hungary, of course, as we can see on the Batthyány estates in the Rohonc–Szalónak area in Vas county, protected as they were from Ottoman campaigns. But if we were to expect a similar growth to that in Austria and the Bohemian lands, the 3.3 million population should have expanded to around 4 million.

This suggests that a decline in population in absolute terms of 300,000–500,000 was one of the gravest consequences of the country being turned into a battlefield. The large part of the expected growth over a century was annulled by persistent warfare and the damage that accompanied it (arson, starvation, and disease). Within this phenomenon, however, it is worth distinguishing between the aforementioned fortress wars (1552–1566) and the slightly calmer "wartime peace years" (1568–1591), on the one hand, and the sultan's great campaigns (1521–1543) and the century's last decade and a half of conflict (1591–1606) on the other.

Contrary to general opinion, the installation of the Ottoman rule did not always incur such catastrophic destruction as historians have tended to describe. For example, in the sanjak of Buda, which can be considered the center of Ottoman Hungary, a mere 8.2 percent of the population emigrated in the period 1546–1559.[2] This, too, shows that the network of settlements had not yet suffered irrevocable damage during the fortress wars of the 1550s, and neither had its residents been marked for catastrophe or escape. The population of the broad belt of the front line even managed to survive the Ottoman-Hungarian incursions for a prolonged period, rebuilding ravaged houses and working its lands anew. In the border areas, the power of places having churches to retain their residents was impressive. Until the end of the sixteenth century, Hungarian society proved its extraordinary resilience, flexibility, and ability to rebuild. The real blow would be brought by the Long Turkish War, which decimated Hungary's population (see part 1, chap. 11).

It was the Hungarian population that was most affected by the destruction and disease wrought by great military campaigns and by Ottoman incursions. Large armies and incursion forces generally proceeded along the rivers, streams, and major thoroughfares, areas that had been settled primarily by Magyars ever since they came to the Carpathian Basin. The population drain of hundreds of thousands in absolute terms thus most affected these plain-dwelling Hungarians, while the Romanians, Slovaks, and Ruthenians living in safer upland areas were able to withstand the attacks with fewer losses. The outcome of all this was that the ethnic composition of Hungary in the sixteenth century started to change in a way that was very unfavorable for the Hungarians.

The most marked ethnic change of the century was the very significant inroads made into Hungary by the Serbs. Although the Serbs (also called *rác* in Hungarian, i.e., Rascians) along the Lower Danube and the Sava had represented an important minority (two hundred thousand) by the late medieval period, in the decades after 1526 they moved in great numbers into the areas by the Danube and in Banat that had been devastated by Ottoman incursions and the sultan's campaigns. The settling of the Serbs in Hungary was much favored by the destruction of 70–90 percent of the settlement infrastructure and the inestimable human and material loss in this region. But they were also assisted in laying down roots by the disintegration of their military groups during the 1527 uprising instigated by Jovan Nenad ("The Black"), in the battle between the two Hungarian kings; what remained of these groups was mostly forced to join the Ottoman side. Only one or two smaller groups of Serb soldiers remained in the service of King John Szapolyai, as led by Radić Bošić, and in the service of Ferdinand I, under the orders of Pavle Bakić, the last Serbian despot who fell in the Eszék campaign against the Ottomans of 1537. It was from ranks of these groups that the soldiers of the royal Danube fleet based at Komárom would emerge. These soldiers, who would become Magyarized but remain Orthodox, were called *naszádosok* ("little boatmen") after the best-known rowing boat of this period, the *naszád*.

While the settlement of the Serbs was vital for the economic recovery of the war-torn southern regions, the ethnic composition of these parts of the country would now be irreversibly transformed. Temesköz/Banat, for example, which before 1526 had been entirely Hungarian, after 1552 became completely Serbianized. On a map published in Antwerp in 1577, the area of Banat was already annotated with the word *Rasci* (Rascians). The Syrmium region had already appeared on a Venetian map in 1564 as *Rascia* (the country of Rascians, i.e., Serbia). But by the second half of the century, there was a sizeable Serbian population in Transdanubia, mainly in Baranya and Tolna counties but also in Somogy and Fejér counties. Together with them would arrive from the North Balkans members of the animal-breeding Vlach tribe, made up from a mixture of the other South Slav ethnic groups. The number of Orthodox Serbs and Vlachs in the Danube region was so great that in 1585 an Orthodox monastery was established at Grábóc, near Szekszárd, for their spiritual maintenance. Their religion and norms of behavior were so far from those of the Hungarians, however, as to act as an almost complete obstacle to integration. This was all a clear sign that the ethnic composition of the southernmost Hungarian regions had begun to undergo fundamental change.

While the use of Serbs for frontier defense against the Ottomans in the period after Mohács was less than effective, there was a region of the medieval Hungarian-Croatian kingdom in which the refugee South Slav population did not fall victim to the battle between the two Hungarian kings after 1526. On the Dalmatian coast and in the neighboring Croatian areas, resettling the so-called Uskoks (Latin *Uscoci*, meaning refugees) and turning them into mercenaries would be most fruitful; the same would be true for other groups of the aforementioned Vlachs in Slavonia between the Drava and Sava Rivers. In these parts, they played a key role in defense against the Ottomans, alongside the Hungarian border defense army, even if for both Vienna and Istanbul the Croatian-Slavonian borderlands were but a secondary theater of war.

In the latter areas, an enormous migration began in a northwesterly direction after 1526. Refugees from the North Balkans, au fait with Ottoman habits and experts in swordplay, arrived in this period in droves in the Croatian and Slavonian areas to the south of the Drava. Their armed implementation was most expedient in a financial, military, and political sense, and from the 1530s the military leadership in Vienna successfully used this skill, primarily in the defense of Carniola, Carinthia, and Styria. The Uskoks arriving from Bosnia and Herzegovina were soon either resettled or taken into the service of border fortresses. The former took place in a number of waves in the area of Sichelberg (Žumberak), Novo Mesto, Möttling (Metlika), and Tschernembl (Černomelj, then all in southern Carniola, now all in Slovenia), on the north bank of the upper part of the Kulpa River. The resettlement was eased by the area near the front line being an estate of the Habsburg family. In 1535, in a special donation of privilege, the Uskoks were given their freedom (first for twenty years and then lifelong tax exemption, etc.) in return for their military service. In the decades that followed, more migrating families were granted privileges in the adjoining territories. This is what led to the creation, by midcentury, of the so-called Sichelberg district (German *Sichelberger Distrikt*), led by a captain in charge of both military and civic life. The captain in turn answered to the Croatian captains general, and so his district was from the second half of the sixteenth century a particular part of the captaincy general of Karlstadt.

For lack of territory, there was clearly no opportunity for the settlement of larger groups of the Uskoks. Thus, they were taken on partly by the fortresses of the Croatian captaincy general (Zengg/Senj, Karlobag, Slunj, Cetin, and Ogulin) and partly by the ships of the Adriatic fleet. Those who were not needed would further migrate to Carniola and Styria, join the service of the Ottomans, or turn to piracy on the Adriatic. This would cause serious political upheaval by the end of the century, as the Uskoks would show no greater mercy to Venetian galleys than they did to the Ottoman barges. By the turn of the seventeenth century, the conflict between Vienna and Venice had reached the boiling point.

The Habsburg military leadership was more fortunate with the advance of Vlachs in Slavonia. The only solution, again, was settlement in return for privileges to prevent them migrating further into Carniola and Styria. In the sixteenth century, this had not caused many problems, as much of the original population of this part of the country (e.g., Körös county) had already escaped or been destroyed. In the area of the Slavonian captaincy general, the Vlachs would also receive land and various privileges (exemption from taxes and other obligations) in return for their military service. Their efforts as guardians of major roads and crossings complemented well the actions of the German and Croatian army of the border fortresses. But despite their military contribution, their privileges damaged the interests of the Croatian and Hungarian nobles of this part of the country, problems that were not solved even with the general settlement of their privileges (*Statuta Valachorum*) in 1630.

The settlement of the Uskoks and Vlachs in Croatia and Slavonia was made possible by another great wave of migration. Decades of active Ottoman incursions and looting by border defense soldiers forced the Croatian population of the areas south of the Drava to decide to flee en masse in the 1530s and 1540s. As Katalin Svetkovics/Švetković, wife of ban Ferenc Batthyány, put it in 1538, "In every bush you could be afraid of the enemy."[3] This is why everyone in a position to do so moved away from the direct vicinity of an Ottoman front line pushing ever further to the west. The Hungarian and Croatian nobility were first to flee after the terrible devastation wrought by the sultan's campaign of 1532, followed by the serfs. The emigration was voluntary at first, but there would soon be consolidated and even violent acts of deportation. Seeing that they could not prevent the destruction of their southern domains, aristocrats with estates in both Croatian-Slavonian areas and Hungary (the Batthyány, Nádasdy, Erdődy, Keglevics/Keglević, and Zrínyi/Zrinski families, see fig. 16) realized that it was best to rehouse their population in their western Hungarian estates north of the Drava. As there was plenty of as yet uncultivated land here, the acceptance of the fleeing Croatian serfs did not pose any threat—indeed, it was of great economic advantage.

During the relocation process, considerable attention was paid to the rescue of the educated class (priests and the literate) and of craftsmen. In the summer of 1538, in response to the hesitation of Slavonian protonotary (Latin *prothonotarius regni Sclavoniae*) Mihály Raveni, Katalin Svetkovics/Švetković observed, "It would be a shame for such a knowledgeable

Fig. 17. The Kostajnica border fortress on the river Una. Engraving by an unknown master, 1617 (Hungarian National Museum, Budapest).

man to be lost."[4] Raveni would soon be living in Hungary, and from 1548 to 1552 he was already serving as the protonotary for Chief Justice Tamás Nádasdy.

After the great waves of migration of the 1530s and 1540s, the fall of Kostajnica castle on the Una in 1556 (see fig. 17) again meant that crowds of Croats made for Hungary and Styria; their place would in part be taken by the Vlachs. In this way, by the second half of the century, tens of thousands of Croatian nobles and serfs had left their historic homeland and fled to the north and the northwest. As a result, from the Muraköz (Međimurje) right across to the Marchfeld, on the frontier between the Kingdom of Hungary and the Austrian and Moravian territories, a quite broad belt was established in which Croats also lived. Particularly high numbers of Croats (German *Krabaten*, Hungarian *krabótok*) settled in the vicinity of Németújvár, Körmend, Rohonc, Szalónak, Kismarton, Sopron, Vienna, and Pozsony, especially on the estates of aforementioned aristocratic families. By the early 1570s, their number had expanded to such a degree that the Lower Austrian estates requested a secret prohibition on their immigration from Emperor Maximilian II.

Unlike the Serbs, the Croats were Catholic, and yet their integration into the Hungarian society of western Transdanubia was also limited. This can largely be put down to the fact that, in return for short-term privileges (tax exemption and various allowances), they usually established separate settlements in clearings or laid down roots on the territory of ravaged former villages. This is when Nádalja, near Körmend, became Magyarnádalja and Horvátnádalja (Hungarian Nádalja and Croatian Nádalja), while the market town of Rohonc was divided into Hungarian, German, and Croatian districts. Thanks to their dogged preservation of their language and identity, the number of Croats along the Austrian-Hungarian frontier remains significant to this day. In the province of Burgenland, created in the early twentieth century, Croats represent some 6 percent of the population. It was only the leading Croatian noble families that became Magyarized—in the courts, domains, or private armies of the Hungarian magnates, they could only better themselves if they spoke Hungarian.

Overall, the ethnic profile of the Carpathian Basin underwent enormous change during the sixteenth century. With their numbers declining due to war, the Hungarians would start their long journey toward becoming a minority vis-à-vis the South Slav population (Serb, Vlach, Uskok, and Croat) that had sought a new home. All this would have serious consequences for Hungary's long-term development, especially as this negative tendency continued in the seventeenth century, as the reader will soon see (part 2, chap. 7).

Notes

1. András Kubinyi, "A Magyar Királyság népessége a 15. század végén" [The population of the Kingdom of Hungary at the end of the fifteenth century], *Történelmi Szemle* [Historical review] 38, nos. 2–3 (1996): 135–161.

2. Dávid, *Studies in Demographic and Administrative History*, 43–60.

3. Géza Pálffy, Miljenko Pandžić, and Felix Tobler, *Ausgewählte Dokumente zur Migration der Burgenländischen Kroaten im 16. Jahrhundert* (Eisenstadt: Kroatisches Kultur- und Dokumentationszentrum, 1999), 87.

4. Ibid.

Fig. 18. István Kis Szegedi (1505–1572), one of the leaders of Hungarian Protestantism. Woodcut by an unknown master, after Máté Skaricza, 1585 (Hungarian National Museum, Budapest).

9

FINDING FAITH

Hungary's New Religion

It was not only in political, economic, and ethnic terms that the sixteenth century brought changes to Hungary's history that would leave their mark for centuries. The enormous religious realignment taking place in Europe would also have fundamental consequences for the relations between the different confessions. Protestantism, which began in 1517 with Martin Luther's actions in Wittenberg, would in the half century or so after 1526 enjoy enormous success in all parts of divided Hungary. Hungary went from being a mostly Catholic to a majority Protestant country. Although the Ottomans had occupied about 40 percent of the country's territory, almost all of the population remained Christian: by the end of the century, more than half was Calvinist, a quarter was Lutheran, and the rest was Antitrinitarian, Catholic, or Orthodox. Overall, a good 80 percent of the population came to follow Protestantism. Despite wartime conditions, great crowds would display amazing openness to the new faith, but this search for a new faith was not in fact such a simple process.

Although there is a widespread belief that—at least within Ottoman Hungary—the religious tolerance of the Turks played a key role in this religious transformation, this does not really fit the facts. In Hungary's neighbor, Lower Austria, Protestants represented a similar proportion of the population in the second half of the sixteenth century (75–80%), but even in the Holy Roman Empire, in the throes of religious wars, almost half of Catholics would turn to some form of Protestantism. This shows that almost everywhere, the residents of Central Europe were amenable to the new faith, irrespective of which state they lived in. It nevertheless cannot be denied that in the occupied lands the Ottomans rarely put obstacles in the way of the spread of the Reformation. On religious questions, for subjects who paid their taxes, they were indifferent rather than patient.

As new research findings have clarified, the fast spread of Protestantism in Hungary was really caused by the late medieval crisis of the Catholic Church, attempts at reform, and a public wish to choose a new faith.[1] Geographical discoveries extended the world's horizons, the Renaissance shook up the world view of medieval humankind, and all over Europe interest in religious life grew. The overly conservative Catholic Church struggled to adjust to these new needs. Moreover, dissatisfaction with the corruption and lack of erudition of a part of the priesthood increased; the prelates, meanwhile, were mostly involved in politics and occupied eminent national positions of power. There was a pressing need for suitable spiritual support for the faithful and for an internal rejuvenation of the church. Initially, grassroots attempts at such reforms (the restructuring of monastic orders, such as, in Hungary, the Benedictine movement of Máté Tolnai, abbot of Szentmárton [today Pannonhalma]; the founding of lay religious groups; and the distribution of religious literature satisfying these new demands) brought only limited results. In the meantime, the Reformation, striving to transform the Catholic Church, gained much ground, and so the efforts of Catholicism to reform itself would not turn into a genuine reform program for the church until after the Council of Trent (1545–1563).

Paradoxically, the civil war between Ferdinand and King John and military campaigns against the Ottomans nevertheless helped the spread of the Reformation. The Catholic Church had suffered enormous losses in these struggles: seven of the country's twelve bishops (including both archbishops) had fallen at Mohács, while the candidates proposed by the two kings were only reluctantly accepted by the popes. During the civil war, the bishops were hardly able to deal with the ecclesiastical affairs of their dioceses, and a good part of these would fall under Ottoman occupation. The archbishop of Kalocsa's residence became an Ottoman castle in 1541; so did those of the bishops of Esztergom and Pécs in 1543, of Vác in 1544, of Csanád in 1552, and, temporarily, of Veszprém in the same year. The bishopric of Csanád disappeared for a prolonged period, as did those of Várad and Gyulafehérvár in Transylvania after 1560. Despite this, as we have mentioned, prelates continued to be appointed by Hungarian kings to the episcopal chairs of Ottoman Hungary and Transylvania.

It was an even greater tragedy that the lower levels of church institutions would also collapse. In the civil war, rich church estates (belonging to bishops, chapters, and monasteries) were often acquired by local nobles, causing irreparable damage in some parts of the country. With the development of the frontier of border fortresses, however, the Habsburg rulers would purloin most of the remaining church income to supply the defense system. This was, for example, the main reason that the chair of the archbishop of Esztergom was not filled between 1573 and 1596. But in the 1540–1560 period, Ottoman inroads brought the destruction of those monasteries and parishes that had managed to survive the decades of the sultan's campaigns. Every single one of the almost one hundred medieval monasteries of the Veszprém diocese disappeared; of a total of six hundred parishes, only a few dozen survived to the end of the century. By this time, only the Franciscans (e.g., in Jászberény, Szeged, Gyöngyös, and Csíksomlyó in Transylvania) were able to protect a few of their monasteries at a national level; the Paulines did so in the Croatian-Slavonian areas, as did sisterhoods that escaped from Buda to Pozsony or Nagyszombat. Thus, by weakening the position of the Catholic Church by their conquest, the Ottomans unconsciously assisted the Reformation's triumph in sixteenth-century Hungary.

The various Protestant confessions established themselves in Hungary much as they had done elsewhere in Central Europe. An acquaintance with its constantly transforming and then increasingly radical teachings demanded a constant connection between the most important centers of the Reformation (Wittenberg and other German cities) and Hungary, now thrashing around in the jaws of the Ottoman Empire. This constant connection was ensured by growing numbers of Hungarian and Transylvanian students at German universities and by the burgeoning religious literature that Gutenberg's invention brought with it.

This all meant that even dismembered Hungary was largely able to remain part of Europe's intellectual lifeblood. In the midst of Ottoman conquest and a constant war footing, this was a crucial achievement in the long run, too.

The teachings of the Lutheran Reformation were first accepted by a few teachers at the college of Buda in 1521. In addition to students traveling to Wittenberg, the Reformation's initial expansion was assisted by the German bourgeoisie of the medieval Hungarian capital and by the openness of certain members of the king and queen's court. German burghers of towns in Western Hungary, the Szepes region, and Transylvania (especially in the Saxon Lands) soon became acquainted with the new confession whose articles of faith had been laid down by Philipp Melanchthon. As these had been accepted in 1530 at the imperial diet of Augsburg, the original name for the Lutheran church—the Evangelical Church of the Augsburg Confession—was given by the city. In the Carpathian Basin, however, it would be a long while before this confession had a developed teaching syllabus (dogma) and established ecclesiastical apparatus. The first of the Transylvanian Saxons to take a step in this direction was Johannes Honterus, a parson and map engraver from Brassó (German *Kronstadt*); the first of the German burghers of Upper Hungary to do so was Leonhard Stöckel, the rector of Bártfa (German *Bartfeld*), who had studied in Wittenberg. It was the latter who in 1546 edited the first creed of the Hungarian Reformation, the so-called *Confessio Pentapolitana*, with which the five free royal cities of Upper Hungary (Kassa, Lőcse, Bártfa, Eperjes, and Kisszeben) would defend themselves to King Ferdinand I against the charge of heresy.

It was not long before the Lutheran Reformation was spread to Hungarian areas by former Wittenberg students who had become both urban and wanderer preachers. Of its first great popularizers, Mátyás Bíró Dévai (the "Hungarian Luther"), Imre Ozorai, and András Gálszécsi are particularly worthy of mention. In the 1550s and in the period of "tranquility" after the peace of Edirne of 1568, their work was continued by the next generation. That the Lutheran church could put down roots throughout Hungary was first and foremost the work of András Horvát Szkhárosi (a preacher in Tállya in Upper Hungary), the reformer Mihály Sztárai, and the preacher and wanderer printer Gál Huszár. They used literary works (congregational hymns, psalms, polemical plays, and poetry histories) and missionary work to convey Melanchthon's message to Hungarian market towns, villages, and the estates of a few prestigious high nobles (Péter Perényi, Elek Thurzó, Tamás Nádasdy, Péter Petrovics, etc.).

It is important to emphasize that in the first half century or so of the acceptance of the Reformation, some of its teachings were still distinctly provisional. As the various confessions came into being (a process known as *Konfessionsbildung* in German, while its expansion into the social and institutional sphere is called *Konfessionalisierung*), the faithful would at first choose between elements of the different schools to fit their needs—they would often convert from an old teaching to a new one or accept certain details from both. For this reason, until the century's end, movements often regarded by posterity as homogenous were in fact marked by diversity. An excellent example of this is the variety of polemics and synods from the middle of the century, which led the various movements gradually to focus their approaches, thanks to which their creeds began to be refined and the foundations of their ecclesiastical structures laid down.

The confession of the aforementioned five free royal towns in Upper Hungary was followed in 1559 by that of the similarly German-speaking seven mining towns along the river Garam (*Confessio Heptapolitana*), then by that of the fourteen towns of the Szepes region (*Confessio Scepusiana*). Meanwhile, the structure of the church started to be established. In 1545, with the support of Anna Báthory, widow of Hungarian aristocrat Gáspár Drágffy, the first Protestant synod was held in Erdőd, Szatmár county. And not even a decade passed before the first Lutheran diocese was formed: the Transylvanian Saxon *superintendentia* at Berethalom in 1553. In Transdanubia, however, the Sopron-Vas diocese did not come into being until 1595, and north of the Danube that of Zsolna (Slovak Žilina) was formed only in 1610, primarily for the Slovak-speaking Lutheran congregation. This can all be put down primarily to the fact that at the end of the sixteenth century it was not the Lutheran Reformation so much as the Helvetian one following the teachings of Ulrich Zwingli, then John Calvin, and finally Heinrich Bullinger and Théodore de Bèze that would become the predominant Protestant confession in Hungary (see fig. 19).

The fast proliferation from the 1550s onward of the Reformed Church movement in the area beyond the Tisza in Eastern Hungary was greatly assisted first by the diligence and aggressive iconoclasm of Márton Sánta Kálmáncsehi, former canon of Gyulafehérvár, and then by István Kis Szegedi (see fig. 18) and his pupil Péter Juhász Melius, able as they were to influence the bourgeoisie of the market towns, the peasantry, and the frontier military. Kis preached all over Ottoman Hungary, and, through his significant work as a writer, he played a key role in the establishment of the so-called Lower Dunamellék diocese. Meanwhile, Melius, as vicar of Debrecen, reinforced the movement in the eastern territories, creating the Transtibiscan diocese in 1557 and drawing up the Debrecen creed of 1562. He forcefully defended his teachings both against the Catholics and against the Lutherans; from 1565 he found himself in increasingly bitter polemical exchanges with the radicalizing Ferenc Dávid. Although in 1564 the latter had himself founded the Transylvanian Calvinist diocese with its center in Nagyenyed (through Giorgio Blandrata, the Italian court doctor to Prince John Sigismund), he would soon be leading the Antitrinitarian movement. Finally, as in the Lutheran case, the Calvinist diocese of Transdanubia was established late in the day (in 1595) and only as a result of the definitive break between Lutherans and Calvinists in the western part of the country. In the northeast of Hungary, meanwhile, were the so-called crypto-Calvinists, who presented a separate set of views differing from Lutheran orthodoxy, especially as regards Holy Communion.

The most radical branch of the Reformation to be established as a church was the Antitrinitarian movement. As their name suggests, they did not accept Jesus's divine nature and rejected the Holy Trinity. Their church, the Unitarian church, would take on a solid structural framework only at the end of the sixteenth century, in large part thanks to the efforts of bishops Demeter Hunyadi and György Enyedi. In Transylvania, however, great swathes of the Kolozsvár population were drawn to the new teachings by the brilliant orator and terrifying polemicist Ferenc Dávid, and by the 1580s almost half of the Hungarian population of the principality professed Antitrinitarian beliefs. In fact, from the 1560s and for many long years, the Unitarian college of Kolozsvár offered sanctuary to more radical freethinkers persecuted for their religious views even in Protestant countries (e.g., Jacobus Palaeologus

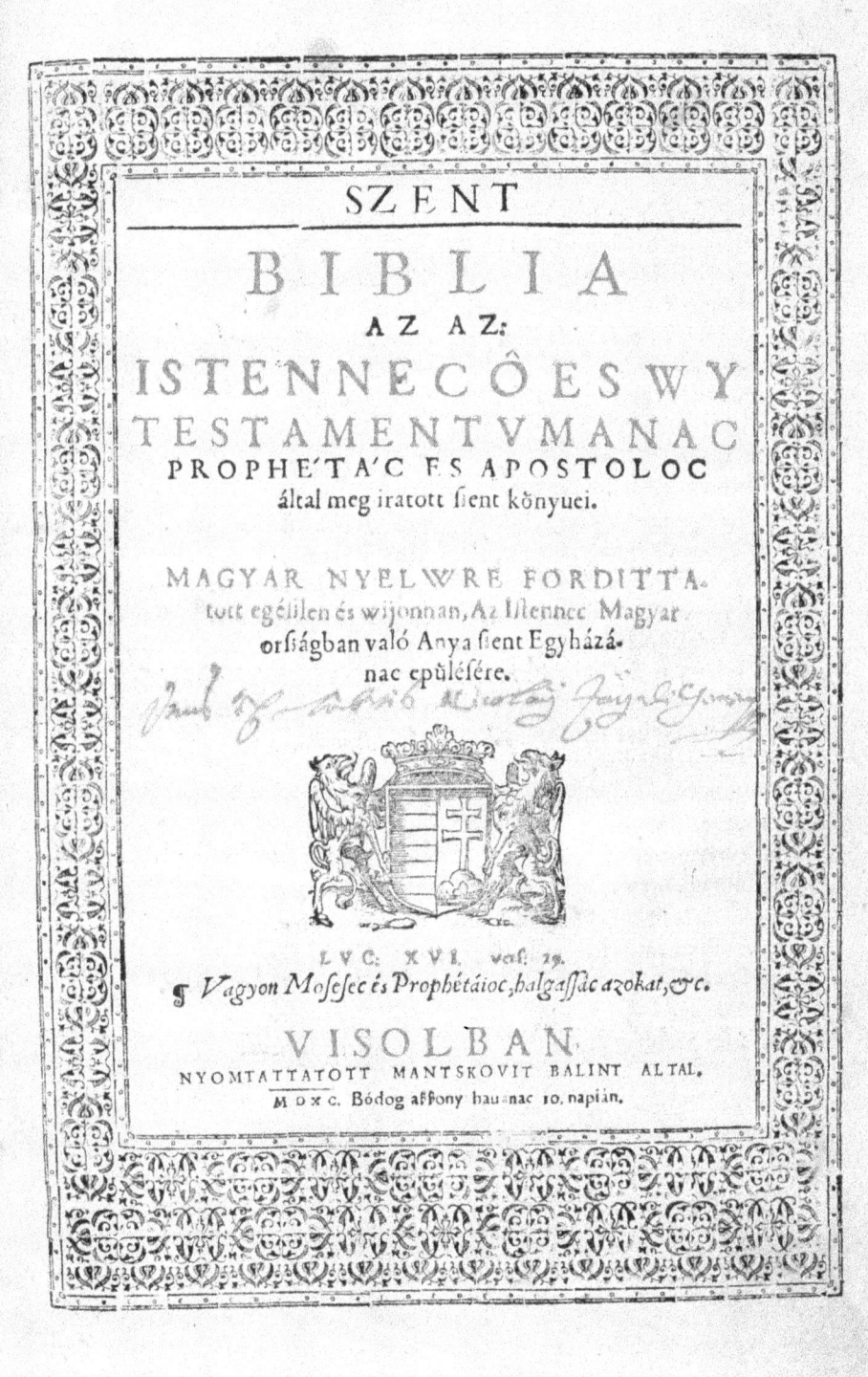

Fig. 19. Front page of the Vizsoly Bible, the first complete Bible translation into Hungarian, 1590 (Széchenyi National Library, Budapest).

and Matthias Vehe-Glirius). Branching out from their Transylvanian base, the Antitrinitarians established modest positions along the Körös and Maros Rivers, in Ottoman Baranya county, and in Nagymaros (near Visegrád) on the banks of the Danube, thanks to the already mentioned double agent and trader János Trombitás (see part 1, chap. 7).

The diversity of the Hungarian Reformation, its so-called confessional pluralism, meant it stood out in the context of European development. As none of the confessions enjoyed any absolute dominance, no Protestant national church could emerge as in the case of Scotland or the Scandinavian countries. The various movements bridged different social classes alongside one another, establishing their ecclesiastical frameworks in the same areas and at the same time. The career of Ferenc Dávid, who was born a Catholic, is an excellent example of the plasticity of Transylvanian Protestantism in the sixteenth century: in 1557 he was still bishop of the Transylvanian Lutherans, and in 1564 he was elected to this status by the Calvinists at the synod of Várad, only to become bishop of the Antitrinitarians by 1576. He was capable of going even further with the flow after this, toward nonadorantism (the denial of the adoration of Christ), which would cost him his life. He died in the prison at Déva in November 1579.

The turn of the seventeenth century saw the dividing lines between the various confessions become clear-cut. The followers of the most popular Calvinist church came primarily from the Hungarian nobility, the urban middle class in market towns, the peasantry, and the frontier military, especially from the central and eastern areas of the dismembered country. The Lutherans were squeezed out to the periphery of the kingdom, principally to the estates of a few high nobles in Transdanubia and Upper Hungary, but the German burghers, Slovak peasants, and German frontier soldiers were also members of this church. The faith of this last group was fortified by a number of members of the Austrian elite in charge of frontier defense (e.g., David Ungnad, president of the Aulic War Council [i.e., the "minister of defense" of the Habsburg Monarchy]; Andreas Teufel, captain general of Győr; Andreas Kielman of Komárom; and Hans Rueber of Kassa), who often mobilized their political and military connections to generate support for education and book publication.

This was also excellent proof of the ecumenicity of Hungarian Protestantism. Aside from a diaspora in Ottoman areas, it was only in Transylvania that the Antitrinitarians enjoyed significant success, although here their strength was striking. For all this, the Catholic Church did not disappear, though it remained dominant in only a few larger cities (e.g., Pozsony and Nagyszombat), on noble estates that remained Catholic throughout, and in the Szekler Land in Transylvania. To the south of the Drava, however, the Reformation had little effect on the Croats, with most of them remaining Catholic. The Serbs who had spread over Ottoman Hungary also retained their Orthodox faith under the authority of the patriarchy of Peć (today Peja, Kosovo), as did the growing Romanian population of Transylvania.

Religious division in the sixteenth century could be observed even within individual families. For example, Zsigmond Forgách, who was quick to fall in line with Protestantism, had three sons. One of them, Simon, one of the best-known frontier officers in the country, was aulic but Protestant, and he supported the eminent preachers Gál Huszár and Péter Bornemisza. Yet the latter's real patron was not Simon but his younger brother Imre, who, through his correspondence with many of Europe's great humanists of the age (Hugo

Blotius, András Dudith, etc.), became a key voice on the continent's intellectual lifeblood, the international *respublica litteraria*. Meanwhile, their brother Ferenc became one of the best-known figures in sixteenth-century Hungarian Catholicism. After being catholicized by Miklós Oláh, archbishop of Esztergom, he followed the tradition of the medieval humanists by studying in Padua and then pursued an eminent church career. In the summer of 1565, for example, he conducted the funeral mass for Emperor Ferdinand at the Stephansdom in Vienna. He later left for Transylvania, where he became chancellor to the Catholic Prince Stephen Báthory. But Ferenc's nephews, Mihály and Ferenc (the sons of Simon), would also continue the family tradition for religious divide. Mihály studied at the universities of Strasbourg and Wittenberg and was the first known Hungarian to get a reply from Justus Lipsius, the eminent professor at the University of Leiden and perhaps the best-known figure in late humanism. Meanwhile, the younger Ferenc followed his namesake and uncle and was converted to Catholicism in 1584, becoming bishop of Veszprém and then of Nyitra, and finally archbishop of Esztergom in 1607. Furthermore, in the early seventeenth century, he became one of the leading figures first of the militant and then of the peaceful Catholic Reformation.

Although, as in German history, the sixteenth century would in Hungary become "the century of the Reformation" as far as religion was concerned, the career of the younger Ferenc Forgách already showed that the rejuvenation of Catholicism had begun. This was principally thanks to the reforms accepted at the Council of Trent of 1545–1563 (strengthening church discipline, prioritizing pastoral work, expanding the training of priests, etc.) and to the Jesuit order founded by Saint Ignatius of Loyola in 1540. But we see the same trend in the fact that, as recent research has shown,[2] re-Catholicization began long before the activity of Péter Pázmány, later eminent archbishop of Esztergom (1616–1637). Following the first converts (Pázmány himself in 1582 and the famous poet Bálint Balassi in 1586), the turn of the seventeenth century would see the conversion of such great figures as Miklós Esterházy, later palatine, and the Upper Hungarian magnate György Drugeth de Homonna. Like the Reformation itself, this Catholic revival was peaceful to start with, turning into more forceful action only in the early seventeenth century, with more violent methods in many ways similar to those of the radical Protestants.

Contrary to the traditional view, the reform of Catholicism was not simply a response to the Reformation (namely, a "counter-Reformation")—thus, the general usage of this term has been brought into question by recent international scholarship. After attempts at reform in the late Middle Ages that came from below, there was also an institutional reform movement from above, led by the papacy. In the second half of the sixteenth century, after the Council of Trent, the two phenomena would complement one another. This made it possible for the Catholic Church to find a way out of one of the deepest crises in its history. So was the case in Hungary, though the church's enormous losses brought great difficulties before these innovations could be implemented. The only advantage was that in these decades the most important secular positions in the Kingdom of Hungary (royal governor, chancellor, and president of the Hungarian Chamber) were provided by prelates.

The cradle of the Catholic revival would become Nagyszombat, the new base for the archbishopric and chapter of Esztergom. Led by the great prelate-politician of the age, Archbishop Miklós Oláh, the reform movement had begun in tandem with the Council of Trent.

This is worthy of note even from a European perspective. The humanist archbishop not only was able to fortify the positions of his church against the secular elite (e.g., by being alone in placing the Holy Crown on the head of Maximilian of Habsburg at the first coronation of Pozsony in 1563) but also began the reorganization of the tattered system of Catholic institutions and the preparation for the adequate pastoral care of the faithful. To aid this, in 1554 he merged the city school and the chapter school in Nagyszombat and then established a diocesan seminary (1558). Between 1559 and 1562, he also arranged canonical visitation to the church of his main diocese, while from 1560 to 1566 there were five synods at which he passed laws to deal with omissions of the Catholic Church. By 1561 he had succeeded in settling the Jesuits, whom he had entrusted with the running of the now reformed school in Nagyszombat.

Although this experiment was only temporarily effective, if only for financial reasons, the Jesuits, leaving Hungary in 1567, would return within two decades. Starting in 1586, they were assisted in founding a new college by György Draskovics, archbishop of Kalocsa; it was eventually opened in Znióváralja, Turóc country, in 1591. The fathers then relocated from there to the more favorably located Vágsellye after Győr was retaken from the Ottomans in 1598. Despite the wartime circumstances, the monastery continued to operate right until the ravaging advance of Stephen Bocskai's troops in 1605 (see part 1, chap. 11). Although this renewed Jesuit experiment was only of local significance, it nevertheless came to be crucial for the later activities of the order. The Jesuits began to acquaint themselves with the state of affairs in Hungary and learned the basic techniques of pastoral work. Indeed, many of their eminent exponents would begin their careers at Znióváralja and Vágsellye: Sándor Dobokay, György Forró, and the Bible translator István Arator Szántó, an important figure in Catholic Reformation prior to Pázmány, as well as Pázmány himself. So could the two little Jesuit colleges become the cradle for Catholic renewal in the kingdom.

In the second half of the sixteenth century, Jesuits laid down roots in the easternmost bastion of European Protestantism, Transylvania. In a clear sign of the princely power, following the rule of the Protestant John Sigismund, the Catholic Stephen Báthory was able to settle the Jesuits in the former Benedictine monastery at Kolozsmonostor in 1579. For political reasons and given the great distances involved, however, they were to arrive not from the Austrian province but from Poland. Their work would soon bring impressive results. By 1581 they were able to settle in the former Franciscan monastery in Kolozsvár, and with time they were able to establish their order in Gyulafehérvár, while they also operated in a smaller mission in Várad. By the middle of the decade, their school in Kolozsvár was more popular than the Unitarian one.

Even in the principality, these initial achievements soon came to an end. In 1586 the plague took more than half of the forty-five members of the order, while at the end of the year the death of Prince Stephen Báthory opened a new era in their history. In 1588 the Protestant estates were able to see that the young Sigismund Báthory signed a law on the exclusion of the Jesuits. This required them to leave Transylvania, but in 1595 the prince they had brought up again guaranteed their safe return. They settled in Kolozsmonostor, Kolozsvár, and Gyulafehérvár anew, where, despite the adversity brought by the long war with the Ottomans (in 1603 their monastery was destroyed by the troops of the pretender to the throne, Moses Székely), they managed to remain until they were again expelled in 1607.

The progress of this Catholic revival was most unusual in Ottoman Hungary. As it was in this part of the country that the Catholic Church was damaged the most, this was where the rejuvenation was most difficult. While the former episcopal offices continued to be nominated by the Hungarian kings, these prelates could really have a significant role only in places where the Franciscan monasteries had survived (Jászberény, Szeged, and Gyöngyös). In other areas, such as Baranya county, with no priests present, secular Catholic preachers (so-called licentiates) maintained the Catholic faith of some of the villages. Amid the Orthodox Serbs and Vlachs now settling in the area and the Calvinist Hungarians, a key part was played in the survival of the Catholic communities—especially along the Danube and in the southern territories—by the Ragusan and Bosnian merchants who oversaw trade with the Levant. The Holy See was quick to recognize the opportunities they offered, and in 1572 it began its missionary organization in the northern half of the Balkan Peninsula, the first phase of which lasted until 1607. In this period the papacy sent apostolic visitors to survey the religious circumstances not only in the Balkans but also in the southern parts of Ottoman Hungary, by this time populated mostly by South Slavs. This was necessary because the jurisdiction of the bishops of the Kingdom of Hungary no longer extended to these areas.

The first visitations to the Balkans and to Southern Hungary to be based on a unified framework took place during the papacy of Gregory XIII (1572–1585), principally led by Pietro Cedulini, Alessandro Comuleo, and Bonifacio di Ragusa. The Ragusan Franciscan monk, formerly theological expert to the Council of Trent, was the first papal visitor to Ottoman Hungary in 1581. It was on the basis of these surveys (of Catholic communities, need for priests, etc.) that missions could be organized in the decades that followed. The southern part of Ottoman Hungary represented the northernmost part of the Balkan arrangements to be made—that is, the last area the organizers of the missions had to reach—as has all been revealed by the research findings of the last two decades.[3] In these areas, in this period, mostly Bosnian Franciscans and Ragusan Benedictines, Franciscans, and Dominicans, as well as a few Jesuits, were active, with a papal mandate. But from the 1570s to the end of the century, this was only really reconnaissance work. Real missionary work would begin only after 1612 and would fully include the Jesuits (see part 2, chap. 8).

Notes

1. Katalin Péter, *Studies on the History of the Reformation in Hungary and Transylvania*, ed. Gabriella Erdélyi (Göttingen: Vandenhoeck und Ruprecht, 2018), especially 50–103.

2. László Lukács and Antal Molnár, "A homonnai jezsuita kollégium (1615–1619)" [The Jesuit theological school of Homonna, 1615–1619], in *Művelődési törekvések a korai újkorban. Tanulmányok Keserű Bálint tiszteletére/Kulturelle Bestrebungen in der frühen Neuzeit: Festschrift für Bálint Keserű*, ed. Mihály Balázs et al. (Szeged: JATE Régi Magyar Irodalom Tanszék, 1997), 357–359.

3. István György Tóth, ed., *Politique et religion dans la Hongrie du XVIIe siècle: Lettres des missionnaires de la Propagande Fide* (Paris: Champion, 2004); Antal Molnár, *Le Saint-Siège, Raguse et les missions catholiques de la Hongrie Ottomane 1572–1647* (Rome: Accademia d'Ungheria, Roma, 2007); Antal Molnár, *Confessionalization on the Frontier: The Balkan Catholics between Roman Reform and Ottoman Reality* (Roma: Viella, 2019).

Fig. 20. Poet Bálint Balassi (1554–1594). Unknown Hungarian painter, seventeenth century (Christian Museum, Esztergom).

10

SEEKING A LANGUAGE

A Cultural Golden Age

IN THE SIXTEENTH CENTURY, WARS AND THEIR TERRIBLE consequences significantly transformed Hungary's political, military, and ethnic circumstances. But the Muses were not silent on the frontier between the two empires. In fact, in the 1570s and 1580s, which brought relative peace and increased prosperity, we can speak of a cultural golden age, as recent research has shown.[1] The Hungarian language was enjoying its first flourish, producing the first treasures of Hungarian literature. Huge advances in book publishing meant literature could reach a broader section of society, and there were publications in the languages of all the different ethnic groups. Meanwhile, thousands of noble, bourgeois, and peasant students attended European universities, and in the various intellectual centers in the Kingdom of Hungary and in Transylvania, humanist scholarly groups operated at a European level. Indeed, the intellectual life became a career possibility, which was a good sign that literacy had improved by leaps and bounds from the very low levels of medieval times. As in the case of economic progress, this period of cultural transformation, one of the most important in Hungarian history, was the product of decades of progress and of enormous diligence of a great many people of all confessions and ethnic groups.

Although Latin was the official language in Hungary until 1844 and thus in this period remained the language of politics, public administration, the legal system, and scholarship, the Hungarian language nevertheless started to play an increasingly active role both in literacy and in culture from the end of the Middle Ages onward. From the first half of the sixteenth century, Hungarian gradually became the most important language for everyday correspondence; indeed, in the Principality of Transylvania—where the break from the kingdom was particularly favorable for the development of Hungarian culture—the official language of legislation became Hungarian as early as the 1550s. It was initially used in rather rough-and-ready fashion, as there was no official correct spelling, and it was hard to form Hungarian consonants with diacritics (e.g., *ő* and *ű*) or two digits (e.g., *gy*). Yet every line that was written or printed in the language would help increase its significance.

Contrary to popular belief, this was not only related to the Bible translations into the vernacular as encouraged by Luther. It is true, however, that processes begun previously were given great impetus by the Reformation, and—in line with the transformation of the country's confessions, as discussed in part 1, chapter 9—by the end of the sixteenth century, the lion's share of literature in Hungarian was by Protestant authors. The foundations were laid by the monks and nuns of the early years of the century, who translated and copied codices in Hungarian by the dozen (e.g., the Winkler codex in 1506, the Döbrentei codex in 1508, the Cornides codex in 1514–1519, the Jordánszky codex in 1516–1519, the Érdy codex in 1524–1526, the Székelyudvarhely codex in 1526–1528, and the Kriza codex in 1532). They were followed by the Catholic nobles and gentry already corresponding in richly composed Hungarian, a process that would be completed by the humanists of the age from the 1530s and then by Protestant preachers and schoolmasters.

While in this era we cannot speak of a national identity in the modern sense of the term—this would come into being only in the nineteenth century—the connection to the Hungarian language became ever closer: it began to be developed and organized in a deliberate fashion and to be discovered both at home and abroad. This is why the humanists, irrespective of their confession, published the first dictionaries and glossaries and the first Hungarian grammars; meanwhile, interest in the language abroad was growing. The six-language travel dictionary (*Nomenclatura sex linguarum*) published in Vienna in 1538 by Gábor Pesti, who worked at the Hungarian Aulic Chancellery, would be followed at the end of the century by the glossaries by Balázs Fabricius Szikszai (1590) and Faustus Verancsics (1595). The latter would list the Slavic loan words in Hungarian in the form of an etymological dictionary. The results of the linguistic progress of the period would be excellently summarized by Albert Molnár Szenci in his Latin-Hungarian and Hungarian-Latin dictionary (*Dictionarivm Latinovngaricvm, Dictionarivm Vngaricolatinvm*) published in 1604 in Nuremberg, the first to have the Hungarian language as its reference point.

The most important of these grammar books was the Latin-Hungarian grammar (*Grammatica Hvngarolatina*) by János Sylvester, still written in Latin, which was published in 1539 by Tamás Nádasdy's press in Sárvár-Újsziget, Vas county. In his postscript, Sylvester announced a manifesto for the increased use of Hungarian: "If we are not afraid to use this national language of ours, this treasure—which hitherto has been hidden from us, which we have discovered for the first time, unearthed and brought into the light—we can soon go from being impoverished to being filthy rich."[2] His efforts soon brought him followers. The Hungarian-language grammar (*Orthographia Vngarica*) by Mátyás Bíró Dévai, which was published in its second edition in 1549, was the first official guide to Hungarian spelling. In 1598 the Protestant humanist historiographer János Decsi Baranyai, from Marosvásárhely in Transylvania, enriched the Hungarian language with a book of phrases.

Alongside the humanists deliberately working on it, a vital role in the development of the Hungarian language was also played by the reformers, even if the language was for them of course primarily a means to their religious ends. Protestantism brought with it a real intellectual buzz: its adherents spoke in their mother tongue and encouraged the reading of religious and literary works in Hungarian, and so their activities did much to enrich Hungarian language and literature. The role of Bible and psalm translations was particularly significant. Of the former, the most influential was the Vizsoly Bible (1590) (see fig. 19 in part 1, chap. 9), the first complete Hungarian Protestant translation of the Bible, by Gáspár Károli, who had studied in Wittenberg; its style and turns of phrase would soon enter common parlance. The most important of the psalm translations were the prose ones of István Székely (*Zsoltárkönyv* [Book of psalms], 1548) and Gáspár Heltai (*Zsoltár* [Psalms], 1560) and the verse manuscript by the Antitrinitarian Miklós Fazakas Bogáti. The first complete book of psalms (*Psalterium Ungaricum*) was also published by Albert Molnár Szenci in 1607. The influence of the many collections of sermons and congregational hymnbooks was also considerable. Meanwhile, a strengthening of patriotism because of defense against the Ottomans boosted the development of the Hungarian language; festivals were now sung almost exclusively in Hungarian. The era of the fortress wars would be recorded for posterity in a historical song by the legendary Sebestyén Tinódi (*Cronica*, 1554), while György Tardi would do likewise for the victory of 1588 near the market town of Szikszó in Upper Hungary.

Thanks to all this, the Hungarian language enjoyed its first golden age in the second half of the sixteenth century. Its basic structure did not change, but it became more colorful and more flexible, its vocabulary grew, and the formal form of address was established, which survives to this day; meanwhile, Hungarian had the Turkish-speaking occupiers to thank for a new sound (the *dzs*). As those developing the language, the humanists and reformers, were also those writing its literature, thanks to them a Hungarian literary tongue would come into being by the end of the century. Although, even before 1526, the main cultural arenas alongside the royal court in Buda were the ecclesiastical and aristocratic centers, as well as the various monasteries, in the Kingdom of Hungary the Ottoman occupation and the relocation of the court to Vienna meant that—in addition to the new capital (Pozsony) and the new headquarters of the archiepiscopate of Esztergom (Nagyszombat)—the magnates' residences would overwhelmingly act as the main centers for culture. This was true of the Nádasdy family's court at Sárvár, the Perényi one at Sárospatak, and the Batthyány residence at Németújvár. In Transylvania this role was played by the princely court. Finally, in Ottoman Hungary, the Protestant schools in market towns and village churches operated as small-scale cultural "workshops." The impact of the humanist intellectual group of the Hungarian Aulic Chancellery in Vienna was also considerable.

The first exponents of post-1526 Hungarian literature were the so-called Hungarian Erasmians (Benedek Komjáti, Gábor Pesti, and János Sylvester), followers of the uncrowned prince of the humanists, Erasmus of Rotterdam.[3] Their work in promoting the Hungarian language was founded on thorough literary principles, which are evident in Sylvester's words to his patron, Tamás Nádasdy: "A few years ago other nations would chide us, saying that when even the Russians now have the scriptures in their own tongue, we Hungarians do not. While, apart from this one thing, not only are Christian nations not able to chide us, they should envy us, for our language is so special, they cannot even emulate it. Which foreign nation would be surprised to find someone able to write any kind of poem in Hungarian, following the Latin and Greek example?"[4] In 1541, it was in this spirit that Sylvester published, at his patron's expense, his translation of the New Testament, which included the first Hungarian poem to scan (see fig. 21). He can thus rightly be considered one of the founders both of Hungarian linguistics and of Hungarian literary criticism. Gábor Pesti also transposed part of the New Testament into Hungarian; his translation, entitled *Esopus fabulái* [Aesop's fables] and published in 1536, would already be a work of real literary merit.

The work of the Erasmians was continued by the reformers and by the humanist prelates, who were great patrons. The activities of these overlapping groups together formed an organic whole. Perfect evidence for this are the vigorous theological debates in the late 1570s

Fig. 21. Front page of the New Testament as translated by János Sylvester, the first book to be published in Hungary in Hungarian. Sárvár, 1541 (Széchenyi National Library, Budapest).

and early 1580s between the Protestant Péter Bornemisza and Miklós Telegdy, bishop of Pécs, which took place in the form of Hungarian masterpieces (*Fejtegetés* [Discussion] in 1578 and *Felelet* [Response] in 1580). It was only with decades of hard work that Bornemisza and his peers could create the characteristic religious genres of Reformation literature (Bible and psalm translations, collections of sermons, congregational hymns, paraphrases of psalms, and Biblical histories). The noted reformer Mihály Sztárai was already writing quality polemical dramas (e.g., *Igaz papságnak tiköre* [Mirror to the real priesthood], 1559).

The greatest Protestant literary personalities of sixteenth-century Hungary were the preachers and printers Gáspár Heltai and Péter Bornemisza. Although Heltai (born Kaspar Helth) was from a Transylvanian Saxon family and his mother tongue was German, he learned Hungarian so well that most of his works were published in Hungarian. His works are particularly noteworthy for their variety and their witty use of language. In addition to his best-known work, *Száz fabula* (Hundred fables, 1566), based on Aesop's fables, he wrote a small volume entitled *A részegségnek és tobzódásnak veszedelmes voltáról* (The dangerous nature of drunkenness and saturnalia, 1552) and *Háló* (1570), about the dramatic Inquisition story of a defrocked Spanish monk. Neither was he insignificant as a historiographer. In 1565 he was the first—beating the humanist Johannes Sambucus—to discover and then publish part of the Latin historiographical work of Antonio Bonfini, the Italian historiographer of Matthias Corvinus, which he also used in preparing his celebrated historiographical survey (*Chronica az magyaroknak dolgairól* [Chronica of the affairs of the Hungarians], 1575).

Péter Bornemisza's oeuvre is also mostly made up of prose works. Initially he was also supported by Tamás Nádasdy, and so as a student in Vienna he was able to publish the Hungarian version of Sophocles's *Electra* in 1558. This is one of the greatest achievements of Protestant humanism and the first Renaissance tragedy in Hungarian. Then in 1573 he founded a mobile press, which published his enjoyable works on a constant basis. His most influential book was *Ördögi kísértetek* [Devilish temptations] (1578), which transfixed its readers with its thrilling subject and gripping style. But his five-volume *Postilla* also established him as a talented author of sermons.

By the end of the sixteenth century, completing half a century of progress after 1526, high-level Renaissance literary Hungarian would be established by Bornemisza's pupil Bálint Balassi (see fig. 20). Balassi, who loved the free life of the frontier army but was unsuitable as a captain general, enterprising lord, or politician, had an extraordinary talent in the "field of the Muses." While the subjects of his poetry were influenced by his adventurous life experiences (particularly his passionate love stories) and by the vivid religious nature of his era, his poems reflected more than just this. Unlike the preachers, he was no longer using the language as a means to an end (e.g., to achieve religious objectives) but rather deliberately turning it into poetry, displaying the emotional world and the habits of his age in a distinctly modern fashion. Particularly worthy of note are the cycles of his Renaissance romantic poetry, which provide an animated picture of his own romantic world that can equally be felt by a modern reader. His religious poetry, which taken as a whole stands above differences between confessions, has a similarly unique voice; his tender, personal relationship to faith was almost modern. In all this, Balassi made expert use of ancient conventions and applied the methods of neo-Latin poetry, and yet he was also able to transform the poetic form and to bring a new genre into being (the court drama: *Szép magyar comoedia* [Beautiful Hungarian comedy], 1588). It was with Balassi that melody and lyrics in Hungarian literature would finally become separate, though he annotated his earlier poems with a musical score pertaining to their melody. He was also a pioneer in the way he deliberately edited his poems into cycles.

Balassi's love poems would establish love poetry in Hungarian, and his religious poems made him the first great figure in Hungarian religious poetry; despite the fact that not one of his poems would be published in printed form in his lifetime, in manuscript form they managed to circulate. In *Egy katonaének* [A soldier's song], celebrating the frontier life, he used a masterfully closed and proportioned structure to describe the heroic attitude to life in the frontier army in the form of an ode. His literary objectives, achieved thanks to his enormous talent, were summarized in the first lines of the *Comoedia* as follows: "I wrote this comedy with the most eloquent of words I could muster. . . . I wanted to enrich the Hungarian language so that all could witness that what is possible in other languages is also possible in ours."[5]

Balassi's circle of poets—which included Kata Telegdy, the first female Hungarian poet—was also partly responsible for the late sixteenth-century trend for verse stories on the subject of love, even erotica, known as *beautiful stories* (Hungarian *széphistóriák*). They usually saw the light of day in pamphlet form and as pulp printings, ones that readers would as good as thumb into rags. The nicest of these was the fairy tale by Albert Gergei (*História egy Árgirus nevű királyfiról és egy tündér szűzleányról* [Story of a prince named Árgírus and a fairy virgin girl]), which was the source for the classic nineteenth-century work by Hungarian poet Mihály Vörösmarty, *Csongor és Tünde* [Csongor and Tünde]. Works of public verse (historicizing, patriotic, and prisoners' songs and verse chronicles) were written in even more everyday style and, largely irrespective of confessional, social, and cultural considerations, were in a language accessible to the broader public. Péter Selymes Ilosvai became famous for his work about Miklós Toldi (it was principally on the basis of this that the great Hungarian poet János Arany wrote his *Toldi* in the nineteenth century); Sebestyén Tinódi for his songs, written to a melody, easy to remember, and thus spread by word of mouth; and Ferenc Wathay for his songbook compiled while in prison in Constantinople.

By the last decades of the sixteenth century, the Hungarian language, which at the end of the Middle Ages was still only being formed, had—thanks to its deliberate development, to its being put to the service of the Reformation, and to the first achievements of its literature—become a fully developed literary language. The result of this successful search for an accepted Hungarian language was perhaps best described by János Rimay, Balassi's pupil: Hungarian had gone from "a bitter blackthorn to a fully ripe sweet Hungarian cherry, resplendent in its splendid red."[6] The fruit of this progress was to be savored no longer by the select few, at court and in the aristocratic and intellectual class, but by an increasingly broad section of society. Advances in printing and the education system allowed the last third of the century to become one of the golden ages for Hungarian culture.

Gutenberg's invention would play a role both in the creation of a literary language and in the blossoming culture of reading and writing in Hungarian. The newly established presses—the first being the one founded in Sárvár by Tamás Nádasdy—no longer published volumes only in Latin and German but now also published ones in Hungarian. Yet the first Hungarian-language printed book came into being earlier, outside Hungary: in 1533, with the support of the highly influential magnate Péter Perényi, Benedek Komjáti published a Hungarian translation of the epistles of Saint Paul, in Krakow. It can be seen as symbolic that this was followed in 1541, the year of the fall of Buda, by the first Hungarian book published in Hungary, János Sylvester's aforementioned version of the New Testament. The printer of the latter, Benedek Abádi, would be followed by numerous others: in Transylvania and Debrecen by Georg Hoffgreff and Gáspár Heltai and in the Kingdom of Hungary by Gál Huszár, Péter Bornemisza, and Raphael and Rudolf Hoffhalter, and then at the turn of the century by Bálint Mantskovit (creator of the Vizsoly Bible) and Joannes Manlius. A number of them (Heltai, Huszár, and Bornemisza) were craftsmen of the Hungarian language and leading writers of their day; they thus changed the language of printed works, further refining it.

Printers, often forced to move as their patrons changed, were crucial to the increasing interest of the population of the Kingdom of Hungary and the Principality of Transylvania in Hungarian—indeed, often secular—literature, and in the written or printed Hungarian word in general. By the second half of the century, book publishing had also become a significant commercial enterprise. One sign of this was the spread of pulp-like "people's books" (Biblical, historical, love stories, sometimes piquant ones), ever cheaper and smaller in size; another was the emergence of books in the Carpathian Basin in the language of its every ethnic minority and for all of its social echelons. Among the approximately nine hundred publications published in the sixteenth century, we find the German-language works of the Saxons of the Szepes region (mostly published in Bártfa), the Croatian-language edition of István Werbőczy's *Tripartitum* (Nedelic, 1574), and Cyrillic books in Romanian and in Old Church Slavonic in Transylvania. The Hungarian translation of the *Tripartitum* was published in Debrecen (*Magyar decretum*) in 1565, while the first Hungarian book on botany, the *Herbarium* by Péter Juhász Melius, was published in Kolozsvár in 1578. Furthermore, the Carniolan-born Manlius published the first Hungarian work on medicine, Gergely Frankovith's *Hasznos és felette szükséges könyv* [Useful and even necessary book] (1582–1585). This was also the first book published in Hungary to be decorated with copper engravings.

The most beautiful book of the sixteenth century is considered to be *Foliopostilla*, Péter Bornemisza's single-volume book of sermons published in Detrekő, Pozsony county (1584); the greatest printing achievement is thought to be the Vizsoly Bible, completed in the summer of 1590 after a year and a half's work, over 603 printer's sheets in length and in seven to eight hundred copies. The demand for books was reflected in the development of book culture, with a number of significant libraries: in addition to those of the humanist prelates (such as András Dudith, Miklós Oláh, Miklós Telegdy, and Demeter Náprágyi), we need only think of those of Boldizsár Batthyány, the magnate interested in French literature, or, in the Transylvanian case, of Giovanni Michaele Bruto, the Italian historiographer to Stephen Báthory.

While many among the peasantry and the poorer gentry would for many decades still know nothing of penmanship, the demand for learning to read and write grew in all social classes. Indeed, the Hungary of the early seventeenth century had reached a level of development at which anyone with a great desire and real need for literacy could relatively easily acquire it at some basic level. This was all assisted by the Hungarian school network, flourishing thanks to the Reformation (in addition to small schools in villages and market towns, there were the Protestant colleges of Debrecen, Sárospatak, Pápa, Eperjes, Várad, Gyulafehérvár, Marosvásárhely, Kolozsvár, and Brassó). From these schools, with the help of a patron, a student could move on to the best universities in Europe, whether German (Wittenberg, Strasbourg, Heidelberg, Tübingen, Jena, etc.), Italian (Padua, Bologna, and Rome), Austrian (Vienna and Graz), Polish (Krakow), or English (Oxford and Cambridge)—this was the *peregrinatio academica*. Having got their fill at the continent's intellectual powerhouses, the peregrines would return home with new scholarly achievements brought at first hand, often passing on their knowledge in the school of some settlement in the Kingdom of Hungary, in Transylvania, or in the Ottoman-occupied areas, while continuing their studies.

Many humanist intellectual workshops in the kingdom and in Transylvania helped the dismembered Hungary in the sixteenth century to remain a key part of the continent's cultural lifeblood. Humanism, which permeated the intellectual scene of Europe and appeared in Hungary in the mid-fifteenth century, retained many followers even during the constant military campaigns after 1526. Indeed, the "big family" of humanists further grew with the expansion of Protestantism, developing a Protestant branch, mostly following the spirit of Melanchthon's teachings. The exponents of this in Hungary, the Protestant humanists (e.g., Balázs Fabricius Szikszai, Zsigmond Torda Gyalui, and János Decsi Baranyai), made significant contributions in the field of Hungarian-language literature, as well as promoting the Latin language, as we saw above. In contrast, the prelates still followed earlier tradition and promoted Latin and Greek culture and the continued heritage of the first Hungarian golden age of humanism, the reign of Matthias Corvinus. Despite Archbishop Miklós Oláh, the father of the Catholic revival in the Kingdom of Hungary, burning Melanchthon's teachings, and despite the often harsh conflicts between confessions, humanism managed to remain a universal intellectual movement that stood above religion.

In the mid-sixteenth century, the court of Archbishop Oláh was a bastion of humanism. The former royal secretary, having escaped after 1526 to the Netherlands with Queen Mary of Habsburg and even become acquainted with Erasmus himself, returned home in 1542 to become both one of the country's most prominent politicians (as archbishop of Esztergom and royal governor) and one of its leading intellectuals. The political and bureaucratic class that he nurtured, both church and secular, would until the end of the century not only determine the kingdom's domestic politics and judicial system but also continue its master's support for and development of humanist culture. Oláh's was quite an act for his disciples to follow: in the Netherlands he had written his work *Hungaria*, compiled his book of correspondence, and put a few Latin and Greek poems to paper. At home, as prelate and politician, he was then best known for his patronage of art and literature. His palaces in Vienna, Nagyszombat, and Pozsony were centers of culture and indeed repositories for antiques and books. In his school at Nagyszombat, meanwhile, Greek was taught by one of Europe's most famous experts on Aristotle, Flanders-born Nicasius Ellebodius.

The archbishop's followers were true to his intellectual legacy. His successor as royal governor (1568–1572), Pál Abstemius Bornemisza, bishop of Veszprém, Transylvania, and then Nyitra, was not one of Oláh's students but rather one of his like-minded intellectual peers, as was the polymath, diplomat, and bishop of Eger, Antal Verancsics, who collected *Corvinas* in Istanbul. Bornemisza was not only a dependable politician, a keen supporter of the Jesuits, a hugely knowledgeable humanist, a historiographer, and a founder of schools but also a well-respected art and book collector. Visiting the various areas of the country for King Ferdinand I, he attempted to save as much as he could of the treasures scattered by the civil war and the Ottoman advance, often having these items restored.

Of those who really were Oláh's students, it was István Radéczy, bishop of Eger and royal governor (1573–1586), who most excelled in the reviving of culture. In Pozsony, the antique-collecting humanist prelate established one of the most important intellectual workshops of the second half of the century: the gardens of his palace became a center for scholarship and literature. The members of the intellectual elite of the period would often seek the protection of the linden tree standing in the middle of the Garden of the Muses (*hortus Musarum*), of which many a song would be written. There they read their latest poems to each other and reported on their correspondences with foreign friends or the books or works of art they had just purchased. These meetings were often attended by Miklós Istvánffy, who had studied in Padua and Bologna and who would be the author of the most thorough summary of Hungarian history in the sixteenth century (*Historiarum de rebus Ungaricis libri XXXIV*).

Istvánffy's tutor in Padua, Johannes Sambucus, also known as a poet, was another external member of the circle of scholars in Pozsony. As a poet, philologist, doctor, and historian, the humanist Sambucus, born in Nagyszombat, was one of the esteemed Renaissance polymaths of the group. He pursued his studies for over two decades, from Wittenberg to Paris to Padua, and then he settled in Vienna as a court historian and imperial physician. As his house in Vienna was a meeting place for the international scholarly world, his relations with the members of the Radéczy Circle would reinforce the European connections of the Hungarian humanists. His oeuvre is of incalculable worth both to European and to Hungarian culture. He published works by many Ancient Greek and Latin authors and wrote a considerable number of poems and epistles, which were published in Europe's intellectual centers (Padua, Basel, Antwerp, Vienna, etc.). In 1568 he was the first to publish a complete edition of Antonio Bonfini's famous work *Rerum Ungaricarum decades*, a summary of Hungarian history up to 1496. A year later he published the poems of his great predecessor Janus Pannonius, the fifteenth-century poet, and in 1566 he published a new edition of Hungary's first printed map, that of *Lazarus secretarius*, first published in 1528. His collection of books and manuscripts would later form the basis of the court library (*Hofbibliothek*) in Vienna.

The intellectuals gathered in Pozsony formed a genuine humanist circle. Not even religious differences could interfere with their shared interest in literature, scholarship, and the fine arts. Bishop Radéczy's garden played host to ardent Catholics such as Istvánffy and prelate and jurisprudent Zakariás Mossóczy, the first publisher of Hungarian legislation (1584); equally and without incident it did the same to eminent Protestants such as Georg Purkircher, the Pozsony doctor and prolific poet, who had studied in Wittenberg and Padua, and the famous Dutch botanist Carolus Clusius. Other visitors included Elias Corvinus, the well-known scientist and poet, and Hugo Blotius, the scholar in charge of the court library in Vienna; even the English poet and diplomat Sir Philip Sidney would sometimes be among the guests. We have the famous Dalmatian-born engraver Martino Rota—who came to Hungary at the invitation of Antal Verancsics—to thank for portraits of them.

Although in their tastes the participants in this intellectual circle were closest to the Habsburg court at Vienna and Prague, their activities were not political in nature; they were instead dedicated to the universal spirit of humanism and scholarship. This was why they could maintain good relations with the eccentric lord from Németújvár, Boldizsár Batthyány, Clusius's patron. Their former studies at Padua also connected them to the members of the humanist school of Gyulafehérvár (chancellors Ferenc Forgách, Farkas Kovacsóczy, and Márton Berzeviczy, as well as Pál Gyulay), who had also studied there and became known as "the Paduans." The role played by the latter in the patronage of culture was particularly significant in the second half of Stephen Báthory's reign and then at the Italian-style Renaissance court of Sigismund Báthory, welcoming as it did excellent Italian artists (mostly musicians). For this reason, the golden age of Hungarian culture in the late sixteenth century can also be regarded as the second golden age of Hungarian and Transylvanian humanism. The warm words of famous philologist Nicasius Ellebodius to the humanist Gian Vincenzo Pinelli, written from Hungary to Padua in 1573, are a fitting testament to this: "If God grants this country peace, then it is one of the most suitable places in which to accomplish academic goals."[7]

Notes

1. Péter, *Studies on the History of the Reformation*, 160–163.

2. János Sylvester, *Grammatica Hungarolatina. Sárvár, 1539*, facsimile, ed. Péter Kőszeghy (Budapest: Akadémiai Kiadó, 1989), M 1.

3. Cf. Pál Ács, *A magyar irodalmi nyelv két elmélete. Az erazmista és a Balassi-követő* [Two theories of literary Hungarian: The Erasmist and the follower of Balassi] (Budapest: Akadémiai Kiadó, 1983).

4. Tibor Klaniczay, ed., *Janus Pannonius: Magyarországi humanisták* [Janus Pannonius: Humanists in Hungary] (Budapest: Szépirodalmi Könyvkiadó, 1982), 735.

5. Bálint Gyarmati Balassi, *Szép magyar komédia* [Beautiful Hungarian comedy], ed. Péter Kőszeghy and Géza Szabó (Budapest: Szépirodalmi Könyvkiadó, 1990), 7, 12.

6. Pál Ács, ed., *Rimay János írásai* [The writings of János Rimay] (Budapest: Balassi Kiadó, 1992), 51.

7. Tibor Klaniczay, "Nicasius Ellebodius és poétikája" [Nicasius Ellebodius and his poetics], *Irodalomtörténeti Közlemények* [Literary history bulletin] 75, nos. 1–2 (1971): 29.

Fig. 22. Stephen Bocskai, prince of Transylvania and Hungary (1605–1606). Engraving by Crispin van Passe, 1605 (Hungarian National Museum, Budapest).

11

LOOKING IN VAIN FOR A WAY OUT

The Long Turkish War, 1591–1606

At the end of the sixteenth century, a great military conflict brought an end to this blossoming of the economy and culture, a conflict that from 1591 to 1606 covered almost every part of the Carpathian Basin in flames for exactly a decade and a half. The Long Turkish War was Hungary's first modern conflict, and the period was a turning point in early modern Hungarian history. By this time the two empires were pitting themselves against one another no longer merely in individual military campaigns but in attacks led year in, year out by their enormous military apparatuses. The damaging effects of these attacks would be left on the development of the kingdom, the principality, and the Ottoman areas, too. Although it would have been by no means the first time in history that a great power found in a war a way out of other problems, it soon transpired that this experiment was conducted in vain.

In 1591 it would again be the eastern great power that would decide Hungary's fate. The Ottomans escaped the crisis in their empire by fighting the war, which grew from a local skirmish along the Croatian-Slavonian and Transdanubian frontiers to a national conflict by 1593. (This is why some researchers consider 1593 to be the year the war began.) While Ottoman state power kept the economy and society under close inspection, it struggled to overcome the constant flow of new problems it encountered. The cost of the oversized army increasingly presented a problem, as did the collapse of the financial and tax system, population growth, the crisis in cereal production, natural disasters, and a good number of uprisings. Meanwhile, every echelon of state power was gradually turning into an enterprise that could be bribed. And the long war with the Persians (1578–1590) in its turn exhausted much of the empire's resources. Even though the coffers in Istanbul were empty, the sultan's administration nevertheless decided to go to war—as recent studies have described.[1]

The Ottoman divisions in Bosnia and Hungary had for years been eagerly awaiting these expeditions and the plundering they offered; indeed, with the support of Hasan, the aggressive pasha of Bosnia, they did their best to see that the campaign quickly spread to as large an area as possible. They first took an important spot along the Kanizsa frontier area, the fortress of Kiskomárom, in 1591; then, in 1592, they took the Croatian captaincy general's bulwark of Bihać (see map 9). This clearly shows that the war was in full flow by this stage, and there could hardly be any road back to peace. The Ottomans' unexpected defeat at Sziszek (Croatian *Sisak*) on June 22, 1593, would bring decisive success to the military lobby at the

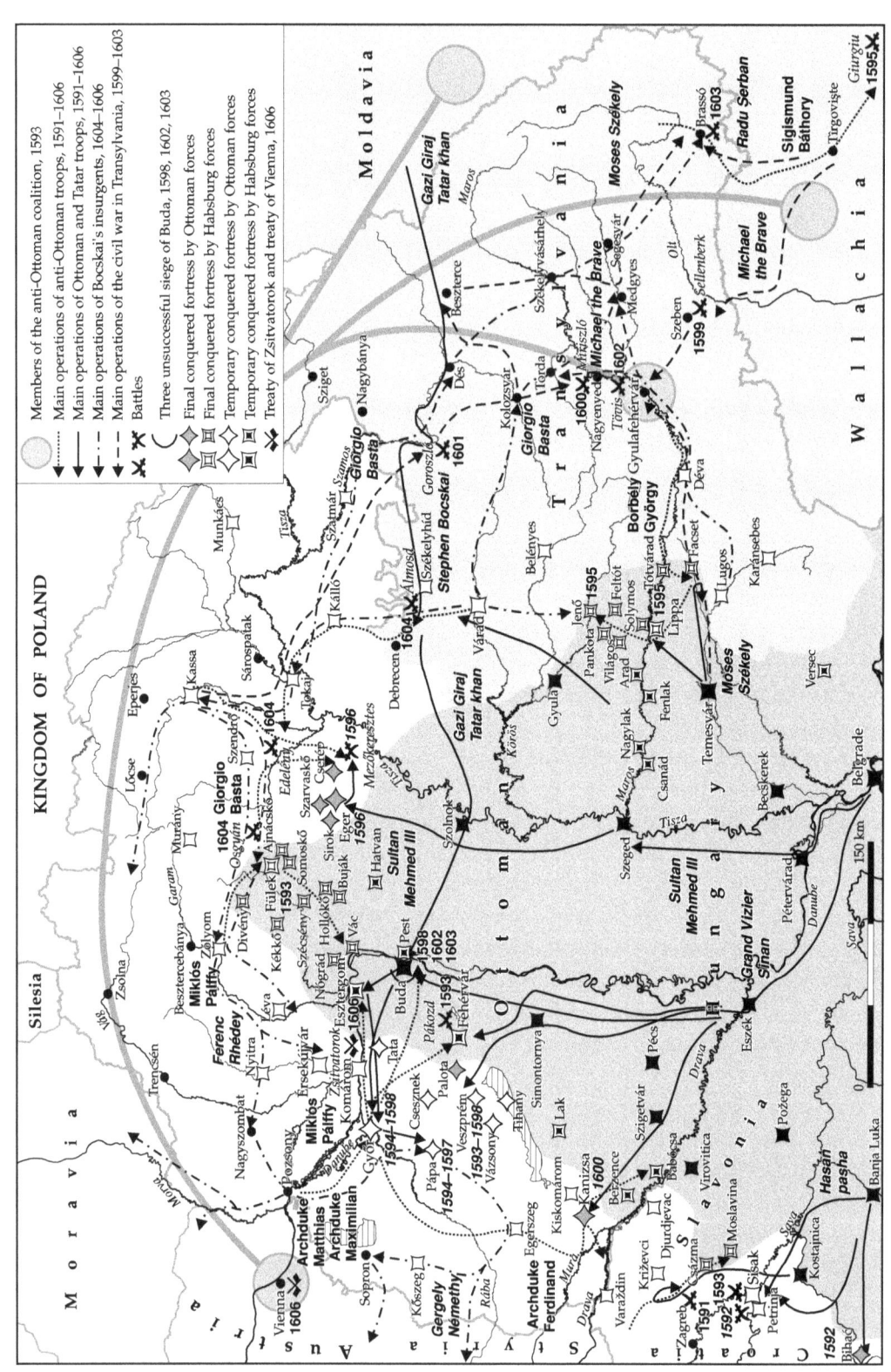

Map 9. The Long Turkish War, 1591–1606, and the Bocskai uprising, 1604–1606.

seraglio that was demanding a European military campaign, even if the Habsburg court in Prague, with its millions in debt, was in no mind to fight a war. The Ottoman military leadership decided on complete mobilization, and so, in the years that followed, either the grand vizier or the sultan himself would lead the empire's troops against Hungary. The Ottoman strategy would remain the same: the goal continued to be the taking of Vienna. For this, of course, it was vital to occupy the border fortresses near the itinerary that the campaign would take along the Danube.

In 1593–1594, the Ottomans made enormous gains toward their objectives in two campaigns led by Grand Vizier Koca Sinan. Applying the strategy that had been successful with John Szapolyai, they tried to make offers to win over as tax-paying vassals the great landowners in the parts of the country furthest from the main path of their invasion (Ferenc Nádasdy in the west and Chief Justice István Báthory and Ferenc Dobó in the east). On this occasion, however, their calls, intending to divide and conquer, fell on deaf ears. Nevertheless, in October 1593 tens of thousands of Ottoman troops took Veszprém and Várpalota; then, in autumn 1594—much to the alarm of the Habsburg Monarchy—they took Győr and the whole of northern Transdanubia. This put the imperial city in immediate danger, with only Komárom left in Christian hands.

In the years that followed, the Ottomans failed to capitalize on this unparalleled opportunity. They might have organized small but militarily overpopulated vilayets in Győr and Pápa to show their intention to advance, but in 1595 the Treaty of Prague (January 28) between Sigismund Báthory, prince of Transylvania, and Emperor Rudolf II, followed by the Christian seizure of Esztergom (September 3), made the Ottoman position difficult. The inclusion in the war of the Ottoman vassal Transylvania and, through it, the two Romanian principalities (Wallachia and Moldavia) opened a new front to the east (on October 29, there was a Christian victory at Giurgiu, along the Danube), while the taking of Esztergom meant that Győr, in Ottoman hands, came under pressure. After the Ottomans took Eger in 1596, it would thus require very serious effort on the part of the new sultan, Mehmed III, to use the modest and fortunate victory at the battle of Mezőkeresztes (October 26–28) and via Transylvania to consolidate Ottoman authority over Wallachia and Moldavia as Istanbul so dearly needed.

The spreading of the war to the entire territory of the Carpathian Basin soon meant that the two empires were unable to face one another on the battlefield. Yet this prolonged standoff would cause a decade of devastation—much to the ill fortune of Hungary and Transylvania. While the Ottomans were incapable of making the most of the strategic advantage provided by the size of their army and their excellent supply lines, the imperial and royal armies also failed to achieve comprehensive victories, despite their military superiority and being equipped, thanks to the Military Revolution,[2] with the most modern armaments of the age. Habsburg military supplies and logistics were built on the financial subsidies, carriages, and workhorses determined by the estates in the countries of the monarchy. The slow pace at which these were provided often rendered the Christian armies immobile. So was it possible that the Ottoman troops could go from Edirne to Buda in less time than it took the Austrians to reach the camp of Magyaróvár near the Austrian-Hungarian border.

Seen as a whole, the war, which had exhausted both sides by the turn of the seventeenth century, would give the Ottomans—who from 1603 renewed hostilities with the Persians—a slight edge in terms of victories. Following on from the vilayet of Eger, established in 1596, the foundation was laid for another new Ottoman territory with the annexation of Kanizsa in 1600 (see fig. 23), while—when losing the respective fortresses—they had to give up on the vilayets of Pápa in 1597 and Győr in 1598. The Ottomans were thus able to significantly extend the territory of Ottoman Hungary in southwest Transdanubia as well as in Croatia; indeed, in early October 1605, they were able to retake Esztergom. It was only to the north of Buda that they had to face a conspicuous loss of territory. At the turn of 1593–1594, Miklós Pálffy retook Fülek, which had been lost in 1554; Kékkő and Divény, lost in 1575; and a number of other smaller frontier locations. On the frontier of the Transtibiscan region, on the other hand, the Ottomans lost Lippa, Solymos, and Jenő, which all fell under the control of the princes of Transylvania. Yet none of these victories could begin to compensate for the enormous destruction that accompanied the renewed military attempts to reunite the kingdom and the principality.

Both Michael the Brave (Mihai Viteazul), voivode of Wallachia, and the Habsburg military leadership—sometimes together, sometimes in competition—tried to exploit the indecision of Sigismund Báthory, who departed the throne on four occasions, to acquire Transylvania. Voivode Michael, first supported by Vienna and later desirous of independence, would end up enduring the same fate as the self-appointed pretenders to the throne in the decades after 1526 (see part 1, chap. 4). In August 1601, the imperial general Giorgio Basta had him killed. The residents of the principality, increasingly deserted and ravaged by famine, experienced the hard-handed Transylvanian governorship of the famed military commander (1602–1604) less as an attempt to unite the country and more as a destructive occupation. Although this occasion was probably the most favorable moment to reunite the kingdom and the principality before the end of the seventeenth century, the Ottoman-controlled areas wedged into the middle of Hungary made any lasting attempt to unite the country little more than an illusion.

There was, likewise, little real hope of the uprising led by Stephen Bocskai (see fig. 22) in October 1604 unifying the country—even if one school of Hungarian historiography contentiously considers this to be the first Hungarian war of independence and national unification movement. Rather, the Bocskai uprising was initially an attempt to reestablish Transylvania's dependence on the Ottoman Empire—that is, the reality of the time. It was also the rebellion of groups of soldiers looking for a way out of a morass—soldiers justifiably dissatisfied with a series of mistakes made by the Habsburg government, left without pay in the middle of a war, often losing everything they had. Bocskai and his hajduk soldiers cannot have hoped for an independent Kingdom of Hungary, as this would never have been possible without the genuine support of the Hungarian political elite (first and foremost the aristocracy and the nobility), as recent research has revealed.[3] Bocskai was first elected prince of Transylvania by the Transylvanian estates on February 21, 1605, in Marosszereda, and then elected prince of Hungary on April 20 in Szerencs by the nobles of the kingdom who supported him (only a minority of said political elite). However, on November 11, on the fields by the Rákos brook near Pest, he accepted the Ottoman crown brought to him by

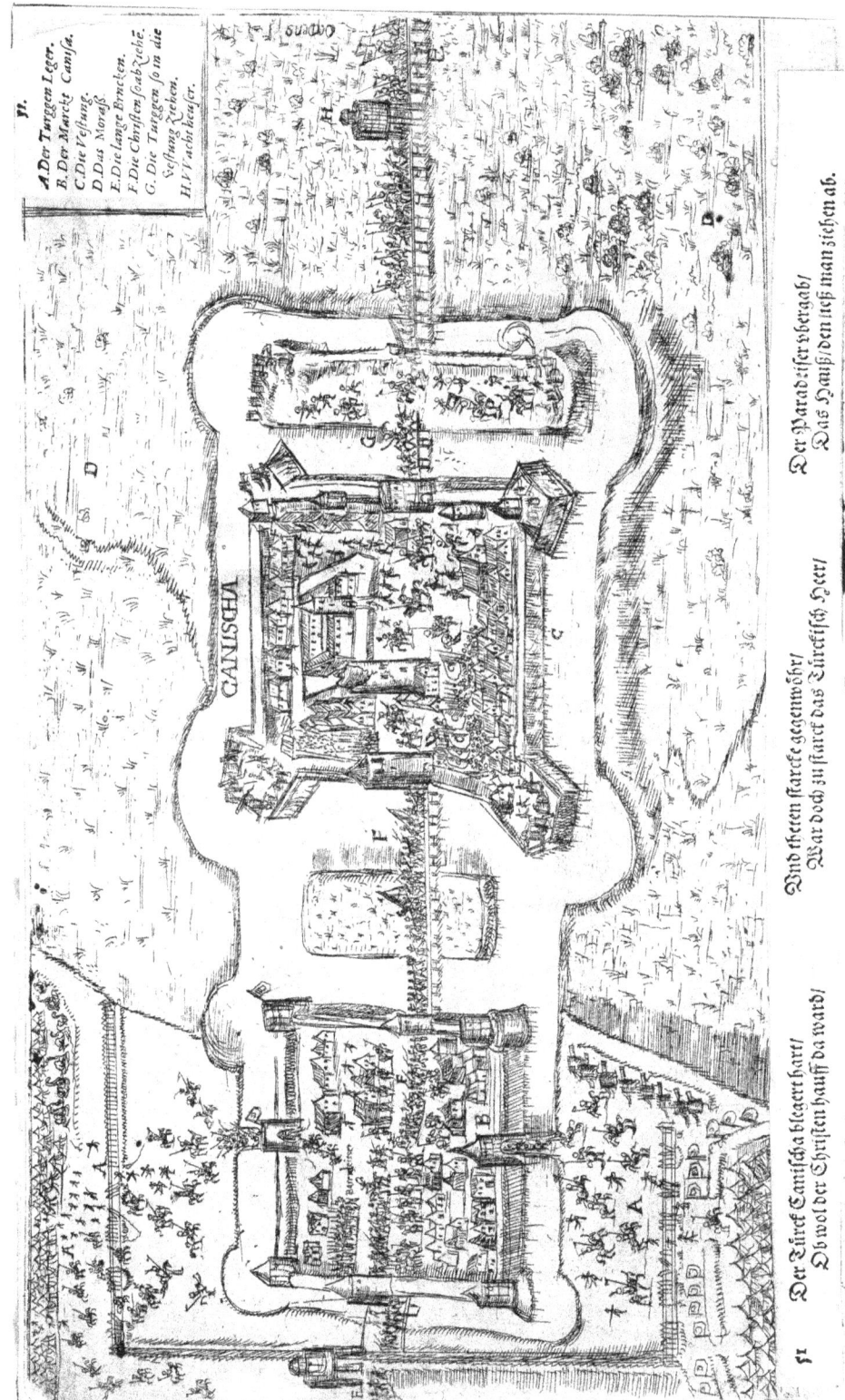

Fig. 23. The Ottoman siege of Kanizsa, 1600. Etching by Wilhelm Peter Zimmermann, 1603 (Hungarian National Museum, Budapest).

Grand Vizier Lala Mehmed and that he had himself requested. This meant the acceptance of Ottoman vassalage, even if Bocskai's European propaganda, understandably, emphasized precisely the opposite—as new research has found.[4]

Behind Bocskai's loud rejection of the Ottoman crown (today housed in the *Schatzkammer* in Vienna) stood the perspicacity of his adviser István Illésházy. Cheered by fast if ephemeral military successes (e.g., the victory at Álmosd in Eastern Hungary on October 15, 1604) and by his being elected prince, Bocskai had started—as John Szapolyai had once done (see part 1, chap. 4)—to believe in the illusion that he could establish an "independent" Hungarian state with Ottoman backing. Illésházy, meanwhile, understood that this would bring utter destruction to Hungary. Even in June 1605, in the midst of hajduk successes, Bocskai's top adviser saw that it was only with the help of the Habsburg Monarchy that the Kingdom of Hungary could manage to survive in the face of the Ottomans: "I cannot even imagine. If the emperor would take his hand off Hungary, how could we maintain the border fortresses in Slavonia, in Transdanubia, and Cisdanubia?"[5]

Illésházy could not be accused of having any special attachment to the Habsburgs. During the long war, he had been one of the main victims of the series of mistakes that the court in Prague, on the verge of bankruptcy, had made. During the war, the Aulic Chamber—with the support of part of the Hungarian political elite—had instigated show trials of a number of large landowners loyal to the court, to ease its financial difficulties by taking back estates given to them as indemnity. The most notorious case was precisely the one brought against Illésházy in 1603. Threatened with the loss of his worldly goods and even of his life, he fled to Poland, and it was on his return from here that he became adviser to Bocskai, who had also had his property confiscated.

The nationwide disapproval generated by these fiscal trials was exacerbated by the leaders of the Catholic Church using the war and the assistance of the imperial and royal troops to improve on their weakened position, breeding enormous resistance in countries that had converted to Protestantism. The great uproar was caused by the occupation of the Lutheran (formerly Saint Elizabeth) Church in Kassa (January 6, 1604). Then came an unprecedented transgression. Arbitrarily, Emperor Rudolf added a separate piece of legislation (law 22) to the decisions taken by the diet of Pozsony in spring 1604, which confirmed the anti-Protestant judgments that had been made while stating that the issue of religion could not be debated at the diet. This led to enormous dissatisfaction on the part of the Protestant Hungarian estates, who were in the majority, and on the part of the gentry in particular. In September 1604, at a meeting held at Gálszécs, Zemplén county, the estates of Upper Hungary threatened a military response if the legislation were not retracted. So in autumn 1604, Bocskai was quickly able to find supporters in their ranks. This was how the hajduk rebellion Bocskai led became the Hungarian estates' first armed movement to confront the court of Habsburg. But there was never to be a national independence struggle or war of independence! It should also be noted that Bocskai drifted into the ranks of the dissatisfied not out of conviction but by necessity. He had been deliberately driven to the rebels' side by Gabriel Bethlen, leader of the Turkophile Transylvanian politicians who rejected any Habsburg occupation of the principality, and later its prince, by having letters sent to the Habsburg commanders about his negotiations with the Ottomans.

The hajduks, accustomed as they were to the conflict of frontier incursions, only occasionally enjoyed success against imperial-royal mercenaries experienced in regular warfare. Yet their movement, supported by the estates of Upper Hungary, brought very real results. Bocskai was aware of their social problems, and so, in return for their military service, on December 12, 1605, he rewarded almost ten thousand hajduks and in March 1606 a further thousand—primarily in the hajduk towns (Dorog, Böszörmény, Szoboszló, Nánás, Hadház, Polgár, and Vámospércs)—with significant privileges (inheritable tax exemptions and jurisdictional and local government privileges). In other words, he settled them in as the nobility en bloc. Though this solved only some of the problems caused by exclusion from society, the privileges granted to the hajduks represented a historical precedent. The residents of the mentioned hajduk towns would not fall under feudal jurisdiction even after the Ottomans were banished, instead forming a separate administrative unit, the hajduk district (*Hajdúkerület*). It was out of this that Hajdú county was born in 1876, which, despite repeatedly being renamed, continues to exist to this day (as Hajdú-Bihar county).

The real winners of the hajduk movement were the Hungarian estates, who were interested less in independence and more in privileges and the strengthening of religious freedoms. Their situation would be emphatically reinforced by the Peace of Vienna, the treaty signed on June 23, 1606, between Emperor Rudolf and Bocskai's envoys after months of negotiations and, finally, the patronage of István Illésházy and Archduke Matthias of Habsburg. The treaty established the free practice of religion (overturning law 22 of 1604); it stated that the estates could again elect a palatine at the next diet and could reserve the most important offices for Hungarians; and it guaranteed the return of the Holy Crown from Prague, while the free royal cities could also retain their privileges. At the same time, Bocskai himself was granted Transylvania and the Partium for his lifetime, as well as the counties of Ugocsa, Bereg, and Szatmár. The prince's death on December 29, 1606, however, meant this all lasted only a few months.

The Treaty of Vienna also stipulated that a peace had to be signed with the Ottomans. This would come to pass on November 11, 1606, at the confluence of the Zsitva (Žitava) and Danube Rivers. The Peace of Zsitvatorok, applicable for twenty years, established peace on the basis of the current borders, along with the reciprocal release of prisoners of war taken by both sides. Emperor Rudolf also had to send a single sum of two hundred thousand florins to Sultan Ahmed I, thus releasing him from the obligation to send an "honorable gift" of thirty thousand florins a year to the Ottomans. With this, the sultan recognized the leader of the Habsburg Monarchy as a ruler (emperor) of equal rank to himself. Transylvania would remain a vassal of the Ottoman Porte, however. The dual treaties of Vienna and Zsitvatorok brought the long war that began in 1591 to a close—and allowed both exhausted empires to breathe a sigh of relief.

Most of all, it was the population of the Carpathian Basin that had been waiting for the peace. A decade and a half of war had completely uprooted their previous existence. Until the 1590s, despite the fortress wars and Ottoman-Hungarian incursions, Hungarian society had retained a real ability for flexibility and survival, even energy for renewal. But during the great military campaigns, repeated year after year, and as the Tatar and Walloon armies spent the winter on the battlefield (not to mention the devastation wrought by the hajduks), there was no scope for rejuvenation. Military conflicts mobilizing tens of thousands of troops a year brought destruction of an entirely different nature from everyday incursions. The Ottoman auxiliary troops, repeatedly laying ruin, alongside Bocskai's hajduks, to the western parts of Lower Austria and Styria as well as to the Hungarian lands, would themselves admit that "only the era of the conquering Süleyman has been witness to such rack and ruin we have experienced, along with such valiant reputations and such rich spoils."[6] Even the most resistant parts of the population could not recover from this series of devastating attacks. The same was true in all parts of Europe across which armies of many thousands would march or where conflict dragged out over many years. To cite just one nearby example, at the time of the siege of Vienna in autumn 1529, the outskirts of the city were completely destroyed, while the city's population declined from some thirty thousand to around half that number. For all the fast pace of development in the emperor's city, such an unprecedented level of ruination took many decades to recover from.

This is why the Long Turkish War represents a real watershed as regards both the Hungarian network of settlements and the loss to the Hungarian population. There could no longer be any escape from the destruction wrought by the repeated advance of thousands of soldiers in a broad flank, together with the associated acts of arson, the starvation, and the diseases decimating animals and people (plague, dysentery, typhoid, malaria, or a particular mixture of these, the so-called Latin *morbus Hungaricus* or German *ungarisches Fieber*). And this was irrespective of whether this involved the "champions" at the vanguard of the Ottoman army's looting, the Tatars, or the thieving Walloon and German mercenaries of the imperial-royal armies, or the hajduks, who were often even more madly merciless than the Ottomans. In the space of a few years, the battlefield had completely cleared, and now the only question was how many more settlements would be destroyed during the next set of military operations.

A clear sign of the extent of the devastation is that from 1598 to 1604 the number of taxable houses in all parts of the Kingdom of Hungary declined by 65–75 percent, while there were counties in Ottoman Hungary where almost 70 percent of the settlements were destroyed. Meanwhile, the area of the country's military route along the Danube became almost entirely depopulated in a mere three years from 1593 to 1595, during the Ottoman and Christian sieges of Győr and Esztergom. After Esztergom was retaken in 1595, Miklós Pálffy, the new captain general of the fortress, had to use military force to relocate Hungarian and Vlach villages from the area around Buda and even from the distant Tolna and Baranya counties in order partially to restore agricultural output around Esztergom.

Together, these examples give us a picture of how, in certain parts of the country, the damage to the network of settlements, to the population, and to material goods was so great as to be recoverable only over a period of decades, if at all. Furthermore, the war damage again affected the Hungarian population most of all. This in turn brought new gains for the Serbs and Vlachs in Ottoman Hungary and for the Romanians in Transylvania, especially in the central, so-called Mezőség (Transylvanian Plain) region. But during the war even highly profitable long-distance trade was crippled. In 1603 the Hungarian Chamber in Pozsony was forced to realize that the Hungarian traders who had previously kept cattle had left their homes to live in Nagyszombat, Pozsony, or Vienna, areas less affected by the conflict. The key question after the end of the Long Turkish War was whether after 1606 there would be a few peaceful decades to allow for regeneration.

Notes

1. Pál Fodor, *The Business of State: Ottoman Finance Administration and Ruling Elites in Transition (1580s-1615)* (Berlin: Klaus Schwarz, 2018), 38–53.

2. Cf. Clifford J. Rogers, ed., *The Military Revolution Debate: Readings on the Military Transformation of Early Modern Europe* (Boulder, CO: Westview, 1995); József Kelenik, "The Military Revolution in Hungary," in *Ottomans, Hungarians, and Habsburgs in Central Europe: The Military Confines in the Era of the Ottoman Conquest*, ed. Géza Dávid and Pál Fodor (Leiden: Brill, 2000), 117–159.

3. Géza Pálffy, *Győztes szabadságharc vagy egy sokféle sikert hozó felkelés? A magyar királysági rendek és Bocskai István mozgalma (1604–1608)* [Victorious war of independence or an uprising bringing a variety of achievements? The estates of the Kingdom of Hungary and the movement of Stephen Bocskai (1604–1608)] (Budapest: MTT, 2009); Sándor Papp, *Török szövetség—Habsburg kiegyezés: A Bocskai-felkelés történetéhez* [Ottoman alliance—Habsburg compromise: To the history of the Bocskai uprising] (Budapest: L'Harmattan, 2014).

4. Kees Teszelszky, "A Bocskai-korona mítosza: A koronázás körülményeinek leírása a fikció és a valóság tükrében" [The myth of the Bocskai crown: The description of the coronation, the fact and the fiction], in *Magyarország védelme—Európa védelme* [Defense of Hungary, defense of Europe], ed. Tivadar Petercsák and Mátyás Berecz (Eger: Dobó István Vármúzeum, 2006), 239–246.

5. Kálmán Benda, *A nemzeti hivatástudat nyomában: Történelmi, történelemelméleti, művelődés-történeti, iskolapolitikai és csángómagyar tanulmányok, írások, interjúk* [On the trail of patriotic awareness: Writings and interviews on history, philosophy of history, intellectual history, educational policies, and Csango Hungarian studies], ed. János Lukáts (Budapest: Mundus Magyar Egyetemi Kiadó, 2004), 136.

6. As recorded by the eminent Ottoman historiographer, Ibrahim Peçevi: József Thúry, "Bocskay István fölkelése" [Uprising of István Bocskay], *Századok* [Centuries] 33 (1899): 119.

II

DECAY AND REJUVENATION: THE JANUS-FACED SEVENTEENTH CENTURY, 1606–1711

Fig. 24. Matthias of Habsburg, Holy Roman emperor (1612–1619). Engraving by Lucas Kilian, 1612 (Hungarian National Museum, Budapest).

1

PEACE OR CIVIL WAR ON THE BORDER OF THE TWO EMPIRES?

After the treaties of Vienna and Zsitvatorok brought the long war of the turn of the seventeenth century to a close, it seemed that they could usher in a fresh period of enduring peace in Hungary. While the peace with the Ottomans prohibited incursions, it was clear that even in a best-case scenario it would in fact be *Kleinkriege*, a warring time of peace, just as the almost quarter century of growing prosperity after the Treaty of Edirne in 1568 had been. The two empires, drained by the great war, genuinely desired (or rather needed) peace. This desire was confirmed by the regular extensions of the Treaty of Zsitvatorok. In this period, every time a new sultan came to the throne or the peace was flouted, such extensions would be agreed on no longer in the Ottoman Empire but rather—what with the strengthened role of the palatine (the leader of the Hungarian secular elite)—in Vienna (1615), Komárom (1618), Gyarmat (1625), and Szőny, by the Danube (today part of Komárom) in 1627 and later in 1642. It was only more than half a century after 1606, in 1658, that significant numbers of Ottoman troops would again step onto Hungarian (more precisely Transylvanian) soil, led by Grand Vizier Köprülü Mehmed Pasha. Their arrival was to punish Prince George II Rákóczi, who had marched into Poland without the Ottoman Porte's permission (see part 2, chap. 2).

For the Ottomans, peace in the Hungarian theater of war in the first half of the seventeenth century was crucial. They had again been at war with their great rival to the east, the Persians, since 1603; indeed, the talented Shah Abbas (1587–1629) was proving a formidable adversary. In Ottoman style, he kept a standing army equipped with gunpowder weapons, with which he was able to take back one Persian area after another lost in previous wars. With various interruptions, the war footing would last right up to 1639, presenting the Porte with great challenges. But they could still not breathe a sigh of relief in Istanbul: a protracted struggle ensued from 1645 in the eastern basin of the Mediterranean Sea, with Venice, primarily for control of the island of Crete, and in 1620–1621 they also fought a smaller war with Poland. And while war on a number of fronts was not rare in the empire's history, the seraglio of the sultan also had to confront a multitude of internal power and economic problems. From the beginning of the century, the so-called *Jelali* (*Celali*) revolts occurring in Anatolia and Syria caused serious difficulties. In these, as in the case of the Hungarian hajduks, arms-bearing groups squeezed to the periphery of society during the wars sought a way out of their predicament, led by self-proclaimed pashas.

It would take almost a quarter of a century for the Ottomans to climb out of the financial-economic and power crisis of the turn of the century. For this, they had completely to reorganize the tax and financial system, reform the army, and settle the relationship between the provinces of the enormous empire and its center. During these reforms, a plethora of new state taxes were introduced, the extraordinary war tax was made permanent, the sanjak registers were abolished, and the growing army was reorganized. As a result, the spahis and fortress soldiers previously paid with *timar* service estates now had to collect their income themselves; meanwhile, the beylerbeys, already equipped with considerable private armies, became increasingly powerful. From the first half of the seventeenth century, the sultan's authority wavered: it was no longer the formerly omnipotent padishahs who decided on key matters of state but the women of the harem and the janissary officers allied to them.[1]

All of these processes would, within a few decades, lead to the sale of positions across the empire, to corruption, and to a series of janissary rebellions and internal conflicts. Yet the dynasty's control was not at risk. For all the signs of crisis, it would be a mistake to regard the Ottoman Empire as a weakened power, as it would become in the nineteenth century. Despite all its problems, Istanbul always had enough strength to resolve the issues of the Hungarian frontier or of vassal Transylvania. But from 1606 to 1658, on account of its foreign and domestic political problems, it insisted on maintaining the peace in the Danube basin (see fig. 25).

In the first half of the seventeenth century, the Habsburg political and military leadership also strove to keep a lasting peace in the Hungarian theater of war. The Long Turkish War had proved that the time to repel the Ottomans had not yet come, and neither was it possible to occupy Transylvania. The long peace was necessary not just for the rebuilding of Hungary, however, but also because of the crises that had shaken the Habsburg dynasty and the monarchy, and then the great European war (1618–1648).

The first of these crises was the only sibling feud seen in the modern history of the dynasty. During the Long Turkish War, Emperor Rudolf II became increasingly isolated from his relatives, who were unhappy with his military and political failures, his reckless spending, and the declining role of the monarchy. In spring 1606 in Vienna, the Habsburg archdukes declared as head of the dynasty Archduke Matthias (see fig. 24), one of the most successful generals in the Turkish war in Hungary and then the creator of the Treaty of Vienna signed with Bocskai. The family conflict that ensued would turn into a brotherly feud or *Bruderzwist*. This saw Matthias, allied with a confederation of Austrian, Hungarian, and Moravian estates, march to Prague against Emperor Rudolf in late spring 1608, accompanied by the troops of the Austrian-Moravian estates and by Hungarian hussars. The armed clash was ultimately avoided, as the emperor "voluntarily" abnegated his kingship of Hungary, as well as the Austrian hereditary lands and ultimately Moravia, too (Treaty of Libeň, June 25). He kept the Bohemian crown until May 23, 1611, but only by making very great concessions, though he did remain emperor until his death in January 1612. In the final months of his life, he was little more than the shadow of an emperor who had lost his power.

In return for their supporting his rise to power, Matthias was forced to make significant concessions to the estates in all of his countries. It was the Holy Roman Empire that was in the most difficult situation: here the estates had broken up into the Protestant Union and the

Fig. 25. Ottoman-Hungarian duel in the seventeenth century. Etching by Isaac Maior, circa 1620 (Hungarian National Museum, Budapest).

Catholic League in 1608–1609. And so, quite understandably, for him the maintenance of the peace in the Kingdom of Hungary was a vital objective. It would remain so for his successors, Ferdinand II and then Ferdinand III. While for the former the greatest challenge was getting recognition of his succession, for the latter it would be the prolongation of one of the greatest European conflicts of the seventeenth century. As Matthias had no children, the question of succession brought the very existence of the Habsburg Monarchy into doubt when, on May 23, 1618, the Bohemian estates began their uprising with the famous defenestration. Indeed, in late August 1619, when the estates in Prague elected Frederick V, elector of the Palatinate, to be the Bohemian ruler instead of Ferdinand II, who had already taken the throne in the Kingdom of Hungary (March 20), there was a danger that the Habsburg dynasty could lose the control it had enjoyed over the Holy Roman Empire since 1437. This could even have led to the collapse of the Central European Habsburg Monarchy, as the group of elector princes supporting the Habsburgs was wavering. Finally, at the imperial assembly in Frankfurt in September 1619, and facing very real difficulties, Ferdinand managed to attain the imperial crown. Indeed, on November 8, 1620, at the White Mountain (Hill) near Prague, his troops were victorious over the Bohemian rebels, leading to the kingdom of Bohemia permanently becoming a hereditary province (*Erbland*).

This did not put an end to the conflict, however. The German Protestant princes and Gabriel Bethlen, prince of Transylvania, joined it on the Bohemian side, as did Danish ruler Christian IV (1588–1648) from 1625, urged by French diplomats, and Swedish king Gustav Adolph (1611–1632) from 1630, to restrict the expansion of the Habsburgs in the Baltic. Finally, France joined in 1635 and George I Rákóczi, prince of Transylvania, from 1644. Thus did the Thirty Years' War (1618–1648) become a conflict and religious war that affected all of Europe and brought tragic destruction to Austrian, German, Bohemian, and Hungarian areas alike, a war that would use up every resource and reserve at the Vienna treasury. And while the Peace of Westphalia, signed on October 24, 1648, after lengthy negotiations in Münster and Osnabrück, settled long-term power relations in Central Europe and the political and religious questions facing the Holy Roman Empire, in the decades that followed Vienna's main rival would remain the Sun King, Louis XIV, striving as he was for European hegemony. As a result, the Hungarian-Ottoman frontier that had been so important in the sixteenth century (see part 1, chap. 3) now became a secondary theater of war in the Habsburg Monarchy, where the maintenance of the peace would, as for the Ottomans, remain of fundamental importance to Vienna.

Despite both empires' needs to maintain peace, the half century after 1606 was not a real period of peace in Hungary. This claim may seem strange, given that almost every historical summary mentions a lasting peace. Despite the regularly extended peace treaties between the two great powers, in reality there was almost constant civil war in the area of the Kingdom of Hungary from the late 1610s until the mid-1640s. This was provoked not by the great powers but by the series of anti-Habsburg campaigns (in 1619–1621, 1623–1624, 1626, 1644, and 1645) of the Transylvanian princes, Gabriel Bethlen and George I Rákóczi, which served their political ends very well, as well as by the imperial and royal counterreactions to these and the tragic consequences of both (see map 10). In this period, the interests—particularly the foreign policy interests—of the kingdom and the principality were so at odds that the princes

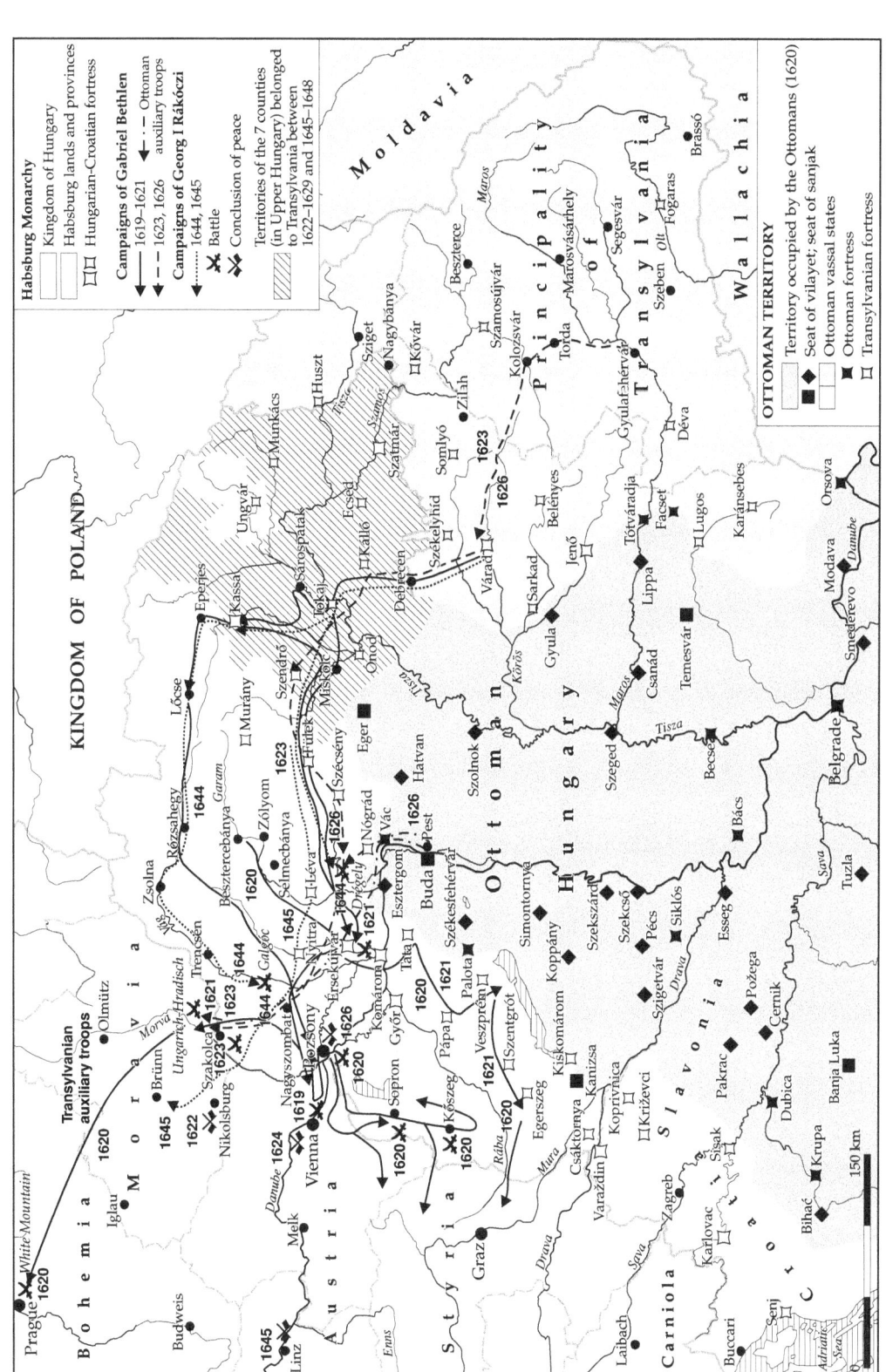

Map 10. The campaigns of the princes of Transylvania in Hungary, 1619–1645.

were not discouraged from sending expeditions even to the kingdom, with its Hungarian population. During the Thirty Years' War, these expeditions were instigated by joining the anti-Habsburg alliances: Bethlen joined the Bohemian rebels and Rákóczi the Swedes, as we discuss later (part 2, chap. 4). The princes' campaigns meant that Hungary experienced similar wartime circumstances to those seen during the Long Turkish War.

In discussing the 1620s and 1640s, it is no exaggeration to speak of civil war conditions in Hungary. During the aforementioned campaigns, first hussars and hajduks of the Transylvanian army marched regularly across the kingdom, followed by the imperial and royal German and Hungarian troops who fought them back; given their lack of supplies, they all ravaged the local population as the much-feared Tatars or Walloon mercenaries had done before them (see part 1, chap. 11). Of course, their ranks were soon boosted by thieves, vagabonds, and others keen to take up arms and who were finding themselves on the periphery of society in ever greater numbers. A good illustration of the nature of the civil war is that the Hungarian frontier soldiers (e.g., those in Pápa and Veszprém in 1621), joining forces with Bethlen, began regular raids into the areas of the castles and towns still under Habsburg control, then went on to loot Lower Austria, Styria, and Moravia. But the (in no small part German) troops marching against the princes were not to be outdone; the Hungarian population of the kingdom would regard them as "foreign invaders."

The real tragedy, nevertheless, was that these civil war conditions came into being in 1619 before Hungarian society had been able to recover from the destruction wrought by the largest military conflict in its history, the Long Turkish War, which ended in 1606. The short-lived period of regeneration in the 1630s was similarly brought to an end by the military campaigns of George I Rákóczi in 1644–1645. This meant that the increasing ruin and destruction was inevitable and fundamentally determined the Kingdom of Hungary's opportunities to develop. This is one reason the famous politician, general, and writer Miklós Zrínyi (1620–1664) complained in the early 1650s, in the preface to his work of military theory, *Vitéz hadnagy* [Valiant general], that the Almighty "placed me in the *saeculum* [century] of Hungarian decline."[2] And Zrínyi was not to know that the real decline would be brought by the great Turkish wars (in 1660–1664 and 1683–1699) and *kuruc* uprisings (in 1672–1685 and 1703–1711) of the following half century.

Notes

1. Recently, cf. Fodor, *Business of State*, 55–331.
2. Sándor Iván Kovács, ed., *Zrínyi Miklós összes művei* [The collected works of Miklós Zrínyi] (Budapest: Kortárs Kiadó, 2003), 257.

Fig. 26. Grand Vizier Kara Mustafa (1676–1683). Engraving by Johann Martin Lerch, 1683 (Hungarian National Museum, Budapest).

2

NEW OTTOMAN CAMPAIGNS TO ACHIEVE AN OLD GOAL

The Ottoman Porte always allowed and even supported Gabriel Bethlen and George I Rákóczi's series of military campaigns in Hungary, for these—with its own military resources tied up on other fronts—weakened the great rival, the Habsburgs (see part 1, chap. 2). But the Porte did not tolerate George II Rákóczi's prohibited expedition to Poland in January 1657. For one thing, the prince had previously repeatedly intervened in the relations between the Romanian voivodeships. Although the Venetian fleet had dealt a serious blow to the Ottoman navy in late June 1656 at the Dardanelles, a few months later (on September 15) no less a figure than Köprülü Mehmed Pasha was elected to the post of grand vizier, and in May 1658 he would personally march against Transylvania.

With out-and-out terror, the replacement of thousands of tax collectors and state functionaries, firm austerity measures, and a ruthless war on corruption, the distinctly senior Köprülü Mehmed was able relatively quickly to solve the empire's recurrent problems and to restore its mainland army and its fleet. Then, in contrast to the soft touch of his predecessors, he decided that he would use the concept developed in the era of Süleyman the Magnificent to put an end to the independent foreign policy ambitions of Transylvanian vassal George Rákóczi, who had strayed from the narrow path one too many times and was now even stepping into forbidden territory. Rákóczi's ambitions—as we see in part 2, chapter 4—were to establish a Polish-Transylvanian dynastic formation of Eastern European states that he would lead. Unlike in the time of Stephen Báthory's reign (see part 1, chap. 5), however, this was not now at all in the Porte's interests.

On September 14, 1658, Grand Vizier Köprülü Mehmed finally placed a new ruler in charge of Transylvania: Ákos (Achatius) Barcsay. In the meantime, Tatar, Ottoman, and Cossack armies had for a long time put an end to the flourishing of the principality (see map 11). But Rákóczi, who continued to enjoy strong domestic support, refused to resign and instead turned to Emperor Leopold I for assistance. All this led to a destructive civil war in Transylvania beginning in autumn 1658 and continuing with the punitive campaigns of Seydi Ahmed, pasha of Buda, in 1659–1660, and of Serdar Köse Ali Pasha in August 1660, after the crushing of Abaza Hasan Pasha's Aleppo uprising and now with the main Ottoman army. In the course of these campaigns, Rákóczi died of his wounds during the defeat at the Battle of Szászfenes (May 22), and then the gate to Transylvania, the fortress at Várad, was lost (August 27) to become another center of a vilayet for the Ottomans. Furthermore, the

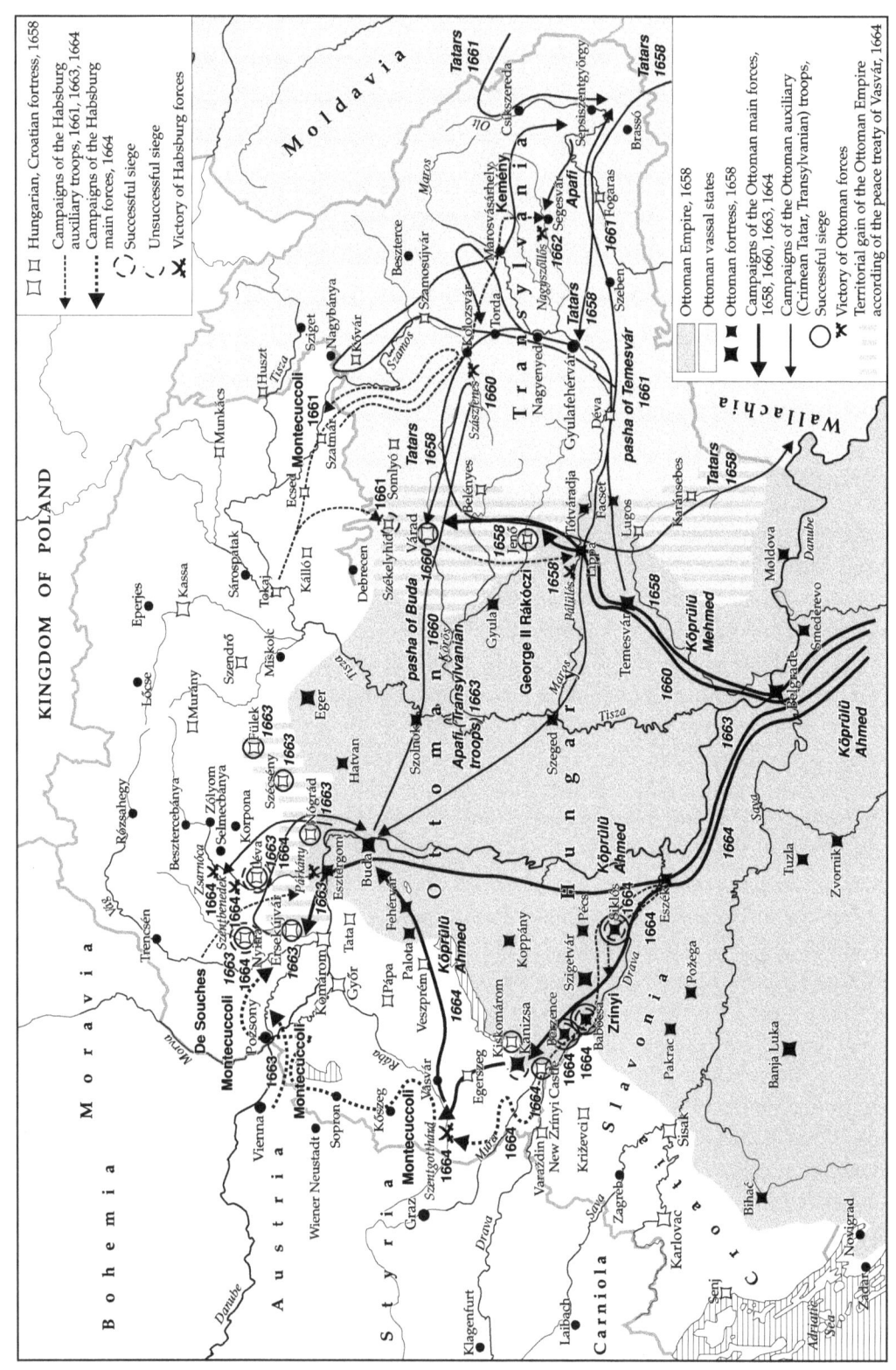

Map 11. The Turkish war in Hungary and Transylvania, 1658–1664.

successful Ottoman campaigns against Transylvania led within a few years to another great conflict breaking out in Hungary between Habsburgs and Ottomans.

The reason for this conflict was that the military leadership in Vienna had intervened in the Transylvanian civil war—at the invitation of John Kemény, formerly Rákóczi's field general, who was elected on January 1, 1661, to be prince instead of the retired Barcsay but who did not enjoy the Porte's support. Although the imperial and royal troops were led by the famous field marshal Raimondo Montecuccoli, their entry into Transylvania in autumn 1661 brought almost complete failure, not to mention enormous destruction both to Upper Hungary and to Transylvania. Köse Ali Pasha, also leading the Porte's troops into Transylvania, did not ultimately occupy the principality; instead, he again placed his own prince on the throne (on September 14, 1661) in the person of Michael Apafi, in place of Emperor Leopold's ally Kemény. However, the intervention of the Habsburg armies, together with the continued presence of German guard forces at a number of more significant fortresses (Kolozsvár, Székelyhíd, Kővár, and Szamosújvár), quickly expanded the conflict beyond Transylvania's borders.

Though John Kemény died during the Battle of Nagyszőllős (January 22, 1662), the civil war in Transylvania continued through to the summer of 1662. Küçük Mehmed, beylerbey of Temesvár and Jenő, in fact remained in the principality, under the eye of the German frontier forces, right until 1663. In this period, that is, both empires had troops stationed for a longer time in Transylvania, something that had previously been seen only during the Long Turkish War at the turn of the century (see part 1, chap. 11). Meanwhile, the Ottoman Porte came to a decision about the campaign against the Habsburgs who were interfering in events in Transylvania and keeping their troops there. Although in these years the idea of a complete occupation of Transylvania had repeatedly been raised in Istanbul, the Ottomans ultimately did not lose sight of Sultan Süleyman's original plan. The old objective of a conquest directed toward Vienna remained more important than the occupation of this eastern vassal state.

In April 1663 Köprülüzade Fazıl Ahmed Pasha, son of the famous grand vizier, led the Ottoman troops in the direction of the Austrian imperial city. The Ottomans marched toward Vienna for the first time since 1594 (see part 1, chap. 11). Although Emperor Leopold continued to make attempts to resolve the conflict by diplomatic means, the Ottoman military leadership casually rejected this, referring to Montecuccoli's retaking of Székelyhíd fortress and to Miklós Zrínyi's building of the New Zrínyi Castle, completed in 1661, on the left bank of the Mura River (i.e., on Ottoman territory). Of course, the real casus belli was an ill-considered intervention in Transylvania's affairs, one that Vienna and the Kingdom of Hungary would ultimately pay a high price for.

The tens of thousands of Ottoman troops originally preparing to attack Vienna decided instead in mid-July 1663 to besiege Érsekújvár, the center of the Captaincy General Defending the Mining Towns. They defeated the troops of Captain General Ádám Forgách in the Battle of Párkány on the Danube on August 7, and on September 25, after a thirty-nine-day city siege involving enormous firepower, they gained control of one of Hungary's most modern fortresses. This caused enormous consternation in the nearby imperial capital and in Austrian and Moravian areas, especially as the Tatars were ravaging the length and breadth of Moravia in the meantime. In late September, the Holy Crown was even taken from Pozsony to Vienna for safekeeping. The few thousand German, Hungarian, and Croatian troops and Hungarian noble insurgents lined up along the Danube were capable of no more than disturbing the Ottoman army's raids. Thus, in late 1663 the Ottomans could set about building their last vilayet in Hungary. The occupation of Érsekújvár and the creation of this new Ottoman province also meant that the inner areas of Hungary were now a frontier zone. The Hungarian capital, Pozsony, was now within the reach of the Ottoman raids. Overall, the part of the country to the north of the Danube would again undergo terrible devastation after 1644–1645. Again, there was no hope for regeneration.

In the following year, war and the ruination it brought extended to Transdanubia and Ottoman Hungary. It would also have a distinctly positive effect, however. In early 1664 the Hungarian, Croatian, Styrian, and German imperial forces led by Croatian ban Miklós Zrínyi and Julius Wolfgang Count of Hohenlohe would, after half a century, enjoy a victory against the Ottomans, one small in scale but large in resonance. In the so-called winter campaign, during a large diversionary operation into the area of Ottoman Hungary, they retook a number of castles and burned down the bridge at Eszék on the Drava, a key link in the Ottoman supply line. The goal of this scorched-earth strategy, of destroying Baranya and Somogy counties, was, as Zrínyi put it, "to ruin that piece of Turkey now so that they won't be able to come to us for many a year."[1]

The operation did not deliver on these expectations, however. Although the great Hungarian-Croatian general stated with satisfaction on February 19, 1664, that "we have set light to all the villages; in short, we have burned up the whole province,"[2] the Ottoman armies, served with a good supply line and mostly reinforced from the Balkans, were nevertheless capable of rebuilding the bridge at Eszék and marching on quickly, with the grand vizier's leadership. Indeed, in early June they liberated Kanizsa, which the Christian side, thanks to the dithering of the military command in Vienna, had besieged too late (April 28); the Ottomans then took New Zrínyi Castle, which, along with nearby Kiskomárom fortress, they would blow up in July.

The great clash would not be avoided on this occasion, either. On July 19, Jean Louis Raduit Count de Souches, a French-born general long in the employ of the Habsburg emperor, defeated the army of the pasha of Érsekújvár near Léva. Meanwhile, Zrínyi's triumph at Eszék inspired the previously hesitant German estates to provide more significant support; French support troops also arrived. The great test of strength finally came on August 1 at Szentgotthárd–Mogersdorf. In this battle, the allied troops achieved a convincing victory over the Ottomans, if not the complete annihilation described by earlier historians; Ottoman troops only partly managed to cross the Rába River, and many of them remained unharmed on the other side. Even if it was not such a great triumph, it did succeed in stopping the Ottomans heading to Vienna in their tracks.[3] Indeed, by this stage the sultan's troops were struggling with very real supply problems.

The burning of the bridge on the Drava did not change things in the short term, but it would be seen in a different light in the longer term. Despite Zrínyi's plans, the winter campaign did not fully achieve its goals, but the diversion did genuinely save Hungary. If the grand vizier, enjoying considerable superiority in numbers, had begun an attack along the Danube in late spring of 1664, even Vienna could have been under serious threat. In the event, the defeat of the sultan's main army, so long awaited, gave hope to many in Hungary and in Europe that the Ottomans could perhaps be driven back, as well as put an end to notions of Turkish invincibility. As a result of the successful propaganda of the *Rheinbund* and Zrínyi, which pursued a special political battle against Emperor Leopold, Europe's eyes again turned to the Hungarian theater of war. This led a number of the Hungarian political elite to hope for a chance to drive the Ottomans back. They were nevertheless unable to get a fair hearing for their ideas in Vienna.

The top leaders of the Habsburg Monarchy would in the end come down firmly on the side of the peace being maintained. We should not forget that the conditions of the peace treaty had been dictated not by Vienna but by the grand vizier, even after the Ottoman defeat at Szentgotthárd. A number of factors were at play in the decision made by the privy councilors in Vienna: on the one hand, the victory at Szentgotthárd, which they too would embellish but which was in fact only partial; and on the other hand, the events in the French theater of war and the monarchy's military and economic potential. They saw quite realistically how the diplomatic, military, and economic conditions for an international anti-Ottoman coalition were far from solid. Without their support, the overly optimistic propaganda of Zrínyi and the Confederation of the Rhine, urging war against the Ottomans, would mean little. The expulsion of the Ottomans would require not diversionary operations and half-baked victories but the decisive triumphs in open battle of armies of tens of thousands of men, great and fruitful sieges of fortresses, and strong, long-lived blockades. This would all demand serious military reforms and lengthy diplomatic preparations.

As a result of all this, the peace treaty signed on August 10, 1664, at Vasvár favored the Ottomans, who still enjoyed a dominant position. The Sublime Porte was able to retain Várad and Érsekújvár; indeed, the military command in Vienna was obliged to destroy Székelyhíd Castle and to pull its troops out of the Principality of Transylvania. With this, Vienna recognized Transylvania as a territory that remained under the control of the sultan. Yet, despite the prince regularly being replaced, the principality never became an Ottoman vilayet; this was a great bonus for the Habsburgs and the Hungarian estates. After the enormous devastation wrought by the renewed Ottoman attacks over almost the entire Carpathian Basin from 1658 to 1664, the Peace of Vasvár could not bring any real relief. Indeed, it caused enormous consternation among the Hungarian nobility, which had been encouraged by the delight of the long-awaited military successes, and it led to a clean break being made with part of the Hungarian political elite, as we will see in more detail later (part 2, chap. 3).

The Ottomans took the Hungarian political crisis as an opportunity to get involved in other theaters of war in the 1660s and 1670s. In the autumn of 1669, after a quarter century of struggle, they were finally able to occupy Candia in Crete. They would soon also give a lesson to Poland, which, in the treaty signed with Russia in January 1667 at Andrusovo (near Smolensk), had divided up Ukraine along the Dnieper River. The war would end up taking place in 1672, when the Porte hurried to the assistance of Western Ukrainian Cossack ataman Petro Doroshenko, who accepted Ottoman vassalage and whom both the Poles and the Russians tried to dislodge. The war, started by Köprülü Ahmed Pasha, would end up lasting until 1676, and overall it brought Ottoman success. Polish king John III Sobieski

Fig. 27. The second Ottoman siege of Vienna, 1683. Etching by Balthasar Bouttats, 1683 (Hungarian National Museum, Budapest).

(1674–1696) had no choice but to lose Podolia and Western Ukraine to the sultan at the Treaty of Zurawno (October 16, 1676). With this, the Ottoman Empire reached the peak of its seventeenth-century conquests in Europe.

Not even these new military successes were able to resolve the empire's internal problems. But after the Russo-Ottoman War (1677–1681) fought against a resurgent Russia, and given the discord in Ukraine, the successor to Grand Vizier Köprülü Ahmed, Kara Mustafa Pasha (see fig. 26), thought it was time to return to Sultan Süleyman's great plan to occupy Vienna (see part 1, chap. 2). Yet even though his enormous army (about forty thousand regular troops and twice as many irregular ones) besieged the imperial city from mid-July 1683 for almost two months, and he was on the verge of success, this in fact became a painful defeat (see fig. 27). The Ottoman military leaders had failed to take into account that on the very day their Viennese campaign began, March 31, Polish king John Sobieski entered into an alliance of mutual assistance with Emperor Leopold I. Even if they had been aware of this, there was hardly any way back; indeed, Imre Thököly's uprising made the situation in Hungary seem suitable for their campaign. There had not been an example of such cooperation between the Polish king and the Habsburg ruler since 1526—Poland had always striven to keep its distance from the Habsburg-Ottoman conflict.

In this case, the agreement was not merely on paper. On September 12, 1683, the Polish, Bavarian, Saxon, imperial, and Hungarian troops liberated the imperial city at the Battle of Kahlenberg, outside Vienna, dealing a crushing blow to the Ottomans. Almost a month later, on October 9, the allies won another battle, near Párkány on the Danube, against the troops of Kara Mehmed, pasha of Buda; by the end of the month, they retook Esztergom. With this, the tide of the war turned. There could be no turning back, not even for the politicians in Vienna who had opposed war with the Ottomans. While Kara Mustafa would pay for the ill-considered campaign with his life (he was strangulated with silk rope), the liberation of Hungary had begun. And if the sultan's campaigns would now lose their old great goal of Vienna, Hungary's multiethnic population would have to wait almost thirty years for a real peace.

Thus, by the end of 1683, the time had come for the Hungarians to put into action their old plans of restraining the Ottomans. Unlike in 1663–1664, the international diplomatic situation was favorable: in the summer of 1684, a cease-fire had been signed at Regensburg with France. In the two decades that had passed since the last great Turkish war, the Habsburgs' standing army had improved by leaps and bounds. Its size would grow by half again, and its structure and supply meant that an important step had been taken toward becoming a real permanent army. The Habsburg Monarchy had begun its journey to becoming a fiscal-military state.[4] And on this occasion the Hungarian political elite supported the possibility of liberation with a united voice; the only exception to this was a self-styled aristocrat, the Ottoman vassal Imre Thököly (see part 2, chap. 4). But even in the seventeenth century, the road to this broad alliance of Vienna and the Hungarian estates would be a bumpy one.

Notes

1. Kovács, *Zrínyi Miklós összes művei*, 764.
2. Ibid., 770.

3. Recently, Karin Sperl, Martin Scheutz, and Arno Strohmeyer, eds., *Die Schlacht von Mogersdorf/St. Gotthard und der Friede von Eisenburg/Vasvár: Rahmenbedingungen, Akteure, Auswirkungen und Rezeption eines europäischen Ereignisses* (Eisenstadt: Amt der Burgenländischen Landesregierung, 2016); Ferenc Tóth and Zágorhidi Czigány Balázs, eds., *A szentgotthárdi csata és a vasvári béke: Oszmán terjeszkedés—európai összefogás* [The Battle of Szentgotthárd and the peace treaty of Vasvár: Ottoman advance—European collaboration] (Budapest: MTA BTK, 2017).

4. Cf. Christopher Storrs, ed., *The Fiscal-Military State in Eighteenth-Century Europe: Essays in Honour of P. G. M. Dickson* (Burlington, VT: Ashgate, 2009).

Fig. 28. Miklós Esterházy, palatine of Hungary (1625–1645). Unknown painter, 1645 (Hungarian National Museum, Budapest).

3

THE RISE OF THE HUNGARIAN ESTATES AND THE BREAK WITH VIENNA

Relations between the Hungarian estates and the court in Vienna continued to face serious conflicts in the seventeenth century, which would even lead to a temporary break in relations. None of this can be seen as a Hungarian specialty. In those parts of Europe where the estates had significant power, absolutist efforts saw conflicts grow and grow. And as the Kingdom of Hungary, despite the strong centralization of its most important affairs, remained a sovereign state within the Habsburg Monarchy to a significant degree (unlike Bohemia, included in the hereditary lands from the 1620s), the role and power of the Hungarian estates could not be compared to those of the Bohemian and Austrian ones. Without them Hungary was ungovernable.

In contrast to the notions applied in retrospect in later centuries, the leaders of the estates at this time were made up not of the burgeoning, largely Protestant gentry but rather of eminent Hungarian secular and Catholic figures. Only in the eighteenth century would the former take over the latter's role. During the seventeenth century, that is, the Hungarian elite governing the kingdom were mostly from the aristocratic families represented in the upper house of the diet. Like the privy councilors who ran the monarchy, in most cases—on account of their differing political, family, regional, economic, and other interests—they did not and could not present a united front. It was only ever a given subject that decided how various interest groups at the court would find supporters and detractors in the Hungarian political elite and vice versa. This all means that the system of connections between the Hungarian estates and the Vienna court cannot be seen as a conflict between national and foreign interests, as they were so often seen by Hungarian historiography of the nineteenth and twentieth centuries. It makes much more sense to inspect the network of interdependencies between the Habsburg court and the Hungarian estates according to the role played in the running of the country.

The basic structure of central administration in the Kingdom of Hungary did not change in the seventeenth century: the lion's share of its foreign, military, and financial policy was decided in Vienna. At the beginning of the century, however, the estates strengthened their hand for a number of reasons. The Hungarian political elite was very clever in using Stephen Bocskai's movement to strengthen its own privileges and religious freedoms—first in the Peace of Vienna of June 1606, then as part of the confederation with the estates of Lower Austria and Moravia, established in early 1608. It was also true that King Matthias II was forced to make very considerable concessions to the Hungarian estates at the Pozsony diet in the autumn of 1608, in return for military and political support from the Hungarians in his sibling war with Emperor Rudolf. This brought the first compromise of the seventeenth century between Vienna and the Hungarians, as new studies have revealed.[1]

A good sign of the unique quality of the compromise is that Matthias of Habsburg was forced, in an almost unprecedented fashion, to accept a special item of legislation even before his coronation on November 19, 1608—nothing like this had even occurred in this period. On the one hand, the Hungarians usually ring-fenced estate privileges to suit their own interests. On the other hand, to satisfy the greatest requirement of the gentry, they announced the freedom of religion (precoronation law 1; at the same time, they banned Jesuits from owning property in the country, in precoronation law 8) and obliged royal free towns to accept nobles (precoronation law 13). Yet it served the interests of the aristocracy that the most important Hungarian positions could in the future be awarded only to Hungarians (precoronation laws 5 and 11), while the Hungarian Council was given ever-greater jurisdiction over so-called Hungarian subjects (precoronation law 10). In addition, a Hungarian magnate would fill the office of palatine, empty since 1562, in the person of Bocskai's former chief adviser, István Illésházy. But, for the first time in Hungarian history, a separate item of legislation recorded the bicameral structure of the diet, the main arena for the estate opposition (postcoronation law 1), while the procedure for electing the palatine was established for future reference (precoronation law 3). They also legislated for the mode in which the Holy Crown, the greatest symbol of Hungarian statehood, would return to Pozsony from the Prague court of Emperor Rudolf according to the terms of the Peace of Vienna and would be kept secure in Pozsony castle (precoronation law 4, then postcoronation law 16).

The diet of 1608 really became a decisive step in the rejuvenation of the estates when, thanks to the newer compromises of the following decades (Sopron in 1622 and Pozsony in 1647), the Hungarian political elite was able to implement most of the items of legislation listed above. The position of palatine was continuously filled until 1667; the procedure meant that the estates always had to select from between two Catholic and two Protestant candidates. The delegation of these four individuals remained the prerogative of the ruler, however, though the most influential aristocrats and prelates could have an effect on it. The posts of captain general of Upper Hungary and of the frontier opposite Kanizsa, previously held by top foreign officers, would during this century be filled by Hungarian aristocrats; the latter, for example, was held from 1633 by members of the Batthyány family on a hereditary basis. But the German councilors employed at the Hungarian Chamber in the sixteenth century also disappeared, while the role of the members of the better-organized Hungarian Council and of the palatine grew. In addition to directing domestic policy, they were given a role in the frontier diplomacy conducted with the Ottomans and in the negotiations with the Transylvanian princes, although final decisions were usually not taken by them and were instead made by the privy councilors in Vienna in response to their submissions.

In this regard, Palatine Miklós Esterházy (1625–1645) is particularly worthy of mention (see fig. 28): he played a key role during the Thirty Years' War at the aforementioned revivals of the peace with the Ottomans (in 1625, 1627, and 1642). All this coincided with the interests of the political leadership in Vienna at the time. In the midst of the great European war, the palatine, the aulic Hungarian lords, and the archbishops of Esztergom, who occupied the position of high chancellor of Hungary (particularly Péter Pázmány [1616–1637] and György Lippay [1642–1666]), relieved the Viennese councilors, who were often inexperienced in these matters, from many of their duties not only at the Ottoman and Transylvanian diplomatic negotiations but sometimes even at the Roman and Polish ones.

It was a good sign of the growth of the role of the Hungarian secular and church dignitaries that, from György Thurzó and Péter Pázmány onward, the palatines and archbishops of Esztergom and even the Hungarian chancellors were often invited to the sessions of the Privy Council that touched on Hungary's key issues, and as such they could have a greater influence over Hungarian affairs. In the 1660s, following Palatine Pál Pálffy and archbishop of Esztergom György Lippay, and as a consequence of this process, Palatine Ferenc Wesselényi, ban of Croatia Miklós Zrínyi, and Chief Justice Ferenc Nádasdy were real privy councilors. This meant they could participate more often at the sessions of the most important decision-making body of the Habsburg Monarchy, even if they were not always able to serve Hungarian interests at these sessions. But this was all connected to the fact that in the whole Habsburg Monarchy only two estate dignitaries, the Hungarian palatine and the archbishop of Esztergom, had free access to the locations of auditions with the emperor, which was enjoyed in similar fashion only by cardinals, imperial princes and elector-princes, foreign ambassadors, high dignitaries at the Vienna court, privy councilors, generals, and real chamberlains.

Another symbol of estate renewal was the Hungarian Holy Crown not leaving the territory of the Kingdom of Hungary over the course of the century, except in the emergency war situation during the Ottoman campaigns from 1663 to 1664 and from 1683 to 1687, when it was taken to Vienna for safekeeping (in 1683 it was even taken as far as Passau). Indeed, the crown would enjoy an increasingly important role in the representation of the "estate nation." Its significance grew when the crown guard Péter Révay was the first to summarize its history (*De Sacrae Coronae Regni Hungariae ortu . . . brevis commentarius*, Augsburg, 1613), building on earlier traditions and legends to establish a veritable cult for the country's most important symbol. He presents the particular balance created between the court and the estates after 1608 and how the Holy Crown would from this point on become a key symbol not only of the ruler's power but also of the Hungarian estate elite and of the sovereignty of the state.

In the first half of the seventeenth century, a very particular circumstance was decisive in the enormous improvement of the positions of the Hungarian estates. Stephen Bocskai provided ammunition for the defense of estate rights not only with his uprising but also with his political will and testament. This gave special instructions for how the estates of the kingdom could make use of the Principality of Transylvania: "As long as the Hungarian crown is in the hands of that stronger nationality of the Germans, and the Kingdom of Hungary revolves around the Germans, it is always useful and necessary to maintain a Hungarian prince in Transylvania, to act in the interests and serve the needs of [the population of the Kingdom of Hungary]."[2] In the seventeenth century, this was to become one of the guiding principles of Hungarian estate politics. So, for the Hungarian political elite, Transylvania would, like the Ottomans, become a winning card to be played against the court in Vienna.

Although the Hungarian campaigns of Gabriel Bethlen and George I Rákóczi brought enormous devastation nationwide, various groups among the estates very cleverly exploited them to defend their own interests. This cannot be seen as a unique Hungarian phenomenon: the German imperial estates similarly kept their ruler in a corner by demanding his financial support for the defense against the Ottoman threat to protect their Protestant faith. The Hungarian estates would play their trump card of a possible alliance with the Transylvanian princes in order to safeguard their freedom of religion and to improve their positions as held after 1608, as well as to retain their privileges. It was for this reason that they had their own demands written into the treaty between the Hungarian rulers and the Transylvanian princes. This was not a great challenge—the Protestant princes were very much in support. The issue of religion had become one of the century's most pressing political problems, one that could often give civil war conditions a religious slant.

This meant that at the most important meetings of the diet, the Hungarian rulers were regularly forced to make guarantees as to estate privileges and the freedom of religion. Indeed, after the peace of Nikolsburg signed with Bethlen, at the diet of Sopron in summer 1622, the estates forced Ferdinand II to enter the *diploma inaugurale* of 1618 into law, which guaranteed the estates' freedoms—the first ruler in Hungarian history to do so. This custom would then continue for centuries until the last Hungarian coronation in 1916. In and of itself, this showed that after the break brought by Bethlen's campaigns into Hungary (1619–1621), another important compromise had been established between Vienna and the estates.

It was a reflection of how special this compromise was that at the Sopron diet in June 1622, the Lutheran Szaniszló Thurzó, who in 1620–1621 had been one of the captains general of the prince of Transylvania, was elected palatine. Yet the example of Thurzó was not unique. A good many of the great landowners of Upper Hungary (Menyhért Alaghy, Péter Melith, István Nyáry, Ferenc Perényi, György Széchy, etc.) were forced to change sides to the prince, who had made successful advances with his armies from 1619 onward and then settled in Kassa. Within the kingdom, the northeast part of the country was also in the particular situation that its greatest landowner was the Rákóczi family—the source, after Bethlen's death, of the princes of Transylvania. For a time, Bethlen also enjoyed the support of the Calvinist Transdanubian magnate Ferenc Batthyány, though he was not joined by any of the Croatian-Slavonian estates.

From 1622 the aristocracy also saw to it that the important public administration post of chief postmaster of Hungary, one formerly filled by members of the German Paar family, instead for many decades was given to Hungarian nobles. Similarly, the estates made use of Bethlen's military campaigns to see that the Aulic War Council in Győr—in line with the precoronation law 11 of 1608—should again, after many decades, fill the post of the Hungarian deputy captain general. In addition, a large part of the German army stationed in Hungary was driven out of the country. This is particularly noteworthy because it had continuously been one of the key demands of one part of the estates.

The second compromise of the seventeenth century thus significantly strengthened the positions of the Hungarian estates. It also brought considerable political realignment. In early August 1622, the holders of more than half of the Hungarian high offices—and all the leaders of the district captaincies general led by the estates—were replaced. Even in the context of the sixteenth and seventeenth centuries, this was a pretty extraordinary development. The Sopron diet of 1622 really brought the start of a new cooperation between Vienna and the estates—and in such a way that the new distribution of offices and power would simultaneously allow compensation for the pro-Habsburg high estates, reassurance for the former supporters of Bethlen, and a guarantee of peaceful functioning of the Kingdom of Hungary (and its defense against the Ottomans and against Bethlen, too).

The fact that part of the Hungarian political elite joined forces with Gabriel Bethlen, whether under constraint or voluntarily, would have serious long-term political consequences. As the prince's attacks came at one of the most critical moments in the history of the Habsburg Monarchy, a sort of general distrust of Hungarians gradually developed among the political leaders in Vienna. The alliance with the Transylvanian princes—at least for some of the privy councilors—meant indirect collaboration with the Ottomans. Given the state of the principality as an Ottoman vassal and Istanbul's authorization of the campaigns into the Kingdom of Hungary, this assumption was not entirely unmerited.

Indeed, in the 1620s and 1630s the elite of the Vienna court underwent a radical transformation. An aristocracy had begun to develop that stood above nations and was loyal only to the dynasty and to the court. This supranational aristocracy increasingly thought in terms of the interests of the empire as a whole, not of regions or countries. Thus, anything that favored the protection of estate rights would harm the power of the Hungarian political elite in Vienna. The Hungarians who entered partial or temporary alliances with Bethlen, then in 1644–1645 with George Rákóczi, would in the decades that followed increasingly be described as "rebels."

In these decades, only a handful of families (the Draskovics, Erdődy, Esterházy, Forgách, and Pálffy families, and, to a lesser degree, the Batthyány, Csáky, Liszthy, Nádasdy, Serényi, and Zrínyi families) were able to establish closer contact with the aristocracy that ran the monarchy and, to varying degrees, to become a part of that aristocracy. Hungarians only rarely entered the central institutions of government in the seventeenth century; those who did were from these families. The Pálffy family was the only one to build a crypt in Vienna (in the Augustinerkirche) when in the 1630s the members of the new aristocratic elite essentially divided up the churches of the city between themselves, to reflect their attachment to the Habsburg court. The members of these great Hungarian landowning families, in no small part because of their loyalty to the court, occupied most of the key Hungarian offices in this century. For example, five palatines and more than twenty-five other dignitaries were from the Draskovics, Erdődy, Esterházy, Forgách, and Pálffy families.

The Treaty of Linz, signed by Ferdinand III and George I Rákóczi in December 1645, which ended the armed conflict caused by the principality's campaigns in 1644–1645, again guaranteed the estate positions. Indeed, as the third compromise of the century, the Pozsony diet of 1646–1647 confirmed these positions. Thus, in the Kingdom of Hungary the estates rose to the height of their powers exactly when a new elite was born in Vienna and as government attempts toward re-Catholicization and absolutism were growing constantly. The conditions in Hungary were far from right for the introduction of these attempts, even if a few leading Catholic clerics (such as archbishop György Lippay) favored more radical action. With the end of the Thirty Years' War, the Hungarian political elite, divided by their confessions, by differing political, family, and group interests, and by the significant discrepancies between different parts of the country, confronted such new absolutist measures with fuller force. But this united estate front was often weakened not just by the lobbying of individual families but also by the power rivalry between the palatines and the archbishops of Esztergom.

In the 1650s the estates constantly objected to the German companies of the burgeoning Habsburg standing army being marched into Hungary and being stationed in barracks there, even if there was a need for this, if only to guarantee the Ottoman frontier. While these units did not fall under the jurisdiction of the captains general of the border fortresses, provision of supplies for them brought enormous new burdens for the country's population. Thus, their presence was not in the interests either of the aristocracy or of the gentry. Although in the long term the restraint of the Ottomans would be possible only with a modern permanent army that was constantly being developed, the country, drained by the campaigns of the Transylvanian princes, was in no mood to house German mercenaries. Especially not ones that would—with arms, if necessary—assist the Hungarian Catholic Church's efforts at re-Catholicization.

Increasingly tense relations between Vienna and the estates were only worsened when, after Leopold I took the throne in 1657 (see fig. 29), the Hungarian political elite found it harder and harder to come to agreement with the members of the new select government body, the Privy Conference (German *Geheime Konferenz*), which replaced the Privy Council. Furthermore, many of the elite's members saw the obstacle to the implementation of absolutist measures in Hungary in its strong estate structure. Amid these ever-worsening relations, some Hungarian lords even entertained the thought of an independent Hungarian kingdom, particularly when they found that, despite their strong influence in Hungary, their opinions fell on ever-deafer ears in the imperial city. The efforts of Transylvanian prince George II Rákóczi may have played a part in this development: he was also tempted by the less than realistic idea of a Hungarian kingdom—of course one led by him. Neither is it inconceivable that the former plan of the famous French minister, duke of Sully, could have had an influence on the Hungarian high dignitaries, who—in line with the great power policy of France, which intended to break up the Habsburg Monarchy—thought in terms of there being separate Hungarian, Bohemian, and Polish elective monarchies on the map of Europe. Of course, this could succeed only in the event of Hungary being liberated from the Ottomans. Given decades of peaceful intentions on the part of the Porte, many in the Hungarian political elite were—with rather too much optimism—confident that this liberation could come to pass. So, with increasing regularity, they were urging that the Habsburg Monarchy finally turn its forces against the Ottomans.

The events of the latest great Turkish war from 1660 to 1664 further poisoned relations between the court and the estates. As the military leadership in Vienna (as we saw in part 2, chap. 2) intervened with particular clumsiness in the events in Transylvania and in 1663–1664 sought to escape from the war as soon as it could, even the most loyal members of the Hungarian political elite started to waver. Although in these years they attended many military conferences, it seems these conferences had little influence on the privy councilors, who thought the issues of the Habsburg Monarchy's western frontier and its internal problems to

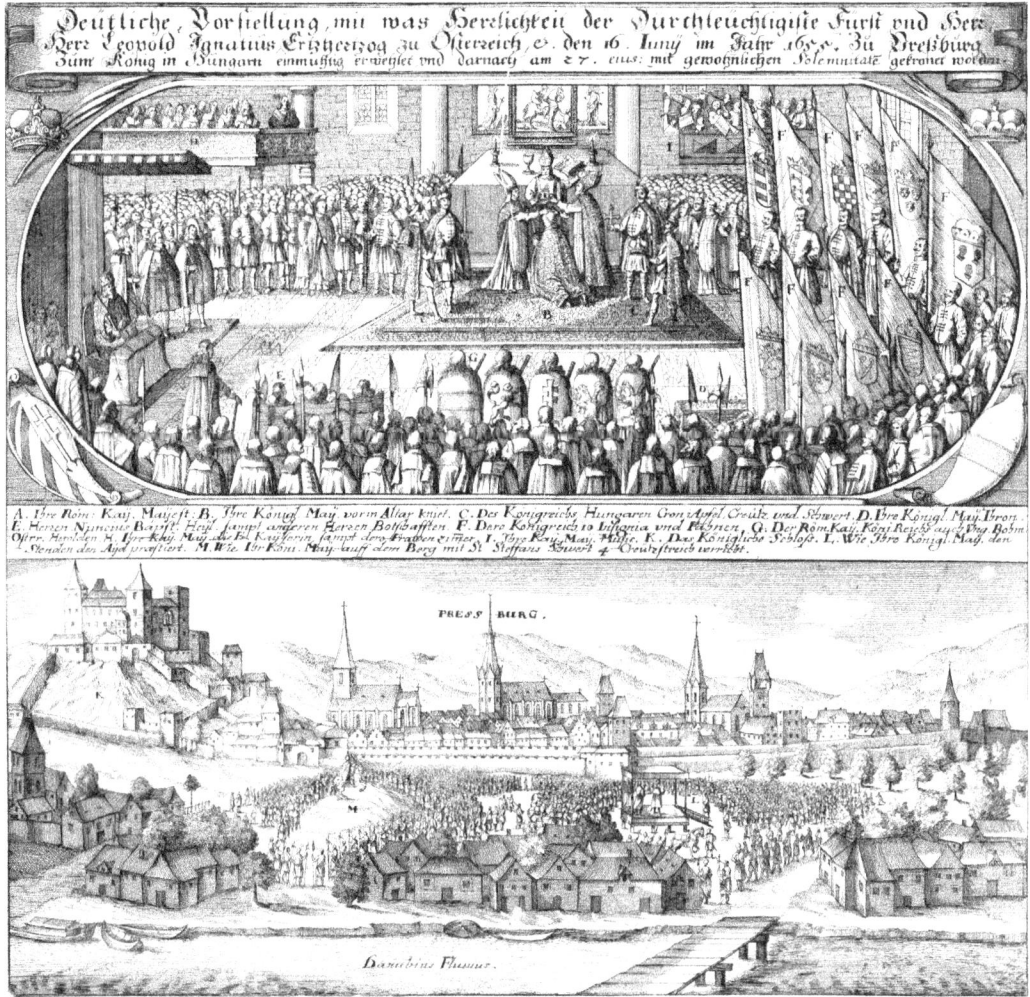

Fig. 29. The Hungarian coronation of Leopold I in Pozsony on June 27, 1655. Engraving by an unknown master, 1655 (Hungarian National Museum, Budapest).

be the most crucial and who mostly desired peace with the Ottomans. This despite the fact that during the existential threat posed by the grand vizier's great campaign, they attempted to put their previous differences behind them and to cooperate, as urged by Chief Justice Ferenc Nádasdy in late June 1663: "We find ourselves in times in which we ought not to nourish tastelessness and hatred for one another, but rather we should strive to bring such vengeful and hateful thoughts instead to agreement and lasting affection."[3] As a result, in autumn 1663 Palatine Wesselényi, Chief Justice Nádasdy, and Ban Miklós Zrínyi obliged one another to the unified enforcement of their interests in a treaty letter, even though it was only with great difficulty that they were able to put their debates about jurisdiction to one side.

Despite this unusual policy of high estate unity, the Hungarian lords would nevertheless be disappointed. In August 1664, the court signed the Peace of Vasvár without asking their opinion; this was entirely at odds with the practice established in the previous decades of extending peace treaties with the Ottomans. Vienna had little choice in the matter: despite the defeat at Szentgotthárd, the peace conditions were still dictated by the grand vizier. Given the tense domestic atmosphere, this only added fuel to the fire, even if, what with the internal relations of the Habsburg Monarchy, it was more realistic than beginning an ill-prepared anti-Ottoman war.

For all this, the Hofburg was to make fundamental errors: in the treaty, without asking the opinion of the Hungarian political elite, it forfeited the central areas of the Kingdom of Hungary that directly neighbored the lands of the Hungarian lords and the archbishop of Esztergom. They had good reason to believe that even if they represented the country's interests in a unified way, they were able to achieve precious little. So even Archbishop Lippay, who for decades had been a dedicated ally of the court, started to find himself on the same side as his former domestic enemies enraged by the peace treaty. Indeed, on November 18, 1664, he made the following outburst: "It is easy, to be sure, for the good Germans to feel good about a peace, while we will find ourselves lost."[4] What is more, Vienna employed enormous propaganda to present the treaty agreement so criticized by the Hungarians as saving Christianity and making peace between the two empires. But the court would in the process upset the balance established in the preceding decades—at least this was how the Hungarian dignitaries and nobles saw it.

The clean break was made when a key group of formerly aulic supporters in the political elite—Palatine Wesselényi, Ban Péter Zrínyi/Petar Zrinski, and Chief Justice Nádasdy—sought a way out of this seemingly hopeless predicament. It had become clear in the half century after 1526 that as long as the Kingdom of Hungary was part of the Habsburg Monarchy (see part 1, chap. 3), the ultimate decisions on the most important issues would be brought by the central government institutions in Vienna; the one way out of this vicious circle would be a complete break with Vienna. Although the Hungarian magnates were all essentially aware of this, it was only in their final despair—after many unsuccessful negotiations held with Viennese councilors on the future of the country and after the ratification by both sides of the Treaty of Vasvár by spring 1666—that they sent envoys on August 27 from Murány, the castle of the Wesselényi family, to the Ottoman Porte. They were prepared to recognize the legitimate authority of the sultan—and thus, in a sense, to sign their own "special peace" with Istanbul—and to pay tens of thousands of golden florins annually in return for guarantees of estate privileges and the free election of kings. This would have assisted the birth of a Hungarian state similar to the Transylvanian one: while a more favorable arrangement, it would still have been an Ottoman vassal. Their desperate attempts would have been rendered more urgent as Ottoman taxation extended to the kingdom became more assertive after 1664.

For all this partial acquiescence to the Ottomans, Wesselényi and the others wished to preserve the integrity of the kingdom. In looking for a way out, they may well have believed that along the border of the two empires there could exist a compromise solution that might allow the creation of an independent Hungarian "estate nation" or even an independent Hungarian foreign policy. In the same way that King John Szapolyai had after 1526 (see part 1, chap. 4), however, they found themselves in cloud-cuckoo-land. This search for an Ottoman alliance in summer 1666 upset the balance established with Vienna from 1608 (and indeed partially undid the network of connections established with the Habsburg

Monarchy after 1526; see part 1, chap. 3) just as much as this balance had been rocked by the actions of councilors (especially court chancellor Johann Paul Hocher) bewitched by absolutist measures and coming to dominance in the Hofburg by the end of the 1660s. What is more, Vienna soon used its wide-reaching propaganda to paint the lords' efforts as a huge "Hungarian-Croatian conspiracy" in order to legitimize its own absolutist actions—despite the fact that the Ottomans had not even deemed the offer of the Hungarian magnates worthy of reply.

In the decade that followed, it soon transpired that this disturbance of the balance condemned both parties to a risky and humiliating failure. Despite its limited sovereignty, the Kingdom of Hungary did have its own legitimate place within the Habsburg Monarchy, one that even the methods of absolutism could not dismantle. Of course, this was not what the more radical groups in Vienna thought during the actions of the magnates in 1666–1668 or when the armed insurrections of Péter Zrínyi and Ferenc Rákóczi were quickly exposed in 1670. Though they were right to fear that a Kingdom of Hungary allied to the Ottomans could bring disaster to the imperial city and to the central parts of the monarchy, they decided on harsh reprisals instead of a quick agreement that could bring compromise to both sides. In retrospect, of course, it was clear this was the wrong choice. Based on illusions rather than a fuller acquaintance with the conditions in Hungary, they thought the time was right to push the estate structure to one side to implement their absolutist plans. This was every bit as ill-considered as had been the experiment with Ottoman acquiescence in summer 1666 on the part of Palatine Wesselényi (who died in 1667) and the others.

Vienna's reprisals, which enjoyed the support of part of the Hungarian Catholic Church, were decidedly harsh. And yet not even the execution of Péter Zrínyi/Petar Zrinski, Ferenc Kristóf Frangepán/Franjo Krsto Frankopan, Ferenc Nádasdy, and Ferenc Bónis (April 30, 1671) had any real effect. The same could be said of the special trial of Protestant preachers who were then sent to the galleys (1673–1675), the abolition of the estate constitution, a partial military occupation of the country, and then coercive re-Catholicization in the 1670s. Meanwhile not even the few reforms, which in the long run could have helped the country free itself from the Ottomans, had any success.

The Gubernium, which was founded in 1673 to manage domestic policy but was alien to the Hungarian system of administration, soon became inoperable, as the estates, the nobility, and the counties all resisted its actions. The new tax system, a necessary development but one elaborated without the involvement of the diet, also failed as a result of the resistance of the nobility and the serfs. The same was true of the terribly timed attempt to restructure the frontier military into a regular form, into permanent units, even though this was also an inevitable change in the long run. Many thousand nobles and soldiers fled the reprisals to Transylvania and the Partium (hence their Hungarian name, *bujdosó*, referring to someone in hiding), creating a problem that it was not possible to solve for many decades. Upper Hungary, which had a particular status within the kingdom, became a burning hotbed of strife for a prolonged period, what with the dissatisfaction of the nobility and then the uprising of the *bujdosók* that began in 1672.

After many years of preparation, it was at the Sopron diet of 1681 that equilibrium between the court and the estates would finally be restored. The fourth compromise of the seventeenth century was assisted by the international situation: in the west, the French had again begun military conflict with the Habsburgs, while the Ottomans hesitated as to whether to renew the Treaty of Vasvár, which was about to expire. But many domestic policy factors were also in play. First, in Vienna the more pragmatic political and military leaders recognized that any further ill-considered actions might even force the Hungarian estates completely onto the side of the Ottomans. Second, the successes of the *bujdosók* and the election of Imre Thököly as their leader in 1679 represented an ever-greater danger in military terms. Third, the Hungarian political elite was increasingly desirous of the restoration of the former order and not least of the peace. Key figures in this were György Szelepchény (Szelepcsényi), archbishop of Esztergom and also royal governor in 1670–1681; Pál Esterházy; Ban Miklós Erdődy; and the former president of the Hungarian Chamber, István Zichy. Although the prelate was one of the leaders of the armed re-Catholicization process, he nevertheless attempted to limit the court's openly absolutist measures. Esterházy, meanwhile, would with his clever organizational efforts convince a good part of the Hungarian aristocracy to support the agreement with Vienna.

Even so, the old balance could be reestablished in Sopron in 1681 only after seven months of hard negotiation. Unlike the practice of the 1660s, it seems that on this occasion the privy councilors were more responsive to the opinions of the Hungarian councilors they were in talks with. It was a sign of the restoration of the estate constitution and the dualist system of government that for the first time since 1655 the estates could again elect the palatine (Law 1), in the person of Pál Esterházy. Leopold I officially dismantled the Gubernium (Law 2) and restored the jurisdiction of the Hungarian Council (Law 4), to include the question of the peace with the Ottomans. He also provided a general guarantee of estate and noble freedoms (Law 10) and restored the operation of the national judges (Law 28). The recognition of religious freedom was an important result for the Protestant gentry (even if, in Transdanubia, this was only thanks to the so-called articular places; Laws 25–26), as was the removal of foreign chamber officials (Law 13). There would also, at least in principle, be a restoration of the old structural framework of the frontier military (Law 5); the new taxes and existing debts on them would also be abolished (Law 12).

This all meant that, even after such a serious break with the court, the estates were able to reclaim their role in the running of Hungary even as absolutist measures were strengthening. At the Pozsony diet in early November 1687, encouraged by the retaking of Buda in the previous year, the upper and lower houses accepted that the male line of the Austrian branch of the Habsburgs would be the hereditary kings of Hungary (Laws 2–3) and annulled the so-called opposition clause of the Golden Bull of 1222 (Law 4). Nevertheless, the estates retained most of the positions they had affirmed at the compromises of 1608, 1622, 1647, and 1681, despite the fact that by this stage the Hungarian estate institutions were in many regards out of date (this is why the Hungarian Royal Court Chancellery was created as a modern institution in Vienna in 1690). Meanwhile, noble privileges were often a hindrance to the development of public administration. Yet the resilience of the estates played a key role in the Kingdom of Hungary managing to retain its special sovereignty within the Habsburg Monarchy and to play a so-called *Sonderweg* in the eighteenth century. It is no accident that after Hungary was taken back from the Ottomans, Vienna attempted to squeeze the estate high dignitaries out of the new system in the country (see part 2, chaps. 10–11). This would again prove only partially successful.

Notes

1. Géza Pálffy, "Le siècle des ruptures et compromis: Nouvelle approche de l'histoire du Royaume de Hongrie au cours du XVIIe siècle," *Histoire, Economie et Société* 34, no. 3 (2015): 78–89; Géza Pálffy, "Jahrhundert von Trennungen und Ausgleichen. Die Geschichte des Königreichs Ungarn im 17. Jahrhundert in einem neuen Licht," *Historisches Jahrbuch* 137 (2017): 248–267.

2. István Sinkovics, ed., *Magyar történeti szöveggyűjtemény* [Collection of Hungarian historical texts], vol. 2/1, *1526–1790* (Budapest: Tankönyvkiadó, 1968), 376.

3. MNL OL, Budapest, Magyar Kamara Archívuma, E 185, Archivum familiae Nádasdy, Ferenc Nádasdy to László Rákóczi, June 25, 1663, Pottendorf.

4. Péter Tusor, ed., *"Ich schreibe es Euer Gnaden so, wie ein gerechter Ungar an einen gerechten Ungarn": Die Briefe von György Lippay, Bischof von Wesprim und Erlau, Erzbischof von Gran an die ungarischen Aristokraten, Adeligen (1635–1665)* (Budapest: Gondolat Kiadó, 2015), 458, no. 446.

Fig. 30. Gabriel Bethlen, prince of Transylvania (1613–1629). Engraving by Matthäus Merian, 1620 (Hungarian National Museum, Budapest).

4

TRANSYLVANIA FLOURISHES, THEN DECAYS

In the seventeenth century, the Principality of Transylvania would—to quote Péter Apor's celebrated work, *Metamorphosis Transylvaniae*[1]—undergo multiple metamorphoses. In this series of transformations, the chaos of civil war in the early years of the century was followed by the golden age of the reign of Gabriel Bethlen and George I Rákóczi, then the less successful rule of George II Rákóczi. As the latter would tread on forbidden ground with his Polish campaign of 1657, the principality, which had been flourishing in the previous decades, in 1658 fell victim to the hellish destruction of the Ottoman-Tatar forces arriving to regulate it (see map 11). The ruin was worsened by the failed intervention of the German troops of General Montecuccoli in 1661, to which were added many years of civil war for the princely throne, as the reader has seen in the previous chapters (part 2, chaps. 1–3). And although the principality enjoyed a revival for three decades (despite the fall of Várad in 1660), its "independent" statehood ended with the expulsion of the Ottomans from Hungary. In 1690 the political leadership in Vienna did not join it to the Kingdom of Hungary, instead making it a province governed from the center of the Habsburg Monarchy as part of the Hungarian Crown (Latin *membrum Coronae Hungariae*). This decision was affected by the transformations of the principality in the seventeenth century, the princes' anti-Habsburg policy, and the interests of the Transylvanian estates.

At the treaties of Vienna and Zsitvatorok in 1606, it became clear that after the death of Stephen Bocskai, Transylvania could continue its independent statehood under Ottoman guardianship (see part 1, chaps. 5 and 11), and yet there was rarely much calm in the principality until Gabriel Bethlen came to power in autumn 1613 (see fig. 30). The interests of those claiming the throne, some magnates from the kingdom (Sigismund Rákóczi, Bálint Drugeth de Homonna), some magnates from the principality (Gabriel Báthory, András Ghiczy, Gabriel Bethlen), the as yet unresolved hajduk question, and the lax policy of Gabriel Báthory all played crucial roles in allowing the conditions of civil war to emerge. On account of its domestic difficulties, it was not hard for Istanbul to accept one self-proclaimed prince after the next, but it would not stand for Prince Báthory extending his influence into Wallachia in early 1611.

Of the self-proclaimed magnate rulers, Sigismund Rákóczi, Bocskai's former governor of Transylvania, led the principality only from February 1607 to March 1608, when he as good as fled from it during the attack of Gabriel Báthory in alliance with the hajduks who had risen up in Transtibiscan area. During his five-year reign (1608–1613), Báthory was not able to establish order, despite the partially successful new relocation of the hajduks (in

Bihar and Torda counties). He was less suited to leadership than his predecessors, however. His aimless and yet often merciless domestic policy and his overly ambitious foreign policy often rendered Transylvania's position unstable. During his reign, the principality was repeatedly ravaged—first by the hajduks, who were used for political gain by Radu Şerban, the voivode of Wallachia, in the summer of 1611; then again by Zsigmond Forgách, captain general of Upper Hungary, who was also intervening in events; and finally by the troops of the beylerbey of Temesvár.

Meanwhile, in spring 1610, the estate opposition led by István Kendi even attempted an assassination of the ruler, though without success. In the interests of preserving his power, Báthory would in April 1613 have been willing to enter into an alliance even with Emperor Matthias of Habsburg, but it was again the Ottoman Porte that was to decide the principality's fate. In September 1612, Gabriel Bethlen, Báthory's court captain general, had turned his back on his volatile boss and, realistically weighing up the relations between the two great powers, looked to the Ottomans in order to unseat him. But he lost no time informing the Hungarian palatine György Thurzó that, with the sultan's assistance, he intended to establish order in Transylvania, where the civil war had been almost continuous since 1606.

Bethlen acquired the throne of the principality in the most unusual of circumstances. To assist his rise to power, he was capable of attracting the fullest support from Sultan Ahmed I, who desired a long-term peace in Transylvania. Together with the troops of Iskender Pasha, beylerbey of Temesvár, and of Magyaroglu Ali, pasha of Silistra, as well as of the voivodes of Wallachia and Moldavia and of the Tatar khan, he entered Transylvania in the summer of 1613. Then on October 23, at the diet convened by the beylerbey, they appeared, and "in line with the wishes of the Turkish emperor and the pashas, they freely elected"[2] Bethlen as their ruler. He was the one ruler in the history of the principality to be helped to power by a foreign army, in return for which he would even be forced to return Lippa Castle to the Ottomans in summer 1616; nevertheless, his ascent to the throne brought long-term peace to Transylvania. Bethlen did not nurture illusions: he was well aware that it was a deathly error to confront the Ottomans, as it was only by making an agreement with them that his country could avoid a further civil war or, worse, being turned into an Ottoman vilayet.

Of course, if in the summer of 1616 Bethlen had lost to the latest Habsburg-backed pretender to the throne, György Drugeth de Homonna, he would no doubt have been remembered by history—along with a number of his Transylvanian peers—as a prince who collaborated with the Porte. But this did not come to pass. With his unrivalled talent, ambition, and ability to adapt, Bethlen was to become one of the greatest of the principality's rulers. With a few further concessions, he was able to acquire the complete trust of the Porte; indeed, in late July 1617 at Nagyszombat, he also made a truce with Emperor Matthias. So did he manage to make himself accepted by both empires.

Perhaps even more importantly, he would, in the space of a few years, establish order in Transylvania with unprecedented political and economic skill, albeit also with a strong hand. Gyulafehérvár again became its center. After a quarter century of fighting wars, this order and these peaceful decades were precisely what the population of his country yearned for. Bethlen delivered this to them. He cleverly made peace with the Saxons, who always had one eye on Vienna; and he came to agreement with the Hungarian nobility, while he guaranteed the Szeklers their former rights. All this brought domestic tranquility, which would constantly be preserved by the strongly centralized institutions of the state. He as good as exorcized the estate assembly from power, for example, always deciding on important questions himself, though he did select his advisers with great care. His economic power was founded on his great personal wealth; with an instinctive sense and a number of successful reforms (e.g., the control of the minting of coins, commercial monopolies, and the development of salt mining), he put almost the entire Transylvanian economy back on its feet. The estimated annual income of the princely treasury may have been around six hundred thousand florins. This paid for his opulent court, his splendid construction projects, and his generous support for Protestantism, scholarship, and the arts, as well as for the indulgent provision of entertainment.

Thus did Gabriel Bethlen become one of the greatest rulers in Transylvanian history, if also one of the cruelest. After protracted destruction, the principality became a peaceful and fast-developing country and one of the centers of Hungarian culture, one that its residents would still grieve for many decades, even centuries later. This nostalgia was already succinctly characterized in 1659 by John Kemény, Bethlen's former page and later his successor as prince, who had lived through the terrible destruction Transylvania suffered in 1658: "Never since King Matthias [Corvinus] has there been a king like Stephen [Báthory], and could not even hope for one. . . . Oh Lord, better he had never lived, or that he had lived forever!"[3]

Thanks to his unparalleled brilliance, Bethlen was able to stray from the proverbial narrow path (see part 1, chap. 5). He liked to wage war—but not within his own country. Enjoying the trust of the Ottomans, in 1619 he joined the uprising of the Bohemian estates with an army of some eighteen thousand men. His objective was partly to improve the principality's room for maneuver in foreign policy, partly to expand Transylvania with some of the eastern parts of the Kingdom of Hungary, and finally to support the attempts of the Protestant Hungarian estates to defend their freedom of religion. Unlike the anachronistic portrayals projected onto him by later historiography,[4] he did not think in terms of a Hungarian national kingdom, Hungarian national independence movement, or unified Hungarian state—though neither could he have thought as an Ottoman vassal. Yet, in contrast to many of his predecessors, he understood there was no point in attempting to head in the direction of Wallachia or Moldavia, Istanbul's key sources of food supplies. So he quickly turned the Thirty Years' War to his own advantage, attacking the Kingdom of Hungary, the frontier bastion of the Habsburg Monarchy, at its most critical moment. His calculation was a good one: his campaign from 1619 brought significant territorial gains for Transylvania (see map 10 in part 2, chap. 1). In the Treaty of Nikolsburg signed on December 31, 1621, Emperor Ferdinand II ceded seven counties in Eastern Hungary (Szatmár, Szabolcs, Bereg, Ugocsa, Zemplén, Abaúj, and Borsod) to the prince for the extent of his lifetime in return for the Holy Crown, which Bethlen had taken in Pozsony in autumn 1619, and for Bethlen abandoning his claim on the Hungarian royal title. Bethlen would then settle his court in the city of Kassa in Abaúj county (i.e., in the area taken from the Kingdom of Hungary).

What finally made Bethlen a ruler of great stature was his ability to set a limit to his unprecedented ambition. While he was elected king by the Hungarian estates that had been annexed to him at the assembly of Besztercebánya in August 1620, he never allowed himself to be crowned, even though at this stage he was in possession of the Holy Crown. He recognized that were he truly to be king, this would only hasten an Ottoman occupation of Hungary, which could also mean the loss of Transylvania. As he wrote to his envoys to the Porte in March 1620, "If I had had myself crowned, there would never have been a prince more crazy or pitiful than I, as [the Porte] would have immediately wanted to have me give up the country's border fortresses, and if I had not done so, would have threatened to attack me, alongside the Germans."[5] But he was also well aware that the strength of the Hungarian estates was incomparably greater than that of the estates of Transylvania that he himself regulated, and so it would never be possible to create a centralized state similar to that in Transylvania against their will.

Bethlen thus knew how far it was possible to stray from the narrow path. As he wrote, also in the spring of 1620, "I am staying in Kassa, and will do so until my downfall."[6] Until then, he would bravely march on, and he established for himself the greatest possible room for maneuver between the two empires. As John Kemény also wrote of him, "He would keep both powerful emperors in equilibrium with himself and with his country."[7] Yet, quite understandably, it was only really the interests of his own state, that of Transylvania, not so much those of the Kingdom of Hungary and Croatia as governed by the Habsburgs, that drove him in initiating his military campaigns. This all went to show that in the seventeenth century, despite the new unity of the country that the estates had so long wished for, the "one (Hungarian) country"[8] did not exist, at least not in political and military terms. Standing at the two conflicting sides of the two empires, there was no way it could exist.

It is possible to establish this fact, even if Bethlen's propaganda—proclaiming Protestantism and the safeguarding of estate rights—achieved great successes among the Hungarian nobility, especially in Upper Hungary. At least it did until, during his first campaign, his soldiers wrought as much devastation as the imperial and royal armies that had fought him back, or indeed the Ottoman-Tatar troops that would soon come to his aid. The prince did not, that is, weigh up just how serious the political, economic, and social consequences of his campaigns could be for the Kingdom of Hungary. As the interests of his own state lay elsewhere, he expended little energy on this consideration. Thus, during his reign, Transylvania flourished, while the Kingdom of Hungary was exposed to his series of military attacks and the Hungarian political elite he was for a while allied with increasingly became the "rebel nation" in Vienna (see part 2, chap. 3).

So it was fortunate for the Kingdom of Hungary that after Bethlen's death and the short reign of his widow, Catherine of Brandenburg (1629–1630), the rule of George I Rákóczi would be a more peaceful one. Although in 1630 the prince had no choice but to abandon the seven Hungarian counties, peaceful growth could continue, and the kingdom could also breathe a sigh of relief. For the most part, Rákóczi continued Bethlen's policies. He too used cruel methods to crush any internal opposition (trials confiscating lands and wealth) and enormously increased his own private wealth (from ten domains to thirty-two), a good part of which lay in the northeast part of the Kingdom of Hungary. But he also maintained his predecessor's legacy as a patron of the arts; his wife, the Calvinist Zsuzsanna Lorántffy, was an enthusiastic partner in this. So the boom in Calvinism, Hungarian-language culture, the fine arts, and scholarship continued in Transylvania into the 1630s and 1640s. We need only think of the foundation of the press in Várad, of more beautiful late Renaissance buildings being constructed, or of the enlargement of the princely library.

Unlike Gabriel Bethlen, however, Rákóczi only rarely came off the narrow path set by the Ottomans. In the autumn of 1636, he successfully repulsed the Ottoman troops from Buda arriving in his country as well as a pretender to the throne, Stephen Bethlen. Then, after a prolonged wait, he too joined the Thirty Years' War. In line with the Swedish-Transylvanian Treaty concluded in Gyulafehérvár in November 1643, in early 1644 Rákóczi began an attack on Emperor Ferdinand III in Hungary (see map 10). Like Bethlen, he did so in the name of defending the Protestant right to religion, while in point of fact continuing his predecessor's anti-Habsburg foreign policy. In March he had already invaded Kassa, but after his Swedish allies could no longer come to his assistance because of the Danish attack on their country, he suffered a defeat at Galgóc, Nyitra county (April 9). He soon had to give up most of the devastated kingdom. Although in his newest expedition in 1645 he would finally join forces with the Swedish chief commander, Lennart Torstensson, at Brünn, he had to make a retreat when the Porte ordered it.

As part of the Treaty of Linz, signed with Emperor Ferdinand on December 16, 1645, Rákóczi was given the seven Hungarian counties for the rest of his life, and indeed Szabolcs and Szatmár counties also for the lives of his sons, while he attained solid consolidation for his domains in the kingdom (Tokaj, Tarcal, Regéc, Ecsed, etc.). In return for this, he had to terminate his anti-Habsburg agreement with the French and Swedes, to retract his troops from the kingdom, and to pledge that he would no longer intervene in Hungary's affairs. Overall, his two campaigns against the Habsburgs would hugely strengthen not just Transylvania's position but also his own power. The golden age of the principality could continue (see fig. 31).

His son and successor George II Rákóczi, who took the throne in 1648, entertained more dangerous dreams than the rulers before him, rich with illusions. His marriage to the last member of the Báthory family of Somlyó, Zsófia, and the earlier successes and personal ambitions of their two families must have led him to believe that he could acquire the Polish throne—or that he could create a composite state run by the Rákóczi dynasty, just as Polish king Stephen Báthory had been able to do in the second half of the sixteenth century (see part 1, chap. 5). The only thing he did not grasp properly was the most important one. While Báthory's Polish kingdom had at that time enjoyed the support of the Ottoman Porte, in the 1650s Istanbul did not want to hear about it—even less about a Transylvania that would take Moldavia and Wallachia, the breadbaskets of the Ottoman capital, under its control to use them to grasp the Polish throne. Yet this is precisely what Rákóczi did: first he turned the Moldavian voivode into a subordinate in 1653; then he did likewise for the Wallachian one in 1655. Although, on account of the war with Venice, the Porte for a time observed Rákóczi's actions without response, it then forbade its vassal, which now wanted to get involved in the Swedish-Polish War and the Cossack question, from going to war. Rákóczi did not judge his room for maneuver realistically. His lax policy would bring great devastation first to Transylvania and then, during the aforementioned Ottoman War, to the Kingdom of Hungary.

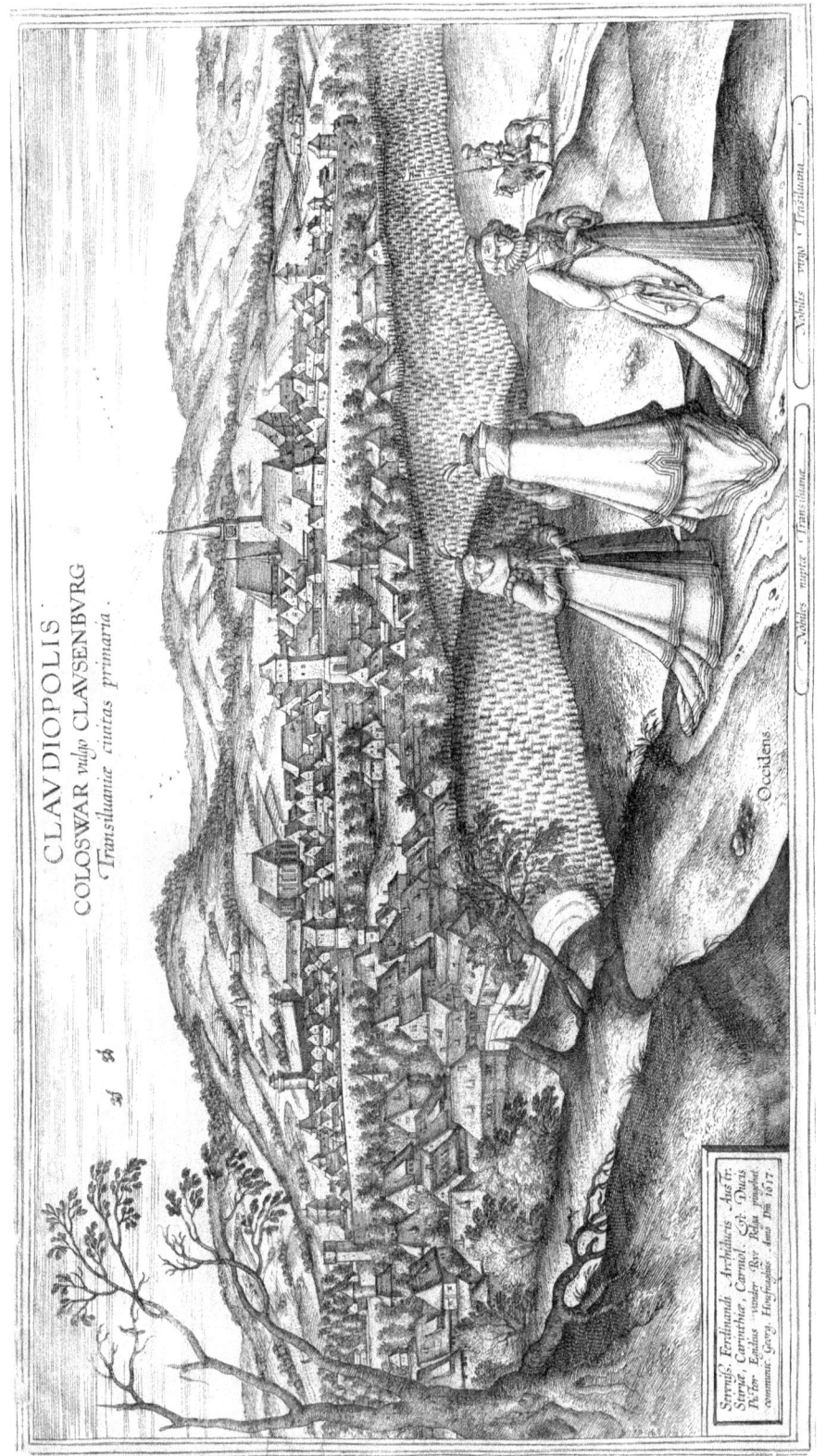

Fig. 31. The city of Kolozsvár in the seventeenth century. Engraving by Georg Hoefnagel, 1617 (Hungarian National Museum, Budapest).

Rákóczi's ill-considered decisions brought an end to the more than four decades in which the principality had been flourishing. While in the course of the Polish campaign the great and good of the Transylvanian nobility fell into Tatar captivity, in early autumn 1658 Ottoman, Tatar, Cossack, Moldavian, and Wallachian troops burned and looted more or less the entire territory of the principality. The damage particularly affected the Barcaság (*Burzenland*), Háromszék, and Fogarasföld (*Fogaraschland*) areas, the richer cities (such as Marosvásárhely, Nagyenyed, and Torda), and the residence city of Gyulafehérvár. This is when the gravestones of the princes were destroyed, together with the library and the archives, but there was hardly a place in Transylvania that did not suffer tremendous damage both in terms of human life and in terms of agricultural and material goods. The return of Rákóczi, who would not hear of resigning the throne, and then the intervention of the imperial troops, as described above (see part 2, chap. 2), led to years of bloody civil war. To make things even worse, in 1660–1661 the famine concomitant with this destruction brought plague with it.

George II Rákóczi straying into forbidden territory thus meant that from 1658 Transylvania was condemned to a decline that would at best take decades to recover from. If with some exaggeration, a report from Kolozsvár in 1662 states that "the whole country is in such turmoil, the Turks have dragged so many residents off into captivity, that Transylvania seems almost desolate."[9] Transylvania's golden age was at an end, even if Prince Michael Apafi, with his dedicated organizational efforts from the mid-1660s, did all he could for the country's recovery. As the vassal of the Porte, and for all his protestations, he could not of course avoid his troops supporting the grand vizier's campaigns heading toward Vienna in 1663 and then again in 1683. Indeed, in October 1663 he was even forced in a proclamation to call on the residents of Hungary to acquiesce to the Ottomans. It was with justification that Leopold I composed a riposte to this on November 10. A week earlier, Palatine Ferenc Wesselényi had already written a letter to the Hungarian counties encouraging them to be resilient. In this letter the palatine raised the following question: "Why does his highness [Prince Apafi] not arrange some permanent and peaceful free existence for our noble Transylvanian country?"[10] These lines make vividly clear just how much more useful it would have been for the progress of both the Kingdom of Hungary and Transylvania if the seventeenth century had been one of peace rather than of wars started from the principality that brought destruction to it after a golden age of forty years.

What Apafi did purely out of military necessity was soon outdone voluntarily by a Hungarian magnate in a tight squeeze. After Vienna introduced a series of reprisal measures in the 1670s in response to the actions of the Hungarian magnates (see part 2, chap. 3), in Eastern Hungary the growing number of dissatisfied members of the gentry and soldiers (refugees who were increasingly referred to as *kurucok*) found in June 1679 a leader in the person of Imre Thököly, an aristocrat with a troubled childhood and passion for writing and who enjoyed Prince Apafi's support. This was how the ruler of Transylvania tried to keep the parts of the soldiery that had broken off from society and were mostly living from looting at a distance from the principality. His plan did work, but Thököly, offered support by the king of France and by the Porte and with real power ambitions despite increasingly being exploited, had a growing desire to have a state of his own in the power vacuum that had come into being between the Kingdom of Hungary and Transylvania.

In 1679 the political and military leadership in Vienna, stubbornly sure of its strength, was not willing to compromise with the *bujdosók*, who since 1675 had been leading a series of campaigns into Upper Hungary. Therefore, Thököly increasingly thought it was high time to establish a state with Ottoman assistance. No amount of absolutist measures was enough to make the majority of the political elite in the Kingdom of Hungary support such a new state, especially as it had repeatedly experienced the terrible destruction of the desperate *bujdosók*. Thököly's propagandistic catchphrases were freedom of religion, justice, and patriotism, but even his peers were well aware he was not exclusively driven by such lofty goals. After his troops in 1680–1681 had ravaged their way through the entire northern part of the kingdom (later referred to as the "Thököly devastation"), and while the court in Vienna and the Hungarian political elite were in the midst of signing the compromise in Sopron in 1681 (which, with his armed campaign, he had helped bring into being), Thököly resolved to take a historic step. In the interests of creating an Ottoman vassal state led by himself, he turned to the Porte with an offer: in return for being made ruler of Hungary, he would undertake to place the Kingdom of Hungary under Ottoman control within two years. Istanbul was open to his proposal, given the difficult predicament it would mean for its main rival, the Habsburg dynasty. There was no precedent for this, but after the Russo-Ottoman War (1677–1681), there were many in the seraglio again pushing for an expedition against Vienna.

So it came to pass that in late 1681 a Hungarian magnate forced into a corner rose to the challenge from which both Bocskai and Bethlen had consistently shrunk back. In mid-September 1682, under Fülek Castle, Uzun Ibrahim, pasha of Buda, created a new Ottoman vassal state on the Transylvanian model, in return for the payment of annual taxes of forty thousand thalers: Thököly's northern Hungarian principality, which Turkish sources referred to as *Orta Macar*, or Central Hungary (see map 12). This meant that, come 1685, Hungary's medieval territory had been split into four parts and was exposed to yet another series of devastations on account of the desperate policy of a lord attached to his power.

Although the romantic schools in Hungarian historiography would in retrospect carve Thököly into a national hero defending Hungarian statehood, and in the 1950s, as part of the "nationalism" of the communist system,[11] a statue of him was even added to the national pantheon on Heroes' Square in Budapest, in truth the "craziest and most pitiful" Ottoman vassal (to quote Gabriel Bethlen, above) became one of the unfortunate rogues of Hungarian history. It was not without reason that in early 1683, Prince Apafi wrote to Palatine Pál Esterházy that Thököly "seeks only his own advance and gain . . . and has completed nothing for the security of the Hungarian nation; if he pretends otherwise, it is but a colorful act."[12] Apafi's words were not objective, of course: Thököly's movement played a vital role in the defense of Protestant freedom of religion.

There could be no question of independent Hungarian statehood in the case of Thököly's vassal state. In the summer of 1683, he even provided assistance to the Ottomans with their advance on Vienna—that is, to the preparations for the intended occupation of the whole of Hungary's territory, significantly increasing the size of his own country in the process. In August 1683, by forcing a number of other Hungarian magnates to join him, albeit for just a few weeks, he ran the risk of a complete Ottoman occupation of the Kingdom of Hungary. But the most tragic aspect was that Thököly did not change his policy even when, with the

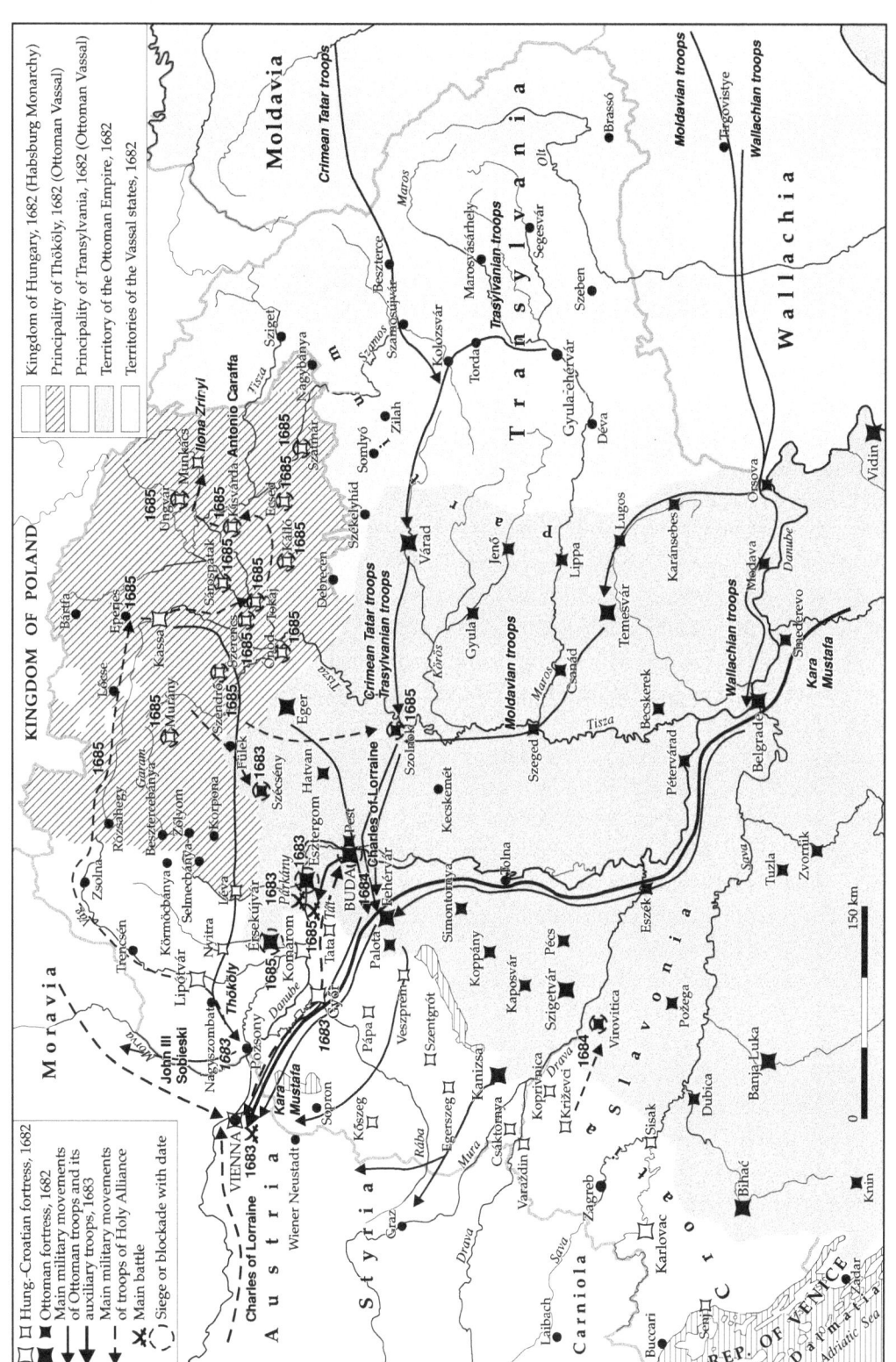

Map 12. Hungary in four parts, 1682–1685.

relief of the second Ottoman siege of Vienna, the liberation of Hungary began and he was no longer obligated to serve the Ottomans. In this drifting between two empires, Thököly, unlike Bethlen, seemed not to have even the smallest amount of good sense. So while Bethlen became a ruler of great stature, Thököly's princedom is now seen by the latest research work as one of the low points of Hungarian history.[13]

It was not only in the sixteenth century that the great powers rejected self-appointed pretenders to the Kingdom of Hungary (see part 1, chap. 4). Thököly had not yet had to face the music in full: his rule was quashed in October 1685, and then the pasha of Várad had him captured. After soon being released from the sultan's captivity, he did not return; indeed, after the death of Prince Michael Apafi in April 1690, he even attempted to acquire the Transylvanian throne with Ottoman, Tatar, and Wallachian troops—that is, he tried again to make the liberated Transylvania into an Ottoman vassal. On September 22, after his victory at Zernyest (Zernescht in Barcaság, German *Burzenland*) on August 21, the terrified Transylvanian estates elected him prince, but in late October an alliance of the imperial-royal and Transylvanian armies was able successfully to oust him. He died an émigré in the Ottoman Empire in Izmit in September 1705.

The history of the independent principality had ended in October 1690. In the Treaty of Balázsfalva (October 27), Charles of Lorraine, the commander in chief who had entered the country in autumn 1687, pledged to retain its independence after its liberation from Ottoman vassalage, but this did not happen. In May 1688, at Fogaras, General Antonio Caraffa had already forced the estates to recognize the hereditary kingship of Leopold I and his descendants. But they steadfastly urged that the aged Apafi stay on the throne, followed after his death by his son Michael II Apafi (who had already been elected as his successor in the summer of 1681), and that the free election of princes should continue, while the prince, subservient to King Leopold, could be higher in rank than the Hungarian palatine. The *Diploma Leopoldinum*, published on October 16, 1690, after the death of Apafi in April, then amended on December 4, 1691, would ultimately be the compromise solution for these attempts. Transylvania ceased to be an independent state; as a part of the Hungarian Crown, even without properly being rejoined to the kingdom, it became a province governed by the Habsburgs from Vienna.

The settlement of Transylvania's legal status in this way was the result of a special compromise between the court in Vienna and the Transylvanian political elite. There could be no doubt, of course, that after the armed liberation it was Vienna that held the stronger hand. As the seventeenth-century foreign policy of the princes toward the Kingdom of Hungary had still not been forgotten in the imperial city, to assist stricter oversight Transylvania was not reannexed to Hungary. What we often forget is that this separation was very much in the interests of the Transylvanian political elite (especially the Apor, Bethlen, Bánffy, and Haller families). Should Transylvania have been returned to the kingdom, they would have been no match for the Hungarian aristocrats (the Esterházys, Pálffys, Batthyánys, Erdődys, etc.) in terms of either political or economic power. At the new governing council (Latin *Gubernium*) established in Nagyszeben (Hermannstadt) in 1690 to run Transylvania, it was no accident that the members of these families were given pride of place; they then tried to retain as much as they could from the former practice of administering the principality. And although the fate of the arrangements of 1690–1691 depended on the outcome of the Turkish war that was still very much in progress, the Peace of Karlóca (Karlowitz) in 1699 settled things for good: Transylvania would remain an eastern frontier bastion and special province for the Habsburg Monarchy that, with the help of the Transylvanian Court Chancellery established in Vienna in 1693 and the local political elite, would retain much of the former system of institutions of the principality and the privileges afforded the estates yet would nevertheless be controlled from the imperial city.

Notes

1. Baron Péter Apor of Altorja, *Metamorphosis Transylvaniae*, trans. Bernard Adams (London: Paul Kegan, 2013).

2. László Makkai, ed., *Bethlen Gábor krónikásai: Krónikák, emlékiratok, naplók a nagy fejedelemről* [The chroniclers of Gabriel Bethlen: Chronicles, memoirs and diaries about the great prince] (Budapest: Gondolat Kiadó, 1980), 216.

3. Éva V. Windisch, ed., *Kemény János és Bethlen Miklós művei* [The works of János Kemény and Miklós Bethlen] (Budapest: Szépirodalmi Könyvkiadó, 1980), 99.

4. László Nagy, *Bethlen Gábor a független Magyarországért* [Gabriel Bethlen for an independent Hungary] (Budapest: Akadémiai Kiadó, 1969); recently, cf. Ágnes R. Várkonyi, *A Királyi Magyarország 1541–1686* [Royal Hungary, 1541–1686] (Budapest: Vince Kiadó, 1999), 76–77.

5. *Török-magyarkori történelmi emlékek*, part 1, *Okmánytár*, vol. 3 (Pest: Eggenberger Ferdinánd, 1868), 214.

6. Ibid., 216.

7. Windisch, *Kemény János*, 99.

8. Cf. István György Tóth, *Három ország—egy haza* [Three states, one country] (Budapest: ADAMS Kiadó, 1992), 16–20.

9. S. V., "Zani gróf levelei Erdély állapotáról 1661–1664" [Count Zani's letters on the state of Transylvania], *Századok* [Centuries] 26 (1892): 607.

10. Győr-Moson-Sopron Megyei Levéltár Győri Levéltára, Győr vármegye levéltára, Közgyűlési iratok [Győr branch of Győr-Moson-Sopron County Archive, Archives of the historical county of Győr, records of public meetings] II/13/1663.

11. Cf. Aladár Mód, *400 év küzdelem az önálló Magyarországért* [400 years of struggle for an independent Hungary], 7th enlarged and revised ed. (Budapest: Szikra, 1954).

12. MNL OL, Budapest, P 125, Esterházy család hercegi ágának levéltára, Esterházy Pál nádor [Archive of the princely branch of the Esterházy family, Palatine Pál Esterházy], no. 1718.

13. János J. Varga, *Válaszúton: Thököly Imre és Magyarország 1682–1684-ben* [At the crossroads: Imre Thököly and Hungary, 1682–1684] (Budapest: MTA TTI, 2007).

Fig. 32. Imre Thököly, prince of Hungary (1682–1685). Engraving by Johannes Meyer, 1683 (Hungarian National Museum, Budapest).

5

MILITARIZATION AND SELF-ADMINISTRATION
Changes in Society

WHILE THE SIXTEENTH CENTURY BROUGHT STRIKING CHANGES TO the structure of society and the forced migration of a number of groups (see part 1, chaps. 6 and 8), the seventeenth century would first and foremost leave its mark on the condition of society. The greatest victim of the decline brought by destructive military campaigns was the broad mass of society. It is well known that the Thirty Years' War set the economic and social development of German areas back by many decades, and in the Kingdom of Hungary the situation may well have been even worse. Between 1591 and 1711, the country lived through two wars, both lasting a decade and a half and causing immense damage (1591–1606 and 1683–1699); a Turkish war over a number of years (1658/60–1664); and the constant campaigns of the Transylvanian princes (1619–1621, 1623–1624, 1626, and 1644–1645). In addition, it suffered a number of peasant revolts (in Upper Hungary in 1631–1632 and in the Croatian territories in 1653–1659), then the attacks of the *kurucok* of Imre Thököly (1672–1685) (see fig. 32), and finally the Hegyalja uprising in Eastern Hungary (1697) and the Rákóczi War of Independence (1703–1711). Meanwhile, its territory was also often ravaged by the soldiers stationed at the two empires' opposing chains of border fortresses.

The greatest tragedy was that society, which after 1526 had shown a real capacity for regeneration (see part 1, chap. 6), was so drained come the seventeenth century that it seemed incapable even of temporary renewal. Broad sections of it were squeezed out of the parameters of everyday life, forced to take up an armed, militarized lifestyle, even turning into wanderers or loitering looters. It was a good reflection of the war-stricken everyday life of the period that, regarding the properties of the Hungarian nobles joining his side, in 1620 Prince Gabriel Bethlen was forced to order his soldiers "under no circumstances to dare to damage, ravage, loot, rob or to take anything against their will and without payment."[1] Another sign of the corrupt state of public affairs was the way in which the Ottoman-Hungarian slave trade along the border for ransom would by the middle of the century turn into a veritable kidnap industry. Meanwhile, vagrant elements increasingly formed into gangs in order to blackmail some more prosperous settlement or other. Indeed, the period from the 1650s to the 1670s was the most active one for the military courts for the frontier soldiers, which shows that even royal soldiers often followed the path of the wrongdoers threatened by the strict punishments listed in the criminal code of the time.

Finally, in the Long Turkish War at the end of the seventeenth century (see part 2, chap. 10), it often happened that the imperial military command would, to save the population of some enfeebled region, recommend temporary relocation, or the pasha of Buda would give Christian villages direct warning that the Crimean Tatars were approaching. Wartime conditions thus transformed and indeed undermined everyday life for broad sections of society. The results of these processes included the considerable militarization of society, the forced settlement of arms-bearing elements removed from everyday life in return for services provided, the preparation and organization of the local population for self-defense, and the continuous hajduk, peasant, and then *kuruc* uprisings.

The militarization of the Ottoman-Hungarian frontier and the awarding of privileges in return for military services had already begun in the sixteenth century, but then it was only really in the Croatian-Slavonian areas that it was significant in size, as we saw with the examples of the Uskoks and Vlachs (see part 1, chap. 8). Given their continuous Balkan supply line and the limited degree of the more or less merged Croatian-Slavonian territories, not even the partial settlement and the use in border fortress service would solve the problems of the refugees. In the case of the Uskoks in the Senj region, this led to a proper war between Venice and Vienna (1615–1618). The military command at Graz even considered relocating them beyond the Tisza, though this was no more realistic than the relocation of the Teutonic Order in Hungary as sometimes planned in the sixteenth and seventeenth centuries. In 1630 Emperor Ferdinand II attempted to settle the problem of the Slavonian Vlachs (especially those from the Körös, Ivanics, and Kapronca regions), reinforced by tens of thousands from northern Serbia during the Long Turkish War, with a general letter of privilege (*Statuta Valachorum*). This provided detailed regulation of the privileges granted and reciprocal services expected of the Vlachs living in specially fortified settlements. Meanwhile, the soldier peasants, who led a half-military, half-peasant lifestyle and so were in daily conflict with the Slavonian nobility and serfs, were put under the authority of the Slavonian captain general. As a result, a privileged free peasant military society, militarized and under military supervision, developed south of the Drava along the broad band of the Ottoman frontier.

Similar changes began to the north of the Drava from the start of the seventeenth century. There were a number of reasons for this. First, a larger and better protected hinterland had remained everywhere here, in which the Hungarian lords had better-populated domains. Second, despite the wars, the population of this area had not changed as much as that of Slavonia, where it had been more or less completely replaced. Third, as we have seen, the Hungarian population was for a while capable of unparalleled revival. But in the seventeenth century, the constant wars and the deterioration of public life meant that sooner or later this would not be possible even in these parts of the country. Bocskai's large-scale settlement of hajduks was symptomatic of how the problems began. The number of arms-bearing elements successively breaking away from society added to the altered significance of the Hungarian theater of war. During the Thirty Years' War, Vienna was forced to reduce the number of frontier soldiers by many thousands, for financial reasons. Over a few decades, their military value also lessened, as, with the decline of assistance arriving from abroad, more and more of them looked to add to their income by taking on civilian work activities (such as breeding livestock, keeping vineyards, practicing agriculture, or making handicrafts). This meant there was an increasingly urgent need across the country for the granting of land—in return for privileges—to the frontier soldiers, hajduks, and other military elements.

The Hungarian and Croatian large landowners along the frontier and the Transylvanian princes were all aware of this. From the 1610s onward, more populous groups were settled in the hinterland of the border fortresses and given collective privileges in return for keeping watch. While the princes established settlements for hajduks or soldier peasants mostly along the Körös Rivers in Bihar county and Szabolcs county further to the north, in the Kingdom of Hungary the Rákóczis did so in the regions of the Sajó, Hernád, and Bodrog Rivers, the Batthyány family along the Rába River, and the Zrínyis in the Muraköz region (Međimurje). By the 1650s and 1660s, that is, behind the border fortresses, from along the Mura to the Bihar areas near Transylvania, a system of guard buildings and settlements had emerged, protected by military elements living a life that was part military, part civilian, effectively acting as an additional line of frontier defense. Relative to the conditions in Croatia and Slavonia, however, there was the significant difference that in both Hungary and the Partium the contracts signed with landowners meant that there was a greater variety of privileges and of types of settlement. Indeed, their residents would never come under the jurisdiction of the captains general of the border fortresses. The only exception to this was that of the residents of Bocskai's hajduk towns, who from 1608 were subordinate to the captains general of Upper Hungary. Some of the peasant soldiers granted privileges (e.g., in Transdanubia, in the Muraköz, or on the Rákóczi estates) also served in the private armies of the large landowners.

This all meant that by the middle of the seventeenth century the everyday life of the population living in the ever-broader band of the border fortress system would be defined by the bearing of arms, whether systematic or occasional, and defense against hajduks, thieves, and the incursions of frontier soldiers. It is hard to make precise estimates, but at this time around eighty to one hundred thousand people may have been in partially armed service. Taken together with their family members, this means that this class may have made up some 20–25 percent of the kingdom's population. Such large-scale militarization of society had enormous risks, and by the end of the century, it would have increasingly damaging consequences. Every new campaign and period of civil war boosted the size of this class, and it was not possible to grant privileges to each new group that was forced to the periphery of society. So arms-bearing groups blossomed, breaking away from society for good to seek their fortune along the frontier region between the two empires—mostly by robbery, as usual for free soldiers. Miklós Zrínyi had reason to worry about the country's fate because of them: "As long as there is this freedom in public order in Hungary, we should expect no good of our affairs. We must use our every strength to abolish this free soldiery, which is not good for anything, not for its country, not for its lords, not for itself."[2]

The Croatian ban and imperial general Zrínyi—a man well versed in warfare—was quite right. Were but a few thousand of the privileged soldier class to lose their livelihoods (as happened, for example, during the Ottoman war of 1664 and after the badly timed attempt at restructuring the frontier army in the 1670s) and to become mercenaries or outlaws, they could, with the right propaganda methods, be put in the service of just about any cause one could think of. This was particularly true in the northeastern counties of Hungary, where the hajduk settlements had mushroomed and where the gentry and the hajduks had since the time of Bocskai always been ready to defend their hard-earned rights and their Calvinist faith. But their privileges stood only as long as their armed service justified them.

With the liberation of Hungary, beginning in 1683, this heterogeneous social class gradually lost its raison d'être. The same was true of those members of the royal frontier army who, attached to the place in which they lived and to a semicivilian lifestyle that they had become accustomed to over many decades, were unable to assume service in an imperial-royal standing army that embodied the next step in military progress. The great war of the end of the century had gone to show that the vocation of the border fortress soldiers, which had played a key role in defending the country for a century and a half, was no longer required. (Its development had become so acclimatized to frontier warfare and the semimilitary lifestyle that once this stopped being a border area it would itself be reduced to insignificance.) It is no surprise that the armies of Imre Thököly and later Francis II Rákóczi were made up mostly of these soldiers, who had lost their privileges or even their all and been squeezed to the edges of society.

So, all in all, the military and civil war conditions that lasted for decades from the 1610s onward would break off a large and constantly replenishing mass from the body of Hungarian society whose problems not even successful settlements could fully solve. The resolution of their situation, which had become even worse by the end of the century, became one of the newly liberated country's greatest difficulties, one that could even conceal the seed of a potential armed conflict. This is why these men could form the basis for Rákóczi's war of independence (see part 2, chap. 11).

In the seventeenth century, on account of the large-scale impoverishment and militarization of society, anyone able to would try to acquire privileges, as these would partially or fully exempt them from the various taxation burdens. In addition to the collective freedoms granted to hajduks and soldier peasants, the most favorable such solution was the acquisition of a charter of ennoblement (Latin *litterae armales*, Hungarian *nemeslevél*). This was an aspiration equally for the burghers in royal free cities, for the residents of market towns, and for frontier soldiers, Transylvanian princely bodyguards, private landowning hajduks, and even the more prosperous peasants (see fig. 33). It was precisely the "century of decline" that brought the golden age of the phenomenon of "noble inflation." A great many frontier soldiers were granted nobility by dint of their military service, as were a number of those in the employment of great families by the intervention of their lords, as well as many hundreds of urban burghers and even richer peasants, thanks to their connections and to bribery. Though it is hard to estimate the number of those granted nobility during the century, there may have been many thousands. In vain did the richer nobles attempt to limit this process at the Pozsony diet of 1630, complaining that "some are hugely assertive in requesting charters of ennoblement, despite showing no merit or worth."[3] They were unable to halt the unstoppable flow of ennoblement throughout the century.

This is when the Hungarian nobility set off along the path that, by the eve of the 1848 Revolution, led to its representing some 5 percent of the population. In Europe at this time, only in Poland did the nobility represent a higher proportion of the citizenry as a whole. In addition, the number of noble communities inhabited almost entirely by the gentry (single

Fig. 33. A Hungarian noble and noblewoman in the seventeenth century. Etching by an unknown Italian master, A. S. (Hungarian National Museum, Budapest).

plot owners, armalists, curialists, etc.) grew across the country in the seventeenth century; in these communities, life was increasingly regulated by written rules (statutes or charters). Although their residents hardly enjoyed a higher standard of living than the more prosperous peasants of the time, their unique self-administration served the maintenance of their tax exemption, the safeguarding of their Calvinist faith, and their economic interests. Even if they were under the supervision of the noble counties, wartime conditions saw their self-administration, and thus their social status, strengthen.

The self-administration and judicial system of the noble counties also consolidated in the course of the century (see map 13); they, too, established one self-regulating statute after the next. These institutions also enjoyed the first golden age of their early modern history. Nevertheless, and despite the general opinion of Hungarian historiography and the situation that would develop by the start of the nineteenth century,[4] the noble county in the seventeenth century was not yet the arena for resistance to the Habsburg government. It was, rather, the defender of local estate rights, the implementer of central orders, and the keystone of the district captaincies general that made up the backbone of the system of border fortresses. The only exception was the 1670s, which brought a clean break, when it was largely the noble counties that crippled the new system of taxation and the measures taken by the Gubernium.

There was also self-administration among smaller communities and those with no privileges. The official seals are a good example: they were increasingly used by smaller settlements, even by the serf villages, and then became widespread. But by the middle of the century, the growing number of thieving soldiers meant that even the peasantry prepared itself for self-defense. The main task of the so-called peasant noble counties (Hungarian *parasztvármegyék*) that came into being on the frontier of Ottoman Hungary[5] was defense against frontier soldiers, free hajduks, thieves, and looters; the protection of markets; and the general maintenance of public order in peasant communities. Even the Christian prisoners suffering in Ottoman Buda prison established a "local government" to protect their interests. They selected so-called prisoner owners (Hungarian *rabgazda*) to run this government, and from the 1640s they even produced their own seals to help defend themselves against the outlaws who masqueraded as prisoners.

The seventeenth century also brought a highly difficult period for the citizenry of the free royal towns. The acquisition of privilege at the individual and community levels (a noble title or status as a royal free city) was one of their most important goals, too. Hence, the number of citizens acquiring nobility grew and grew, as did the list of royal free towns (Korpona, Zólyom, Breznóbánya, Modor, Bazin, Szentgyörgy, Kőszeg, Kismarton, Késmárk, Ruszt, and, at the end of the century, Debrecen). Kőszeg, for example, which, along with other towns in western Hungary, was returned to the Kingdom of Hungary in 1647 after being pledged to the Habsburgs for two centuries, would the following year pay an enormous price (25,000 golden florins and 132 hectoliters of wine), about ten times the town's yearly income, in order to achieve free royal town status and to have representation at the diet (in the lower house). The same was achieved by the town of Kismarton (Eisenstadt). And yet the horizons of the urban citizenry were much restricted by wartime conditions and the strengthening of the nobility of the noble counties. This was particularly true in Upper Hungary, which

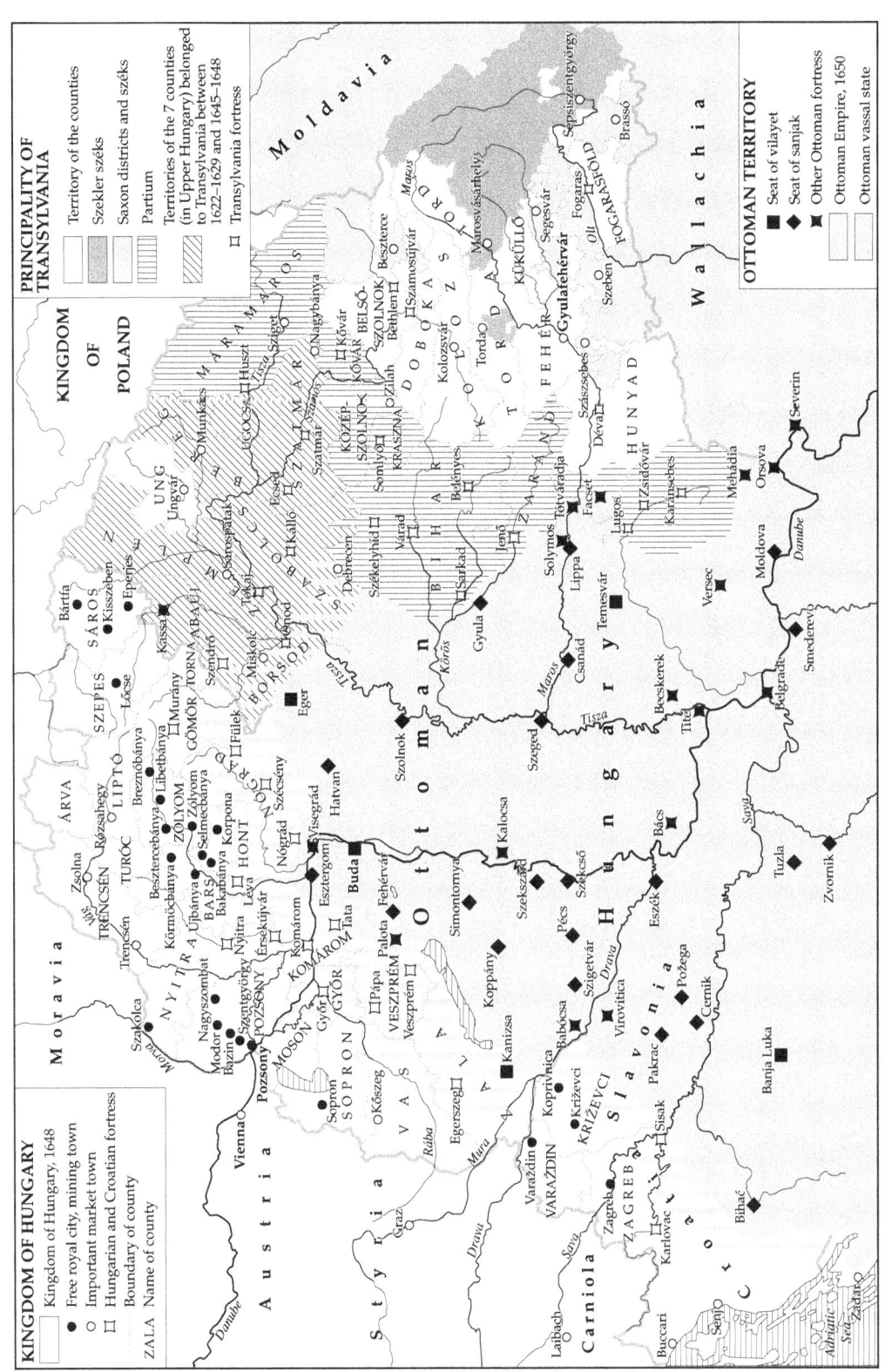

Map 13. Administration in the mid-seventeenth century.

enjoyed but a handful of peaceful years from the invasion of Gabriel Bethlen in 1619 until 1711. Meanwhile, the nobility limited the bourgeoisie's chances of becoming stronger not just by moving into the towns (as attested to by the prevalence throughout Hungary of the street name *Úri utca*, meaning the "street of the nobles") but also by getting a swathe of antiurban legislation accepted by the diet.

Indirectly, militarization would even affect the aristocracy, as the most important families (e.g., the Batthyány, Esterházy, Nádasdy, Rákóczi, Thurzó, and Zrínyi families) commanded respectable private armies. The aristocracy that controlled the house of lords was made up of some fifty to seventy families. And while this class underwent a significant transformation after 1526 (see part 1, chap. 6), in the seventeenth century, rare was the *homo novus* who rose up through their ranks. Those who did rise included the Esterházy family, advancing with excellent marriages; the Melith, Szunyogh, Kéry, Koháry, Bercsényi, and Károlyi families, joining the elite mostly by dint of their military service; the Zichy family, managing to combine careers on the frontier and at the chamber; and the Csáky family, which had moved from Transylvania. To a considerable degree, these families took over the lands and positions of the Alaghy, Dobó, Dóczy, Mágochy, Török, and Thurzó families, which had all died out. But the already mentioned Balassi, Batthyány, Bánffy, Czobor, Draskovics, Erdődy, Forgách, Frangepán/Frankopan, Drugeth de Homonna, Keglevics, Liszthy, Nádasdy, Nyáry, Pálffy, Pethő, Rákóczi, Serényi, Széchy, Thököly, and Zrínyi families, occasional fluctuations notwithstanding, all retained their leading positions. Administrative and intellectual careers enjoyed increasing significance, as did work as the *familiaris* of an aristocratic family, and these helped the Apponyi, Berényi, Cziráky, Horváth of Veglia, Horváth-Kissevics, Lippay, Viczay, and Vízkelethy families join the ranks of the magnates.

In this era, magnates were understood to refer not only to the country's high dignitaries and to aristocrats with the Hungarian baronial title (Latin *liber baro*, German *Freiherr*, Hungarian *báró, mágnás*). In the seventeenth century, under German influence but also based on certain Hungarian precedents, the title of count (Latin *comes*, German *Graf*, Hungarian *gróf*) would also be given to high noble families. In the course of the century, this title was awarded to the Thurzó (1606), Bánffy (1622), Esterházy (1626), Batthyány (1630), Nyáry (1632), Pálffy (1634), Draskovics (1635), Forgách (1640), Széchy (1645), Wesselényi (1646), Croatian Konsky (1647), Kéry (1654), Thököly (1654), Liszthy (1655), Balassi (1664), Rákóczi (1664), Pethő (1666), Szunyogh (1669), and Illésházy families (1678), and finally, at the end of the century, to the Koháry (1685), Barkóczy (1687), Ráttkay (1687), Bercsényi (1689), and Pekry (1692) families and a few foreign families. Unlike in Bohemia, however, the title of imperial prince never took hold in Hungary: in the seventeenth century, it was only Pál Esterházy (1687) and Francis II Rákóczi (1697) who were to receive the German *Reichsfürstentitel*.

It was also true that from the middle of the century the Austrian, German, Bohemian, Moravian, Italian, and indeed often supranational aristocracy would increasingly often and in ever-greater numbers be granted Hungarian "citizenship" (*indigenatus*). But, what with the constant war conditions and poor state of law and order, it was only after the end of the Long Turkish War at the end of the century that they actually settled in Hungary. Their advance in the first third of the eighteenth century then brought another thorough transformation of the Hungarian high nobility. Another key factor in this was that many Hungarian families (the Festetics, Ghillány, Grassalkovich, Mednyánszky, Szapáry, Széchényi, and Szirmay families, etc.) made clever use of the new economic and political opportunities afforded by the liberation from the Ottomans, thereby rising into the ranks of the aristocracy that played such a key role in the country's life.

Notes

1. Péter Dominkovits, "Bethlen Gábor levelei Vas vármegye rendjeihez (1620)" [Letters of Gabriel Bethlen to the estates of Vas county], *Lymbus. Magyarságtudományi Forrásközlemények* 3 (2005): 69.

2. Sándor Iván Kovács, ed., *Zrínyi Miklós összes művei* [The collected works of Miklós Zrínyi] (Budapest: Kortárs Kiadó, 2003), 422.

3. *Magyar törvénytár. (Corpus Juris Hungarici) 1608–1657. törvényczikkek* [Acts of 1608–1657], with explanatory notes by Dezső Márkus (Budapest: Franklin-Társulat, 1900), 296–297 (1630: Law 30).

4. Péter Dominkovits, "Das ungarische Komitat im 17. Jahrhundert: Verfechter der Ständerechte oder Ausführungsorgan zentraler Anweisungen?," in *Die Habsburgermonarchie 1620 bis 1740: Leistungen und Grenzen des Absolutismusparadigmas*, ed. Petr Maťa, and Thomas Winkelbauer (Stuttgart: Franz Steiner, 2006), 401–441.

5. Ferenc Szakály, *Parasztvármegyék a XVII. és XVIII. században* [Peasant counties in the seventeenth and eighteenth centuries] (Budapest: Akadémiai Kiadó, 1969).

Fig. 34. Austrian cameralist Johann Joachim Becher (1635–1682). Engraving by Wolfgang Kilian, 1675 (private collection of Géza Pálffy, Budapest).

6

ECONOMIC DECLINE AND REORGANIZATION

In the seventeenth century, as in other centuries, the potential for economic development was essentially determined by the political and economic circumstances in Europe, and by the military situation in Hungary. After 1526, despite the dismemberment of the country and sultan's great campaigns, these circumstances allowed for relatively consistent economic growth, and after the Treaty of Edirne in 1568 for a period of greater affluence (see part 1, chap. 7), but they would be less favorable for the progress of an economic framework partially crippled by the Long Turkish War (see part 1, chap. 11). Yet after the upswing of the sixteenth century, there is nevertheless no cause for speaking of a speedy economic downturn or of the "destruction of the Hungarian merchants," as Hungarian economic history had done for so long.[1] The economy of the century after 1606 would more faithfully be characterized by a crash coming after a brief revival, then a gradual decline, culminating in a series of reorganizations resulting from the actions of interest groups responding in various ways to crisis phenomena.

The peace brought by the treaties of Vienna and of Zsitvatorok in 1606 must have brought hope to those involved in economic activity that the boom enjoyed before 1591 would now return. Such confidence was not ungrounded. Commercial ties had begun to be reestablished from 1610 onward; meanwhile, Vienna represented a certain market, mines were less affected by military strikes, and peace would be constant until 1619. It was a sign of this consolidation that from 1607 the annual income from the thirtieth customs levy grew both in Western and in Upper Hungary. The records from 1615–1617 of the water customs at Petronell in Lower Austria and of the road customs at Maria Ellend (near the Hungarian border) show the same rate of exchange of goods as during the best times in the previous century. Neither were the traders of Debrecen, Kolozsvár, and Várad restricted in their economic ties to the Habsburg Monarchy by the Transylvanian princes' anti-Habsburg military campaigns into Hungary. Indeed, even during the wars of the 1620s, they made most of their purchases of manufactured goods directly in Vienna.

All this coincided with the interests of the great merchant bankers with prestigious stockpiles in the imperial city (e.g., the Henckel, Pietsch, and Wolfart families from Vienna; the Probst, Ernst, and Pilgram families from Nuremberg; the Österreicher family from Augsburg; the Zollikofer family from Sankt Gallen; and the Italian Pestaluzzi, Joanelli, and Negroni families). For this reason, in the autumn of 1615, they combined to encourage the upkeep of the old commercial ties, based as they were on the invaluable role of Hungarians from the kingdom, from Ottoman Hungary, and from Transylvania in exchanging goods as far as Vienna. The most profitable (if by this period partially flooded) copsper mines along the Garam River were also rented by members of this interest group, namely the Henckel and Paler families until 1612, the Rehlingens of Augsburg (related to the latter) and the Henckels until the 1620s, and later the Joanelli family, suppliers to the Habsburg court. The continued enormous economic significance of these mines is well displayed by the fact that in 1626/27, in Hamburg, one of the key points of sale for copper from Besztercebánya, 3,830 *mázsa* (similar to hundredweight), or around 200 tons of copper was sold, around half of which was transported further to Amsterdam. But the exports to Spain remained also very significant.

Yet the fleeting revival of the 1610s and 1620s would soon come to a standstill, followed by decline. This was primarily thanks to the crippling of Central Europe's formerly blooming economic relationships and to the permanent military footing Hungary was on. The Thirty Years' War that erupted in 1618 would within a decade generate uncertainty in the Austrian, German, and Bohemian lands. As the series of battles did not spare the key trading centers for Hungarian livestock (the southern German cities), their population, economic strength, and thus their purchasing market constantly decreased. The fate of Augsburg is a good example of the altered economic circumstances of the Holy Roman Empire as a whole by the middle of the seventeenth century. Huge special taxes had repeatedly been levied on the town, some eight thousand of its citizens fled measures taken against Protestants, and it was under Swedish occupation for three years from April 1632. All in all, it lost more than half of its former population of forty-eight thousand. Although the state of war, arson, famine, and plague mostly affected military routes and the repeatedly besieged towns, the population in the whole of the Old Empire fell by some 15–20 percent, and its economy and purchasing power were drastically weakened, while conditions for trade also became uncertain. The situation was worsened by general indebtedness, while the consumption of meat among the German burghers and peasants became limited to feasts. Similar circumstances held in the lands of the Bohemian Crown; in the first half of the century, even the population of Italy, less affected by the wars, declined.

In summary, while in the sixteenth century Hungary's economic development had been greatly assisted by the sharp increase in the population of Austrian, German, Bohemian, and Italian territories and by the agricultural boom and the price revolution (see part 1, chap. 7), the Thirty Years' War brought trends antithetical to these. The agricultural boom and the price revolution evaporated, while the war conditions in Germany placed what commercial ties remained under ever-greater strain. Alongside plummeting cereal prices, the value of cattle also declined from the 1620s, assisted by ever-cheaper cows being bred in Schleswig-Holstein and Denmark.

In addition to international trends, the war conditions in Hungary played a key role in this economic collapse (see fig. 35). Of course, this negative impact was felt not immediately but only after some decades. The campaigns of the Transylvanian princes and declining conditions of public life made trade harder and more expensive and did nothing to help investment in mines, while the impoverishment of society weakened its purchasing power. Furthermore, Hungarian society faced much greater burdens after the drying up of foreign assistance (primarily from the Holy Roman Empire) formerly given for frontier defense against the Ottomans. The increasingly prosperous nobility, however, strove to pass these

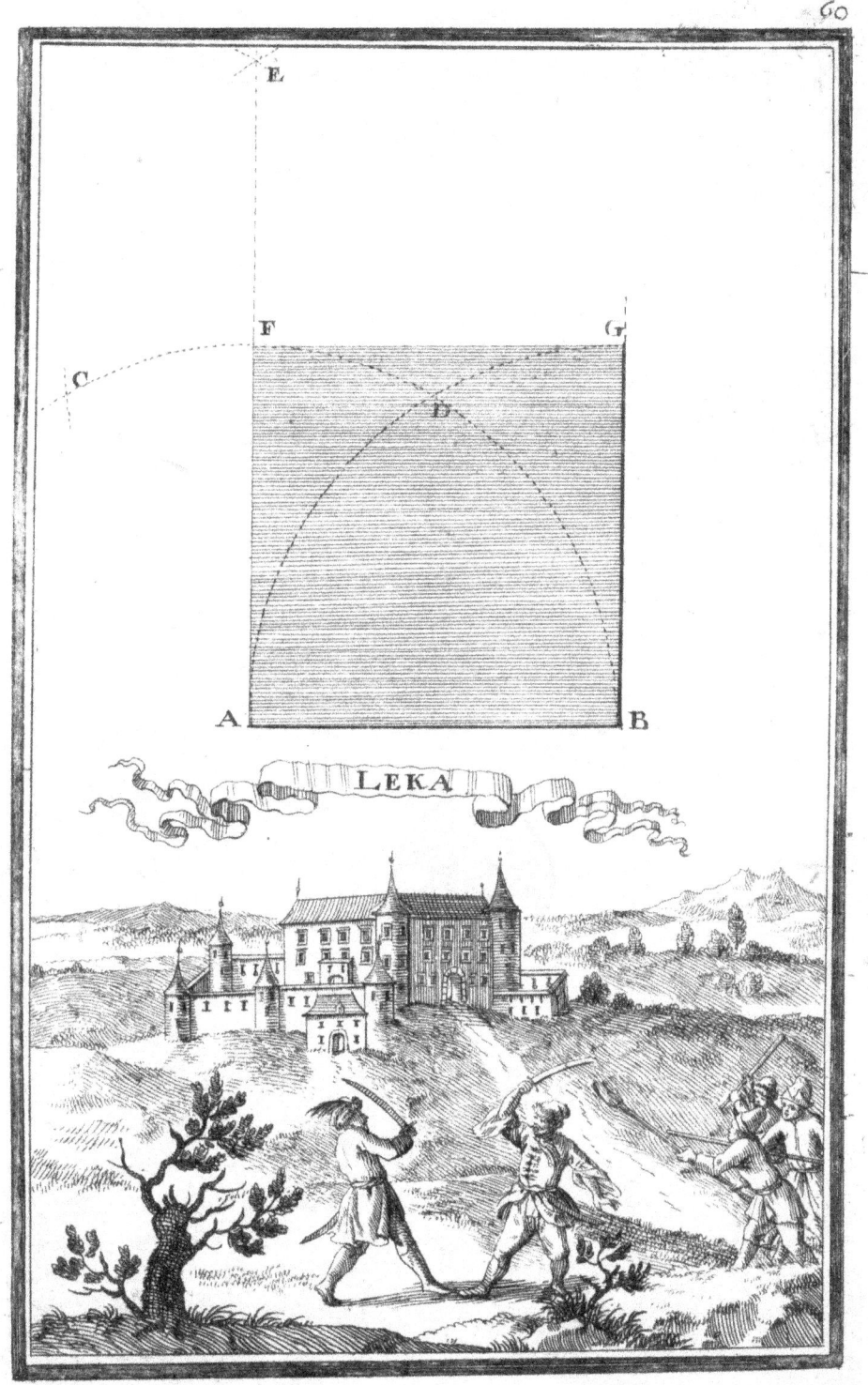

Fig. 35. Hungarian soldiers in front of Léka Castle (today Lockenhaus, Austria). Etching by Justus van der Nypoort, 1686 (Hungarian National Museum, Budapest).

burdens on to the ever-poorer peasantry, to the free royal cities, and to the merchants of Hungary. While the latter were burdened by the so-called half-thirtieth tax levied by the Hungarian estates from 1635 onward to pay for the border fortresses, the diets also turned the temporary tax on the cities into a permanent and increasingly significant levy. The city of Kassa, for example, still known as an important lender in the sixteenth century, would thereby run up ever more serious debts and ultimately have to take loans itself.

From the 1650s onward, the accommodation of regular German regiments would bring with it further taxes and levies, while the growing number of free military elements would destroy agricultural resources on a daily basis. This destruction spread to Transylvania after 1658, while the Ottomans' renewed campaigns in the 1660s (especially in Várad and Érsekújvár) also inflicted terrible economic damage. Neither was the progress of the economy helped by the creation of the privileged military bases or by "noble inflation." The number of taxpayers kept falling, while increasing numbers tried to use their privileges to share the declining benefits reaped from the economy. Dániel Rauch, head thirtieth-tax collector for Slavonia, observed in 1655 that all of the trading peasants and burghers were "attempting to acquire charters of ennoblement, particularly with a view to avoiding customs and the thirtieth tax."[2]

For all these crisis attributes, Hungary remained part of Central Europe's economic lifeblood, if to a smaller degree. Even if the estimated export of livestock may have fallen by some tens of thousands, the Hungarian territories continued to be the breadbasket of Vienna and of the Austrian, Bavarian, and North Italian provinces. In the summer of 1649, Miklós Turós, vice captain of Kiskomárom fortress, had reason to brag to his superior, captain general Ádám Batthyány, that "we know what kind of livestock is needed by the Italians and by the Bavarians, as it is twenty-five years since I first sold beef to Bavarians."[3] Even during the great conflict of 1663–1664, beef exports were not in any terminal crisis, as they continued to provide the lion's share of customs income in Győr, in Magyaróvár, and at nearby offices for the thirtieth tax. Of particular significance was the supply of Vienna and the Habsburg court with beef, lamb, pork, smoked meats, poultry, fish, cereals, wine, honey, and leather. Thanks to the continued growth of wine production in Hegyalja, wine exports to Poland were also considerable.

All in all, the unfavorable Hungarian and international factors eventually led to a series of economic transformations. Yet this did nothing to question the role of the Hungarian merchants necessary for the operation of long-distance commerce any more than it questioned the role played by Hungarian magnates in border defense. Thus, this was not about the exclusion of Hungarian merchants, as that would have presumed that foreign traders would come across to the Great Plain themselves to collect cattle, through parts of the country with everyday dangers, which in the sixteenth century they had still not been willing to do. The change effectively consisted of increasing numbers trying to take their cut of the trade, which was still the success story of the economy. For this reason, it was not the economy's direction or the composition of its goods that changed but rather, as a result of the competition between various interest groups, the form of its management, its techniques, and the distribution of its profits. While the price of Hungarian cattle on the Austrian and German market declined, in Hungary it rose, and so the margin between the purchase price and selling price, and thereby the profit margin, constantly fell.

This increase in price was in part a sign of the economy's realignment. The customs revenue so important to the court and merchants' income had declined as a result of breeding difficulties caused by hard winters, great floods, a bad fodder harvest, and regular animal disease. Moreover, from the 1620s to the 1660s, declining civilian conditions meant that everyone wished to earn their part of income that was dependable. This was particularly true of the flourishing, privileged parts of society: frontier soldiers, the aristocracy, and the gentry, as well as noble burghers. During the great European war, frontier soldiers across the country, able to attain "neither money nor cloth," became increasingly active in the livestock trade in order to complement their income. As thirtieth-tax collector Rauch noted in 1655, just as aptly, "they are soldiers, and demand freedom for themselves"—that is, they demanded exemption from customs levies.[4]

Furthermore, the frontier soldiers were in league with the aristocrats filling the posts of captains general, especially the Batthyány and Zrínyi families, who supported the soldiers in their movement of animals, as they could demand protection money from the traders in return for the security they provided. The Batthyánys could herd animals through their lands in Vas county, mostly to Vienna, Lower Austria, and Styria; the Zrínyis could do the same across their estates in Muraköz (Međimurje) and through Carniola and the Istrian peninsula to Venice, thus completely avoiding customs on their own territory. From their Adriatic port at Buccari, the Zrínyis conducted significant trade in salt, wood, and iron with the city-state. The increased activity of enterprising frontier soldiers and high nobles greatly reduced the profits of civilian and peasant commerce.

Similar processes were brought into being when the commercial activity of merchants, gentry, and peasants was often restricted on the estates of the high nobles, either by the raising of new customs or with violence. The introduction of new levies was an almost universal phenomenon, thanks to which costs further increased. Indeed, in the second half of the century, the large landowners of Western Hungary (e.g., Ferenc Nádasdy, Pál Esterházy, and Ferenc Kéry) and the top German officers at the fortress city of Győr increasingly often took Jewish traders under their wing, who, in return for the loans they gave, received various levels of privilege from the Aulic Chamber and who, thanks to their connections to the Jews at the Habsburg court and in Buda, had increasingly significant economic clout. The captains general of Komárom did the same with the Greek and Serbian traders who had settled in the town and who also had profitable connections in Ottoman Hungary.

In Transylvania and the Partium, it was in this period that the associations for so-called Greek (in fact Serbian, Greek, Armenian, Dalmatian, Bulgarian, and Albanian—i.e., non-Muslim) traders (e.g., the *Compania Graeca* based in Brassó and Nagyszeben) received privileges. Of course, the Hungarian and Saxon merchants had a close relationship with them. While the Jews and Serbs in the kingdom dealt in goods from the west, the Greeks and Armenians brought manufactured goods and luxury items from the Levant to Hungary and Transylvania, and from there on to the Habsburg Monarchy or the Ottoman Empire.

Alongside the magnates, the nobles residing near the border and even the aforementioned armalists (a poor part of the gentry) and noble burghers of market towns wanted to avail themselves of the tax exemptions concomitant with noble privilege. Although in principle this applied only to goods grown on one's own lands and purchased for domestic needs, the impossibility of verifying this led to widespread abuse of the system. The whole situation that emerged was described in 1668 by the customs inspector of Wiener Neustadt: "Whether with letters of exemption or without, the magnates and nobles take huge quantities of food, cereal, honey, pork, bacon, poultry and other items to the town [viz. Wiener Neustadt], to the weekly market, returning with all kinds of goods, carrying great amounts of wood material, without paying any thirtieth tax."[5] This customs-free trade was accompanied by the establishment of new, illegal trade routes of various sizes near the main ones. In the course of the century, the chambers were thus repeatedly forced to establish new branches (Latin *filiale*) of the larger customs centers in new locations. Another considerable challenge was the growth in smuggling, in which the nobility played the leading role, alongside the frontier soldiers.

All of these changes had an effect on agricultural production. As they had joined the trade in cereals and other crops, the magnates (the Batthyány, Esterházy, Nádasdy, and Zrínyi families in the west and the Thököly, Rákóczi, and Wesselényi ones in the east) strove to increase the size of the worked land on their estates, to produce as much grain as they could or to create new grazing land out of clearings and barren land. The growth in grain production meant more forced work for serfs; indeed, their taxes were increasingly demanded in kind, as produce, partly to feed burgeoning private armies and staff, and partly to allow involvement in local commerce. This led to the odd state of affairs in which serfs had to buy back the wine they themselves had produced and submitted as tax in kind at a higher price at the local taverns.

The victims of all these processes were primarily the burgher and peasant traders, as well as the increasingly impoverished social groups living near the frontier lands. A clear sign of the dwindling purchasing power and falling living standards of the lowest social classes was the increasing presence in the still significant import of textiles and manufactured goods of cheaper goods of middling or lower quality from Thuringia, Silesia, and Moravia. The only exceptions to this were the more sheltered and urban western areas of the country (Sopron, Kismarton, Ruszt, Pozsony, and the surrounding areas), for which Vienna presented an almost insatiable market. The wine-producing regions (particularly the market towns in Tokaj-Hegyalja: Szerencs, Tokaj, Tállya, Mád, Tolcsva, Tarcal, Sárospatak, and Sátoraljaújhely) were also in a more favorable position, as the price of wine remained stable throughout the century.

From the 1620s the court at Vienna played an increasingly active role in the process of economic reorganization. There were a number of reasons for this. The most pressing was that the supply of meat to the imperial city and to the court had to be ensured at any cost. This was at least as important a consideration as that of the defense of the Kingdom of Hungary's border against the Ottomans. Custom-free noble commerce and large-scale smuggling had seen customs revenue decrease drastically, however, and both the Aulic Chamber and the Hungarian Chamber, constantly obliged to take loans, sought more secure sources of income. In Vienna they also wished to make circular commerce, which in the sixteenth century had passed through far fewer hands and routes, simpler and more transparent again. The Austrian and Italian merchant bankers who had a special interest in this nevertheless had to face the fact that the nobles and frontier soldiers, who knew the conditions in Hungary extremely well and made use of the wartime circumstances and their privileges, would make this less and less likely. With their profits falling from having to be shared among so many, the large-scale traders attempted, first individually and then by forming associations, to gain preemptive rights (monopolies) for certain goods and areas from their rulers in return for loans and a given profit share. That is, to ensure the supply to the central areas of the monarchy and to guarantee its income, the debt-laden treasury allied itself with the monarchy's economic elite in the competitive struggle in Hungary. While this was not directly aimed against the Hungarian merchants, without whom the system would have been unworkable, there is no doubt that many of them in time became the victims of this new practice.

The preemptive right meant that the price previously dictated by the market was replaced by a set purchase price—that is, the big traders could have access to livestock at a restricted price. For example, in 1626 Matthia Guallandro was given an exclusive right to drive cattle to Italy (a so-called *apaldo*); in 1622 traders from Southern Germany and Austria set up their first association, the Landsverlegerische Viehkompanie. With this they acquired the privilege for exporting beef and leather to Vienna and Austria. Although this attempt would ultimately fall foul of resistance from the German imperial cities, from the Hungarian Chamber, and from the nobility, the activity of the individually privileged traders from Austria and Northern Italy was a success for many decades, as it ensured the continuous supply of meat to the Austrian and Italian territories.

In the 1650s and 1660s, as the trade conducted by the nobility and the frontier soldiers further grew, the imperial grand traders tried again. The company Kaiserliche Ochsenhandlung, founded in 1651, would nevertheless be only a temporary phenomenon. The so-called first Orientalische Handelskompanie, created in 1667 for the exclusive export of beef and for the import of iron and cloth, survived right through to 1683. The further worsening of public conditions, the regular armies driven through Hungary, and the supply of Vienna all made the company indispensable. But its success was also assisted by the mercantilist-protectionist economic policy devised by the so-called cameralists (Johann Joachim Becher, Philipp Wilhelm Hörnigk, and Wilhelm von Schröder) (see fig. 34).

Contrary to the popularly held view, this company did not squeeze out the Hungarian merchants. In Győr, to take but one example, it entered into a contract with the nobility of the noble county; elsewhere it did so with the merchants. Thus, the greatest problems for the merchants were caused not by commercial ties being broken but rather by the low price set, as well as those factors—further declining public conditions and occasional natural disasters—that the privileged nobility and groups courting ever-greater favor (German and Italian large traders, Jews, Serbs, Greeks, etc.) had no interest in. As a result of all this, their profits became ever leaner, and from the 1660s many were forced to stop their commercial enterprises. Except the most prosperous in their ranks, their place would by the first third of the eighteenth century be taken by the large foreign enterprises that formed a special alliance with the political elite of the Holy Roman Empire and Hungary and gained monopoly positions. After this, the peasant-burgher class would retain significant positions mostly only in local breeding and production and in trade limited to local markets.

These developments were only reinforced by the advent of the Long Turkish War in 1683 (see part 2, chap. 10). To pursue its military campaigns, the Habsburg court was in need of enormous loans, as well as the continuous supply of weapons and an at least partially satisfactory supply of provisions to its tens of thousands of troops. These could not be provided by Hungarian merchants, whose capital was limited and who were further impoverished by the terrible devastation that war brought. This required large enterprises: rich in capital, credit worthy, and with extensive economic connections throughout Europe. Occasionally, however, a few ambitious citizens from market towns (e.g., the Gindly and Fördős families from Győr) could avail themselves of the opportunities and become suppliers to the capitalist giants.

The most successful military supplier of the period, awarded the titles *Oberhoffaktor* and *Oberkriegsfaktor*, was the "court Jew" (German *Hofjude*) Samuel Oppenheimer. Using his monopoly position, he became the largest supplier of army provisions, weapons, and ammunition both to the Hungarian theater of war against the Ottomans and to the western one against the French, while loans he provided would on more than one occasion save the treasury in Vienna from complete collapse. Indeed, by the end of the century, Oppenheimer's companies also controlled trade in copper and mercury in the Holy Roman Empire and the trade in salt in Hungary and Transylvania.

Thus, while without Oppenheimer and his capital-rich peers (Lazarus Hierschel, Simon Michael, Samson Wertheimer, etc.) Hungary could never have been liberated from the Ottomans, the reorganization of the economy and the destruction wrought by war would, by the end of the century, reach such a level as to make it impossible for the class of Hungarian burgher and peasant traders to emerge from the "century of decay." In the sixteenth century, by ensuring the exchange of goods between Vienna and Ottoman Hungary, this class had been partly responsible for keeping Hungarian trade in the European economic system, but they would then become victims of the very liberation the country had so long wished for. The same was true of the large part of the free royal cities, for they, too, greeted the new century in debt, exhausted, and with decreased populations. Although the reorganization that lasted for a good five decades from the middle of the seventeenth century did not completely uproot the Hungarian economy from that of Central Europe, during many decades of wartime conditions and civil war it fell even further behind the areas of the Habsburg Monarchy that had been allowed to develop in peace from 1648 onward.

Notes

1. In particular, under the influence of a work by Sándor Takáts entitled "A magyar tőzsérek és kereskedők pusztulása" [The ruination of Hungarian merchants and traders], in *Szegény magyarok* [Wretched Hungarians] (Budapest: Genius Kiadás, 1927), 129–247.

2. "Rauch Dániel szlavóniai főharmicados jelentései a vámokról, 1655" [Reports of Dániel Rauch, head thirtieth tax-collector for Slavonia, on customs levies], *Magyar Gazdaságtörténeti Szemle* [Hungarian economic history review] 5 (1898): 577.

3. MNL OL, Budapest, P 1314, A herceg Batthyány család levéltára [Archives of the family of Prince Batthyány], Missiles no. 50293.

4. "Rauch Dániel szlavóniai főharmicados jelentései," 577.

5. Lajos Gecsényi, "Nyugat-Magyarország kereskedelmi viszonyai egy harmincadvizsgálat tükrében (1668)" [Commercial relations in western Hungary as reflected in a thirtieth tax report (1668)], *Győri Tanulmányok* [Studies on the history of Győr] 16 (1995): 64.

Fig. 36. Romanian peasants. Watercolor by Franz Neuhaser, circa 1800 (Hungarian National Museum, Budapest).

7

HUNGARIAN POPULATIONS FALL—OTHER ETHNIC GROUPS RISE

The development of the demographic and ethnic makeup of Hungary in the seventeenth century was determined by the same constant war and civil war conditions that had led to large-scale social decline and the reorganization of the economy. The devastating effects of military campaigns (arson, famine, disease, decline in public conditions, and poverty) only reinforced the trends of the preceding century (see part 1, chap. 8). While in a social sense the greatest victim of this decline was the poorest stratum of society, in an ethnic sense it was primarily the Hungarian-speaking population that suffered.

In the seventeenth century, too, we have to rely on estimates when ascertaining the size of the population: even the tax records that cover a large part of society survive only partially and for different periods, meaning that this data can be used only with considerable caution. Thus, there can be variances of many hundreds of thousands between different estimates. Yet more recent research is nevertheless rather consistent in placing the population of historical Hungary at the start of the eighteenth century at around 3.8–4 million, on the basis of national contributions records from 1715 and 1720.[1] Relative to the 3.5–3.7 million level estimated for the period around 1600, this represents a modest increase of a little less than 10 percent, similar to that seen in the Austrian, German, and Polish territories, those most affected by wars. Given the significant newer waves of immigration presented in this chapter, however, it is more correct to speak of population stagnation.

Thus, the theory of a population decline of 1–1.5 million over the whole of the sixteenth and seventeenth centuries, as held by early twentieth-century historiography, does not hold weight. Yet the maximum growth of 20 percent from the end of medieval times (3.3 million) to the start of the eighteenth century (3.8–4.0 million) includes a significant amount of immigration. Thus, real population growth fell far behind the figures as high as 50–90 percent seen in the European regions developing in more peaceful circumstances in this period (Scandinavia, Britain, and the more sheltered Swiss and German territories). There also continued to be great differences in population density depending on the region. At the start of the eighteenth century in the Kingdom of Hungary, for example, there were often two, three, or even five or six times as many people living per square kilometer as in certain parts of the liberated Ottoman Hungary.

The modest increase in population in the Carpathian Basin in the seventeenth century was merely the appearance of growth. Although population growth slowed all over the continent during the century referred to as the Little Ice Age, what might otherwise have been a 20–30 percent increase was depleted by constant warfare and the damage it wrought. Particularly harmful was the period on a constant war footing from 1660 to 1711, including the Long Turkish War (1683–1699), which mobilized tens of thousands of men (see part 2, chap. 10). Transylvania, meanwhile, was unable even by the early eighteenth century to fully recover from the Turkish-Tatar devastation of 1658–1660 (see part 2, chap. 4). By 1660, as we have seen, tens of thousands of men found themselves forced to the periphery of society in Hungary, who would then be the first to fall foul of the famine and the nationwide plague epidemics that war brought with it, especially in the first half of the 1660s, then in 1676–1679 and 1690–1691, and finally in 1708–1712. In the most intensely affected areas, rejuvenation would be possible only after many long decades.

In this century, too, wars and their consequences, as well as the everyday destruction wrought by gangs of thieves, mostly affected the areas around the larger rivers and more important thoroughfares, as well as the Hungarian population, living as it did in richer agricultural lands. The Long Turkish War at the end of the century also brought enormous losses of life to the Serbian population. Looked at overall, it was the Hungarian population that was most affected by the loss of population in absolute terms, while there was continuous immigration of Romanians into Transylvania (see fig. 36) and the Partium, and of South Slavs into the territory of Ottoman Hungary. A more significant migration of Romanians was noted by Zacharias Geizkofler, the imperial master of payments (German *Reichspfennigmeister*) as early as 1602: "There were few Romanian villages in Transylvania previously, but now they have spread widely in the hills, as, in contrast to the destruction of the flatlands, the uplands have become built up."[2] Meanwhile, the Serbian emigration to the north was summarized in a report to Palatine Miklós Esterházy of 1629 as follows: "Before the approach of Sinan Pasha [1593] and the siege of Eger [1596] the Rascian population between the Tisza and the Danube stretched from Titel right across to Jánoshalma, Szeged and Kiskunhalas. . . . Before the arrival of Sinan Pasha, in Transdanubia there were few or no Rascians except in Mohács, Szekszárd, Baranya and Somogy counties; they were all Hungarians."[3] But this was only the start of these processes; both the Romanians and Serbs would make real inroads only in the half century after 1658.

After the ravaging of Transylvania in the early seventeenth century and particularly the Turkish-Tatar devastation of 1658–1660, it was in the interests of the Hungarian landowners to return every last ruined piece of land to active agricultural use. In order to revive production, they relocated ever-larger groups from the already Romanian population of the uplands (the valleys of the Southern Carpathians, Fogaras land, the Hátszeg area, and Máramaros county)—a population that had begun to trickle down of its own accord—to the desolate areas formerly populated by Hungarians (e.g., the Mezőség). The Romanians, mostly working as shepherds, were given temporary tax exemptions; they were usually granted lower-quality parts of land that were harder to work. Despite having to make ends meet in harsher conditions, the everyday life of part of the Romanian population was transformed, though large swathes of it still lived as seminomadic livestock breeders. In addition to this organized immigration, the more favorable opportunities in Transylvania relative to the less secure political and economic conditions in Wallachia and Moldavia also encouraged voluntary migration. The two Romanian voivodeships, that is, represented a limitless source of reserves for the Romanian population of Transylvania.

The new immigrants were hardly touched by assimilation: their Orthodox faith and different way of life meant that they did not usually blend into the neighboring Hungarian, Saxon, or Szekler ethnic groups. The only exception to this was that some of the Romanians converted to Protestantism in Hunyad county. And as the Romanians were not an estate nation in their own right, their leaders responsible for the relocations (especially in Hunyad, Máramaros, and Bihar counties), after acquiring goods and estates for their services, soon joined the Hungarian nobility (e.g., the Kendeffy and Macskássi families), leaving the masses to the fate of serfdom. But princely authority intervened in their lives only when, from the 1620s onward, it attempted to force the nomadic peasants to move into feudal plots and to pay taxes. In the second half of the sixteenth century, indeed, the Catholic prince Stephen Báthory even established a bishopric for them, and his successors would continue to pay great attention to their church life. Thus, it should be emphasized that the continuous growth of the Romanian population generated almost no problems for the Transylvanian principality. And while the great military campaigns and worsening tax burdens during the Long Turkish War at the turn of the seventeenth century meant less emigration to the Romanian voivodeships, overall, by the early eighteenth century, both in Transylvania and in its antechamber of the Partium, the development of a largely connected strip inhabited by Romanians had continued apace.

In 1629 Palatine Esterházy must have sensed that even more radical changes were taking place in the southern parts of Ottoman Hungary. The growth of the South Slav population, which had begun in the late Middle Ages and was still evident after 1526, continued into the seventeenth century. Yet it was only with the second Long Turkish War at the end of the century that more fundamental change occurred (see part 2, chap. 11). Although the repulsion of the Ottomans meant that considerable numbers of Serbs left the country, a good number of them entered into an alliance with the generals of Emperor Leopold I, then participated in the occupation of Belgrade in 1688 and of further territories in northern Serbia and western Bulgaria in the years that followed. But in autumn 1690, the grand vizier's armies retook Belgrade, together with the rest of Serbia, and so those Serbs who had joined the imperial forces fled to Hungary to avoid Ottoman reprisals. Although we are not aware of the exact numbers, tens of thousands moved to Hungary, led by Arsenije III Čarnojević, patriarch of Peć (today Peja, Kosovo) and head of the Serbian national church. In the 1690s Leopold I would repay their loyalty with three charters of privilege (in 1690, 1691, and 1695). These ensured their freedom of religion and the election of their own leaders and even exempted a good part of the Serbian population from the jurisdiction of the noble counties and Hungarian magnates.

Some of the Serbs led by Čarnojević found their new home in Hungary's interior, in Szentendre, Izbég, Pomáz, and Budakalász, as well as boosting the existing Serbian population of the Tabán and Víziváros (Water Town) districts of Buda. In return for the privileges previously granted to the aforementioned Slavonian Vlachs, the greater masses of Serbs were given the opportunity to serve in the Sava, Danube, Tisza, and Maros districts of the Military Border (German *Militärgrenze*, Serbian *vojna krajina*)—that is, the new defense system against the Ottomans that gradually expanded from the 1690s onward. The Serbian peasant soldiers serving in guardhouses known as *čardaks* became the defining element of the new border defense system. Their duties complemented the activities of the German regular divisions of the great border fortresses. And as Hungarian frontier soldiers were not keen to serve in these unknown and considerably ravaged southern territories that were under separate military jurisdiction of the Aulic War Council in Vienna, the role of the Serbs in the employ of the imperial and royal army in protecting the frontier would become invaluable.

All of these processes fundamentally transformed the ethnic map of Hungary's southern regions. Although the German settlement of the eighteenth century would later form considerable German blocs in these areas, overall, the Serbs and Serbianized Vlachs would form the majority in the territory between the Danube and Tisza Rivers. Meanwhile, their presence also became dominant in southern Transdanubia, in Tolna and Fejér counties, to some degree in Somogy county, and in Szentendre. Indeed, as a result of early seventeenth-century immigration, the Serbian population of Győr and Komárom remained significant, although it would, with time, become more Magyarized. Thus, by the end of the seventeenth century the fundament of Ottoman Hungary had become an area of irreversibly South Slav ethnicity. The contemporary sources rightly refer to it as *Rascia* (Hungarian *Rácország*), which now encompassed a growing part of the southern area of maps of Hungary. The changes brought by the Ottoman invasion meant that these territories lost their Hungarian populations. In fact, the area mostly populated by Serbs "moved up" north to the former Hungary.

Although Hungarian historiography often regards the South Slavs living in the territory of Ottoman Hungary as being universally Serb, this rough-and-ready picture has been rendered more precise not only by Serbian and Croatian research findings but also by recent Hungarian research into the history of missionary work.[4] While the lion's share of the immigrant South Slav population was indeed made up of Serbs and Vlachs of Orthodox faith, tens of thousands of Catholic Bosnians also arrived, together with smaller numbers of Croats and Roma people. The main homogenous blocks of Bosnians were established first between the Drava and Sava, in the eastern parts of the erstwhile Pozsega county and in Valkó, and then in the vicinity of Pécs city. At the turn of the seventeenth century, the Bosnians, continuously replenished by further immigration, also settled in the Bácska region (e.g., in Bács, Baja, Jánoshalma, Zombor, and Szabadka). Contemporary sources already refer to these groups as *sokácok* (*Šokci*) and *bunyevácok* (*Bunjevci*). One of their folk traditions, the *Busójárás* of Mohács, is a living testament to their memory.

The increase in the South Slav population was assisted by the army enforcing the Ottoman system and the civil population arriving with it. Most of these almost one hundred thousand people would not be fully fledged Turks but rather South Slavs, especially Bosnians and Serbs. This is revealed by the latest research findings about the ethnic makeup of the fortress army of the Buda vilayet.[5] These findings show that from the outset more than 90 percent of those serving in the castles in the Hungarian theater of war were from Bosnia, Macedonia, and Serbia. From the 1550s this proportion rose even further. By this time, the fortress soldiery was replenished almost exclusively from Bosnia, Herzegovina, Northern Serbia, and the area between the Drava and the Sava. While those from Bosnia and Herzegovina were mostly Muslim and thus brought their Balkan Muslim customs with them, the

Serb and the Vlach soldiers who mixed with them would preserve their Orthodox customs in Hungary.

The most influential military and administrative echelons of the Hungarian society created by the Ottomans, the beylerbeys and *sanjak-beys*, the officials of varying importance, and the leaders of religious life (imams and various monks), were also mostly from the Balkans. The traders and craftsmen living in the cities with more significant burgher populations (such as Buda, Pécs, Belgrade, Temesvár, and Bács) also originated from the Balkans or in part from Ragusa in Dalmatia. This is borne out by the large amount of ceramics uncovered by archeological digs that were of Balkan style, made on a handwheel and baked until dark gray or black. A good part of the Ottoman and Turkish loan words in Hungarian entered it via Slavic languages. Indeed, a Turkish language book written in Hungary in 1668 claimed that those living there spoke a Bosnian dialect of Turkish. So, in fact, life in the Ottoman border fortresses and the larger towns was not so much a Turkish world as a Bosnian and Serbian one. The songs sung in Ottoman Hungary may have been heard in Bosnian or Serbian. The famous Turkish traveler Evliya Çelebi (1611–1684) had reason to state in the 1660s that "the entire population of Buda is Bosnian from Bosnia."[6] (See fig. 37.)

For all this, in both centuries, in the elite intellectual laboratories (djamis, schools, and monasteries) of certain centers of vilayets and sanjaks (Buda, Temesvár, Eger, Pécs, etc.), the best-known poets of the Ottoman Empire appeared for a certain amount of time. Their poems, however, were written in a specially crafted version of the Ottoman language, full of Persian and Arab expressions and with its own grammar, that was incomprehensible to the majority of ordinary soldiers.

Unlike in the case of the Serbs, the settlement of Croatians in Hungary in the seventeenth century was not significant. An important change nevertheless took place south of the Drava. Within the space of a century, as it moved northward, the Croatian nobility took over the administration of Slavonia (Zagreb, Körös, and Varasd counties), a region that in the Middle Ages had always belonged to the Kingdom of Hungary but that had a majority Croatian and only minority Hungarian population. The nobility did so with exceptional ability to integrate and with great success. This process would ultimately lead to the gradual unification of Croatia and Slavonia. With the formerly coastal kingdom of Croatia being almost completely occupied by the Ottomans, Croatia, so to speak, slid up northward to Slavonia. In 1643 this unusual unification of territories caused by the Ottoman occupation was summarized in a pithy Latin epigram by János Szakmárdy (Croatian Ivan Zakmardi), Croatian-Slavonian protonotary and later Hungarian royal Personal: "*Illa ego Sclavonia, ac iam dicta Croatia tellus*" ("This is the territory of Slavonia, which they now call Croatia").[7]

A good sign of the merging of the Croatian and Slavonian territories was the fact that from 1557, the Croatian and Slavonian estates almost always held common assemblies (*sabor*). The noble society of Croatia and Slavonia, which formerly had distinct customs, were ever more strongly starting to blend into one. Despite this, the characteristic Hungarian institutions of local administration, the noble counties—which were not present in the territory of coastal Croatia—did not cease to exist. The Croatian nobility fleeing northward saw an excellent opportunity for advance in a structure that had operated effectively and that, thanks to the medieval Hungarian-Croatian union, they were to some degree acquainted

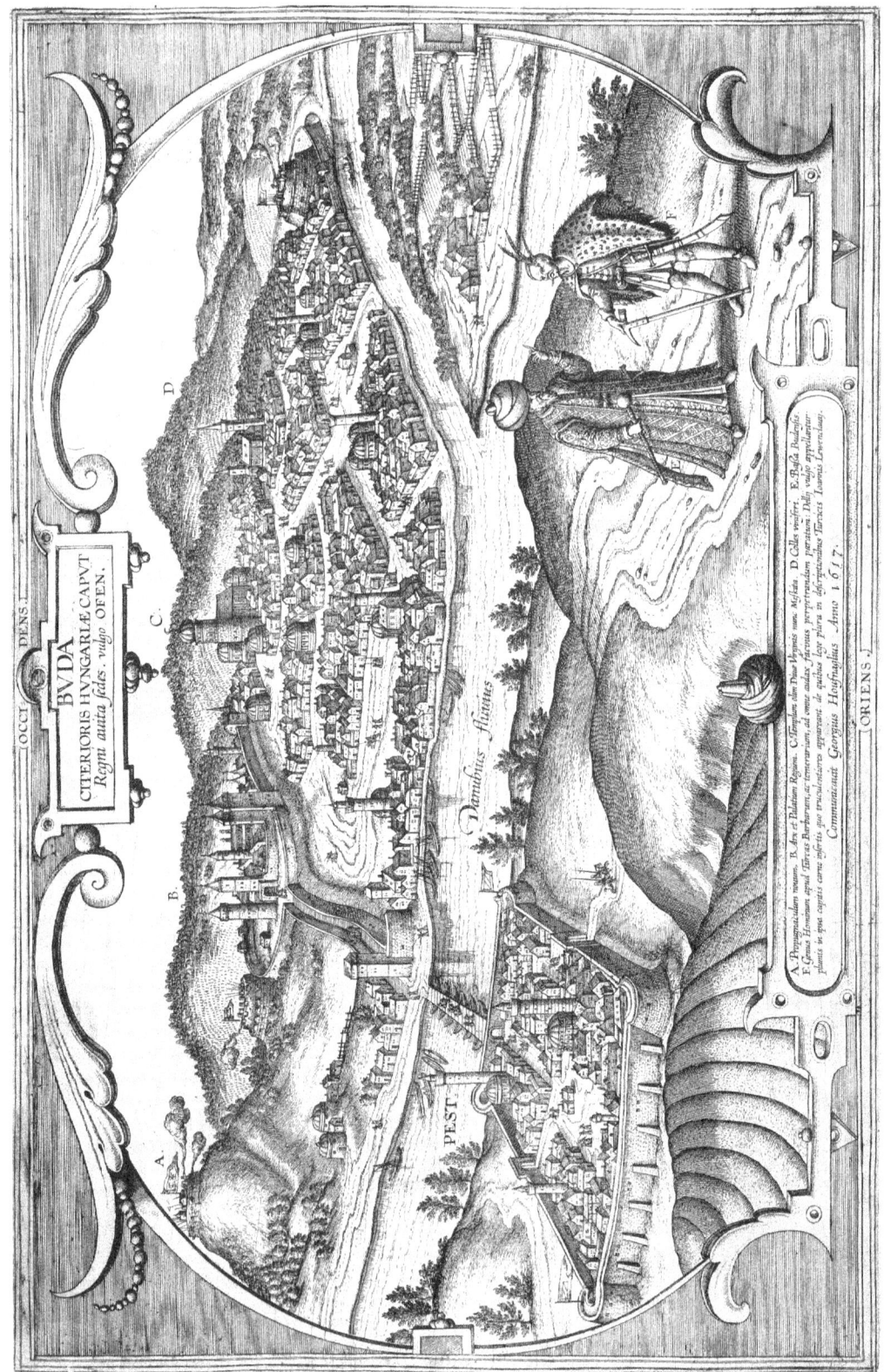

Fig. 37. Ottoman Buda in the seventeenth century. Engraving by Georg Hoefnagel, 1617 (Hungarian National Museum, Budapest).

with. And they were able to make the best of this opportunity. Indeed, after liberation from the Ottomans, eminent Croatians quickly achieved positions in the eastern, formerly Hungarian part of the area between the Drava and Sava—that is, in the former Pozsega, Valkó, and Szerém/Syrmium counties. Then, in the early eighteenth century, these regions were reorganized into new noble counties very different from the medieval ones, under the direction and jurisdiction of the Croatian-Slavonian ban.

All in all, these processes began to circumscribe a region south of the Drava more or less homogeneously inhabited by Croats—that is, the territorial parameters of modern Croatia. This was assisted by the fact that from the mid-seventeenth century growing numbers of the Croatian nobility and the members of Zagreb Chapter became believers in broad political autonomy within the Kingdom of Hungary, in independent Croatian estate representation, and in the beginnings of a program of Croatian-language culture. The leading exponents of this movement were Juraj Ráttkay, canon of Zagreb, and then, at the end of the century, the writer, historian, and publisher Pavao Ritter Vitezović. The camaraderie brought from defense against the great common enemy of the Ottomans, however, forced Croatians and Hungarians still to cooperate closely, even though, despite living together, certain political and ecclesiastical conflicts would emerge in this period. The eighteenth and nineteenth centuries would bring unfortunate negative changes in this regard.

In the case of the Slovaks and Ruthenians living in the northern regions of the Kingdom of Hungary, similar processes had not begun in the seventeenth century, though they were also less affected by the military campaigns than the Hungarian population had been. Although the Slovaks had in part started to descend to the Hungarian areas of the northern Great Plain destroyed during the wars, they would, except a few groups, mostly become Magyarized. The Ruthenians, first Orthodox and then from the middle of the century mostly Greek Catholic, and living in the counties of Máramaros, Ugocsa, Bereg, Ung, Zemplén, Sáros, and Szepes, appeared sporadically along the river valleys in the northeast. Yet it was only later, in the eighteenth century, that all this brought significant reorganization.

Overall, from the end of the Middle Ages to the early eighteenth century, the ethnic map of Hungary changed enormously. The Hungarian population, decreased as a result of war, ended up in a minority alongside the South Slav (Serbian, Vlach, Croatian, and Bosnian) and Romanian population. While at the end of the fifteenth century the native language of some 75–80 percent of the population of the Kingdom of Hungary was Hungarian, the national contributions of 1720 reveal a mere 45–50 percent of the population to be Hungarian. Hungary had irrevocably become a multiethnic, multiconfessional, and multicultural country. In fact, the ethnic boundaries observed at the end of Ottoman rule would essentially persist, with declining Hungarian strength, until the early twentieth century.

In the sixteenth and seventeenth centuries, the coexistence of various ethnicities, natural assimilation, and migration did not yet cause any kind of ethnic tensions. In this period the important divisions were on class lines, not ethnic ones. At this time every resident of Hungary was *Hungarus* (possibly *Pannonicus*), those in the Principality of Transylvania were *Transilvanus*, and those living in the united Croatia and Slavonia were *Croata*, all irrespective of which ethnic group one belonged to, the language one spoke, and indeed whether one spoke Hungarian at all. The continual decline of the Hungarian population, until it came to be in a minority, would nevertheless have enormous significance during the formation of modern nation-states in the nineteenth century. In the long run, this would be one of the longest-lasting consequences of the Ottoman occupation of Hungary and of the great wars fought between the two empires.

Notes

1. Dávid, *Studies in Demographic and Administrative History*, 1–13.
2. József Deér and László Gáldi, eds., *Magyarok és románok* [Hungarians and Romanians], vol. 1 (Budapest: Teleki Intézet, 1943), 513.
3. László Szalay, *Galantai gróf Eszterházy Miklós Magyarország nádora* [Count Miklós Esterházy of Galánta, palatine of Hungary], vol. 3 (Pest: Lauffer Vilmos, 1870), 518–519.
4. Cf. Molnár, *Le Saint-Siège*; Molnár, *Confessionalization on the Frontier*.
5. Klára Hegyi, "Les origines ethniques et la confession des soldats de l'armée turque servant dans les châteaux forts en territoire hongrois (XVIe-XVIIe siècles)," *Histoire, Economie et Société* 34, no. 3 (2015): 54–64; Klára Hegyi, *The Ottoman Military Organization in Hungary: Fortresses, Fortress Garrisons and Finances* (Berlin: Klaus Schwarz, 2018), 235–253.
6. Pál Fodor, ed., *Evlia Cselebi török világutazó magyarországi utazásai 1660–1664* [The journeys to Hungary of the Turkish explorer Evliya Çelebi, 1660–1664], 2nd ed. (Budapest: Gondolat Kiadó, 1985), 288.
7. Juraj Rattkay, *Spomen na kraljeve i banove Kraljevstva Dalmacije, Hrvatske i Slavonije*, ed. Mirko Valentić, 2nd ed. (Zagreb: Hrvatski institut za povigest, 2016), 81.

Fig. 38. Péter Pázmány, archbishop of Esztergom (1616–1637), one of the leaders of the Catholic revival in Hungary. Engraving by Lucas Kilian, circa 1635 (Hungarian National Museum, Budapest).

8

THE REVIVAL OF CATHOLICISM—A PROLONGED WAR OF RELIGION

As in the case of the German lands, the sixteenth century in Hungary can justifiably be seen as "the century of the Reformation" (see part 1, chap. 9). But the seventeenth century would also bring fundamental change to the religious landscape. Reforms affected even the Catholic Church, indeed at the same time as the Reformation, though the first important consequences of this would be seen only in the last third of the sixteenth century, mostly as a result of the Council of Trent (1545–1563). More recent studies in ecclesiastical history consider early modern (Hungarian) Catholicism, like Protestantism, to have been an integral part of confessionalization.[1] By the second half of the seventeenth century, Catholicism was almost as different from the Christian church of the late Middle Ages as Protestant confessions were. We can thus justifiably speak of Catholic reform, even of the "Catholic Reformation."

As with the relationship between the estates and the court (see part 1, chap. 3, and part 2, chap. 3), Hungarian historiography for a long time portrayed the relations between Protestantism and Catholicism as the antithesis between the national and the foreign or between progressive and reactionary interests, but it has since largely dismissed this outdated view. The connection between Protestantism and Catholicism cannot realistically be understood in this national romantic and anachronistic framework prevalent from the nineteenth century. The relations between the two cannot be mapped in any useful way unless we treat them as equals, study their almost constant changes during the early modern period, and investigate how the competition between them was able to lead to the repeatedly exacerbated wars of religion of the seventeenth century.

The essence of Catholic reform, like that of the Reformation, was the announcement of a return to the ways of the ancient church, while in practice it meant the modernization of a church in crisis. Protestantism and the reborn Catholicism made use of almost the same methods: both elaborated the confessions, established new religious and secular institutions to distribute them, and renewed the liturgy. In addition, the church regularly inspected its reformed internal activities, while it kept ever more precise records of its members thanks to the registry books it introduced at about this time. What with the spread of book publishing and literature, it was happy to use its increasingly effective propaganda to achieve this. As Protestants made use of the prince's power in Transylvania, so Catholics used royal authority to achieve their goals and to regain their lost positions in the Kingdom of Hungary.

While the first stage in this Catholic renewal was, as we have seen, the activity of archbishop Miklós Oláh and György Draskovics in the sixteenth century (the first synods, diocese visitations, the foundation of schools, the attempts of the Jesuits to settle, and the first wave of conversions of the high nobles; see part 1, chap. 9), its real achievements came in the decades after 1606.

At first, Catholic reform progressed with peaceful methods. But just as Protestantism was quick to become radicalized (we need only think of iconoclasm), its initial successes and failures drove Catholicism to tougher, more violent means, especially once it received support for this from state power and from the magnates converting to Catholicism. And as at this time the representatives of all confessions were resolutely convinced that salvation could be attained only through the dogma they themselves presented, in general not even dramatic polemics could bring substantive agreement. Religiosity pervaded the worldview of the people of the period to such a degree that a lack of willingness to compromise would often and quickly drive leaders of a confession to the point of radical action against their enemies.

At the turn of the seventeenth century in Lower Austria, a revealing example of this was how the Lutheran Ferdinand Count of Hardegg, former captain general of Győr, and Georg Paradeiser, former captain general of Kanizsa, were both put on the gallows after show trials (in summer 1595 and in 1601, respectively) not for surrendering their border fortresses in Hungary to the Ottomans (in 1594, and in 1600) but rather for their Protestant faith. In the course of the Long Turkish War, the "Austrian model" soon found favor in Hungary. A few more radical prelates (e.g., Ferenc Forgách, Márton Pethe, and István Szuhay) used imperial mercenaries to occupy Protestant churches and schools and to expel priests and teachers. The best-known act was the retaking of the Lutheran church of Kassa in January 1604, assisted by captain general of Upper Hungary Giacomo Barbiano Belgiojoso, as discussed in part 1, chapter 11. The situation produced by this harsh behavior came to a head a few months later in the form of the anti-Protestant law 22 of 1604, arbitrarily appended at the Prague court to the decisions made by the Pozsony diet. While the confessional question was one of the most divisive subjects of debate of the diets in the sixteenth century, the wartime aggressive attempts at re-Catholicization all assisted the hajduk uprising led by Stephen Bocskai to turn into both an estate movement against the court and a civil war on religious lines.

The Hungarian Catholic elite was quick to learn from the profound effect of armed counter-Reformation. The destruction of the Jesuit college in Vágsellye at the hands of Bocskai's hajduks in 1605 may have been a strong enough message for the most eminent Catholics in Pozsony and Nagyszombat: violent acts would be met with an equally violent response from their opponents. To achieve a true rejuvenation of the church, rough methods had to be replaced by more peaceful and effective ones. That this was the right direction in which to proceed was also shown by the Treaty of Vienna of 1606 and the precoronation law 1 of 1608, which ensured the freedom of religion for Protestant nobles, frontier soldiers, and the citizens of the royal free cities and the royal market towns. This meant that the law turned the freedom of religion into an estate privilege—indeed, into a significant political trump card in the Kingdom of Hungary (see part 2, chap. 3).

In the first half of the seventeenth century, the Catholic Church used the new, peaceful methods to achieve what it had been unable to achieve in the shadow of weaponry in the Long Turkish War. One of the key principles of this new program based on persuasion was summed up in poignant fashion by Péter Pázmány in one of his polemics written to the Calvinist preacher from Kassa, Péter Alvinczi: "You need to fight me not with a sword, but with a pen; not with blood, but with ink."[2] While the first steps had been taken by his predecessor, Ferenc Forgách, archbishop of Esztergom (1607–1615) and former believer in re-Catholicization by force, it was Pázmány who would carry out the real series of reforms (see fig. 38). In 1608 Forgách founded a printing press in Pozsony, and in 1611 he held a regional synod in Nagyszombat, which developed a comprehensive program in the spirit of the reforms of the Council of Trent. Although its decisions were announced only by the bishoprics of Esztergom, Győr, and Zagreb, the implementation of the more important reforms (diocese synods, regular church visitations, unblemished life for the priesthood, education for priests, etc.) did nevertheless begin.

Meanwhile, the Jesuits laid down roots in Hungary again. They established their college in Nagyszombat in 1615; within three years, it had almost eight hundred students, and it soon became the most important educational institution in the kingdom. In addition, and thanks to György Drugeth de Homonna, who converted around 1601, they established themselves for a few years (1615–1619) right in the middle of mostly Calvinist Upper Hungary, in Homonna in Zemplén county. The Jesuits strengthened the Catholic Church not only with their schools but also with their evangelism carried out on the estates of the ever-greater number of magnates converting to Catholicism, whether for political or financial motives or from genuine conviction. By the 1610s these aristocrats did not shy away from expropriating Protestant churches and expelling preachers, which met with an increasingly agitated response from the Protestant estates.

The most effective exponent of peaceful Catholic reform was Péter Pázmány, the Jesuit teacher turned archbishop of Esztergom and then made a cardinal in 1629. His extraordinary influence can be put down to his masterful implementation of every method of renewal. He wrote works of lasting importance in all genres of religious literature (polemical and theological works, sermons, and prayer books), and not only in what remained the language of the Catholic liturgy, namely Latin, but also in Hungarian (see fig. 39). In order to alleviate the chronic lack of priests and to encourage the preaching of Catholic teachings at a high level, he put particular emphasis on ensuring the next generation of priests. It was for this reason that in 1623 he established the seminary in Vienna that would be named after him: the Pázmáneum. A Jesuit lycée was established in the center of domestic political life, Pozsony, in 1626; in the following year, another was founded in the fortress city at Győr. The latter, alongside the college in Graz, would throughout the century be the prominent educational establishment for the nobility and urban bourgeoisie of Transdanubia and Slavonia, as well as frontier soldiers keen to learn. In the decades that followed, Jesuit lycées spread (to Sopron, Ungvár, Trencsén, Komárom, etc.), challenging the Calvinist colleges both in terms of the quality of teaching and in terms of student numbers. In the cultural realm, Pázmány's most important act was the founding of University of Nagyszombat on May 12, 1635. This was the predecessor of today's prestigious Eötvös Loránd University (ELTE) in Budapest.

In addition to all of this, the hard-working archbishop held diocesan, regional, and national synods, arranged regular church visitations at his parish churches, and demanded

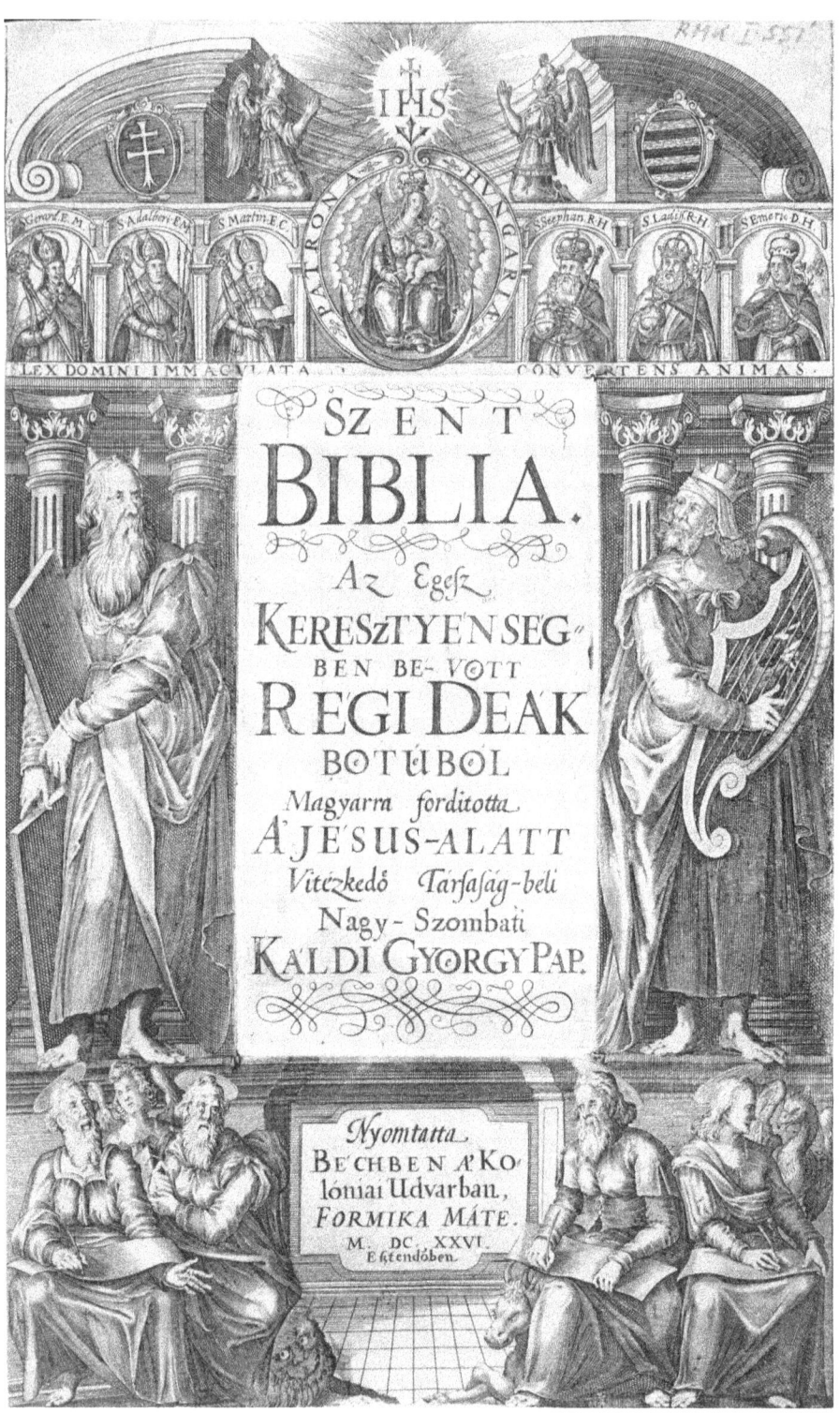

Fig. 39. Front page of the first complete Catholic translation of the Bible into Hungarian by György Káldi, Vienna, 1626 (Széchenyi National Library, Budapest).

exemplary behavior and strict celibacy from his priests and generous pastoral care from his congregation. Neither did he lose sight of the monastic orders (alongside the Jesuits, principally the Franciscans and the Paulines), and he was able to regain a number of church goods and sources of income that had previously been withheld. At the same time, his charismatic personality and his engaging sermons, able to speak to all social classes, helped numerous magnates (e.g., Ádám Thurzó and György Zrínyi) and many members of the gentry to convert. Pázmány was thus not a key exponent of the militant counter-Reformation but rather the leading figure in peaceful Catholic reform. His energetic, even snide style was limited to his polemic writings, in which, applying his amazing knowledge of the classical texts of theology, he defended the articles of the Catholic faith and did not fail to respond to the attacks the church had endured. As a result of his exceptionally effective activities, the Catholic Church regained ever greater areas of Hungary. Albeit with a touch of exaggeration, his peers would say of him after his death, "He was born in a Protestant country and died in a Catholic one."[3]

While Pázmány's successors as archbishop (Imre Lósy, canon lawyer, 1637–1642; György Lippay, politician and prelate, aspiring to the cardinal's hat, 1642–1666) enthusiastically continued the modernization of the church, overall their results were less impressive. Their greatest achievement was the continuation of the Pázmány era (further synods, visitations, foundations, founding of seminaries and schools, etc.), though there would now increasingly often be more violent acts as supported by the Catholicized magnates. They were unable to make any real change to the relative sizes of the different confessions, and the number of influential synods was small, and so their activities were directed mostly at nurturing internal church life and the continued patronage of the Jesuits.

As a result of all this, by 1650 the Jesuits had a total of four colleges, eight residences, and fourteen missionary stations (with a total of 149 staff) in Hungary. Significant pastoral, teaching, and missionary activities were also undertaken by the Franciscans, who also established new religious houses (in Győr, Kismarton, Érsekújvár, Szombathely, Körmöcbánya, etc.); by the Paulines, who remained in the Croatian-Slavonian areas; and by the Piarists, the teaching order settling in Podolin in the Szepes region in 1642 and in Privigye in Nyitra county in 1666. Another sign of the increased prominence of the monastic orders was the return of the Benedictines in 1639 after half a century to their monastery in Szentmárton (today's Pannonhalma). A year earlier, the Dominicans opened a new friary in Szombathely, while from 1630 the chapter of Veszprém could again operate in the border fortress by the Séd River. By midcentury, the large part of the Catholic priesthood was recruited from better-educated curates who had attended a seminary. It is no surprise that Catholic religious literature would, both in quantity and in quality, become a worthy rival of its Protestant equivalent.

Catholic modernization was a great success, especially in the western reaches of the country. While the Protestant confessions used similar techniques (synods, visitations, and then particularly the foundation of presbyteries) to defend their positions, their almost constant internal crisis made thorough reform difficult. There were nevertheless modern reform movements within all Protestant confessions from the turn of the new century. After a number of Calvinist reformers (e.g., Imre Újfalvi, author of a well-known Debrecen song book [1602] and a great figure in Protestant humanism), there were the representatives of the Puritanism that had its origins in Britain, who urged a church that was cleansed of the remnants of Catholic teaching and liturgy. For the Lutherans, it would be the Pietist movement, with its emphasis on personal religiosity and the practicalities of Christian life, that would then play a similar role. But it was only in the second half of the century that these movements, by introducing church and school reform and by publishing pastoral books, enjoyed results, and modest ones—thanks, for example, in the case of the Puritans, to János Dali Tolnai, active on the Rákóczi estates in the kingdom; to János Csere Apáczai, a teacher in Gyulafehérvár; and to Pál Medgyesi, a minister in Sárospatak.

Both in the Kingdom of Hungary and in Transylvania, the exponents of the inflexible Lutheran and Calvinist orthodoxy continued to enjoy stronger positions. Insistent on their old articles of faith and methods, they often were not even afraid of violent resistance. In Transylvania, for example, the Calvinist bishop István Katona Geleji (1633–1649), sparring partner of the Puritanical reformers pushing for renewal, stood up against the Unitarians and the Greek Orthodox and meanwhile enjoyed considerable cultural and literary influence with his collection of songs entitled *Öreg Graduál* (Old gradual, 1636). For the Unitarians, the situation was further worsened by the decision of the diet of Dés of 1638, the so-called *complanatio of Dés*, which put an end to the independent path taken by a variety of radical movements—including the so-called *szombatisták* (Sabbatarians), who came to prominence from the end of the sixteenth century—by making the more moderate confession the obligatory one. The key representatives of the radicals were charged in court and then sentenced to loss of material goods and to imprisonment.

In the absence of any real internal reform, the representatives of Protestantism were ready to employ ever-tougher methods to defend their positions against Catholicism, which was achieving considerable successes. That freedom of religion became an estate privilege gave them an excellent opportunity to confirm this freedom at meetings of the diet (law 77 of 1618; law 22 of 1625; law 33 of 1630; law 29 of 1635). All this shows just how much Catholicism was recovering its previous positions. Thus, the Protestants, forced to give ground, were not afraid to resort to ever more aggressive, even violent armed methods. The Protestant gentry and urban burghers, who had an important role in Upper Hungary, recognized that they could make great use of Gabriel Bethlen and Georg I Rákóczi's Hungarian military campaigns to strengthen their weakening position (see part 2, chaps. 3–4). And by citing the clause of the Golden Bull (1222) relating to resistance, they even considered the use of armed force to be a legitimate response to Catholicism as supported by the Habsburg rulers. Were their Catholic rivals to do likewise, however, they would consider it violent contravention of the law.

For this reason, the Protestant gentry would from 1619 use every single military campaign led first by Bethlen, then by George I Rákóczi, to achieve their religious goals. This was not difficult, as the princes joined the Thirty Years' War on the side of the Protestant allies. Then, during these campaigns, they expelled or killed Catholic priests and monks (e.g., in Kassa in 1619) and liquidated Jesuit schools (e.g., the aforementioned college in Homonna in 1619 and again in 1644) with the military assistance of the Transylvanian armies—that is, with means just as brutal as those used by the armed counter-Reformation. Thus, for many years, the princely expeditions created not only civil war conditions but also religious war ones, giving further ammunition to ever more irreconcilable religious divisions. Yet the nobles of the noble counties of northeast Hungary managed to include the freedom of religion among the international diplomatic issues: the guarantee of this freedom was always part of the peace treaties between the Habsburgs and Transylvania (Nikolsburg, 1621; Pozsony, 1626; Linz, 1645). The second clause of the Treaty of Linz extended this even to the peasantry: "Peasants must not be limited in their religion or be punished for it."[4] These achievements were later included in the decrees of the Protestant estates (laws 6–19) at the Pozsony diet of 1646/47.

The leaders of the Catholic Church themselves had to employ tougher action increasingly often against the fighting of the Protestants assisted by political, diplomatic, and even foreign armed supporters. At the Pozsony diet of 1647, for example, when it came to the Protestants, hot-headed Archbishop Lippay "wanted to deal with everything with the sword,"[5] not the pen—that is, he considered even the destruction of rival confessions a real possibility. The Vienna court and the Hungarian political elite were able to convince the prelate to temper his ideas.

Things had completely changed by the 1660s. Among the wishes of the absolutist regime in Vienna was the principle of "one state—one religion," which was a boon for the violent re-Catholicization tendencies. And when there was a break in ties between Vienna and the secular elite as the 1660s became the 1670s (see part 2, chap. 3), the Hungarian prelacy as led by archbishop of Esztergom György Szelepchény considered it time for stringent action. The scenario, from the era of the Bocskai uprising and the campaigns of the Transylvanian princes, was a given (see part 1, chap. 11, and part 2, chaps. 1 and 4). Just as from the 1620s to the 1640s the Protestants had called on the support of the Hungarian and Ottoman troops of the Transylvanian princes, so from the 1670s did the Hungarian Catholic elite call on the imperial and royal army, made up mostly of German soldiers, to occupy churches and schools, to expel priests and teachers, and to install those of the Catholic Church in their place.

The armed re-Catholicization of the 1670s and 1680s—which, given its attempt to completely break the back of Protestantism, can justifiably be called a counter-Reformation—managed definitively to turn the uprising of the *bujdosók* and then of Imre Thököly into a war of religion, just as had happened to Bethlen and Rákóczi's Hungarian campaigns as a result of similar actions on the part of the Protestants (see part 2, chaps. 2–4). Thököly's enraged soldiers responded to the Pozsony preacher trial of 1673–1674 and to the occupation of churches by German troops in a series of campaigns (in 1678, 1680–1681, 1682, and 1683) in which they wrought similar devastation on Catholic schools, monasteries, and churches. The counterreaction was of course not slow in coming: after the aforementioned partial solution of the diet of 1681 at Sopron, the regular troops saw to the implementation of another reorganization of affairs during the Long Turkish War at the end of the century. The high point of this series of exaggerated acts of retribution was the blood-soaked executive court of General Antonio Caraffa at Eperjes in 1687. While the number of victims of these show trials was not very high, they had terrible consequences for the political, military, and social situation in the country. The rousing of religious anger meant that civil war conditions would wreak enormous damage in terms of human lives, agricultural and economic means, and cultural assets. These conditions were a key factor in the further collapse of society and in further groups being pushed to its periphery.

In the quarter century after 1670, Catholicism, enjoying as it did the support of Habsburg state power and the army, enjoyed too big a victory for its own good in the liberated Hungary. The number of its believers, churches, schools, and monasteries increased markedly, thanks not only to the violent occupations but also to the construction of churches, monasteries, hospitals, and poorhouses that had begun in the retaken territories (in Buda, Esztergom, Eger, Pécs, etc.). A good example of this growth was that by 1700 the Jesuits ran nine colleges, thirteen religious houses, and eighteen missionary stations (with a total of 423 staff). But this all came at enormous cost. Many victims of almost three decades of religious and civil war after 1670 would from 1703 try to find a way out of their hopeless situation by joining the independence movement led by Francis II Rákóczi (see part 2, chap. 11). The failure of peaceful progress in the liberated Hungary was thus down as much to the armed counter-Reformation as to the earlier military campaigns of the Transylvanian princes and Imre Thököly in Hungary, supported by the Protestant nobility. The Protestantism and Catholicism of the seventeenth century were equals in this regard, too.

Notes

1. Recently, cf. Pál Ács, *Reformations in Hungary in the Age of the Ottoman Conquest* (Göttingen: Vandenhoeck und Ruprecht, 2019).
2. István Bitskey, *Pázmány Péter* [Péter Pázmány] (Budapest: Gondolat Kiadó, 1986), 93.
3. Ibid., 214.
4. István Sinkovics, ed., *Magyar történeti szöveggyűjtemény* [Collection of Hungarian historical texts], vol. 2/1, *1526–1790* (Budapest: Tankönyvkiadó, 1968), 526.
5. Franz Christoph Khevenhüller to *Obersthofmeister* Maximilian von Trauttmansdorff, March 22, 1647, Pozsony, ÖStA, Allgemeines Verwaltungsarchiv, Familienarchiv Trauttmansdorff Ee 2, no. 54, fol. 107–108.

Fig. 40. General, politician, and poet Miklós Zrínyi / Nikola Zrinski (1620–1664). Engraving by Gerhard Bouttats, 1664 (Hungarian National Museum, Budapest).

9

HALF A CENTURY OF CULTURAL PROGRESS—HALF A CENTURY OF MILITARY CRISIS

THE KEY CHANGES BROUGHT BY THE SEVENTEENTH CENTURY would leave their mark on the development of literature, culture, and the arts. The golden age at the end of the previous century (see part 1, chap. 10) and the rejuvenation of Catholicism gave the Kingdom of Hungary a solid basis and momentum for another fifty years of progress; only the military and civil war conditions from the 1660s to 1711 could force it into crisis. In Transylvania it was the prolonged period of peace from 1613 to 1658 that made a period of flourishing possible, until Turkish-Tatar looting and civil war halted it in its tracks (see part 2, chap. 4).

After 1606, that is, the Muses did not fall silent along the frontier between the two empires. The deliberate development of the Hungarian language continued; Hungarian literature was enriched by a few excellent works and the education system by new institutions. This was all closely linked to the wider spread of literacy, while the revolutionary advance of printing and communication in the sixteenth century broadened the horizons of growing sections of society. Alongside the continued existence of the late Renaissance, the first defining traits of Baroque art appeared, while humanist patronage of the arts was increasingly replaced by the artistic patronage of magnates and the Transylvanian princes. Not even the wars after 1660 were able to put a halt to these developments, but it was the hard-fought recovery following the Treaty of Szatmár (1711) that would reveal just what narrow scope the half century of war had allowed these new trends.

Despite the birth of a literary Hungarian language at the end of the sixteenth century (see part 1, chap. 10), the deliberate development of the language continued after 1606. One goal of the grammar published by Albert Molnár Szenci in 1610 (*Novae Grammaticae Ungaricae libri duo*) was to make the learning of Hungarian accessible to foreigners. His work not only discussed syntax but also played a role in creating a unified spelling, especially with its explanation of the use of the letters *u* and *v* and of the use of diacritical marks for long vowel sounds. His successors as Protestant cultivators of the Hungarian language would be István Katona Geleji, János Csere Apáczai, and György Csipkés Komáromi. The *Magyar Grammatikatska* (Hungarian small grammar, 1645), by the Calvinist István Katona Geleji, was a real work of language cultivation, drawing attention to the etymological way of writing; indeed, as an early language reformer, he enriched the Hungarian language with many invented words used to this day (e.g., *emberiség*, meaning "humanity," and *intézet*, meaning "institute"). The orthodox Calvinist bishop also demanded that his opponents, who supported Puritanism, join him in debate. Pál Medgyesi used this experience to write the first book on rhetoric in Hungarian (1650); János Csere Apáczai used many everyday words in his *Magyar Encyclopaedia* (Hungarian encyclopedia, 1655). Unlike his predecessors, György Csipkés Komáromi was directed not by the grammar of Latin but by the operation of Hungarian itself in writing his grammar (*Hungaria Illustrata*, 1655), in which he also urged the consistent marking of long vowels (e.g., the Hungarian *á* and *é*).

The milestones in the Catholic development of Hungarian are usually considered to be György Káldi's complete translation of the Bible (*Szent Biblia*, Vienna, 1626—the counterpart of Gáspár Károli's Calvinist Vizsoly Bible [see fig. 39, in part 2, chap. 8, and fig. 19, in part 1, chap. 9]), then the works of Péter Pázmány, and finally the grammar of Nagyszombat Jesuit Pál Pereszlényi (*Grammatica Lingvae Ungaricae*, 1682). The innovations brought by the last of these were the recognition of vowel harmony and the typification of verb conjugations (indefinite, definite, passive, taking the *-ik* form, etc.). And though written in Latin, it became one of the most important handbooks for teaching Hungarian in the Catholic schools of liberated Hungary. Pereszlényi's grammar took its fair share from the Protestant language cultivators, meaning that even during the "century of decline," the Hungarian language would take strides toward a unified official use.

Thanks to this process, twenty-first-century speakers of Hungarian feel closer to the works of the great writers of the seventeenth century (principally Péter Pázmány, Miklós Zrínyi, and István Gyöngyösi) than to the poems of Bálint Balassi, the creator of Renaissance literary Hungarian. Meanwhile, János Rimay, who, as Balassi's former student and collector of his works, followed in Balassi's footsteps, would in his own poems use more complex textual solutions to create a new style. Mannerist elements (mannered poetic language, shocking similes, melodious rhymes, exaggerations, disharmony, etc.) would dominate. The poet and prose writer, who was well versed in diplomacy, also arranged literary activities and was in constant contact with the Protestant and Catholic intellectual elite of the period. He is considered the first representative of literary criticism in Hungarian for subjecting the court reports (1628) of George Rákóczi's court priest (András Prágai) to biting criticism.

While Rimay's work stood above confessional issues, this was not an option for Péter Pázmány, archbishop of Esztergom (see fig. 38, in part. 2, chap. 8). The greatest figure in Catholic reform was nevertheless a brilliant user of literary Hungarian, which he used to good effect in his often satirical and humorous polemical writings primarily addressed to the Lutheran István Magyari and the Calvinist Péter Alvinczi, including *Felelet* (Response, 1603) and *Öt szép levél* (Five nice letters, 1609). Although the latter work was already a work of literary interest, Pázmány's wide-ranging talent as a writer was perhaps most clearly evident in the crystal-clear logic underlying the first theological synthesis in Hungarian, *Isteni igazságra vezérlő Kalauz* (The guide to divine truth, 1613). In this work, he arranged the articles of the Catholic faith to reject Protestant objections so effectively that his opponents were hardly able to recover from their shock. They even sent the *Kalauz* as far as Wittenberg so that the theologians there might respond to it. The archbishop replied to this in Hungarian. Finally, Pázmány's book of sermons, published in 1636, which remained a model work for centuries, played a key role in the further progress of literary Hungarian in the seventeenth century, which saw its theological, philosophical, and liturgical vocabulary increase dramatically. Pázmány's inimitable writing style would continue to have an influence on the writers of the seminal journal *Nyugat* in the twentieth century.

The most erudite Hungarian military expert and general of the sixteenth and seventeenth centuries, Miklós Zrínyi (Croatian Nikola Zrinski) was the author of works important to the literary development both of Hungarian and then of Croatian (see fig. 40). The magnate possessed one of the most unique libraries of the period; his oeuvre was characterized by diversity and deliberate innovation. He introduced a number of genres to Hungary: he was the first to publish love poems in Hungarian, and he wrote the first Hungarian epic (*Obsidio Szigetiana*, 1645–1648), intended as a tribute to his great-grandfather's heroic death at Szigetvár in 1566. Although his works have been misinterpreted by later generations—for example, Zrínyi was in favor not of an independent national army but merely of a permanent Hungarian military force in the frontier lands that could be mobilized at any time—the image that has remained of his thought has undeniably been that of a strong and independent Kingdom of Hungary, which was, under the rule of Matthias Corvinus in the second half of the fifteenth century, one of the defining powers in Central Europe. As he had to experience the decline of this power on an everyday basis, it is understandable that he revived the traditions of the Matthias cult from the preceding century in his work *Mátyás király életéről való elmélkedések* (Reflections on the life of King Matthias).

In his exceptional works on military theory (*Tábori kis trakta* [Short tract from the camp], after 1646; *Vitéz hadnagy* [Valiant lieutenant], 1650–1653) and his notable programmatic proclamation (*Az török áfium ellen való orvosság* [The antidote to the Turkish disease], 1661–1663), he sought in Baroque literary language an answer to the seemingly insuperable problem of how the "century of decline" could be taken back to the flourishing times of King Matthias Corvinus and how the Ottoman advance could be repelled. In addition to the traditions of antiquity, his works, passionate in tone, bear the hallmarks of almost all the intellectual and ideological movements of his age. They were able again and again to become relevant precisely because the golden age of the late Middle Ages would fail to return even in the centuries following the repulsion of the Ottomans. Finally, Zrínyi published his poetic works (romantic idylls, elegies, philosophical epigrams, etc.) in a separate volume (*Adriai tengernek Syrenája* [Siren of the Adriatic Sea]) in Vienna in 1651, and so these were already able to have an effect on his peers. Indeed, as this anthology was also published by his younger brother Péter Zrínyi (Croatian Petar Zrinski) in Croatian translation (*Adrianszkoga mora Syrena*) in Venice in 1660, for the benefit of the Croatian nobility and frontier soldiery, this work would later also influence the development of Croatian national identity.

While Zrínyi's romantic verse continued the tradition set by Balassi's court poetry, the best-known exponent of this movement was István Gyöngyösi, the leading poetic figure of the second half of the seventeenth century. While Gyöngyösi, trained as a lawyer and employed for the longest period as secretary to Palatine Ferenc Wesselényi, was more popular than Zrínyi in his time, the quality of his work does not come close to that of the poet general. He wrote mostly when commissioned by his magnate patrons (Wesselényi, Pál Esterházy, Imre Thököly, and István Koháry, who was also a poet) or to elicit their praise. His poems were thus more the tools of court representation than of the innovation so typical of Zrínyi, even if Gyöngyösi, too, deliberately worked on developing the Hungarian language.

His virtuoso lyricism, lightness of style, and fluid use of language would by the eighteenth century make him one of the most popular poets.

The best examples of Hungarian prose of the Baroque period, including memoirs, diaries, and autobiographies popular elsewhere in Europe, would have a considerable influence on generations to come. They were particularly well accepted in Transylvania. Here the leading politicians of the day (Prince John Kemény, János Szalárdi, Miklós Bethlen, etc.) became the best exponents of the genre. Although most of their work saw the light of day in print only at a later date, as distributed in manuscript form, they were known across the country.

A further factor in the standardization of the Hungarian language and the development of Hungarian literature was an increase in the number of those it was reaching. While in the decades after 1526 this process was powered mostly by the new network of Protestant schools (see part 1, chaps. 9–10), in the Kingdom of Hungary of the seventeenth century, it would be propelled by the Jesuit lycées mushrooming along with Catholic reforms (by the 1650s, there were colleges in Zagreb, Nagyszombat, Homonna/Ungvár, Pozsony, Győr, Besztercebánya, Trencsén, Sopron, Kassa, and Komárom; in the 1670s, in Lőcse, Eperjes, Kőszeg, and Varasd; and finally, during the Long Turkish War, in Pécs, Esztergom, and Buda). New institutions were also added to the educational system, in which teaching now took place according to a unified, modern syllabus (*Ratio Studiorum*). This flourishing of culture in the early part of the century was completed by the university that Pázmány founded in Nagyszombat (1635), to which, thanks to the will of his successor, Archbishop Imre Lósy, a faculty of law would finally be added in 1667. Nevertheless, in this century, many pursued their higher education studies at the universities of Vienna, Graz, and Olmütz or of Rome, Padua, or Krakow.

In Transylvania, in Debrecen, in Rákóczi-owned Sárospatak, in Pápa in Transdanubia, and in Eperjes in Upper Hungary, Protestant colleges nevertheless operated successfully for many years to come. Indeed, eminent German Protestant professors who fled to Transylvania during the Thirty Years' War (Johann Heinrich Bisterfeld, Johann Heinrich Alsted, Ludwig Philipp Piscator, etc.) brought intellectual sparkle to the college at Gyulafehérvár comparable only to that attracted to Sárospatak by the Puritan reformers in the form of the Bohemian teacher of Europe-wide fame, Johannes Amos Comenius (Komenský). Comenius taught in Sárospatak from 1650 to 1654, and his influential, accessible textbooks (e.g., *Orbis Pictus*, written in Sárospatak) revolutionized pedagogy in Hungary and around the world.

János Csere Apáczai developed and published (primarily abroad) an educational program that was likewise exceptionally innovative and Puritan in spirit, though only a part of this was in fact put into practice in the colleges in Transylvania. Unlike the Catholics, the Protestants did not have a university in Hungary at this time; their students continued to pursue their university studies in the West. In this century, instead of Wittenberg, Hungarian visiting students attended Heidelberg, Jena, Halle, and Herborn in the German lands; Franeker, Leiden, and Utrecht in the Netherlands; Basel in Switzerland; and Oxford and Cambridge in Britain. They continued to bring back new academic discoveries experienced at first hand.

The development of the new Catholic school network in the seventeenth century played a key role in the further spread of literacy across the country; the format and spelling of private correspondence began to be standardized, while careers in administration (e.g., chamber or noble county administration) or the law (e.g., as attorneys or judges) became more common and better respected. But, in addition to the Protestant school system and these new language subjects, the further growth of book publishing played a role in this process. For, in this period, at about the same number of presses, some five times as many books were published as in the previous century. The era of wanderer printers was at an end; such enterprises tended to be longer lasting. While in the kingdom Pozsony and Nagyszombat were the centers for Catholic printing, the presses at Bártfa, Lőcse, Kassa, and Sárospatak mostly published Protestant works. Across the country, meanwhile, the number of nonreligious works and works in Hungarian was growing. By the end of the century, the Nagyszombat university press, in operation since 1648, would lead all the other Hungarian presses in terms of both its number of publications and their print runs. In Transylvania the presses at Debrecen, Várad, Kolozsvár, Gyulafehérvár, Nagyszeben, and Brassó retained their leading role, undertaking a key task in the supply of textbooks for Protestant schools.

Overall, the quality of the typography of the works published would decline, however. This did not prevent this century from seeing the emergence of a few special personalities: early on, Lőrinc Ferenczffy, the Hungarian royal secretary and publisher of more than thirty volumes in Vienna; Jakab Németh, the Jesuit working in Pozsony; Ábrahám Kertész Szenci of Várad; and most of all, the typographer Miklós Kis Tótfalusi, who achieved European renown in Amsterdam and later worked in Kolozsvár, Transylvania.

The growth in printing went hand in hand with the development of book culture and the book trade. As well as the royal libraries (in Vienna and Gyulafehérvár) and those of the prelates, a number of prominent libraries were built by magnate families (in the kingdom, the Batthyány, Zrínyi, Révay, Nádasdy, Esterházy, and Rákóczi families; in Transylvania, the Teleky, Ráday, and Bethlen ones), and the libraries of the gentry and bourgeoisie were also growing. By the end of the century, the country's most significant library (with almost ten thousand volumes) was assembled at Nagyszombat university. There was also an increase in the number of official book traders, most of whom settled after arriving from the large German cities and established bookshops in the more important cities in the kingdom or in Transylvania (Bártfa, Kassa, Lőcse, Pozsony, and Nagyszombat, or Brassó, Nagyszeben, Kolozsvár, etc.).

The development of printing was of particular significance for another reason. The printed newsletters, weekly journals, and newspapers that were now common in the German and Austrian territories (German *gedruckte neue Zeitungen*) provided increasingly constant information about and even visual depictions of events in the Hungarian theater of war against the Ottomans. Interest in the Kingdom of Hungary grew particularly after the war of 1663–1664; one sign of this was the reprinting of a number of sixteenth-century works on Ottoman subjects. The German press materials also reached Hungary, and so Comenius, for example, in the 1650s was able to instruct his pupils at the Protestant college in Sárospatak to spend two hours a week on communal newspaper reading.

But while it was easy to manipulate printed news in the great news centers of Central Europe (Vienna, Nuremberg, Prague, Augsburg, etc.) and turn it to the service of royal or imperial estate propaganda, and indeed to censor it, this was harder to achieve with handwritten newsletters (German *handgeschriebene neue Zeitungen*). This handwritten news grew out of the correspondence of medieval traders (especially in Italy and Germany), becoming so important by the early seventeenth century—with the expansion of commercial connections and the creation of the *respublica litteraria*, as well as of modern diplomacy and state bureaucracy—that in a number of European countries so-called news traders (*Zeitungsschreiber*, *novellista*, *scrittori d'avvisi*) were in operation. They duplicated by hand the news they received; then, in return for payment, they would distribute these to their customers, first on a fortnightly and then on a weekly basis. Palatine Tamás Nádasdy was already receiving such anonymous manuscript news in the sixteenth century; after 1606 a number of his successors (e.g., György Thurzó and Miklós Esterházy) continued to do the same—as the latest research findings have revealed.[1]

The printed and the handwritten channels of news each had their own function and significance. In the space of a century, their progress brought a gradual transformation of communication decisive enough to be referred to as the "information/communication revolution" or "information explosion."[2] Another sign of the increased value of news and the increased openness of people's lives was that in the seventeenth century few private letters failed to include some local or national news in their last paragraphs. Information was increasingly becoming a form of capital—one that could bring with it distinct political, economic, and cultural utility.

All seventeenth-century Hungarian art forms were two-faced. In the kingdom and in Transylvania, the late Renaissance survived to the end of the century in a number of genres. Nowhere was this as true as in architecture: we need think only of the grand palaces of Gabriel Bethlen and the Rákóczis (Gyulafehérvár, Várad, Alvinc, Fogaras, and Sárospatak) or of the castles and mansions of the Transylvanian and Hungarian magnates with their traditional ground plans and corner towers and bastions (e.g. Radnót, Csíkszereda, and Bethlenszentmiklós in the principality or Kéked, Márkusfalva, and Mihályi in the kingdom). The facade decoration typical of the late Renaissance, the cornice rising above the main plinth, would remain in vogue for many years, especially in the castles, bell towers, and town houses of Upper Hungary. Examples of this could also be found in Transylvania (Gyergyószárhegy) and in Transdanubia—for example, in the burghers' houses in Kőszeg, which until 1647 was part of Lower Austria. Meanwhile, in parallel, and only in the kingdom, Baroque would also emerge. Research dates the start of this as 1629,[3] when, with support from Palatine Miklós Esterházy, work began on the construction of the Jesuit church at Nagyszombat, with its enormous nave, extravagantly decorated interior, and side chapels. The two styles then continued to coexist, with the Baroque becoming dominant only in the early eighteenth century.

The gradual inroads made by the Baroque in the Kingdom of Hungary were assisted by commissions from the prelates and Jesuits leading Catholic reform and from the re-Catholicized high nobles. While the Jesuit churches in Győr, Trencsén, and Kassa were built in the style of that of Nagyszombat, the aristocrats loyal to the court, given the danger of war, had only the interiors (hall and chapels) of their already fortified residences refitted in this new style. This led to a golden age for early Baroque frescoes and the stucco decoration that accompanied them. Good examples of this are the ceremonial hall in the Nádasdy castle at Sárvár, decorated with monumental historical battle scenes (the main events of the Long Turkish War, by Hans Rudolf Miller); the row of halls, chapel, and ground-floor *sala terrena* ("cooling hall" with the appearance of a cave, with ocean motifs) in the Pálffy castle at Vöröskő; and the Csáktornya castle of the Zrínyi family and the Batthyány fortress at Rohonc. The first Baroque castle to be palace-like in appearance was the residence of the Esterházy family at Kismarton (German *Eisenstadt*), which was built around a medieval castle with four corner towers in the protected hinterland along the border with Austria.

The era of humanist patronage of the arts was gradually replaced during the seventeenth century by princely participation in Transylvania and by that of the aristocracy in the kingdom. For this, the Renaissance was adequate, and yet Baroque pomp would be even more favorable. The former is shown by Gabriel Bethlen's large-scale building works and support for the arts. He was clearly driven by political motive: he sought to find a suitable artistic reputation to ally with his greater political plans. Historian János Szalárdi would later be correct to write of Bethlen that "he had grand, princely houses built in all his places of residence, the castles of Gyulafehérvár, Radnót, Alvinc, Balázsfalva, Fogaras and Várad . . . in order to give himself an aura of immortality by comparison."[4] His political image was helped by his opulent court, which was a regular customer not only of the excellent Kolozsvár and Nagyszeben jewelers of the time but also of various luxury-goods makers from Germany, Vienna, Venice, and Istanbul. The Rákóczi family did the same in Transylvania, but they also turned their private castle in Sárospatak, in the Kingdom of Hungary, into an ornate residence.

The political and artistic representation of the more important magnate families in the kingdom (the Batthyány, Csáky, Draskovics, Erdődy, Esterházy, Forgách, Pálffy, and Zrínyi families), however, were characterized by their castles displaying the hallmarks of the Baroque. The excellence of their dynasties was emphasized not just by the ceremonial halls in these castles (e.g., Sárvár and Kismarton) but also by the so-called ancestors' galleries, series of paintings depicting family members life-size—for example, in the Pálffy castle at Vöröskő, the Nádasdy one at Pottendorf, or the Esterházy residence in Fraknó, including numerous paintings by the eminent German artist Benjamin Block.

The century's two greatest artistic patrons of the arts, Chief Justice Ferenc Nádasdy and Palatine Pál Esterházy, employed almost all branches of the arts to emphasize the importance of their families and their own political activity, as did the rulers of the period. The former patron's residences at Sárvár, Sopronkeresztúr, and Pottendorf and the latter's residences at Kismarton and Fraknó were on a par with the German, Austrian, or Bohemian high noble castles of the time, in terms not just of their ceremonial halls, libraries, and portrait paintings but also of their rich collections of artworks. These contained brilliant jewelry from Augsburg and Nuremberg as well as valuable jewels, various rock specimens, and skeletons and preparations reflecting the scientific preoccupations of the age.

In 1664, the broad-minded Nádasdy, who had traveled throughout Europe in his youth, published a collection of full-length portraits of Hungarian rulers (*Mausoleum*) at the Endter press in Nuremberg (see fig. 41), establishing a tradition of such depictions that would last many centuries. In addition, the lord, who maintained contact with many famous artists of the age (e.g., the painter Block, Rubens' pupil Jan Thomas, and the architect Carlo Carlone), operated presses in Lorettom (Sopron county) and Pottendorf. Indeed, in Lorettom he founded a Servite monastery and in Léka an Augustine one; he was a committed supporter of the Franciscan order as well. In mid-1663, for example, it was in his name that the

Fig. 41. Front page of the *Mausoleum* of Hungarian kings by Ferenc Nádasdy, Nuremberg, 1664 (Széchenyi National Library, Budapest).

Franciscan church in Győr commissioned one of the century's major works of Baroque art in Hungary from Jan Thomas (the so-called *Köpenyes Madonna* [Cloaked Madonna]). This work wildly exaggerated Nádasdy's real-life defensive role during the Ottoman war, portraying him as the leading figure in the struggle against the Ottomans. It was also at least in part to lift the family's prestige that the chief justice's firstborn son, István, was sent on a *Kavalierstour*, a grand aristocratic study tour of Western Europe.

Pál Esterházy was equally deliberate and skillful in exploiting art to enlarge his own honor and that of his family. Personally compiling musical works as well as supporting theatrical performances, the palatine used every avenue to show, as the century drew to a close, that he was the country's foremost figure and sole imperial prince (*Reichsfürst*). He "celebrated" the attainment of the latter title in 1687 by commissioning the artistic refinement of a five-foot elephant tusk. His power was similarly well represented by his treasury at Fraknó/Forchtenstein (the oldest surviving aristocratic private collection in Central Europe) and by his residence at Kismarton/Eisenstadt. On the facade of this residence, the series of busts of old Hungarian leaders would be joined by likenesses of his father (Palatine Miklós) and himself. The deeply religious Esterházy also excelled in his establishing of Baroque churches and altars and commissioning of frescoes, which all had great influence on eighteenth-century Baroque art as a whole. And, in 1700, taking inspiration from Nádasdy's *Mausoleum*, Esterházy presented the heritage and excellence of his newly ascendant family in a volume (*Tropheum*) richly illustrated with engravings, in which his ancestors, real or imagined, could trace their service to the country right back to Örs, one of the supposed original chieftains of the Magyars.

It may seem odd in the light of all this, but at a national level education, culture, and the arts underwent decades of crisis after 1660. The activities of Chief Justice Nádasdy and Palatine Esterházy, living in a more sheltered nook of the kingdom, were the exception. From 1658/63 right through to 1711, the everyday life of the large part of the kingdom and Transylvania was determined by the almost annually repeated ravages of the Turkish-Tatar, royal and imperial, and *kuruc* (anti-Habsburg) troops. These would bring decades of stagnation and decline not just in society and the economy but also in education and culture. As, with the taking of Érsekújvár in autumn 1663, the Ottomans were given the green light to prey on previously protected parts of the kingdom's territories, the religious civil war restricted or ended the operation of hundreds of Protestant schools and then, in the 1680s and after 1703, many Catholic ones as well. Of the Jesuit colleges, for example, those in Trencsén, Selmecbánya, Lőcse, Eperjes, Sárospatak, Ungvár, and Szatmár were closed, but in 1683 Imre Thököly's troops even forced the fathers teaching in Sopron, in the country's western edge, temporarily to flee. The national crisis in education was sorrowfully hinted at in the words of the later headmaster of the Piarist college in Privigye in 1678: "The number of students is low, but the fear of insurgents is high."[5]

And the 1670s saw only the beginning of the military crisis. The repeated attacks of the aforementioned *bujdosók* were followed by the liberation war and many years of destruction wrought by the imperial and royal troops and then, in the early eighteenth century, by the regular nationwide looting of Francis II Rákóczi's rebel *kuruc* fighters. The number of schools in operation—for all confessions, but particularly for Catholics—declined, and in a few decades the lower student numbers in turn lowered the level of literacy across the country. This is why reports from the first third of the eighteenth century speak of widespread illiteracy. The wartime circumstances had meant that the generation at the turn of the century would hardly partake in the advances in culture and education that their fathers and grandfathers had enjoyed. This also threatened the reception of literature. So it is no accident that we know of fewer authors of great merit from this period. The exceptions to this were the aforementioned István Gyöngyösi, memoirist Miklós Bethlen, Kata Szidónia Petrőczi (a Protestant poet and author of religious works), and Prince Francis II Rákóczi, who later excelled with his memoirs and confessions.

Amid such long-lasting war conditions, intellectual life became increasingly difficult. One sign of this was that there were fewer scientific and literary circles than in the previous, more peaceful period. The number of printed literary works in Hungarian had declined by the end of the century, while any further spread of the Baroque was largely limited by Rákóczi's independence struggle (see part 2, chap. 11). In the years following 1711, after the ruins of devastation of constant military campaigns since 1660 had been swept away, it would take decades of determined effort for Hungarian education and culture to return to the level it had been proud of during its more fruitful period a good half century previously.

Notes

1. Nóra G. Etényi, *Hadszíntér és nyilvánosság: A magyarországi török háború hírei a 17. századi német újságokban* [Battlefield and publicity: News of the Ottoman wars in Hungary in seventeenth-century German newspapers] (Budapest: Balassi Kiadó, 2003); Zsuzsa Barbarics-Hermanik, "Handwritten Newsletters as Interregional Information Sources in Central and Southeastern Europe," in *The Dissemination of News and the Emergence of Contemporaneity in Early Modern Europe*, ed. Brendan Dooley (Surrey: Ashgate, 2010), 155–178.

2. Michael North, ed., *Kommunikationsrevolution: Die neuen Medien des 16. und 19. Jahrhunderts* (Cologne: Böhlau, 2001).

3. Géza Galavics, "Barokk" [Baroque], in *Magyar művészet a kezdetektől 1800-ig* [Art in Hungary from its beginnings to 1800], ed. Géza Galavics et al. (Budapest: Corvina Kiadó, 2001), 317–320.

4. Ferenc Szakály, ed., *Szalárdi János Siralmas magyar krónikája* [János Szalárdi's lamentable Hungarian chronicle] (Budapest: Magyar Helikon, 1980), 94.

5. András Koltai, "A Pálffyak és a piaristák: A bajmóci uradalom katolizációja és a privigyei piarista kollégium első évei" [The Pálffy family and the Piarists: The Catholicization of the Bajmóc estate and the first years of the Piarist college at Privigye], in *Pálfiovci v novoveku: Vzostup významného uhorského šľachtického rodu* [The Pálffy family in the modern age: The rise of a famous Hungarian noble family], ed. Anna Fundárková and Géza Pálffy (Bratislava–Budapest: Spoločnosť Pro História–AEP, 2003), 99.

Fig. 42. Charles of Lorraine (1643–1690). Unknown painter, eighteenth century (Hungarian National Museum, Budapest).

10

A COUNTRY LIBERATED BUT RAVAGED

The Long Turkish War, 1683–1699

Grand Vizier Kara Mustafa led the army of the Ottoman Empire against Vienna for the last time in 1683 (see part 2, chap. 2). This unsuccessful expedition, followed by the victory of Christian troops in Kahlenberg (September 12), near Vienna, was the prelude to a new great war: the second Long Turkish War in early modern Hungarian history (see map 14). By 1699, with the exception of the Banat, this would liberate the area of the medieval Hungarian state from the Ottomans. Key to this military victory were the incomparably preferable circumstances at its outset in early 1684 relative to those at the time of the war of 1663–1664.

In autumn 1683 the allied forces achieved a victory near Vienna that was not partial, as the Szentgotthárd–Mogersdorf one in summer 1664 had been, but decisive. Indeed, in the counteroffensive that soon followed, they retook Esztergom, the Ottomans' furthest Danube outpost (October 27). This was a great success, as it drove a wedge into Ottoman Hungary and was the first time that the anti-Ottoman forces had taken a fortress of this kind since Székesfehérvár in 1601. In fact, as it returned home, the allied Polish army of King John III Sobieski (1674–1696) retrieved a number of smaller castles in northern Hungary from the Ottomans and from Thököly. This was all a source of optimism both for the leadership in Vienna, which had previously sought peace with the Ottomans, and for the political elite in Hungary, and it would be decisive in furthering the war effort.

Of utmost importance for the success of this war was the Holy Alliance, an international diplomatic and military coalition formed in March–April 1684 under the aegis of Pope Innocent XI (1676–1689). Alongside Emperor Leopold I and Polish king John III Sobieski, this alliance would also be joined by the Republic of Venice and then, in 1686, by Russia. And as in mid-August 1684 it had signed a twenty-year cease-fire with Louis XIV in Regensburg—albeit at the cost of significant territorial losses along the Rhine—the Habsburg Monarchy could now focus its military might on the Hungarian theater of war. Furthermore, the imperial and royal army was worlds away from what it had been twenty years previously, in terms of not just its size, its organization, and its military technology but also the supply system it was developing. It was also particularly significant that to ensure the supply of weapons and wages for war, Vienna was able to enter an alliance with the capital-rich great entrepreneurs of Central Europe; the papal court also began a program of

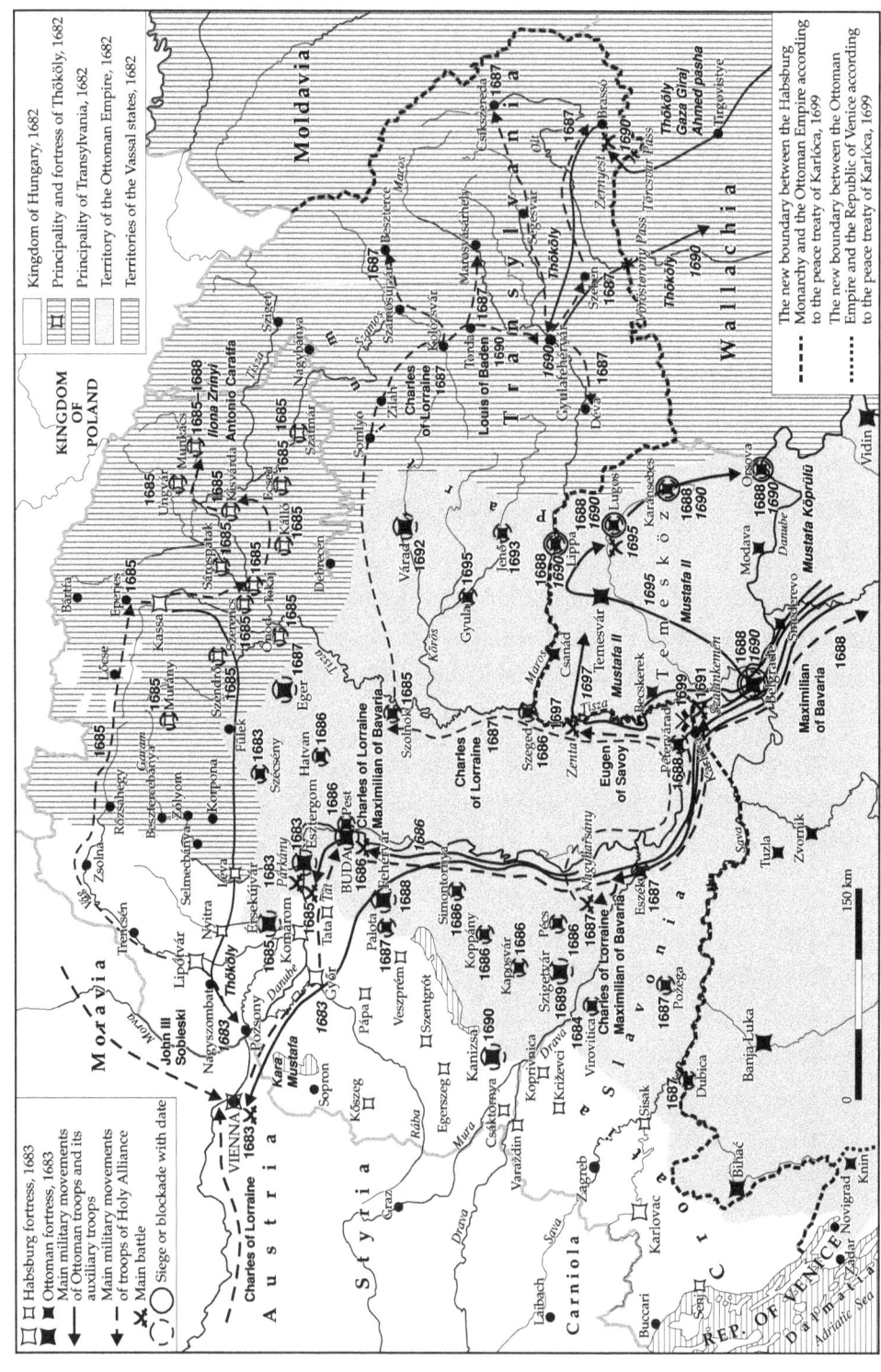

Map 14. The Long Turkish War, 1683–1699.

aid. The only restraining factor was the Hungarian principality of Imre Thököly (see map 12, in part 2, chap. 4), who was persistent in his support for the Ottomans. The pacification of the northeast parts of the country would thus for many years divert thousands of soldiers and enormous resources from the main forces fighting the Ottomans.

Although the siege of Buda in 1684 ended in failure, the international cooperation in the years that followed, against all odds, was a triumph. In the first stage of the war (1683–1686), the imperial forces, after overcoming the defense ring around Buda (Visegrád, Vác, and Pest, in June 1684) and gradually pushing Thököly back, were in the second half of 1685 able to retake the hopelessly squeezed Érsekújvár (August 19) and even Szolnok on the Tisza (October 19). Such successes were crowned by the taking of the former Hungarian capital on September 2, 1686, after a hard siege lasting two and a half months (see fig. 43). The return of Buda would receive an unparalleled response. The Spanish viceroy of distant Naples, for example, "came close to fainting on receiving this wonderful and long-awaited news, and, not knowing how to express the immeasurable joy filling his heart, did so with tears."[1]

Neither did the troops of the three commanders involved in the Buda victory (Commander in Chief Charles of Lorraine [see fig. 42], Maximilian Emanuel, and Louis of Baden) recoil in the second stage of the war (1686–1689). Further successful sieges (of Pécs, Szeged, and Eger) were followed by decisive victories in open battle. The most memorable of these was the so-called second Battle of Mohács fought by Nagyharsány near Siklós on August 12, 1687. Finally, on September 6, 1688, the allies, by now led by Maximilian Emanuel, retook Belgrade, which had been lost 167 years earlier. All in all, these successes brought the liberation of the Great Plain of Hungary and the Croatian-Slavonian areas, even if the defenders of a fewer larger Ottoman bastions (Kanizsa, Szigetvár, and Székesfehérvár) would stand their ground for some years. In 1689 the new commander in chief, Louis of Baden, occupied large parts of northern Serbia (Niš) and western Bulgaria (Vidin), thus rightly acquiring the title *Türkenlouis*. Meanwhile, the speedy liberation of Transylvania began in autumn 1687; only Thököly, freed from captivity, would in August 1690 attempt to return it to its status as an Ottoman vassal with his Tatar and Wallachian troops (see part 2, chap. 4).

With the recovery of Ottoman Hungary and Transylvania, the area of the Habsburg Monarchy grew by almost 150,000 square kilometers in just five years or so. This was a considerable territory, larger than the Austrian hereditary provinces or than the lands of the Bohemian crown. The Habsburgs' significant increase in strength was contrary to the interests of its rival in the west, the Sun King, who annulled the 1684 cease-fire of Regensburg in September 1688 and initiated an attack on the Rhineland Palatinate. Hereafter, the monarchy was forced into a war on two fronts. Many cavalry and infantry regiments were driven to the western front; the commander in chief, until his death in 1690, was Charles of Lorraine.

Even with the imperial army split between two fronts, in the third and last stage of the war (1689–1697) the Ottoman leadership did not have the strength for a decisive counteroffensive. After the Bulgarian and Serbian territories, Grand Vizier Mustafa did retake Belgrade in early October 1690, but he was unable to turn the tide of the war. In the years that followed, key fortresses (e.g., Várad in 1692 and Gyula in 1695) held under the blockade would capitulate in turn, while both sides would enjoy significant advances on the battlefield. On August 19, 1691, at Szalánkemén (Serbian *Slankamen*), Louis of Baden enjoyed victory over

Fig. 43. The siege of Buda, 1686. Painting by Franz Geffels, 1686 (Hungarian National Museum, Budapest).

the grand vizier; on September 21, 1695, on the other hand, the Ottomans triumphed at Lugos over Transylvanian commander in chief Friedrich Veterani. The struggle between the two empires, both increasingly drained by the war, was finally decided by Eugene of Savoy's victory at Zenta (September 11, 1697), during which his masterful strategy saw huge losses of life for the troops of the new sultan, Mustafa II, who had returned to retake Hungary.

A decade and a half of military successes for the allies had been made possible most of all by the Viennese leadership's ability to mobilize significant bodies of troops in many theaters of war at once (Hungary, Transylvania, Croatia, Slavonia, Serbia, etc.) and to provide them with at least partly adequate supplies. Thanks to the establishment of a standing army, that is, it was able to capitalize on the military and tactical advantage it had already attained a century earlier. This presented itself in dramatic victories in battle and successful sieges of fortresses.

The triumph of Zenta made it possible to end the war and to forge a peace between the two empires. With English and Dutch mediation, the envoys of the Holy Alliance and that of the sultan finally signed this on January 26, 1699, at Karlóca (Karlowitz) in Syrmium/Szerém county. This twenty-five-year treaty concluded the long war, preserving the military status quo as it had developed. With the exception of Banat, Hungary would be freed from the Ottoman yoke after a century and a half; Transylvania would lose its vassal status, though also its independent statehood, falling under the rule of Emperor Leopold I. Venice acquired significant territories on the Peloponnesian Peninsula and in the Aegean Sea; Poland was granted Podolia, which it had lost in the 1670s; and Russia was extended to the Black Sea, at Azov. The sultan also promised to ensure free trade, not to support the *kuruc* rebels, and to settle Imre Thököly within his own empire. Meanwhile, the treaty guaranteed the Ottoman Empire's place at the table of the great powers of Europe. In the years that followed, the border between the two empires would be defined precisely, settlement by settlement, and carefully marked on a map. On the Habsburg side, this enterprise was led by the renowned soldier polymath of the period, Luigi Ferdinando Marsigli (Marsili).

Hungary's long-awaited liberation came at a high price. The repulsion of the Ottomans would not have been possible without the imperial and royal standing army of some eighty thousand men and without enormous financial aid from Central Europe. The greatest burden of the hostilities was borne by the population of the theater of war; it was also the local population that suffered the most damaging consequences. For almost two whole decades after 1683, the life of the whole country was characterized by regular war taxes, military quarterage, and coercive requisitions, as well as by the "rivalry" in looting carried out by Ottoman, Tatar, imperial and royal, *kuruc*, and other troops. In November 1686, the noble county of Pest already complained to Palatine Pál Esterházy that "in the last few years, many have been consumed by the pagan Turks and Tatars and their weapons and slavery, while others have died at the hands of hunger, terrible destitution and unbearable penury, or have scattered to distant lands."[2]

In some parts of the newly liberated country, both the population and the infrastructure would repeatedly be decimated by the annual march, winter lodging, and ravaging of the enormous armies on the two opposing sides and then by the famines and diseases that followed (especially the plague of 1690–1691). The regular devastating attacks left even the most resilient populations unable to get back on their feet. In Tolna county, for example, heavily affected by the military advance along the Danube, 120 communities survived the entire length of Ottoman rule, whereas in the early eighteenth century, census records registered inhabitants in only 50. Similar damage was suffered by those regions that had an Ottoman bastion at their center (Kanizsa, Szigetvár, Várad, and Gyula) that the allied leadership had forced to capitulate by means of a blockade. The troops ensuring such a blockade would positively perch themselves on the villages surrounding the fortresses, while both sides, for strategic reasons, repeatedly used scorched-earth tactics. Sometimes the local population would even be forcibly displaced. This was why the younger István Zichy was so resigned in his despair at the start of the protracted blockade of Kanizsa (1688–1690): "There is nothing in the meadows and the fields as far as the eye can see, no wheat, nor other crops like barley or oats; it's as if it were a no man's land. No one except the Lord can say when and with what there will again be bread-baking here."[3] Thus, the second fifteen-year conflict in the Carpathian Basin would leave as lasting a mark on Hungary's settlement infrastructure, population, and material goods (not to mention on its social, economic, and cultural progress and even on its ethnic makeup) as the Long Turkish War had done at the turn of the seventeenth century (see part 1, chap. 11).

Amid a liberation that brought so much devastation, the most pressing question for Hungary was that of how and within what framework its future structures would be developed. In this regard, the interests and objectives of the Habsburg court in Vienna, the Hungarian estates, and the various classes of society were markedly different. This is all clearly reflected in the plans for the future leadership and administration of the country as established in the wake of the Pozsony diet of late 1687, where—as we have seen—the estates accepted the hereditary kingship (*Erbkönigreich*) of the Habsburgs' male Austrian line, annulled the Golden Bull's clause on the right of resistance, and then crowned the nine-year-old Archduke Joseph heir to the Hungarian throne (see part 2, chap. 3). The steps showed that the court, overestimating its military successes but not adequately taking into consideration its critical problems in Hungary, was doing politics based in part on its military might. In Vienna, as the front became more distant, they must have believed, now Hungary had become a hereditary land (*Erbland*) of the Habsburgs, that they were able to significantly restrict the positions of the estates in its administration.

This thinking in terms of a Danubian empire was most of all espoused by the grand-scale settlement plan (*Einrichtungswerk des Königreichs Ungarn*) developed by a seven-member committee between July 1688 and November 1689, led by Leopold Kollonitsch (Kollonich), archbishop of Kalocsa. Of all this, Hungarian historiography since the end of the nineteenth century has tended to focus on a single, exaggerated statement on the settlement of Germans in the country[4]; however, more recent research has shown that the proposal for the future legal, ecclesiastical, political, military, and economic administration of the Kingdom of Hungary, laid down over five hundred pages, did in fact contain numerous positive elements urging the modernization of the country. These elements were all intended to serve the key interests of the monarchy, of course—and to further reinforce the positions of the court on military, foreign, and financial affairs. But, with the possible exception of support for Catholicism, there was no trace in the plans of the drastic absolutist methods employed in the 1670s. Kollonitsch nevertheless felt it necessary to involve the nobility in the burden of public obligations, the defense of the peasantry depleted by war, and the strict specification of its feudal obligations, which would become one of Francis II Rákóczi's slogans in his struggle of independence (see part 2, chap. 11). The proposal also thought it desirable to settle the deserted areas with Hungarians and other groups as well as Germans, in return for tax exemptions; it also urged the elaboration of a civil and criminal book of statutes.

The plan, for the most part made up of positive objectives, was nonetheless mistaken in one key regard: given its thinking in terms of the framework of an extended Habsburg Monarchy, it did not weigh up in realistic fashion the true power of the estates of the Kingdom of Hungary or of the nobility insisting on its privileges. Neither was it fully aware of the real situation facing the masses forced to the periphery during half a century of war, nor did it grasp the real wartime influence of the imperial commanders who sought to share in the territory and spoils of the liberated country. Thus, with the great war still raging, the *Einrichtungswerk* was overly ahead of its time.

In contrast, the plan laid down in September 1688 by the Hungarian estate committee led by Pál Esterházy (the so-called Hungarian *Einrichtungswerk*), which further developed the palatine's April proposal, looked overly to the past. The diet of 1687 sought to restore the country to the pre-1526 state administrative structure, albeit in a modern form and in return for significant estate concessions. The leading role in this structure would have been given to a central administrative and judicial body, the Hungarian Royal Council, led by the palatine and based in Hungary (in Pozsony or in Buda), on a par with the Privy Council in Vienna. At the same time, they would have reinstituted the pre-Mohács office of treasurer and, in the anti-Ottoman frontier defense to be rebuilt, the institution of the areas run by bans, while also planning to establish a Hungarian standing army of some ten thousand men. With the rise of the estates in the seventeenth century, the protection of estate and noble privileges was given a prominent place in the proposal. While the committee agreed to tax armalists and nobles living on serf plots and to be stricter about ennoblement, it nevertheless emphasized that Hungary was the country of the nobility.

Although the estates' plan included many elements on economic modernization and urging revival after the ravages of war, these mostly served the interests of the magnates and nobles. Just as the proposal of Kollonitsch and the others had done, so the concept of the estates was misguided in one key regard: it refused to acknowledge the fundamental changes that had, after 1526, made the Kingdom of Hungary (as its bulwark and breadbasket) a very important and for this reason tightly controlled part of the Habsburg Monarchy (see part 1, chaps. 3 and 7). It also brazenly ignored the fact that the liberation of Hungary, still continuing at a pace, was possible only with the troops of the Danubian empire.

Both proposals were clear evidence of the particular two-facedness of the seventeenth century. The dualist state administration reestablished by the Sopron diet of 1681 could not be abolished by either side. Even in the shadow of the ten-thousand-strong army and with the recognition of the hereditary kingship, there was no opportunity for the Kingdom of Hungary to be annexed by the Habsburg Monarchy, and yet the close-knit relationship with it could not be relaxed either. And so only those elements of the proposals in which the court and the estates were able, after varying periods of debate, to come to a compromise could be implemented in the short term. One example was the establishment of the Hungarian Royal Aulic Chancellery (August 12, 1690): operating as a centralized modern body in the imperial city of Vienna, this new institution was run by the Hungarian elite.

During the long war, the country's fate was determined not by aulic or estate interests but rather by the military and financial considerations of conflict—in short, by the interests of the generals, military suppliers, and chamber administrators. A perfect example of this was the creation of the Commission for New Acquisitions (Latin *Neoaquistica Commissio*) in December 1688. As the country was retaken by the Habsburg army, Vienna intended to govern the liberated areas as it saw fit, on the basis of the law of arms (Latin *ius armorum*). These areas would be returned by the commission operating within the Aulic Chamber to their former Hungarian landowners only if they were able to prove their old property rights and if they were willing to pay the "arms ransom" in cash. This was 10 percent of the estimated value of the estate. Thus did the treasury, alongside new exceptional war taxes, attempt to ease its debt, which had risen to many millions of florins. Given the impoverishment brought by war, however, not all former landowners were in a position to pay the fee.

In return for loans, meanwhile, plenty of the reoccupied territories came into the hands of the war's generals, military suppliers, and chamber administrators, as well as those foreign aristocrats whose ancestors had acquired Hungarian status over the century. But the Chamber Administration of Buda, established in 1686, was subordinated not to the Hungarian Chamber in Pozsony but to the Aulic Chamber in Vienna, which was in charge of financing the army; as such, the Chamber Administration of Buda would play a key role in supplying the divisions of the theater of war along the Danube. Re-Catholicization also gained momentum in the recaptured territories; indeed, in 1702 Leopold I mortgaged the Jászság and Kunság regions (territories of the Iasians and Cumans), which came under the legal and military authority of the palatine and had special governments, to the Teutonic Order as a new acquisition area. After 1687, during the war, there was not even any meeting of the diet. All of these measures evoked ever-greater dissatisfaction and nationwide indignation.

The fate of the new frontier defenses against the Ottomans was similarly decided exclusively by military considerations. The Hungarian estates were given next to no say in the running of the constantly developing Military Border (German *Militärgrenze*, Croatian *vojna krajina*) along the Sava, Danube, Tisza, and Maros Rivers. Neither did Hungarian frontier soldiers play a key role. Unless the former frontier soldiers accepted transfer to the Hungarian hussar divisions created in succession after 1688 (the Barkóczy, Csáky, Pálffy, Batthyány, Zichy, Kéry, Czobor, and Deák regiments) or were willing to relocate to one of the local guard stations in southern Hungary, they found themselves boosting the number of the rogue military groups. Alongside regular company, a good part of the soldiery of the new southern Military Border was made up of Serbian peasant soldiers settled en masse in the deserted southern frontier zone by the Aulic War Council. The estates retained a voice only in the direction of the ban's frontier area (German *Banalgrenze*, Croatian *Banska krajina*), which was restructured both geographically and militarily but still governed by the ban of Croatia. Indeed, given the exclusive oversight of the War Council, the noble county public administration of the southern parts of the country was not reintroduced.

This is how the former dualistic management of the border defenses (by border and district captains general) came to an end. The military leadership in Vienna thereby solved a triple problem. First, it settled the struggle fought with the Hungarian estates in the sixteenth and seventeenth centuries over central and local direction of military affairs. Second, by resettling the Serb population fleeing from Ottoman territory, it removed a focus of social tensions. Third, it constructed a new defense system, which would provide an effective long-term guarantee of the security of the monarchy and Hungary in the face of the Ottomans. Recent research had shown that the large-scale destruction of former fortresses by the Habsburgs was one of the myths of Hungarian historiography.[5] While there were some larger detonations of a few, formerly important but now redundant fortresses (such as Eger and Kanizsa), something Francis Rákóczi would continue later for strategic and other reasons, the construction of new bastions and barracks, of such great significant for future events, meanwhile began in earnest.

The Long Turkish War was not, however, able to provide a solution to one of the greatest problems facing seventeenth-century Hungary: the fate of the military elements finding themselves at the periphery of society or outside society altogether. Although some of them found new leases of life in regular divisions of the Habsburg army and a few thousand would join Thököly in exile in the Ottoman Empire, those who remained in their original places of residence (whether they were frontier soldiers, hajduks of the Transylvanian princes, or private landowners, peasant soldiers, etc.) increasingly risked losing their collective privileges as their armed service became unnecessary. The situation was particularly critical in Upper Hungary, where there was the greatest concentration of hajduk settlements and where hostilities, with the civil war and the war of religion, would be constant from the 1670s onward. Thököly's support for the Ottomans, furthermore, meant that regular troops were sent to this exhausted region; in the 1680s and 1690s, the foreign mercenaries among them would regularly exploit and indeed humiliate Hungarian nobles and peasants who remained loyal to their Protestant religion.

The unbearably tense political-social situation in Upper Hungary in 1695 turned into a peasant uprising in Bereg county and in the summer of 1697 into a peasant uprising that broke out in Hegyalja, one that was joined by former border troops and by the *kuruc* soldiery. While the members of this latter movement attempted to convince the greatest landowner in this part of the country, the younger Francis Rákóczi, to be their leader, he rejected this by departing for Vienna. The imperial and royal troops were able to slow the uprisings but could not eliminate them completely. And as Rákóczi's own circumstances soon underwent radical change, in the spring of 1703 he himself took the lead of the dissatisfied, hopeless crowds in the northeast region of the country.

Notes

1. Ferenc Szakály, ed., *Buda visszafoglalásának emlékezete 1686* [The memory of the retaking of Buda] (Budapest: Európa Könyvkiadó, 1986), 565.

2. Ferenc Szakály, "A felszabadító háborúk történeti helyéről. (Ki felelős a hódoltsági terület pusztulásáért?)" [On the historical location of the war of liberation (who is responsible for the destruction of the occupied areas?],

in *Előadások és tanulmányok a török elleni visszafoglaló háborúk történetéből 1686–1688* [Lectures and studies on the history of the wars of liberation against the Ottomans 1686–1688], ed. László Szita (Pécs: Baranya Megyei Levéltár, 1989), 34.

3. László Szita, "Dokumentumok a kanizsai blokád és a vár kapitulációjának történetéről, 1688–1690" [Documents on the history of the blockade of Kanizsa and the capitulation of its fortress, 1688–1690], *Somogy Megye Múltjából, Levéltári Évkönyv* [From the history of Somogy county: Archival journal] 25 (1994): 80.

4. J. János Varga and János Kalmár, eds., *Einrichtungswerk des Königreichs Hungarn (1688–1690)* (Stuttgart: Franz Steiner, 2010), 74–76.

5. András Oross, "Rendeletek és intézkedés-tervezetek a magyarországi várak lerombolásáról (1699–1702)" [Orders and plans of action for the destruction of Hungary's fortresses, 1699–1702], *Fons (Forráskutatás és Történeti Segédtudományok)* [Fons (sources research and auxiliary disciplines of history)] 12, no. 2 (2005): 257–294.

Fig. 44. Francis II Rákóczi, leader of the first Hungarian war of independence (1703–1711). Painting by Ádám Mányoki, 1707 (Hungarian National Museum, Budapest).

11

INDEPENDENCE MOVEMENT AND CIVIL WAR

The Rákóczi Uprising, 1703–1711

The peace treaty of Karlóca (Karlowitz) in 1699, establishing the country's liberation, should in principle have brought rejuvenation to the Kingdom of Hungary after many decades of war. Yet the treaty settled little more than the country's foreign policy relationships, doing so within the framework of the now strengthened Habsburg Monarchy such that the Hungarian estates—as had been the case for the Treaty of Vasvár in 1664—had no say at all in the treaty's formulation. The Long Turkish War, and the new organization of the country being dictated for a good decade by military interests, again undermined the relationship between the estates and the court that had been resolved at the diet of Sopron in 1681 (see part 2, chap. 3).

The situation became grave when, far from settling its economic and social problems, the liberation of the country instead only exacerbated the tensions that lay within them. Economic and property relations became realigned, to the detriment of the Hungarian nobility and merchant class; the mass suffered great deprivations, and impoverishment was inevitable. Meanwhile, tens of thousands of now unneeded bearers of arms (frontier soldiers, Transylvanian princely hajduks, hajduks belonging to private landowners, soldier peasants, and *kuruc* soldiers), together with their families, were faced with the danger that were they to lose their privileges, they would sink back amid the serfs.

The process of seventeenth-century countrywide militarization and decay would thus have exceptionally tragic consequences (see part 2, chap. 5). Yet neither Vienna nor the Hungarian estates nor the great landowners nor the nobility saw any urgency in resolving the problems of the masses of bearers of arms and peasants who had been flung to the periphery of society. However, the uprisings driven by these dissatisfied groups at the end of the century would not have turned into the first independence movement in Hungarian history if the highly erudite Francis II Rákóczi, one of the richest and most powerful magnates of the turn of the century (see fig. 44), had not taken the helm and mobilized them.

Rákóczi's inheritance was a glittering but very difficult one. His great-grandfather and grandfather (George I Rákóczi and George II Rákóczi) had been real princes of Transylvania, while his father (Francis I Rákóczi) had been its elected prince (1652), who played an active part in the Wesselényi movement (conspiracy, 1667–1670) and was in the end only granted an amnesty thanks to his assistance in the crushing of the uprising and in return for many hundreds of thousands of florins. His stepfather—that is, the second husband to his mother, Ilona Zrínyi—was Imre Thököly. Contrary to popular belief, the latter had only a marginal role in Rákóczi's upbringing, and Rákóczi himself always treated Thököly, a keen servant of the Ottomans, with suspicion. His character was also formed by his studies at the Jesuit college at Jindřichův Hradec (German *Neuhaus*) in Bohemia and at the University of Prague (1688–1692). Thus, by the end of the century, Rákóczi would, as a deeply faithful but tolerant Catholic aristocrat and as an imperial prince (1697) with a German wife (Amalie Charlotte, princess of Hessen-Rheinfels), become one of the greatest landowners not only of mostly Protestant northeast Hungary but of the Kingdom of Hungary as a whole.

Given his father's and grandfather's activities, not even his princely title and enormous wealth could guarantee Rákóczi a career. Yet he was forced to watch as the statehood of the Transylvania his ancestors had led came to an end by the 1690s, while the liberation from the Ottoman yoke failed to bring the rejuvenation that had so long been hoped for. Given his family traditions, his childhood and adolescent experiences, and his faith, however, Rákóczi saw all this in a very different light from his fellow prince, Palatine Pál Esterházy, who also fought a valiant struggle against the court in Vienna. By the end of the 1690s, Rákóczi's driving political principles were as follows: the removal of the Habsburg dynasty from the Hungarian throne (to which end his father had already striven), the rebirth of the Principality of Transylvania led by his grandfather and great-grandfather under its own control (and independent of the Ottomans), and, to achieve all this, an alliance with the key rival to the Habsburgs, King Louis XIV of France.

The years following the Treaty of Karlóca would definitively commit him to these objectives. After the end of the Long Turkish War, he began taking political steps to improve the positions of the estates and to achieve his own personal goals; as part of this, he established contact with the Sun King. For this, he was arrested in mid-April 1701 and then taken to court and charged with treason. In the context of the War of the Spanish Succession (1701–1714) fought between France and the Habsburg Monarchy for the legacy of Charles II, the last Spanish Habsburg (who died in November 1700), the charge was not without foundation. But in November 1701, with his wife's assistance, he succeeded in escaping to Poland from a prison in Wiener Neustadt. There now remained no peaceful path from here toward the realization of his grand objectives. Still only twenty-five years old, the young aristocrat had to choose: he could remain in exile; or, like his father before him, he could, at great cost, compromise with the court and with the Hungarian aulic elite; or else he could attempt to achieve his ambitions through force. In spring 1703, after agonizing over this at length, he chose the last of these options. As there was still a good number of dissatisfied soldiers in Bereg county waiting for a leader, Rákóczi decided to attempt to serve both his own interests and those of these despondent military elements by establishing an anti-Habsburg independence movement. Thus, in a proclamation of May 6, 1703, from Brezan (Polish *Brzeżany*) in Poland, he called all the residents of Hungary, nobles and non-nobles alike, to an armed uprising against the Habsburgs. This marked the outset of the first war of independence (1703–1711) in Hungarian history (see map 15).

While Hungarian historiography has thus far generally considered Rákóczi to have continued the policies of the Transylvanian princes and of Imre Thököly,[1] this stands up to scrutiny only in certain regards (anti-Habsburg sentiment and the protection of Transylvanian

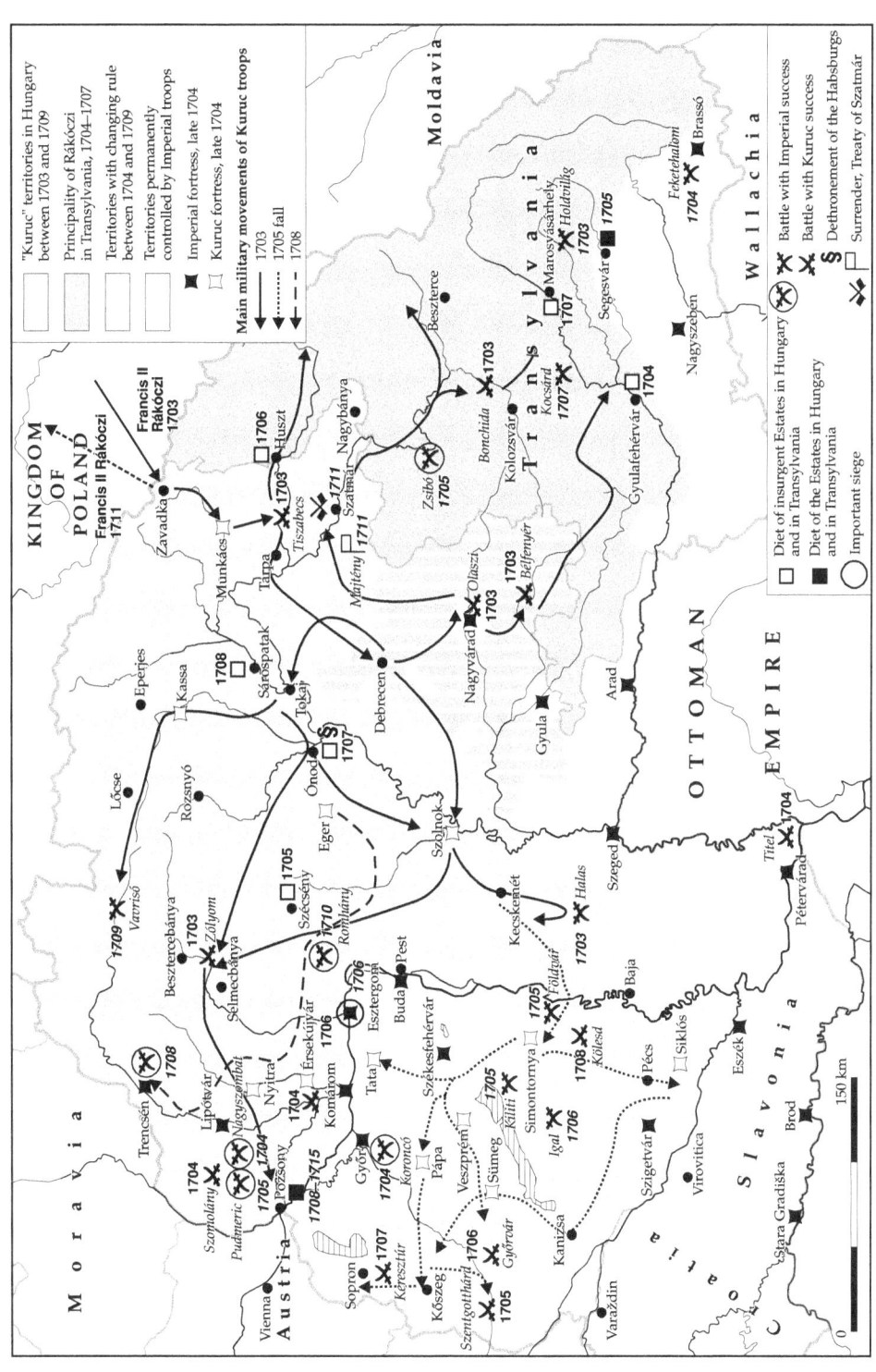

Map 15. The war of independence of Francis Rákóczi, 1703–1711.

independence), not as a whole. As we have seen in some detail, we cannot consider the Ottoman vassal princes of Transylvania or indeed Thököly to have presented any kind of national independence movement (see part 2, chaps. 2 and 4). Rákóczi's actions, meanwhile, can best be compared to those of King John Szapolyai after 1526 (see part 1, chap. 4). Albeit with external diplomatic and military support, if not control, they both attempted to create an independent Hungarian state in opposition to the Habsburgs and in autonomous fashion, founded in the main on their Hungarian political, economic, and social base. A key difference is that Szapolyai did so as a legitimate ruler, with significant political experience under his belt, if soon falling under direct Ottoman influence. The young Rákóczi, on the other hand, despite his limited political experience, did so in sovereign fashion to the end—first as leader of an independence movement and then, after the dethronement of the Habsburgs at the assembly of Ónod (June 13, 1707), as pretender to the throne. In the midst of the Ottoman conquest, King John had no such opportunity.

After the expulsion of the Ottomans and given his enormous estates and the army of tens of thousands that he would soon amass, Rákóczi's room for maneuver seemed distinctly more favorable. However, it was soon clear that in the long term only in the event of the Habsburg Monarchy's collapse could he entertain any hope of creating an independent state. For, like Szapolyai before him, Rákóczi was mostly chasing illusions in domestic as in foreign policy. This held true even if the goal of an independent Hungarian state was a noble one and even if some partial success in implementing it would, in wartime circumstances, be a very considerable achievement.

Rákóczi's foreign policy opportunities initially appeared to be good. The outlook for the independence struggle, initiated at a decidedly favorable moment, seemed all the more rosy when, in the War of the Spanish Succession, erstwhile imperial general against the Ottomans Maximilian Emanuel, elector of Bavaria, entered into an alliance with the French, which in 1703–1704 put the Habsburg military leadership in a very difficult position. But the victory at Blenheim (August 13, 1704) of the Habsburg-British allies over the French-Bavarian troops marching along the Danube was a turning point both for the great European war and for the Hungarian independence struggle. In its wake, and from a diplomatic perspective, only the international recognition of Rákóczi's state could have saved the independence revolt.

Although Rákóczi's followers nominally elected him prince of Transylvania on July 8, 1704, elected him for real on April 5, 1707, and elected him prince in charge of Hungary on September 17, 1705, he was unable to achieve any resounding success in foreign policy terms. Like Szapolyai, he put out feelers to all the powers of importance in Europe (France, Prussia, Sweden, Britain, the Netherlands, the Papal States, and the Ottoman Empire), yet he had neither the time, the money, nor specialists with the right experience to establish a permanent diplomatic apparatus that might have acquired significant financial or military assistance for the uprising. What is more, Rákóczi was too blind in his support of Louis XIV, who never considered him an internationally recognized ally in return. Indeed, in his anti-Habsburg plans, the Sun King assigned hardly more of a role to Rákóczi than French king Francis I had granted to King John Szapolyai after 1526. They never managed to sign a treaty; perhaps the best chances for this were ended for good by the prince's defeat at Trencsén in August 1708 and by France's worsening military and economic circumstances.

French diplomacy nevertheless did everything in its power to prevent Rákóczi and the court in Vienna in their efforts at compromise. The greatest chance for this was presented at the peace negotiations at Nagyszombat held from October 1705 to July 1706, which, despite British-Netherlandish mediation, concluded without success. Vienna would not accept Rákóczi's key conditions, namely the free election of kings and independence for Transylvania—conditions the mediators themselves did not support. The prince, pushed increasingly into a corner on the world stage, tried first an alliance with Russia (Treaty of Warsaw, September 15, 1707) and then one with the Ottomans. The former fell victim to the war of Tsar Peter the Great (1682–1725) against Sweden; the latter was frustrated by the Porte's refusal to enter into renewed conflict with the house of Habsburg.

For a long while, Hungarian historiography was silent about the attempts at alliance with the Ottomans;[2] in fact, in 1709–1710, in his final isolation and desperation, Rákóczi seemed willing to concede significant areas of southern Hungary (the area between the Sava and the Drava, the Syrmium region, and the Bácska region) and to return Transylvania to an Ottoman vassal state under his own leadership, in order to preserve the independence struggle and his own power at least in Transylvania. These diplomatic efforts on his part represented the last stage of the Ottoman orientation that had begun in the late 1520s (see part 1, chap. 4). Their failure would prevent the prince from continuing Thököly's tragic policy and using Ottoman troops to attack Hungary or Transylvania.

Largely as a result of his extraordinary sense of calling, Rákóczi also overestimated his room for maneuver in domestic policy. In his memoirs he would claim that "Divine Providence sent me to my barren homeland as a cry to arms, a cry for freedom. It saw that all the country's people heard the cry. The name of freedom moved people's noble hearts, who mobilized and bore arms to win back their freedom."[3] This was, in fact, the sort of embellishment in retrospect that one might expect of a memoir: from the outset, with only part of the country joining Rákóczi's cause, the independence struggle was also a civil war. The greatest problem was that fewer of the Hungarian political elite stood by him than had once stood by King John Szapolyai after 1526. The prelacy remained overwhelmingly loyal to Habsburg rulers Leopold I and then from 1705 King Joseph I; the same was largely true of the high nobility (except Miklós Bercsényi, Antal and Dániel Esterházy, Simon Forgách, Sándor Károlyi, a number of counts Csáky, and a few other aristocrats). Lacking their support, Rákóczi was unable to establish an independent Hungarian state; at most, he might realistically have had an independent Transylvanian principality in his sights.

Yet even in Transylvania and the Partium, Rákóczi's power was never stable, for the Transylvanian Saxons would always remain loyal to the Habsburg dynasty, while the *kuruc* forces suffered a series of losses against the troops of Transylvanian commander in chief Jean Louis Rabutin, not even managing to take Várad. To make matters worse, in the whole of Europe only France supported Transylvania's independence. But Rákóczi was not even able to convince some of the free royal cities (e.g., Buda, Pest, Pozsony, Trencsén, and Sopron) to join him; indeed, a good number of the former frontier soldiers fought on the imperial and royal side. In military terms, it is telling that the country's most important fortresses—both along the Ottoman border (Pétervárad, Szeged, Arad, etc.) and in the interior (Lipótvár, Győr, Komárom, Buda, Várad, etc.)— failed to join the rebels, with rare exceptions.

Overall, that is, and despite the shared interests of those wanting to protect estate and noble privileges, only a part of the country's population experienced the *kuruc* uprising as an independence struggle. The other part considered it a civil war that was impeding the peace the country had so long desired, especially once it saw that Rákóczi's Hungarian soldiers rivalled German mercenaries in their looting habits. During the war, moreover, no more than a partial solution was found to the situation of the military groups enjoying collective privileges and of the peasantry. Thus, we cannot speak of the liberation of the serfs or of the sharing of social welfare burdens—as emphasized by the historiography of the last half century[4]—but only of the announcement (law 9 of 1708) of the liberation of soldiers with serf status who had persevered to the final victory and of a new form of tax collection, which affected a third of the country and brought only modest returns. Seen realistically, the solution of the social problems of the bearers of arms in possession of privileges was not connected either to the question of independence or to Rákóczi's personal objectives, and so it was usually from necessity that the *kuruc* political leadership gave concessions to its dissatisfied soldiers. This group was greatly reduced in its numbers after the armed struggles of the war of independence and the plague outbreak of 1708–1712; these numbers were further lessened by the thousands fleeing into exile. The situation of those who survived the war would ultimately be settled by the Treaty of Szatmár and by the agreements made with landowners in the years of peace that followed.

As seen in the above, then, the idealized image of the Rákóczi war of independence, fostered first by the national romantic era of the late nineteenth century and then by the nationalism of the communist system from 1949, needs to be nuanced and indeed corrected in a number of respects. Yet there is no case for painting an entirely opposing picture—it is simply that the war of independence needs to be given its just place in Hungarian history. For all its contradictions and however limited its chances, Rákóczi's movement was nevertheless the first Hungarian independence struggle. Thus, even if its leader's actions were full of illusions, he has a leading place among the great figures of Hungarian history, just as no one would question the place that King John Szapolyai has in the line of Hungarian rulers. And Prince Francis Rákóczi had a number of achievements against a background of tough wartime and civil war conditions. But it is misleading to compare his state or his army to the European states developed over long periods of time and their standing armies, as his latest biography has done.[5]

Given the war still being fought, the following can be considered actions of real historic importance: Rákóczi successfully prevented the peasant uprisings in the northeastern counties of Hungary from turning into nationwide dissatisfaction, and he was effective in convincing the nobility and military elements of Upper Hungary to join him. Indeed, he was capable of turning them into a fighting force, although it was only partially of regular form, thanks to a lack of funding and of officers, the fighting etiquette of the former frontier soldiers, and failures in training and in supplies to the army. This explains why, while Rákóczi's troops were able to quickly place some part or other of the country under their supervision (as, for example, the forces of János Bottyán did with Transdanubia in 1705 or other *kuruc* troops did with parts of Transylvania), in open battle they would suffer one defeat after the next (e.g., on December 26, 1704, at Nagyszombat, and on August 3, 1708, at Trencsén).

There were nevertheless some significant administrative achievements in military affairs. They elaborated a military hierarchy based in part on the ranks of the imperial and royal armed forces and in part on the French model; from late 1703 they established the apparatus for military supplies (Hungarian *Hadi és Provincialis Commissariatus*), and then in 1706 they put military public administration into practice, too. Further important achievements included the creation of military medical care, the military judicial framework, and the field chaplain service, as well as the introduction of the unified military regulations (*Regulamentum Universale*) accepted at the 1707 assembly of Ónod.

We can also consider it an important success that those loyal to Rákóczi were able in large part to take over the direction of public administration in northeast Hungary, in parts of the Great Plain, and in Transylvania. The prince himself meanwhile established central bodies to direct the most important affairs of his state: first, in January 1704, the Aulic Council (*Consilium Aulicum*), then, at the Szécsény assembly of autumn 1705, the twenty-four-member Senate and the Economic Council (*Consilium Oeconomicum*). In 1707 the princely Court of Justice was created, and, finally, in March 1710, the Aulic Economic Council, to arrange the affairs of his own great estates. Rákóczi's Transylvanian state system would develop in similar form in 1704–1705 and then at the inauguration assembly at Marosvásárhely in April 1707.

Thanks to the wartime circumstances, Rákóczi's power was highly centralized throughout; his personal influence remained decisive in all areas of state administration. As King John had done before him, he allowed only his most senior senators and generals any say in matters. At his national assemblies (Szécsény, 1705; Ónod, 1707; Sárospatak, 1708), however, he had to pursue a difficult struggle both with the nobles and with the military elements that were on his side, just as had been the case in the estate monarchies of contemporary Europe in peacetime. Neither should we forget that it was Rákóczi who published the first newspaper in Hungary, the *Mercurius Hungaricus* (later *Mercurius Veridicus ex Hungaria*), from late May 1705, if initially on an irregular basis (see fig. 45).

Although, from the perspective both of Hungary's progress and perhaps also of Rákóczi's own fate, it would have been far more favorable had the war of independence ended after the terrible rout at Trencsén in the summer of 1708, the prince, like John Szapolyai before him, refused to give up his power. As such, the negotiations on an armistice that began in November 1708 ended in failure within a few months. The political and military leadership in Vienna, finding itself in an increasingly favorable position, continued sternly to reject one of Rákóczi's key demands, that of retaining Transylvania under his own control. Yet had the prince given ground, the *kuruc* army might have avoided further defeats, and he might have prevented the further devastation of the country over many years, as would all be wrought by the violent reestablishment of order by the imperial and royal forces that was only exacerbated by a nationwide outbreak of plague.

Had he yielded, the prince would likely not have been subjected to such prolonged exiling and such a tragic displacement as would ensue from the aforementioned experiment of giving the Ottomans access to the territory. Yet he was unable—as we can in part understand—to alter his political driving principles. So Hungarian history gained one more story of lengthy exile, the royal French army gained hussar divisions made up of emigrating

Anno Millesimo Septingentesimo Decimo,

MERCURIUS VERIDICUS

ex

HUNGARIA.

Ujvár, *sive* Neuhausel, *quartâ Januarii.*

Elicia nobis Novus Annus producit initia, Parthia enim nostra Equestris, quæ Trans-Vagum ad Annonæ comportationem urgendam excurrerat, cùm Cæsareum Generalem Campi-Marschallum *Heister* parvo comitatu Posonium versùs tendere intellexisset, citato cursu eundem persecuta est, qui nisi spatio mediæ horæ Posonium se recipisset, prout ante duos Annos *Stárnbergius*, ita hic quoq; in captivitatem incidisset. Felicius tamen alteri Parthiæ res cessit, sub Capitaneo *Javorka*, quæ perfidum illum *Ladislaum Otskay*, olim apud nos Brigaderum (qui ejuratâ fide, post Prælium Trentsiniense ad Cæsarianos profugit,) commilitonibus ejus ultra triginta trucidatis, vivum nobis attulit, Militiâ Præsidiariâ inexplicabili cum indignatione patibulum & furcam, antequam vel ad Commendantem nostrum deduceretur, contra eum conclamante, & vix jam ipse Commendans fervorem Militum mitigare poterat, nisi Jure Belli convictum, quà iniqvum Patriæ & Confœderationis Proditorem (pro quo flexis genibus ad minuendam mortis pœnam apud totam Militiam Frater ejus *Alexander* apud nos Vice-Colonellus Institit) hodie manu Carnificis decollandum curasset.

Χ   Casso-

Fig. 45. Front page of the first Hungarian newspaper, the anti-Habsburg *Mercurius Veridicus ex Hungaria*, January 1710 (Lutheran Central Collection, Lutheran Central Library, Budapest).

kuruc fighters, and the Kingdom of Hungary of the early eighteenth century became poorer by one great politician who deserved a better fate and who could perhaps have done more for his country had he remained in it. Rákóczi's movement, the first Hungarian fight for independence, would from the nineteenth century onward have an exceptional influence on the formation of modern Hungarian national identity. This was, of course, a tribute less to the prince and more to the way in which later politicians would variously make use of his independence struggle.

The greatest achievement of the Rákóczi war of independence would ultimately be the Treaty of Szatmár (May 1, 1711) that concluded it. While Hungarian historical popular belief continues to this day to condemn the agreement itself and the two men behind it, *kuruc* general Sándor Károlyi and János Pálffy, the commander in chief of the imperial and royal forces (accusing Károlyi, in particular, of treachery), they did in fact implement a significant historical undertaking. This is all the more true if we consider that there were generals in Vienna who wished to end the uprising with the use of tougher military methods. The peace treaty, meanwhile, not only promised Rákóczi and his followers a general amnesty and the return of their lands in return for an oath of allegiance—it also settled the situation and domestic affairs of the whole Kingdom of Hungary. This would not have been the case without the circumspection of the two aristocratic Hungarian military and political statesmen.

With the Treaty of Szatmár, Vienna accepted that, for all the liberation carried out by the imperial and royal army, Hungary could not merely be an annexed but important and defining part of the Habsburg Monarchy in the running of which the Hungarian elite and estates could be sidelined. Thus, the dualist governance of the country as developed in the decades after 1526 would be retained (see part 1, chap. 3, and part 2, chap. 3), even if the influence of the estates on military matters was reduced even further. The unity of the estate constitution and of estate society divided by civil war was reestablished. But, alongside noble freedoms, the peace treaty guaranteed the implementation of the religious laws (of 1681 and 1687) already in force, even if these fell short of ensuring full religious freedom. The progress of an independent Transylvania came to a halt, however, even if it could now develop within the borders of the Hungarian Crown rather than as an Ottoman vassal, separately governed from Vienna, albeit under the influence of the local estates.

Finally, and, perhaps, most importantly, the Treaty of Szatmár put an end to a state of war that had been in place for almost a century and to a civil war often religious in nature, which had almost made the country "barren, deserted and uncultivated."[6] Within the borders of the Danubian Habsburg Monarchy but as its most sovereign and one of its most important member states, the rebuilding of the country and many decades of peaceful progress could begin. All in all, this marked the beginning of modern Hungary. After two centuries as the ravaged frontier zone between two empires, the Kingdom of Hungary could again become one of the important countries of Central Europe, if one that operated within the framework of a composite monarchy. The spring of 1711 would bring an end to the Janus-faced seventeenth century: after so much devastation, the long-awaited rejuvenation could begin.

Notes

1. Recently, cf. Domokos Dániel Kis and Ágnes R. Várkonyi, eds. *A Rákóczi-szabadságharc* [The war of independence of Francis Rákóczi] (Budapest: Osiris Kiadó, 2004), 317–619.

2. For the most recent clarification of this question, see Sándor Papp, "A Rákóczi-szabadságharc török diplomáciája" [Ottoman diplomacy of the war of independence of Francis Rákóczi], *Századok* [Centuries] 138, no. 4 (2004): 793–822.

3. Francis Rákóczi, *Vallomások. Emlékiratok* [Confessions. Memoirs.], ed. Lajos Hopp (Budapest: Szépirodalmi Könyvkiadó, 1979), 247.

4. Béla Köpeczi and Ágnes R. Várkonyi, *II. Rákóczi Ferenc* [Francis II Rákóczi], 3rd enlarged ed. (Budapest: Osiris Kiadó, 2004).

5. "With consistent hard work, Rákóczi enjoyed more achievements than the Habsburg state, which had built a centralized state administration a century and a half before. They established the sharing of the social welfare burden, and some social groups were coming into being which could have been the foundation for the construction of a modern state within the conditions set by Central Europe's circumstances." Ibid., 395.

6. As late as 1717, Lady Mary Wortley Montague would still see the most affected areas along the Danube in the same way. György Gömöri, ed., *Angol és skót utazók a régi Magyarországon (1542–1737)* [English and Scottish travelers in Old Hungary (1542–1737)] (Budapest: Argumentum Kiadó, 1994), 106.

GLOSSARY

ahdname: Celebratory letter of agreement by an Ottoman sultan (q.v.) to appoint a new ruler.

alispán (**Latin** *vicecomes*): The deputy of the county's *ispán* (q.v.). From the early sixteenth century, the *alispán* was usually elected by the noble community of the county (q.v.).

articular places: The law (Latin *articulus*, German *Gesetzartikel*, i.e., article) 26 of the Hungarian diet of Sopron in 1681 laid down in detail, for each given county (q.v.), the settlements in which Lutherans and Calvinists were allowed to practice their religion in public (hence the name).

Bácska (**Serbian** *Bačka*): A geographical and historical region in the Hungarian Great Plain bordered by the river Danube to the west and south and by the river Tisza to the east. It is divided between Serbia and Hungary. Most of the area is located in the Vojvodina (Hungarian *Vajdaság*) region in Serbia (its capital is Novi Sad). The smaller northern part of the geographical area is located in Bács-Kiskun county in Hungary.

ban (Latin *banus*, **Hungarian** *bán*, **from Avar** *bajan* **or Slavic** *ban, pan* **= lord):** The royally appointed governor of the Kingdoms of Croatia and Dalmatia (q.v.) and/or the region called Slavonia (q.v.). The political importance and income of the ban was significant; he was always a member of the Hungarian royal council.

Banat (Hungarian *Temesköz, Bánát,* **Serbian** *Banovina,* **Romanian** *Banat*): A geographical and historical region between the rivers Lower Danube, Tisza, and Maros in East Central Europe that is currently divided among three countries: the eastern part lies in western Romania, the western part lies in northeastern Serbia, and a small northern part lies in southeastern Hungary.

beylerbey (Turkish *beykerbeyi*): "Bey of beys"; the governor-general of a vilayet (q.v.) in the Ottoman Empire, who usually also held the rank of pasha (q.v.).

bujdosók: "Exiles"; peasants and soldiers who fled from Upper Hungary to Transylvania and the Partium (q.v.) in 1670–1680s and upraised many times against the Habsburgs in the late seventeenth century.

čardak: Guardhouse in the border defense system against the Ottomans, especially in the Croatian, Slavonian, and Serbian military frontier (q.v.).

çelebi: Honorific title for learned men and high-ranking bureaucrats in the Ottoman Empire.

chief justice (Latin *judex curiae regiae*, **Hungarian** *országbíró*): Originally the officer in charge of the royal court and thus the head of household servants, he acquired high judicial functions once the palatine (q.v.) became the itinerant judge of the entire country (c. 1200). From then on, the chief justice of Hungary passed judgment in the name of the king and soon acquired extensive jurisdictional function.

Cis-Danubian area/region: According to the principle of the central territorial view, prevalent at the early modern age, the region seen from the country's "domestic capital," Pozsony (Pressburg, today Bratislava, Slovakia), as being this side of the Danube, namely the areas from Pozsony county across to Liptó county.

comes: See *ispán*.

condominium: "Double ownership"; a broad area of the chain of Habsburg-Hungarian and Ottoman castles of the opposing sides under double ownership and dual taxation in the sixteenth and seventeenth centuries.

Corvinas: Codices and printed books in King Matthias Corvinus's esteemed library at Buda, which generally include the ruler's coat of arms with a raven (Latin *corvus*; hence the name).

county (Latin *comitatus*, **German** *Komitat, Gespanschaft,* **Hungarian** *megye, vármegye,* **probably from a Slavic word meaning "boundary"):** A complex administrative, judicial, and military unit built around the royal domain, the organization of which had probably begun by the rule of King Stephen I, with a castle in its center where the *ispán* (q.v.) also resided.

Croatia and Dalmatia: The kings of Hungary acquired these kingdoms at the turn of the eleventh to twelfth century; thus, they are often referred to as *regna*. The constitutional relation between Croatia and Hungary became a contested issue only in modern times. The territory enjoyed a special status and differing legal procedures throughout the Middle Ages; it was governed by its own ban (q.v.), frequently together with Slavonia (q.v.).

crown: See **Holy Crown of Hungary**.

Cumans (Hungarian *kunok*): Kipchak Turkic nomads who were settled on the Hungarian Great Plain (the region known in Hungarian as *Kunság*) after the Mongol invasion in the 1240s and who were permitted to retain some of their customs and privileges. Their social and cultural integration was complete by the beginning of the sixteenth century, but they preserved their administrative autonomy until the end of the seventeenth century, and separate Cuman practices persisted until the nineteenth century.

defenestration: "Throwing out of window"; the term is a reference to the leaders of the Bohemian estates throwing two royal lieutenants and their secretary out of a window of Prague Castle on May 23, 1618.

defterdar: Treasurer or fiscal director responsible for property and financial affairs both in the capital and in provincial centers of the Ottoman Empire.

diet (Latin *diaeta, comitia*, German *Landtag/Reichstag*, Hungarian *országgyűlés*): General assembly, parliament of the Kingdom of Hungary with two chambers/houses: prelates (clergy) and magnates (q.v.) met in the upper house, the delegates of the common nobility and free royal cities (q.v.) in the lower house.

dualist nature of the government (German *der fürstlich-ständische Dualismus*): Dual system of power-sharing between the ruler (or their central institutions of government) and the estates (q.v.) in late medieval and early modern Europe.

estates (German *Stände*, Latin *status*, Hungarian *rendek*): The territorial assemblies and the leading noble families (magnates) and prelates (clergy) who dominated them.

familiaris: See **noble retainer**.

florin (Latin *florenus*, Hungarian *forint*): Gold florins began to be minted under Charles I of Anjou, c. 1325 (first mentioned in 1326). They were modeled after the Florentine *fiorino d'oro* (hence the name).

fratricide: A brutal tradition that a young sultan rising to the throne had to do away with his brothers in order to strengthen the power of the Ottoman state.

free city (Latin *libera civitas*): A city (usually walled) with a privilege granting the right of the citizens or burghers to elect their magistrate and other liberties, bestowed by royal charter (since the early thirteenth century). Their number and jurisdictional status was fluid. Some were "free royal cities" (Latin *libera regia civitas*, Hungarian *szabad királyi város*), others were subject to the jurisdiction of the master of the treasury (q.v.), and others were mining towns with special privileges.

gentleman of the realm (Latin *regnicola*, lit. "inhabitant of the realm," Hungarian *országlakó*): The term we use for those inhabitants who, as owners of land and lords of tenant peasants, enjoyed political rights; its equation with the "members of the estates" was gradual and hardly complete by the end of the Middle Ages. However, *regnicolae* may occasionally refer to inhabitants (citizens) of the country in general, or inlanders in contrast to foreigners.

Golden Apple (Turkish *kızıl elma*): In the Ottoman ideology of conquest, the Red or Golden Apple was the symbol of world dominance, of constant and successful conquest, which in the fifteenth century originally referred to Constantinople and, after its occupation, always referred to the military targets of the given time (particularly rulers' residences, such as Buda, Vienna, and Cologne).

Golden Bull: An edict issued by King Andrew II of Hungary at the diet of Székesfehérvár in 1222, which was one of the first examples of constitutional limits being placed on the powers of a European monarch by grants of liberties and rights for the Hungarian nobility, including the right to disobey the king when he acted contrary to law (Latin *ius resistendi*). The Golden Bull of 1222 is often compared to England's Magna Carta of 1215.

Gubernium: A six-member council of governors created by Emperor Leopold I in 1673 to lead Hungary, existed only until the diet of Sopron in 1681.

hajduk (Hungarian *hajdú*, plural *hajdúk*): Irregular or mercenary infantry soldiers of the Kingdom of Hungary (and Central and Southeast Europe) in the early modern period with different privileges donated by the kings, the princes of Transylvania, and Hungarian aristocrats. The Hungarian term *hajdú* may derive from *hajtó*, which meant cattle drover.

***hódoltság* (German *gehuldigte Territorien*):** Ottoman Hungary, the areas occupied by the Ottoman Turks.

Holy Crown of Hungary (*Sacra Corona regni Hungariae*): Refers to the royal office, occasionally to the coronation jewel, the so-called St. Stephen's Crown. The regalia were kept from the mid-fourteenth century until the 1530s at Visegrád Castle, later in Vienna and Prague court, and after 1608 in Pozsony Castle.

hussar (Hungarian *huszár*): Light cavalrymen, equipped with sabers and only lightly armed; these played an increasing role in the Hungarian armies, mainly as a counterweight to the Ottoman spahi cavalry (q.v.). By the close of the Middle Ages, some hussars were fitted with armor and, later, with firearms, too.

Iasians (Hungarian *jászok*): Ethnic minority of Ossetian origin who were settled on the Hungarian Great Plain (the region known in Hungarian as *Jászság*) probably in the thirteenth century and who were permitted to retain some of their customs and privileges. Like the Cumans, they preserved their administrative autonomy and practices until the nineteenth century.

imam: Head of a local Islamic religious community, in charge of mosques and people working in them; leader of religious ceremonies.

***insurrectio* (German *adeliger Aufstand*):** The insurrectio was the "feudal" militia or uprising of the nobles and free royal cities in Hungary (existed until 1809).

***ispán* (Latin *comes*; from Slavic *župan*, "local lord"):** Between the eleventh and thirteenth centuries, the royal officer in charge of one of the counties or of a royal forest or border district. From the thirteenth century onward, the word seems to have been used more widely for members of families that had *ispán*s among their ancestors, even though no hereditary *comes* title was granted in Hungary until the later Middle Ages. With the development of the corporation of nobles in every county (q.v.), the *ispán*, who came to be called *főispán* (in modern texts often translated as "lord lieutenant"), remained the royal officer but exercised his duties in concert with the county magistrates and left the actual administration to his retainer, the *alispán* (q.v.).

janissary (Turkish *yeniçeri*): The main infantry force in the Ottoman army from the early fifteenth century onward; janissaries were deployed in increasing numbers in major provincial centers and castles.

kadi: Judge; a key figure in Ottoman administration, who administered justice according to Islamic law; an official who was also responsible for the administration of financial and military matters and for the enforcement of dynastic law.

***Kavalierstour*:** The Grand Tour, i.e., a grand aristocratic study tour that was the traditional trip of Europe undertaken by mainly aristocrat young men of means. The custom flourished from about the middle of the seventeenth century until the advent of large-scale rail transport in the 1840s. It served also as an educational rite of passage.

kaza: Judicial district, jurisdiction of a kadi (q.v.).

kul: Slave, servant of the dynasty, any member of the administrative-military elite of the Ottoman Empire.

***kurucok*:** "Refugees"; the term *kuruc* originally referred to the crusader soldiers of the peasant uprising led by György Dózsa in 1514. In the second half of the seventeenth century, this same term began to be used to refer to soldiers and peasants participating in armed uprisings. Although the precise origin of the term is debated, the most broadly accepted view is that the Hungarian word *kuruc* comes from the Latin *crux* ("cross").

landsknecht: "Servant of the land"; mercenary soldiers who became an important military force through late fifteenth- and sixteenth-century Europe (among the first in the army of Emperor Maximilian I). Consisting predominantly of German mercenary pikemen and foot soldiers, they were the universal mercenaries of early modern Europe.

licentiate: The title referred to the episcopal license (Latin *licentia*) with which this person would lead a parish (hence the name).

magnates: Leading men in eleventh- and twelfth-century Hungary, originally members of the king's retinue. From the late thirteenth century onward and in the early modern age, members of this upper stratum of society (aristocrats) were usually referred to as magnates.

market town (Latin *oppidum*): See **town**.

master of the treasury (Latin *magister tavernicorum regalium*, Hungarian *tárnokmester*): The title of a royal officer, originally responsible for the royal court's provisioning, derived from the Hungarian name for the guards of royal magazines (*tavernici*); from the fourteenth century onward, the master of the treasury was no longer associated with the treasury but was rather the presiding judge of the appeal court of certain royal cities (*sedes tavernicalis*).

Military Border (Frontier) (German *Militärgrenze*, Croatian and Serbian *vojna krajina*, Hungarian *Határőrvidék*): The defense system against the Ottoman Empire straddling the southern borderland of the Central European Habsburg Monarchy and later the Austro-Hungarian Monarchy along the Sava, Danube, Tisza, and Maros Rivers in Croatia, Slavonia, Hungary, and Transylvania from the very late seventeenth century until 1881.

Muraköz (Croatian *Međimurje*): A small historical and geographical region in the historical Hungary in Zala county, today in northern Croatia, comprising the area between the two large rivers, Mura and Drava; in the sixteenth and seventeenth centuries mostly in the domain of the Zrínyi/Zrinski family.

ninth (Latin *nona*, Hungarian *kilenced*): One of the most substantial elements of seigniorial revenues in Hungary from the first third of the fourteenth century onward. Similar to tithing, it meant in fact the "second" tithe, often paid before the ecclesiastical tithe, on wine and grain, but the ninth was frequently demanded after livestock as well.

noble retainer (Latin *familiaris*): A lesser nobleman who chose to accept military or administrative positions in the service of a prelate, magnate, or major landowner in Hungary. He kept his noble privilege and was subject to his senior (*dominus*) only for service, for which he received monetary compensation and occasionally land. The institution resembled West European vassalage but was less formalized and less mutual.

nobleman (Latin *nobilis*): A wide stratum of landowners in medieval and early modern Hungary, normally holding property originally granted by the king and enjoying, in principle, equal rights regardless of wealth and status.

Oberstfeldhauptmann: Commander in chief of a Habsburg campaign in Hungary in the sixteenth and seventeenth centuries.

palatine (Latin *palatinus*, Hungarian *nádor*): Originally the head of the king's household and highest officer in the realm. By the mid-twelfth century, he had become the king's deputy and commander of the royal host; he gradually moved out of the court and served as the king's itinerant judge administering justice to the nobles, later the first person of the secular elite of Hungary. The election of the palatine was a contested issue between king and estates (q.v.) at the diets (q.v.).

parkan: Palisade; defensive structure consisting of a wall built out of timber and earth.

Partium: Area beyond the Tisza River, i.e., the Hungarian "Parts" (*partes Hungariae*; Hungarian *Részek*), an area of varying size in the sixteenth and seventeenth centuries, belonging to Transylvania, hence Partium, of which the princes of Transylvania became rulers.

pasha: High rank in the Ottoman Empire, in the provinces most often held by the beylerbey (q.v.).

peasant / tenant peasant / serf (Latin *jobagio*, Hungarian *jobbágy*; from c. 1250 onward): The word, which originally meant a royal office holder (*jobagio*) was gradually transferred to *rustici jobagiones* (lit. peasant retainers), who had acquired personal liberty but were bound to the lord of the land by having to render seigniorial dues. They were subject to seigniorial jurisdiction but free to move once they had paid their annual dues and obtained a license. This status remained the characteristic legal condition of Hungarian peasants until the Revolution of 1848.

personal (Latin *personalis presentia regia* or short *personalis*, Hungarian *személynök*): Court of royal personal presence, which emerged as early as the thirteenth century. In the Late Middle Ages, it became the main royal court of justice, issuing sentences under the king's judicial seal.

plot (tenant peasant's): A complex made up of a plot in the village, arable land, and rights to commons assigned to one (or more) tenant peasants (Hungarian *telek*; in taxation terms, *porta*).

prefection (Latin *prefectio in filium, in heredem masculinum*, Hungarian *fiúsítás*): Royal privilege by which the king "promoted" the daughter or daughters of a nobleman without male heirs in the third (since 1397, fourth) degree to a son, i.e., authorized her to inherit the paternal fortune just as if she were a man, starting a new kindred.

presbytery (Hungarian *presbitérium*): The most important body in the Calvinist church administration, one elected by the church community to include secular members as well as ministers. The first Hungarian presbytery was founded in Pápa, northern Transdanubia (Veszprém county), in 1615.

protonotary (Latin *prothonotarius*, Hungarian *ítélőmester*, "master in sentencing"): Lawyers who acquired legal training in the secular Hungarian courts of palatine, chief justice, personal, and ban (q.v.). From the mid-fifteenth century, they presided over court sessions in an increasing number of cases.

Rheinbund: "Confederation of the Rhine"; the alliance was established on August 14, 1658, under the leadership of Johann Philipp von Schönborn, the archbishop of Mainz, seen as the imperial opposition to the newly crowned Emperor Leopold I, and between the archbishops of Trier and of Cologne, the elector-count palatinate, the princes of Hessen-Kassel and of Braunschweig-Lüneburg, and Charles X, king of Sweden (as prince of Bremen); on August 15, it was joined by the Habsburgs' main rival, French king Louis XIV.

sabor: General assembly of the Kingdom of Croatia in the Middle Ages, later common parliament of the gradual unified Croatia and Slavonia.

sanjak (Turkish *sancak*): "Flag," "banner"; subprovince, district in the Ottoman Empire, governed by a *sanjak-bey* (q.v.).

sanjak-bey (Turkish *sancakbeyi, bey, mirliva*): The highest-ranking official in a sanjak (q.v.) of the Ottoman Empire, responsible for both military and civilian affairs.

Saxons: The collective name for Rhenish or Swabian German settlers, especially in Transylvania and in northern Hungary (German *Zips*, Hungarian *Szepesség*, today Slovak *Spiš*), who from the thirteenth century onward enjoyed considerable privileges and virtual autonomy in their towns and areas of settlement (Latin *sedes*, German *Stühle*, Hungarian *székek*).

serdar: The commander in chief of an Ottoman campaign.

serf: See **peasant**.

Slavonia: The major part of the region between the rivers Drava and Sava as well as a part of the region south of the Sava (presently the northern part of the Republic of Croatia and partly Bosnia and Herzegovina), which became part of the kingdom of Hungary in the late eleventh century. In the Late Middle Ages and the sixteenth century, Slavonia included the counties of Varasd/Varaždin, Körös/Križevci, and Zagreb. The counties of Pozsega, Valkó, Syrmium/Szerém, and southern Baranya (though all lying between the rivers Drava and Sava) did not belong to Slavonia in this period, only later in the eighteenth century (called then Lower Slavonia). The region was administered by a ban (q.v.), often jointly with Croatia and Dalmatia (q.v.). Its inhabitants and nobles had slightly different rights and duties from those of the rest of the Kingdom of Hungary.

spahi: 1. Cavalryman; member of one of the six divisions of salaried cavalry troops of the Ottoman court. 2. Provincial light cavalry remunerated with *timar* grants (q.v.).

sultan: Ruler, monarch of the Ottoman Empire.

Szekler (Hungarian *székely*, Latin *siculus*): Originally border guards who were moved to Transylvania in the late twelfth and early thirteenth centuries, where they constituted their own privileged community in their towns and areas of settlement (Latin *sedes*, Hungarian *székek*).

szombatisták ("Sabbatarians"): Their name derives from the fact that, following the prescriptions of the Old Testament, they considered Saturday rather than Sunday to be the holy day. Accepting as they did the primacy of the Old Testament, their movement was close to the Jewish faith. Their best-known exponent, Simon Péchi, who translated Jewish prayers from the original Hebrew into Hungarian, was chancellor to prince of Transylvania (1613–1629) Gabriel Bethlen.

***Temesköz* region:** See **Banat**.

thirtieth (Latin *tricesima*, Hungarian *harmincad*): A customs duty on import and export in Hungary that developed out of different types of urban and market tolls.

timar: The category of prebend yielding the lowest annual income (below twenty thousand akçes per year) in the Ottoman Empire.

tithe (Latin *decima*, Hungarian *tized*): Ecclesiastical tithe was decreed by the first kings of Hungary, but the details of its collection were a recurrent issue of debate at the diets through the centuries. In principle, it was to be paid to the bishop (or his tax collector, Latin *dicator*, or the persons to whom it was farmed out) and shared by the cathedral chapter and parishes.

town (Latin *oppidum*, Hungarian *város*): Nonprivileged town or market town (Hungarian *mezőváros*) that was—in contrast to free cities (q.v.)—subject to the jurisdiction of secular or ecclesiastical lords, but with some rights of autonomy (election of mayor and/or parish priest, market rights, etc.). In the early sixteenth century, there were some eight hundred marketplaces in the country.

Transylvania: The mountainous eastern part of the Kingdom of Hungary in the Middle Ages beyond the Királyhágó (Romanian Pasul Craiului) with a mixed Magyar (including Szekler), German (Saxon), and Romanian population, governed by the voivode (q.v.) and enjoying some autonomy and following slightly different legal customs. The Principality of Transylvania developed from this territory in the sixteenth century (see part 1, chaps. 4–5).

***Tripartitum* (Hungarian *Hármaskönyv*):** Customary law of the Kingdom of Hungary summarized by István Werbőczy at the beginning of the sixteenth century and edited in Vienna in 1517.

***Türkenhilfe*:** Turkish taxes and monetary aids paid by the estates of the Holy Roman Empire and the Austrian hereditary lands to maintain the defense in Hungary and Croatia against the Ottoman Turks.

urbarium (German *Urbar*, Hungarian *urbárium*): A register of fief ownership that includes the rights and benefits that the fief holder has over his serf and peasants. It is an important economic and legal source of the early modern age.

uskoks (Latin *Uscoci*, Croatian *Uskoci*): Irregular soldiers in Habsburg Croatia in the sixteenth and seventeenth centuries that inhabited areas on the eastern Adriatic coast and in surrounding territories during the Ottoman wars in Europe.

vilayet: Largest territorial unit of Ottoman civil and military administration, under the command of a beylerbey (q.v.).

village (Latin *villa, possessio*, Hungarian *falu*): The development of fixed village settlements from the summer and winter quarters of seminomadic peoples began in the eleventh century, but "villages" kept moving either to pastures with their cattle or to new lands once the cultivated area was exhausted, probably until the late twelfth century. By 1300, Hungary may have had about two thousand villages; in the early sixteenth century, there were approximately eighteen thousand. The term was used loosely for different types and sizes of settlements.

vizier (Turkish *vezir*): Title held by the grand vizier and several other dignitaries. In sixteenth-century Ottoman Hungary, the rank was rarely granted to the beylerbeys (q.v.); after 1621 it was given to all the beylerbeys of Buda.

Vlach: 1. People of Romanian origin in the Balkan peninsula. 2. Transhumant shepherd. 3. Balkan peasant military people with Vlach legal status, many of whom were settled in Ottoman Hungary.

voivode of Transylvania (Latin *waywoda*, Hungarian *vajda*): Royally appointed governor of Transylvania in the Middle Ages with jurisdiction over the seven Hungarian counties and, as *ispán* of the Szeklers (q.v.), over these former borderland kindreds as well. His court was the first instance in the region with the right to appeal to the royal courts. Thus, the nobility of Transylvania lay in a different jurisdictional position from their fellows in the central areas.

***zsellér* (Latin *inquilinus*):** (Cottar) landless peasants and often wage laborers. The term acquired a more general legal meaning in the Late Middle Ages: persons without at least a quarter of a plot (q.v.), regardless of their economic status.

RULERS AND HIGHEST DIGNITARIES

Emperors of the Holy Roman Empire

Maximilian I (1493–1519)
Charles V (1519–1556/58)
Ferdinand I (1558–1564)
Maximilian II (1564–1576)
Rudolf II (1576–1612)
Matthias (1612–1619)
Ferdinand II (1619–1637)
Ferdinand III (1637–1657)
Leopold I (1657–1705)
Joseph I (1705–1711)
Charles VI (1711–1740)

Sultans of the Ottoman Empire

Selim I (1512–1520)
Süleyman I, the Magnificent (1520–1566)
Selim II (1566–1574)
Murad III (1574–1595)
Mehmed III (1595–1603)
Ahmed I (1603–1617)
Mustafa I (1617–1618)
Osman II (1618–1622)
Mustafa I (1622–1623)
Murad IV (1623–1640)
Ibrahim (1640–1648)
Mehmed IV (1648–1687)
Süleyman II (1687–1691)
Ahmed II (1691–1695)
Mustafa II (1695–1703)
Ahmed III (1703–1730)

Kings of Hungary and Croatia

Louis II of Jagiello (1516–1526)
John I Szapolyai (1526–1540)
Ferdinand I of Habsburg (1526–1564)
John II Sigismund Szapolyai, only *elected king* (1540–1571)
Maximilian I of Habsburg (1564–1576)
Rudolf I (1576–1608)
Matthias II (1608–1619)
Ferdinand II (1619–1637)
Ferdinand III (1637–1657)
Leopold I (1657–1705)
Joseph I (1705–1711)
Charles III (1711–1740)

Princes of Transylvania

John Sigismund (1540/59–1571)
Stephen Báthory of Somlyó (1571–1586)
Sigismund Báthory (1588–1602, with some interruptions)
Andrew Báthory (1599)
Governance of Michael the Brave (1599–1600)
Governance of Giorgio Basta (1602–1604)
Moses Székely, only *elected prince* (1603)
Stephen Bocskai (1605–1606)
Sigismund Rákóczi (1607–1608)
Gabriel Báthory (1608–1613)
Gabriel Bethlen (1613–1629)
Catherine of Brandenburg (1629–1630)
Georg I Rákóczi (1630–1648)
Georg II Rákóczi (1648–1660, with some interruptions)
Francis I Rákóczi, only *elected prince* (1652)
Francis Rhédey (1657–1658)
Ákos (Achatius) Barcsay (1658–1660)
John Kemény (1661–1662)
Michael I Apafi (1661–1690)
Michael II Apafi, only *elected prince* (1681)
Francis II Rákóczi (1704–1711)

Royal Governors (Latin *locumtenens regius*, Hungarian *királyi helytartó*)

Queen Mary of Hungary (1527)
Palatine István Báthory of Ecsed (1528–1530)
Chancellor Tamás Szalaházy and Chief Justice Elek Thurzó (1531–1532)
Chief Justice Elek Thurzó (1532–1542)
Archbishop of Esztergom Pál Várday (1542–1549)
Bishop of Győr Ferenc Újlaky (1550–1554)
Palatine Tamás Nádasdy (1554–1562)
Archbishop of Esztergom Miklós Oláh (1562–1568)
Bishop of Transylvania Pál Bornemisza (1568–1572)
Archbishop of Esztergom Antal Verancsics (1572–1573)
Bishop of Eger István Radéczy (1573–1586)
Archbishop of Kalocsa György Draskovics (1586–1587)
Bishop of Nyitra István Fejérkövy (1587–1596)
Archbishop of Esztergom János Kutassy (1597–1601)
Archbishop of Kalocsa Márton Pethe (1602–1605)
Archbishop of Esztergom Ferenc Forgách (1607–1608)
Palatine István Illésházy (1608–1609)
Palatine György Thurzó (1609–1616)
Palatine Zsigmond Forgách (1618–1621)
Palatine Szaniszló Thurzó (1622–1625)
Palatine Miklós Esterházy (1625–1645)
Archbishop of Esztergom György Lippay (1645–1646)
Palatine János Draskovics (1646–1648)
Archbishop of Esztergom György Lippay (1648–1649)
Palatine Pál Pálffy (1649–1653)
Archbishop of Esztergom György Lippay (1654–1655)
Palatine Ferenc Wesselényi (1655–1667)

Chief Justice Ferenc Nádasdy and Archbishop of Esztergom György Szelepchény (1667–1670)
Archbishop of Esztergom György Szelepchény (1670–1681)
Palatine Pál Esterházy (1681–1713)

Palatines (Latin *palatinus regni Hungariae*, Hungarian *nádor*)

István Báthory of Ecsed (1526–1530)
vacantia (1530–1554)
Tamás Nádasdy (1554–1562)
vacantia (1562–1608)
István Illésházy (1608–1609)
György Thurzó (1609–1616)
Zsigmond Forgách (1618–1621)
Szaniszló Thurzó (1622–1625)
Miklós Esterházy (1625–1645)
János Draskovics (1646–1648)
Pál Pálffy (1649–1653)
Ferenc Wesselényi (1655–1667)
vacantia (1667–1681)
Pál Esterházy (1681–1713)

Chiefs Justice (Latin *iudex curiae regiae*, Hungarian *országbíró*)

Elek Thurzó (1527–1543)
Tamás Nádasdy (1543–1554)
András Báthory of Ecsed (1554–1566)
Gábor Perényi (1566–1567)
Kristóf Országh (1567)
István Bánffy (1567–1568)
Miklós Báthory of Ecsed (1568–1584)
István Báthory of Ecsed (1586–1605)
Zsigmond Forgách (1606–1608)
Bálint Drugeth de Homonna (1608–1609)
Zsigmond Forgách (1610–1618)
György Drugeth de Homonna (1618–1620)
Miklós Esterházy (1622–1625)
Menyhért Alaghy (1625–1631)
Pál Rákóczi (1631–1636)
János Drugeth de Homonna (1636–1645)
Pál Pálffy (1646–1649)
László Csáky (1649–1655)
Ferenc Nádasdy (1655–1670)
Ádám Forgách (1670–1681)
Miklós Draskovics (1681–1687)
István Csáky (1687–1700)
Ádám Batthyány (1700–1703)
György Erdődy (1704–1713)
Pálffy Miklós (1713–1714)

Bans of Croatia and Slavonia (Latin *banus Croatiae et Slavoniae*, Hungarian *horvát-szlavón bán*)

Ferenc Batthyány (1525–1533) and Ivan Karlović (1527–1531)
Lajos Pekry (1531–1537)

Tamás Nádasdy (1537–1539) and Péter Keglevics / Petar Keglević (1537–1541)
Miklós Zrínyi / Nikola Zrinski (1542–1556)
Péter Erdődy (1556–1567)
Franjo Frankopan / Ferenc Frangepán (1567–1572) and György Draskovics (1567–1578)
Gáspár Alapy (1574–1576)
Christoph Ungnad (1578–1584)
Tamás Erdődy (1584–1595)
Gáspár Sztankováchky (1595–1596) and János Draskovics (1595–1607)
Tamás Erdődy (1608–1615)
Benedek Thuróczy (1615–1616)
Nikola Frankopan / Miklós Frangepán (1617–1622)
György Zrínyi / Juraj Zrinski (1622–1626)
Zsigmond Erdődy (1627–1639)
János Draskovics (1639–1646)
Miklós Zrínyi / Nikola Zrinski (1647–1664)
Péter Zrínyi / Petar Zrinski (1665–1670)
Miklós Erdődy (1670–1693)
Ádám Batthyány (1693–1703)
János Pálffy (1704–1731)

Royal Masters of the Treasury (Latin *magister tavernicorum regalium*, Hungarian *tárnokmester*)

Elek Thurzó (1523–1527)
András Báthory of Ecsed (1527–1534)
Tamás Nádasdy (1536–1542)
András Báthory (1544–1554)
Gábor Perényi (1554–1557)
Miklós Zrínyi / Nikola Zrinski (1557–1566)
György Zrínyi / Juraj Zrinski (1567–1603)
Tamás Erdődy (1603–1608)
Zsigmond Forgách (1608–1610)
János Draskovics (1610–1613)
Tamás Erdődy (1615–1624)
Kristóf Bánffy (1625–1643)
István Csáky (1644–1662)
György Erdődy (1662–1663)
Ádám Forgách (1663–1679)
Imre Erdődy (1679–1690)
István Zichy (1690–1693)
György Erdődy (1693–1704)
Zsigmond Csáky (1706–1739)

Presidents of the Hungarian Chamber (Latin *praefectus Camerae Hungaricae*, Hungarian *Magyar Kamara elnöke*)

Miklós Gerendi (1527–1531)
Stefan Pemfflinger (1531–1537)
Albert Pereghy (1537–1546)
Balázs Péterváradi (1547–1549)
Ferenc Thurzó (1549–1556)
János Dessewffy (1557–1561)
János Újlaky (1561–1568)

István Radéczy (1568–1586)
István Fejérkövy (1587–1596)
István Szuhay (1596–1607)
Tamás Vízkelethy (1608–1611)
László Pethe (1612–1617)
Gáspár Horváth of Veglia (1619–1624)
Pál Pálffy (1625–1646)
Gáspár Lippay (1646–1652)
István Zichy (1655–1671)
Leopold Kollonitsch (1671–1684)
Kristóf Erdődy (1684–1704)
Otto Christoph Volkra (1704–1709)
Sándor Erdődy (1709–1718)

Archbishops of Esztergom (Latin *archiepiscopus Strigoniensis*, Hungarian *esztergomi érsek*)

Pál Várday (1526–1549)
vacantia (1549–1551)
Friar Georg Martinuzzi (1551)
Miklós Oláh (1553–1568)
Antal Verancsics (1569–1573)
vacantia (1573–1596)
István Fejérkövy (1596)
János Kutassy (1597–1601)
Ferenc Forgách (1607–1615)
Péter Pázmány (1616–1637)
Imre Lósy (1637–1642)
György Lippay (1642–1666)
György Szelepchény (1666–1685)
György Széchényi (1685–1695)
Leopold Kollonitsch (1695–1707)
Christian August of Saxe-Zeitz (1707–1725)

SELECT BIBLIOGRAPHY
(MONOGRAPHS AND COLLECTED STUDIES)

Abrahamowicz, Zygmunt, et al. *Die Türkenkriege in der historischen Forschung*. Vienna: Franz Deuticke, 1983.
Ács, Pál. *A magyar irodalmi nyelv két elmélete: Az erazmista és a Balassi-követő* [Two theories of literary Hungarian: The Erasmist and the follower of Balassi]. Budapest: Akadémiai Kiadó, 1983.
———. *"Az idő ósága": Történetiség és történetszemlélet a régi magyar irodalomban* ["The antiquity of time": Historicity and historical vision in Old Hungarian literature]. Budapest: Osiris Kiadó, 2001.
———. *Reformations in Hungary in the Age of the Ottoman Conquest*. Göttingen: Vandenhoeck und Ruprecht, 2019.
Ács, Pál, and Enikő Buzási, eds. *Esterházy Pál, a műkedvelő mecénás: Egy 17. századi arisztokrata-életpálya a politika és a művészet határvidékén* [Pál Esterházy, the ambitious patron: A seventeenth-century aristocratic career on the border of politics and art]. Budapest: reciti, 2015.
Ács, Pál, and Gergely Tóth, eds. *"A magyar történet folytatója": Tanulmányok Istvánffy Miklósról* ["Who continued Hungarian history": Essays on Miklós Istvánffy]. Budapest: MTA BTK TTI, 2018.
Acsády, Ignácz. *Magyarország három részre oszlásának története, 1526–1608* [The history of division of Hungary into three parts, 1526–1608]. Budapest: Athenaeum Irodalmi és Nyomdai Részvénytársulat, 1897.
———. *Magyarország története I. Lipót és I. József korában, 1657–1711* [The history of Hungary in the age of Leopold I and Joseph I, 1657–1711]. Budapest: Athenaeum Irodalmi és Nyomdai Részvénytársulat, 1898.
Adamček, Josip. *Agrarni odnosi u Hrvatskoj od seredine XV do kraja XVII stoljeća* [The agricultural situation in Croatia from the middle of the fifteenth to the beginning of the seventeenth century]. Zagreb: Sveučilišna naklada Liber, 1980.
Ágoston, Gábor. *A hódolt Magyarország* [Hungary under Ottoman rule]. Budapest: ADAMS Kiadó, 1992.
Ágoston, Gábor, and Teréz Oborni. *A tizenhetedik század története* [The history of seventeenth-century Hungary]. Budapest: Pannonica Kiadó, 2000.
Almási, Gábor. *The Uses of Humanism: Johannes Sambucus (1531–1584), Andreas Dudith (1533–1589), and the Republic of Letters in East Central Europe*. Leiden: Brill, 2009.
Almási, Gábor, et al., eds. *A Divided Hungary in Europe: Exchanges, Networks and Representations, 1541–1699*. 3 vols. Newcastle upon Tyne: Cambridge Scholars, 2014.
Ammerer, Gerhard, et al., eds. *Bündnispartner und Konkurrenten der Landesfürsten? Die Stände in der Habsburgermonarchie*. Vienna: Oldenbourg, 2007.
Angyal, Dávid. *Magyarország története II. Mátyástól III. Ferdinánd haláláig* [The history of Hungary from Matthias II until the death of Ferdinand III]. Budapest: Athenaeum Irodalmi és Nyomdai Részvénytársulat, 1898.
Arens, Meinolf. *Habsburg und Siebenbürgen 1600–1605: Gewaltsame Eingliederungsversuche eines ostmitteleuropäischen Fürstentums in einen frühabsolutistischen Reichsverband*. Cologne: Böhlau, 2001.
Baďurík, Jozef, ed. *Slovensko a Habsburská monarchia v 16.–17. stor.: Zborník príspevkov z vedeckého sympózia usporiadaného dňa 22. novembra 1994 v Bratislave* [Slovakia and the Habsburg Monarchy in the sixteenth and seventeenth centuries: Collected studies of the symposium organized on November 22, 1994, in Bratislava]. Bratislava: OSI, Pobočka v Bratislave, 1995.
Baďurík, Jozef, and Peter Kónya, eds. *Slovensko v Habsburskej monarchii 1526–1918* [Slovakia in the Habsburg Monarchy, 1526–1918]. Bratislava: Lana, 2000.
Bagi, Zoltán Péter. *A császári-királyi mezei hadsereg a tizenöt éves háborúban: Hadszervezet, érdekérvényesítés, reformkísérletek* [The imperial-royal field army in the Long Turkish War: Military organization, interest representation and reform attempts]. Budapest: Históriaantik Könyvkiadó, 2011.
Bahlcke, Joachim. *Regionalismus und Staatsintegration im Widerstreit: Die Länder der Böhmischen Krone im ersten Jahrhundert der Habsburgerherrschaft (1526–1619)*. Munich: Oldenbourg, 1994.

Bahlcke, Joachim, Hans Jürgen Bömelburg, and Norbert Kersken, eds. *Ständefreiheit und Staatsgestaltung in Ostmitteleuropa: Übernationale Gemeinsamkeiten in der politischen Kultur vom 16.-18. Jahrhundert.* Leipzig: Universitätsverlag Leipzig, 1996.

Bahlcke, Joachim, and Arno Strohmeyer, eds. *Konfessionalisierung in Ostmitteleuropa: Wirkungen des religiösen Wandels im 16. und 17. Jahrhundert in Staat, Gesellschaft und Kultur.* Stuttgart: Franz Steiner, 1999.

Bak, Borbála. *Magyarország történeti topográfiája: A honfoglalástól 1950-ig* [The historical topography of Hungary from the conquest to 1950]. Budapest: MTA TTI, 1997.

Bak, János M., ed. *Coronations: Medieval and Early Modern Monarchic Ritual.* Berkeley: University of California Press, 1990.

———. *Königtum und Stände in Ungarn im 14.-16. Jahrhundert.* Wiesbaden: Steiner, 1973.

Bak, János M., Péter Banyó, and Martyn Rady, eds., trans. *The Customary Law of the Renowned Kingdom of Hungary: A Work in Three Parts Rendered by Stephen Werbőczy (The "Tripartitum").* Introductory study by László Péter. Idyllwild, CA: Charles Schacks, Jr., 2006.

Bak, János M., and Béla K. Király, eds. *From Hunyadi to Rákóczi: War and Society in Late Medieval and Early Modern Hungary.* Boulder, CO: Social Sciences Monographs, 1982.

Bak, János M., and Géza Pálffy. *Crown and Coronation in Hungary 1000-1916 A.D.* Budapest: RCH, 2020.

Balázs, Mihály. *Early Transylvanian Antitrinitarianism (1566-1571).* Baden-Baden: Valentin Koerner, 1996.

Bariska, István. *A Contribution to the History of the Turkish Campaign of 1532.* Szombathely: Institute for Social and European Studies, 2007.

———. *A Szent Koronáért elzálogosított Nyugat-Magyarország 1447-1647* [Western Hungary mortgaged for the Holy Crown, 1447-1647]. Szombathely: VML, 2007.

Barlay, Ö. Szabolcs. *Romon virág: Fejezetek a Mohács utáni reneszánszról* [A flower on ruins: Chapters from the Renaissance after Mohács]. Budapest: Gondolat Kiadó, 1986.

Barta, Gábor. *Az erdélyi fejedelemség születése* [The making of the Principality of Transylvania]. 2nd ed. Budapest: Gondolat Kiadó, 1984.

———. *La route qui mène à Istanbul 1526-1528.* Budapest: Akadémiai Kiadó, 1994.

———. *Vajon kié az ország?* [Whose is the country?]. Budapest: Helikon Kiadó, 1988.

Barta, János, ed. *Habsburgok és Magyarország a XVI-XVIII. században. (Tanulmányok)* [Habsburgs and Hungary in the sixteenth and seventeenth centuries: Essays]. Debrecen: KLTE Történelmi Intézet, 1997.

Barta, János, Jr., and Klára Papp, eds. *"Nincsen nekönk több hazánk ennél . . .": Tanulmányok a Bocskai-felkelés történetéhez* ["We have no other homeland but this one . . .": Essays about the history of the Bocskai uprising]. Budapest: Lucidus Kiadó, 2004.

Barta, János, Manfred Jatzlauk, and Klára Papp, eds. *"Einigkeit und Frieden sollen auf Seiten jeder Partei sein.": Die Friedenschlüssen von Wien (23. 06. 1606) und Zsitvatorok (15. 11. 1606).* Debrecen: Institut für Geschichte der Universität Debrecen, 2007.

Bartoniek, Emma. *A magyar királykoronázások története* [The history of royal coronations in Hungary]. 2nd ed. Budapest: Akadémiai Kiadó, 1987.

———. *Fejezetek a XVI-XVII. századi magyarországi történetírás történetéből* [Chapters from the history of Hungarian historiography in the sixteenth and seventeenth centuries]. Edited by Zsigmondné Ritoók. Budapest: MTA ITI, 1975.

Basics, Beatrix, and Johan Van der Beke, eds. *Hungaria regia (1000-1800): Fastes et défis.* Turnhout: Brepols, 1999.

Beke, Margit, ed. *Esztergomi érsekek 1001-2003* [The archbishops of Esztergom, 1001-2003]. Budapest: SZIT, 2003.

Benczédi, László, ed. *A Thököly felkelés és kora* [The Thököly uprising and its age]. Budapest: Akadémiai Kiadó, 1983.

———. *Rendiség, abszolutizmus és centralizáció a XVII. század végi Magyarországon* [Estates, absolutism, and centralization in Hungary at the end of the seventeenth century]. Budapest: Akadémiai Kiadó, 1980.

Benda, Kálmán. *A nemzeti hivatástudat nyomában: Történelmi, történelemelméleti, művelődés-történeti, iskolapolitikai és csángómagyar tanulmányok, írások, interjúk* [On the trail of patriotic awareness: Writings and interviews on history, philosophy of history, intellectual history, educational policies, and Csango Hungarian studies]. Edited by János Lukáts. Budapest: Mundus Magyar Egyetemi Kiadó, 2004.

———, ed. *Magyarország történeti kronológiája* [Historical chronology of Hungary]. Vol. 2, *1526-1848*. 3rd ed. Budapest: Akadémiai Kiadó, 1989.

Benda, Kálmán, and Erik Fügedi. *Tausend Jahre Stephanskrone.* Budapest: Corvina Kiadó, 1988.

Bene, Sándor, and Gábor Hausner, eds. *A Zrínyiek a magyar és a horvát históriában* [The Zrínyi family in Hungarian and Croatian history]. Budapest: Zrínyi Kiadó, 2007.

Bene, Sándor, et al., eds. *Határok fölött: Tanulmányok a költő, katona, államférfi Zrínyi Miklósról* [Above borders: Studies on poet, soldier, and statesman Miklós Zrínyi]. Budapest: MTA BTK, 2017.

Bérenger, Jean. *Habsbourg et Ottomans (1520–1918)*. Paris: Champion, 2015.

———. *A History of the Habsburg Empire, 1273–1700*. London: Longman, 1994.

———. *La Hongrie des Habsbourg*. Vol. 1, *De 1526 à 1790*. Rennes: Presses Universitaires de Rennes, 2010.

———, ed. *La paix de Karlowitz 26 janvier 1699: Les relations entre l'Europe centrale et l'Empire Ottoman*. Paris: Champion, 2010.

———. *Léopold Ier (1640–1705): Fondateur de la puissance autrichienne*. Paris: PUF, 2004.

———. *Les "Gravamina": Remontrances des diètes de Hongrie de 1655 a 1681*. Paris: PUF, 1973.

Bérenger, Jean, and Charles Kecskeméti. *Parlement et vie parlementaire en Hongrie, 1608–1918*. Paris: Champion, 2005.

Bertényi, Iván. *A magyar korona története* [The history of the Hungarian crown]. 3rd revised ed. Budapest: Kossuth Kiadó, 1986.

Bessenyei, József. *Menekültek . . .: A kereskedelem helyzete Magyarországon 1526 után, Bornemisza Tamás és a budai menekültek működésének tükrében* [Refugees: The state of commerce in Hungary after 1526 in the mirror of the activities of Tamás Bornemisza and the refugees from Buda]. Miskolc: Miskolci Egyetemi Kiadó, 2007.

Bibl, Viktor. *Maximilian II. Der rätselhafte Kaiser: Ein Zeitbild*. Hellerau bei Dresden: Avalun, 1929.

Bireley, Robert. *Ferdinand II: Counter-Reformation Emperor, 1578–1637*. Cambridge: Cambridge University Press, 2014.

———. *The Jesuits and the Thirty Years War: Kings, Courts, and Confessors*. Cambridge: Cambridge University Press, 2003.

Birnbaum, Marianna D. *Humanists in a Shattered World: Croatian and Hungarian Latinity in the Sixteenth Century*. Columbus, OH: Slavica, 1986.

Bitskey, István. *Pázmány Péter* [Péter Pázmány]. Budapest: Gondolat Kiadó, 1986.

Black, Jeremy. *A Military Revolution? Military Change and European Society, 1550–1800*. Atlantic Highlands, NJ: Humanities Press, 1991.

Blažević, Zrinka. *Vitezovićeva Hrvatska između stvarnosti i utopije* [Vitezović's Croatia between reality and utopia]. Zagreb: Barbat, 2002.

Bobory, Dóra. *The Sword and the Crucible: Count Boldizsár Batthyány and Natural Philosophy in Sixteenth-Century Hungary*. Newcastle upon Tyne: Cambridge Scholars, 2009.

Bog, Ingomar, ed. *Der Außenhandel Ostmitteleuropas 1450–1650: Die ostmitteleuropäischen Volkswirtschaften in ihren Beziehungen zu Mitteleuropa*. Cologne: Böhlau, 1971.

Bónis, György, Alajos Degré, and Endre Varga. *A magyar bírósági szervezet és perjog története* [The history of Hungarian court bodies and procedures]. Edited by András Molnár. 2nd ed. Zalaegerszeg: Zala Megyei Bíróság, 1996.

Bonney, Richard. *The European Dynastic States, 1494–1660*. Oxford: Oxford University Press, 1991.

Bracewell, C[atherine] W[endy]. *The Uskoks of Senj: Piracy, Banditry, and Holy War in the Sixteenth-Century Adriatic*. Ithaca, NY: Cornell University Press, 1992.

Branca, Vittore, ed. *Venezia e Ungheria nel contesto del barocco Europeo*. Firenze: Olschki, 1979.

Brandis, Clemens Graf zu. *Die Habsburger und die Stephanskrone*. Zürich: Amalthea, 1937.

Breuer, Dieter, et al., eds. *Das Ungarnbild in der deutschen Literatur der frühen Neuzeit: Der Ungarische oder Dacianische Simplicissimus im Kontext barocker Reiseerzählungen und Simpliziaden*. Bern: Peter Lang, 2005.

Bucholtz, Franz Bernhard. *Geschichte der Regierung Ferdinands I*. 9 vols. Vienna: Schaumburg, 1831–1838. Reprinted with Berthold Sutter's introduction, 1971.

Bucsay, Mihály. *Der Protestantismus in Ungarn 1521–1978: Ungarns Reformationskirchen in Geschichte und Gegenwart*. Vol. 1, *Im Zeitalter der Reformation, Gegenreformation und katholischen Reform*. Vienna: Böhlau, 1977.

Budak, Neven. *Hrvatska i Slavonija u ranom novom vijeku* [Croatia and Slavonia in the early modern age]. Zagreb: Leykam international, 2008.

Budak, Neven, Mario Strecha, and Željko Krušelj. *Habsburzi i Hrvati* [Habsburgs and Croats]. Zagreb: Srednja Europa, 2003.

Bůžek, Václav, ed. *Ein Bruderzwist im Hause Habsburg (1608–1611)*. České Budějovice: JU HÚ, 2010.

Bůžek, Václav, and Pavel Král, eds. *Šlechta v habsburské monarchii a císařský dvůr (1526–1740)* [Nobility in the Habsburg Monarchy and at the imperial court, 1526–1740]. České Budějovice: JU HÚ, 2003.

Bůžek, Václav, and Rostislav Smíšek, eds. *Habsburkové (1526–1740): Země Koruny české ve středoevropské monarchii* [The Habsburgs, 1526–1740: The lands of the Bohemian crown in a Central European monarchy]. Prague: Nakladatelství Lidové noviny, 2017.

Cartledge, Bryan. *The Will to Survey: A History of Hungary*. London: Timewell, 2006.

Crăciun, Maria, and Elaine Fulton, eds. *Communities of Devotion: Religious Orders and Society in East Central Europe, 1450–1800*. Farnham-Burlington: Ashgate, 2011.

Crăciun, Maria, Ovidiu Ghitta, and Graeme Murdock, eds. *Confessional Identity in East-Central Europe*. Aldershot: Ashgate, 2002.

Csaplár-Degovics, Krisztián, and István Fazekas, eds. *Geteilt—Vereinigt: Beiträge zur Geschichte des Königreichs Ungarn in der Frühneuzeit (16.–18. Jahrhundert)*. Berlin: Osteuropa-Zentrum Berlin, 2011.

Csatári, D[ániel], L[ászló] Katus, and Á[gnes] Rozsnyói, eds. *Nouvelles études historiques publiées à l'occasion du XIIe Congrès International des Sciences Historiques par la Commission Nationale des Historiens Hongrois*. 2 vols. Budapest: Akadémiai Kiadó, 1965.

Csepregi, Zoltán. *A reformáció nyelve: Tanulmányok a magyarországi reformáció első negyedszázadának vizsgálata alapján* [The language of the Reformation: Studies based on research into the first quarter century of the Reformation in Hungary]. Budapest: Balassi Kiadó, 2013.

Czigány, István. *Reform vagy kudarc? Kísérletek a magyarországi katonaság beillesztésére a Habsburg Birodalom haderejébe* [Reform or failure? Attempts to integrate the Hungarian soldiery into the army of the Habsburg Monarchy]. Budapest: Balassi Kiadó, 2004.

Dáné, Veronka, et al., eds. *Bethlen Erdélye, Erdély Bethlene* [The Transylvania of Gabriel Bethlen, and the Bethlen of Transylvania]. Kolozsvár: EME, 2014.

Dávid, Géza. *Studies in Demographic and Administrative History of Ottoman Hungary*. Istanbul: Isis, 1997.

Dávid, Géza, and Pál Fodor, eds. *Hungarian-Ottoman Military and Diplomatic Relations in the Age of Süleyman the Magnificent*. Budapest: Loránd Eötvös University, Department of Turkish Studies, 1994.

———, eds. *Ottomans, Hungarians, and Habsburgs in Central Europe: The Military Confines in the Era of the Ottoman Conquest*. Leiden: Brill, 2000.

———, eds. *Ransom Slavery along the Ottoman Borders (Early Fifteenth–Early Eighteenth Centuries)*. Leiden: Brill, 2007.

Deér, József, and László Gáldi, eds. *Magyarok és románok* [Hungarians and Romanians]. 2 vols. Budapest: Teleki Intézet, 1943.

Domanovszky, Sándor, ed. *Magyar művelődéstörténet* [History of Hungarian culture]. Vols. 3–4. Budapest: MTT, 1940. Reprint edition, Szekszárd: Babits Kiadó, 1991.

Dominkovits, Péter, and Csaba Katona, eds. *Egy új együttműködés kezdete: Az 1622. évi soproni koronázó országgyűlés* [Beginning of a new collaboration: The Hungarian coronation diet at Sopron in 1622]. Sopron: MNL Győr-Moson-Sopron Megye Soproni Levéltára, 2014.

Dominkovits, Péter, Csaba Katona, and Géza Pálffy, eds. *Amikor Sopronra figyelt Európa: Az 1625. évi soproni koronázó országgyűlés* [When the eyes of Europe were on Sopron: The Hungarian coronation diet of 1625]. Sopron: MNL Győr-Moson-Sopron Megye Soproni Levéltára, 2020.

Domokos, György. *Ottavio Baldigara: Egy itáliai várfundáló mester Magyarországon* [Ottavio Baldigara: An Italian fort architect in Hungary]. Budapest: Balassi Kiadó, 2000.

Duchoňová, Diana. *Palatín Mikuláš Esterházy: Dvorská spoločnosť a aristokratická každodennosť* [Palatine Miklós Esterházy: Court society and aristocratic everydayness]. Bratislava: HÚ SAV, 2017.

Duindam, Jeroen. *Vienna and Versailles: The Courts of Europe's Dynastic Rivals, 1550–1780*. Cambridge: Cambridge University Press, 2003.

Dybaś, Bogusław, and István Tringli, eds. *Das Wiener Fürstentreffen von 1515: Beiträge zur Geschichte der habsburgisch-jagiellonischen Doppelvermählung*. Budapest: HAS RCH, 2019.

Edelmayer, Friedrich, and Alfred Kohler, eds. *Kaiser Maximilian II.: Kultur und Politik im 16. Jahrhundert*. Vienna: Verlag für Geschichte und Politik, 1992.

Edelmayer, Friedrich, Maximilian Lanzinner, and Peter Rauscher, eds. *Finanzen und Herrschaft: Materielle Grundlagen fürstlicher Politik in den habsburgischen Ländern und im Heiligen Römischen Reich im 16. Jahrhundert*. Munich: Oldenbourg, 2003.

Ember, Győző. *Az újkori magyar közigazgatás története Mohácstól a török kiűzéséig* [The history of Hungarian administration in the modern period, from the Battle of Mohács until the expulsion of the Turks from Hungary]. Budapest: MOL, 1946.

Engel, Pál. *The Realm of St. Stephen: A History of Medieval Hungary, 895–1526*. London: I. B. Tauris, 2001.

Erdélyi, Gabriella, ed. *Armed Memory: Agency and Peasant Revolts in Central and Southern Europe, 1450–1700*. Göttingen: Vandenhoeck und Ruprecht, 2016.

———. *Negotiating Violence: Papal Pardons and Everyday Life in East Central Europe, 1450–1550*. Leiden: Brill, 2018.

Etényi, Nóra G. *Hadszíntér és nyilvánosság: A magyarországi török háború hírei a 17. századi német újságokban* [Battlefield and publicity: News of the Ottoman wars in Hungary in seventeenth-century German newspapers]. Budapest: Balassi Kiadó, 2003.

———. *Pamflet és politika: A hatalmi egyensúly és Magyarország a 17. századi német propagandában* [Pamphlets and politics: The balance of power and Hungary in seventeenth-century German propaganda]. Budapest: L'Harmattan Kiadó, 2009.

Etényi, Nóra G., and Ildikó Horn, eds. *Idővel paloták . . . Magyar udvari kultúra a 16–17. században* [In time palaces: Hungarian court culture in the sixteenth and seventeenth centuries]. Budapest: Balassi Kiadó, 2005.

———, eds. *Portré és imázs: Politikai propaganda és reprezentáció a kora újkorban* [Portrait and image: Political propaganda and representation in the early modern period]. Budapest: L'Harmattan Kiadó, 2008.

———, eds. *Színlelés és rejtőzködés: A kora újkori magyar politika szerepjátékai* [Pretense and subterfuge: Role-playing in the Hungarian politics of the early modern age]. Budapest: L'Harmattan Kiadó, 2010.

Evans, R[obert] J[ohn] W[eston]. *Austria, Hungary, and the Habsburgs: Essays on Central Europe, c. 1683–1867*. Oxford: Oxford University Press, 2006.

———. *The Making of the Habsburg Monarchy 1550–1700: An Interpretation*. Oxford: Oxford University Press, 1979.

———. *Rudolf II and His World: A Study in Intellectual History, 1576–1612*. 2nd corr. ed. Oxford: Clarendon, 1984.

Evans, R[obert] J[ohn] W[eston], and T[revor] V. Thomas, eds. *Crown, Church and Estates: Central European Politics in the Sixteenth and Seventeenth Centuries*. London: Macmillan, 1991.

Fallenbüchl, Zoltán, ed. *Állami (királyi és császári) tisztségviselők a 17. századi Magyarországon: Adattár* [State (royal and imperial) officers in seventeenth century Hungary: A reference book]. Budapest: OSZK, 2002.

———, ed. *Magyarország főispánjai/Die Obergespane Ungarns 1526–1848*. Budapest: Argumentum Kiadó, 1994.

———, ed. *Magyarország főméltóságai 1526–1848* [Highest dignitaries of Hungary, 1526–1848]. Budapest: Maecenas Kiadó, 1988.

Farkas, Gábor Farkas, Zsolt Szebelédi, and Bernadett Varga eds. *"Nekünk mégis Mohács kell . . .": II. Lajos király rejtélyes halála és különböző temetései* ["We do need Mohács, after all . . .": King Louis II's mysterious death and various funerals]. Budapest: MTA BTK, 2016.

Fata, Márta. *Ungarn, das Reich der Stephanskrone, im Zeitalter der Reformation und Konfessionalisierung: Multiethnizität, Land und Konfession 1500 bis 1700*. Münster: Aschendorff, 2000.

Fata, Márta, Gyula Kurucz, and Anton Schindling, eds. *Peregrinatio Hungarica: Studenten aus Ungarn an deutschen und österreichischen Hochschulen vom 16. bis zum 20. Jahrhundert*. Stuttgart: Franz Steiner, 2006.

Fata, Márta, and Anton Schindling, eds. *Calvin und Reformiertentum in Ungarn und Siebenbürgen: Helvetisches Bekenntnis, Ethnie und Politik vom 16. Jahrhundert bis 1918*. 2nd ed. Münster: Aschendorff, 2011.

———, eds. *Luther und die Evangelisch-Lutherischen in Ungarn und Siebenbürgen: Augsburgisches Bekenntnis, Bildung, Sprache und Nation vom 16. Jahrhundert bis 1918*. Münster: Aschendorff, 2017.

Fata, Márta, et al., eds. *Das Trienter Konzil und seine Rezeption im Ungarn des 16. und 17. Jahrhunderts*. Münster: Aschendorff, 2019.

Fazekas, István. *A reform útján: A katolikus megújulás Nyugat-Magyarországon* [In the way of reform: Catholic renewal in western Hungary]. Győr: Győri Egyházmegyei Levéltár, 2014.

Fazekas, István, and Gábor Ujváry, eds. *Kaiser und König. Eine historische Reise: Österreich und Ungarn 1526–1918. Ausstellung im Prunksaal der Österreichischen Nationalbibliothek. 08. März–01. Mai 2001. Katalog*. Vienna: Collegium Hungaricum, 2001.

Fazekas, István, et al., eds. *Frühneuzeitforschung in der Habsburgermonarchie: Adel und Wiener Hof—Konfessionalisierung—Siebenbürgen*. Vienna: Institut für Ungarische Geschichtsforschung in Wien, 2012.

Federmayer, Frederik. *Rody starého Prešporka: Genealogický rozbor obyvateľstva a topografia mesta podľa súpisu z roku 1624* [Families of the Old Pozsony: Genealogical analysis of the population and topography of the city based on the register from the year 1624]. Bratislava: Monada atelier, 2003.

Fekete, Lajos. *Buda and Pest under Turkish Rule*. Edited by Gyula Káldy-Nagy. Budapest: Akadémiai Kiadó, 1976.

Feld, István. *Magyar építészet* [Hungarian architecture]. Vol. 3, *Késő reneszánsz és kora barokk* [Late Renaissance and early Baroque]. Budapest: Kossuth Kiadó, 2002.

Feneșan, Cristina. *Constituirea principatului autonom al Transilvaniei* [The making of the independent Principality of Transylvania]. Bucharest: Editura Enciclopedică, 1997.

Fichtner, Paula Sutter. *Emperor Maximilian II*. New Haven: Yale University Press, 2001.

———. *Ferdinand I of Austria: The Politics of Dynasticism in the Age of the Reformation*. Boulder: East European Monographs, 1982.

———. *The Habsburg Monarchy 1490-1848: Attributes of Empire*. Houndmills: Palgrave-Macmillan, 2003.

Finkel, Caroline. *The Administration of Warfare: The Ottoman Military Campaigns in Hungary, 1593-1606*. Vienna: VWGÖ, 1988.

Fodor, Pál, ed. *The Battle for Central Europe: The Siege of Szigetvár and the Death of Süleyman the Magnificent and Nicholas Zrínyi (1566)*. Leiden: Brill, 2019.

———. *The Business of State: Ottoman Finance Administration and Ruling Elites in Transition (1580s-1615)*. Berlin: Klaus Schwarz, 2018.

———. *In Quest of the Golden Apple: Imperial Ideology, Politics, and Military Administration in the Ottoman Empire*. Istanbul: Isis, 2000.

———, ed. *Remembering a Forgotten Siege, Szigetvár 1556*. Compiled by Péter Kasza. Budapest: HAS RCH, 2016.

———. *The Unbearable Weight of Empire: The Ottomans in Central Europe—a Failed Attempt at Universal Monarchy (1390-1566)*. Budapest: HAS RCH, 2015.

Fodor, Pál, and Pál Ács, eds. *Identity and Culture in Ottoman Hungary*. Berlin: Klaus Schwarz, 2017.

Fodor, Pál, and Szabolcs Varga, eds. *A Forgotten Hungarian Royal Dynasty: The Szapolyais*. Budapest: RCH, 2020.

———, eds. *Több mint egy csata: Mohács. Az 1526. évi ütközet a magyar tudományos és kulturális emlékezetben* [More than a Battle: Mohács—The battle of 1526 in Hungarian scientific and cultural memory]. Budapest: MTA BTK, 2019.

Fraknói, Vilmos. *A magyar királyválasztások története* [The history of the election of Hungarian kings]. 1st ed. Budapest: Athenaeum Irodalmi és Nyomdai Részvénytársulat, 1921. 2nd ed. Máriabesenyő: Attraktor Kiadó, 2005.

———. *Magyarország egyházi és politikai összeköttetései a római Szent-Székkel* [Hungary's ecclesiastical and political relations with the Holy See]. Vol. 3, *1526-1689*. Budapest: SZIT Tudományos és Irodalmi Osztálya, 1903.

Fraknói, Vilmos, and Árpád Károlyi, eds. *Monumenta comitialia regni Hungariae/Magyar Országgyűlési Emlékek történeti bevezetésekkel* [Documents from the Hungarian diets, with historical introductions]. 12 vols. Budapest: MTA, 1874-1917.

Fuchs, Martina, Teréz Oborni, and Gábor Ujváry, eds. *Kaiser Ferdinand I: Ein mitteleuropäischer Herrscher*. Münster: Aschendorff, 2005.

Fuchs, Martina, and Orsolya Réthelyi, eds. *Maria von Ungarn (1505-1558): Eine Renaissancefürstin*. Münster: Aschendorff, 2007.

Fučíková, Eliška, et al., eds. *Rudolf II and Prague: The Court and the City*. London: Thames and Hudson, 1997.

Fundárková, Anna. *Barokový aristocrat: Pavol Pálffy* [A Baroque aristocrat: Pál Pálffy]. Bratislava: VSAV, 2018.

———. *Ein ungarischer Aristokrat am Wiener Hof des 17. Jahrhunderts: Die Briefe von Paul Pálffy an Maximilian von Trauttmansdorff (1647-1650)*. Vienna: Institut für Ungarische Geschichtsforschung in Wien, 2009.

Fundárková, Anna, et al., eds. *Die weltliche und kirchliche Elite aus dem Königreich Böhmen und Königreich Ungarn am Wiener Kaiserhof im 16.-17. Jahrhundert*. Vienna: Institut für Ungarische Geschichtsforschung in Wien, 2013.

Galavics, Géza. *Kössünk kardot az pogány ellen: Török háborúk és képzőművészet* [Let's gird ourselves with a sword against the heathen: The Ottoman wars and the fine arts]. Budapest: Képzőművészeti Kiadó, 1986.

Galavics, Géza, et al. *Magyar művészet a kezdetektől 1800-ig* [Art in Hungary from its beginnings to 1800]. Budapest: Corvina Kiadó, 2001.

Gastgeber, Christian, and Elisabeth Klecker, eds. *Johannes Sambucus / János Zsámboki / Ján Sambucus (1531–1584): Philologe, Sammler und Historiograph am Habsburgerhof*. Vienna: Praesens, 2018.

Gebei, Sándor. *A Rákóczi-szabadságharc 1703–1711* [The war of independence of Francis II Rákóczi, 1703–1711]. Budapest: Kossuth Kiadó, 2009.

———. *Az erdélyi fejedelmek és a lengyel királyválasztások* [The princes of Transylvania and the election of Polish kings]. Szeged: Belvedere Meridionale, 2007.

———. *II. Rákóczi György külpolitikája, 1648–1657* [The foreign policy of George II Rákóczi, 1648–1657]. Budapest: Heraldika Kiadó, 2004.

Gecsényi, Lajos. *Gazdaság, társadalom, igazgatás: Tanulmányok a kora újkor történetéből* [Economy, society, administration: Studies in the early modern history]. Győr: Győr-Moson-Sopron Megye Győri Levéltára, 2008.

———. *Grund- und Hausverzeichnisse der Festungsstadt Győr / Raab 1564–1602*. Győr: GyVL, 2003.

Gergely, András, and Gábor Máthé, eds. *The Hungarian State*. Budapest: Korona, 2000.

Glatz, Ferenc, ed. *Environment and Society in Hungary: Études historiques hongroises 1990 publiées à l'occasion de XVIIᵉ Congrès International des Sciences Historiques par le Comité National des Historiens Hongrois*. Vol. 3. Budapest: Institute of History of the HAS, 1990.

———, ed. *European Intellectual Trends and Hungary: Études historiques hongroises 1990 publiées à l'occasion de XVIIᵉ Congrès International des Sciences Historiques par le Comité National des Historiens Hongrois*. Vol. 4. Budapest: Institute of History of the HAS, 1990.

———, ed. *Settlement and Society in Hungary: Études historiques hongroises 1990 publiées à l'occasion de XVIIᵉ Congrès International des Sciences Historiques par le Comité National des Historiens Hongrois*. Vol. 1. Budapest: Institute of History of the HAS, 1990.

Glatz, Ferenc, et al., eds. *Études historiques hongroises 1985 publiées à l'occasion de XVIᵉ Congrès International des Sciences Historiques par la Comité Nationale des Historiens Hongrois*. Vol. 2. Budapest: Akadémiai Kiadó, 1985.

Gonda, Imre, and Emil Niederhauser. *Die Habsburger: Ein europäisches Phänomen*. Budapest: Corvina Kiadó, 1985.

Gooss, Roderich. *Österreichische Staatsverträge: Fürstentum Siebenbürgen (1526–1690)*. Vienna: Adolf Holzhausan, 1911.

Granasztói, György. *A barokk győzelme Nagyszombatban: Tér és társadalom 1579–1711* [The triumph of the Baroque in Nagyszombat: Place and society, 1579–1711]. Budapest: Akadémiai Kiadó, 2004.

Harai, Dénes. *Gabriel Bethlen: Prince de Transylvanie et roi élu de Hongrie (1580–1629)*. Paris: L'Harmattan, 2013.

Haug-Moritz, Gabriele, and Ludolf Pelizaeus, eds. *Repräsentationen der islamischen Welt im Europa der Frühen Neuzeit*. Münster: Aschendorf, 2010.

Hausner, Gábor. *Márs könyvet olvas: Zrínyi Miklós és a 17. századi hadtudományi irodalom* [Mars reads books: Miklós Zrínyi and military science literature in the seventeenth century]. Budapest: Argumentum Kiadó, 2013.

Hausner, Gábor, and András Németh, eds. *Zrínyi-Újvár. A Seventeenth-Century Border Defence System on the Edge of the Ottoman Empire*. Budapest: Dialóg Campus, 2020.

Hegyi, Klára. *The Ottoman Military Organization in Hungary: Fortresses, Fortress Garrisons and Finances*. Berlin: Klaus Schwarz, 2018.

———. *Török berendezkedés Magyarországon* [Ottoman rule in Hungary]. Budapest: MTA TTI, 1995.

Hegyi, Klára, and Vera Zimányi. *The Ottoman Empire in Europe*. Budapest: Corvina Kiadó, 1989.

Heischmann, Eugen. *Die Anfänge des stehenden Heeres in Österreich*. Vienna: Österreichischer Bundesverlag für Unterricht, Wissenschaft und Kunst, 1925.

Hengerer, Mark. *Kaiser Ferdinand III. (1608–1657): Eine Biographie*. Vienna: Böhlau, 2012.

———. *Kaiserhof und Adel in der Mitte des 17. Jahrhunderts: Eine Kommunikationsgeschichte der Macht in der Vormoderne*. Konstanz: UVK Verlagsgesellschaft, 2004.

———. *Making Peace in an Age of War: Emperor Ferdinand III (1608–1657)*. West Lafayette, IN: Purdue University Press, 2020.
Hiller, István. *Palatin Nikolaus Esterházy: Die ungarische Rolle in der Habsburgerdiplomatie 1625–1645*. Vienna: Böhlau, 1992.
Höbelt, Lothar. *Ferdinand III. (1608–1657): Friedenskaiser wider Willen*. Graz: Ares, 2008.
Hochedlinger, Michael. *Austria's Wars of Emergence: War, State and Society in the Habsburg Monarchy 1683–1797*. London: Longman, 2003.
Hochedlinger, Michael, Petr Maťa, and Thomas Winkelbauer, eds. *Verwaltungsgeschichte der Habsburgermonarchie in der Frühen Neuzeit*. Vol. 1/1–2, *Hof und Dynastie, Kaiser und Reich, Zentralverwaltungen, Kriegswesen und landesfürstliches Finanzwesen*. Vienna: Böhlau, 2019.
Hochedlinger, Michael, and Thomas Winkelbauer, eds. *Herrschaftsverdichtung, Staatsbildung, Bürokratisierung: Verfassungs-, Verwaltungs- und Behördengeschichte der Frühen Neuzeit*. Vienna: Böhlau, 2010.
Holčík, Štefan. *Krönungsfeierlichkeiten in Pressburg 1563–1830*. 4th ed. Bratislava: Ikar, 2005.
Horn, Ildikó. *Báthory András* [Andrew Báthory]. Budapest: Új Mandátum Kiadó, 2002.
———. *Tündérország útvesztői: Tanulmányok Erdély történelméhez* [The labyrinths of the land of the fairies: Studies in the history of Transylvania]. Budapest: ELTE Történelemtudományok Doktori Iskola, 2005.
Illik, Péter. *Minden nap háború: A magyar királyságbeli török kártételek anatómiája (1627–1641)* [Everyday war: The anatomy of Ottoman damages in the Kingdom of Hungary, 1627–1641]. Budapest: L'Harmattan Kiadó, 2013.
Imber, Colin. *The Ottoman Empire, 1300–1650: The Structure of Power*. Basingstoke: Palgrave-Macmillan, 2002.
Inalcik, Halil. *The Ottoman Empire: The Classical Age 1300–1600*. 3rd ed. London: Weidenfeld and Nicolson, 1997.
Ingrao, Charles, Nikola Samardžić, and Jovan Pešalj, eds. *The Peace of Passarowitz, 1718*. West Lafayette, IN: Purdue University Press, 2011.
Ingrao, W. Charles. *The Habsburg Monarchy 1618–1815*. 3rd ed. Cambridge: Cambridge University Press, 2019.
———. *In Quest and Crisis: Emperor Joseph I and the Habsburg Monarchy*. West Lafayette, IN: Purdue University Press, 1979.
Kádár, Zsófia. *Jezsuiták Nyugat-Magyarországon a 17. században: A pozsonyi, győri és soproni kollégiumok* [Jesuits in western Hungary in the seventeenth century: The colleges in Pozsony, Győr, and Sopron]. Budapest: BTK TTI, 2020.
Kann, Robert A. *A History of the Habsburg Empire 1526–1918*. Berkeley: University of California Press, 1974.
Kármán, Gábor. *Confession and Politics in the Principality of Transylvania 1644–1657*. Göttingen: Vandenhoeck und Ruprecht, 2020.
Kármán, Gábor, and Lovro Kunčević, eds. *The European Tributary States of the Ottoman Empire in the Sixteenth and Seventeenth Centuries*. Leiden: Brill, 2013.
Kármán, Gábor, and Radu G. Păun, eds. *Europe and the 'Ottoman World': Exchanges and Conflicts (Sixteenth to Seventeenth Centuries)*. Istanbul: Isis, 2013.
Kármán, Gábor, and András Péter Szabó, eds. *Szerencsének elegyes forgása: II. Rákóczi György és kora* [The wheel of fortune: Georg II Rákóczi and his age]. Budapest: L'Harmattan Kiadó, 2009.
Kármán, Gábor, and Kees Teszelszky, eds. *Bethlen Gábor és Európa* [Gabriel Bethlen and Europe]. Budapest: ELTE BTK Középkori és Kora Újkori Egyetemes Történeti Tanszék, 2013.
Kármán, Gábor, and Márton Zászkaliczky, eds. *Politikai nyelvek a 17. század első felének Magyarországán* [Political languages in Hungary in the first half of the seventeenth century]. Budapest: reciti, 2019.
Károlyi, Árpád. *Illésházy István hűtlenségi pöre* [The impeachment of István Illésházy]. Budapest: MTA Könyvkiadó-Hivatala, 1883.
———. *Néhány történeti tanulmány* [A few studies in history]. Budapest: MTA, 1930.
Karpat, Jozef. *Zákonodarná moc v Uhorsku v rokoch 1526–1604* [Legislative power in Hungary in the years 1526–1604]. Bratislava: Slovenská univerzita, 1944.
Kaser, Karl. *Freier Bauer und Soldat: Die Militarisierung der agrarischen Gesellschaft an der kroatisch-slawonischen Militärgrenze (1535–1881)*. Vienna: Böhlau, 1997.
Kasza, Péter. *Egy korszakváltás szemtanúja: Brodarics István pályaképe* [Witness to a change of era: The career of István Brodarics]. Pécs: Kronosz Kiadó, 2014.
Kaufmann, Thomas DaCosta. *Variations on the Imperial Theme in the Age of Maximilian II and Rudolf II*. New York: Garland, 1978.

Keller, Katrin, Petr Maťa, and Martin Scheutz, eds. *Adel und Religion in der frühneuzeitlichen Habsburgermonarchie: Annäherung an ein gesamtösterreichisches Thema*. Vienna: Böhlau, 2017.

Keller, Katrin, and Martin Scheutz, eds. *Die Habsburgermonarchie und der Dreißigjährige Krieg*. Vienna: Böhlau, 2020.

Kenyeres, István. *Uradalmak és végvárak: A kamarai birtokok és a törökellenes határvédelem a 16. századi Magyar Királyságban* [Estates and border fortresses: The fiscal domains and the border defense against the Ottomans in the sixteenth-century Kingdom of Hungary]. Budapest: Új Mandatum Kiadó, 2008.

Király, Béla K., and László Veszprémy, eds. *A Millennium of Hungarian Military History*. Boulder, CO: Social Sciences Monographs, 2002.

Kirschbaum, Stanislav J. *A History of Slovakia: The Struggle for Survival*. 2nd ed. Houndmills: Palgrave-Macmillan, 2005.

Kis, Domokos Dániel, and Ágnes R. Várkonyi, eds. *A Rákóczi-szabadságharc* [The war of independence of Francis II Rákóczi]. Budapest: Osiris Kiadó, 2004.

Kiss, István N. *Bauernwirtschaft unf Warenproduktion in Ungarn vom 16. bis zum 18. Jahrhundert: Produktion, Schichtung, Markt, Ausfuhr*. Cologne: Forschungsinstitut für Sozial- und Wirtschaftsgeschichte, 1974.

Klaić, Vjekoslav. *Povijest Hrvata od nastarijih vremena do svršetka XIX stoljeća* [A history of the Croats from their origins to the end of the nineteenth century]. Vols. 4–5. Edited by Trpimir Macan. Zagreb: Nakladni zavod Matice hrvatske, 1982.

Klaniczay, Tibor, ed. *Janus Pannonius: Magyarországi humanisták* [Janus Pannonius: Humanists in Hungary]. Budapest: Szépirodalmi Könyvkiadó, 1982.

———. *Pallas magyar ivadékai* [The Hungarian offshoots of Pallas]. Budapest: Szépirodalmi Könyvkiadó, 1985.

———, ed. *Rapporti veneto-ungheresi all'epoca del Rinascimento*. Budapest: Akadémiai Kiadó, 1975.

———. *Reneszánsz és barokk: Tanulmányok a régi magyar irodalomról* [Renaissance and the Baroque: Studies in Old Hungarian literature]. 2nd ed. Szeged: Szukits, 1997.

Koenigsberger, H[elmut] G[eorg]. *Early Modern Europe 1500–1789*. London: Longman, 1987.

Köhbach, Markus. *Die Eroberung von Fülek durch die Osmanen 1554: Eine historisch-quellenkritische Studie zur osmanischen Expansion im östlichen Mitteleuropa*. Vienna: Böhlau, 1994.

Kohler, Alfred. *Ferdinand I. 1503–1564: Fürst, König und Kaiser*. Munich: C. H. Beck, 2003.

Koller, Markus. *Eine Gesellschaft im Wandel: Die osmanische Herrschaft in Ungarn im 17. Jahrhundert (1606–1683)*. Stuttgart: Franz Steiner, 2010.

Koltai, András. *Batthyány Ádám: Egy magyar főúr és udvara a XVII. század közepén* [Ádám Batthyány: A Hungarian aristocrat and his court in the mid-seventeenth century]. Győr: Győri Egyházmegyei Levéltár, 2012.

Kontler, László. *A History of Hungary: Millennium in Central Europe*. Budapest: Atlantisz, 1999. Reprint ed., Houndmills: Palgrave-Macmillan, 2002.

Kónya, Péter. *Az eperjesi vésztörvényszék 1687* [The emergency tribunal of Eperjes, 1867]. Budapest: EOM, 1994.

———, ed. *Doba kuruckých bojov/Kuruc küzdelmek kora* [The age of the *kuruc* wars]. Prešov: VPU, 2014.

———, ed. *Gróf Imrich Thököly a jeho povstanie/Thököly Imre gróf és felkelése* [Count Imre Thököly and his revolt]. Prešov: VPU, 2009.

———. *Pod zástavou kurucov: Protihabsburské povstania v Uhorsku v r. 1670–1711* [Under the *kuruc* flag: Revolts against the Habsburgs in Hungary, 1670–1711]. Prešov: VPU, 2015.

———, ed. *Povstanie Františka II. Rákócziho (1703–1711) v novšom priblížení/A Rákóczi-szabadságharc (1703–1711) újabb megközelítésben* [The revolt of Francis II Rákóczi (1703–1711) in a new light]. Prešov: Prešovská univerzita, v Prešove, Filozofická fakulta, 2005.

———, ed. *Rekatolizácia, protireformácia a katolícka reštaurácia v Uhorsku/Rekatolizáció, ellenreformáció és katolikus megújulás Magyarországon* [Re-Catholicization, counter-reformation and Catholic renewal in Hungary]. Prešov: VPU, 2013.

———, ed. *Zemepánské mestá a mestečká v Uhorsku v ranom novoveku/Mezővárosok a koraújkori Magyarországon* [Market towns in Hungary in the early modern period]. Prešov: VPU, 2013.

Köpeczi, Béla. *Staatsräson und christliche Solidarität: Die ungarischen Aufstände und Europa in der zweiten Hälfte des 17. Jahrhunderts*. Budapest: Akadémiai Kiadó, 1983.

Köpeczi, Béla, and Éva H. Balázs, eds. *Noblesse française, noblesse hongroise: XVIe-XIXe siècles: Colloque franco-hongrois d'histoire sociale. Rennes, 11–13 juin 1975*. Budapest: Akadémiai Kiadó, 1981.

Köpeczi, Béla, and Ágnes R. Várkonyi. *II. Rákóczi Ferenc* [Francis II Rákóczi]. 3rd enlarged ed. Budapest: Osiris Kiadó, 2004.
Köpeczi, Béla, et al., eds. *History of Transylvania*. 3 vols. Boulder, CO: Social Sciences Monographs, 2001.
Korpás, Zoltán. *V. Károly és Magyarország (1526–1538)* [Emperor Charles V and Hungary, 1526–1538]. Budapest: Századvég Kiadó, 2008.
Kósa, László, ed. *A Cultural History of Hungary*. 2nd ed. Budapest: Corvina Kiadó, 2002.
Kosáry, Domokos. *Bevezetés a magyar történelem forrásaiba és irodalmába* [Introduction to the sources and literature of Hungarian history]. Vol. 1. Budapest: Közoktatásügyi Kiadóvállalat, 1951.
———. *Bevezetés a magyar történelem forrásaiba és irodalmába* [Introduction to the sources and literature of Hungarian history]. Vol. 3, *Kiegészítések és névmutató* [Additions and indices]. Budapest: Bibliotheca Kiadó, 1958.
Kosáry, Domokos, et al. *Bevezetés Magyarország történetének forrásaiba és irodalmába* [Introduction to the sources and literature of the history of Hungary]. Vols. 1–4. Budapest: Osiris Kiadó, 2000–2015.
Kovács, Gyöngyi, and Ibolya Gerelyes, eds. *Archaeology of the Ottoman Period in Hungary: Papers of the Conference Held at the Hungarian National Museum, Budapest, 24–26 May 2000*. Budapest: HNM, 2003.
Kovacsics, József, ed. *Magyarország történeti demográfiája (896–1995)* [The historical demography of Hungary, 896–1995]. Budapest: KSH, 1997.
Kropf, Rudolf, ed. *Türkenkriege und Kleinlandschaft*. Vol. 2, *Sozialer und kultureller Wandel einer Region zur Zeit der Türkenkriege*. Eisenstadt: Amt der Burgenländischen Landesregierung, 1986.
Kropf, Rudolf, and Wolfgang Mayer, eds. *Kleinlandschaft und Türkenkriege*. Vol. 1, *Das südliche Burgenland zur Zeit der Bedrohung durch die Türken im 16.–17. Jahrhundert*. Eisenstadt: Amt der Burgenländischen Landesregierung, 1983.
Kruhek, Milan. *Krajiške utvrde i obrana Hrvatskog kraljevstva tijekom 16. stoljeća* [Border fortresses and the defense of the Croatian kingdom in the sixteenth century]. Zagreb: Institut za suvremenu povijest, 1995.
Kruhek, Milan, et al., eds. *Hrvatsko-mađarski odnosi 1102.–1918: Zbornik radova* [Croatian-Hungarian relations, 1102–1918: Collected studies]. Zagreb: ISP, 2004.
Kubíková, Blanka, Jaroslava Hausenblasová, and Sylva Dobalová, eds. *Ferdinand II. Erzherzog von Österreich aus dem Hause Habsburg—Renaissance-Herrscher und Mäzen: Zwischen Prag und Innsbruck*. Prague: Národní galerie v Praze, 2017.
Kubinyi, András. *König und Volk im spätmittelalterlichen Ungarn: Städteentwicklung, Alltagsleben und Regierung im mittelalterlichen Königreich Ungarn*. Herne: Tibor Schäfer, 1998.
Kühlmann, Wilhelm, Anton Schindling, and Wolfram Hauer, eds. *Deutschland und Ungarn in ihren Bildungs- und Wissenschaftsbeziehungen während der Renaissance*. Stuttgart: Franz Steiner, 2004.
Kühlmann, Wilhelm, Gábor Tüskés, and Sándor Bene, eds. *Militia et Litterae: Die beiden Nikolaus Zrínyi und Europa*. Tübingen: Max Niemeyer, 2009.
Kurz, Marlene, et al., eds. *Das Osmanische Reich und die Habsburgermonarchie: Akten des internationalen Kongresses zum 150-jährigen Bestehen des Instituts für Österreichische Geschichtsforschung Wien, 22.–25. September 2004*. Vienna: Oldenbourg, 2005.
Laczlavik, György. *Kettős pecsét alatt: Várday Pál esztergomi érsek, királyi helytartó (1483–1549)* [Under a double seal: Pál Várday archbishop of Esztergom, royal governor, 1483–1549]. Pécs: Kronosz Kiadó, 2014.
Laubach, Ernst. *Ferdinand I. als Kaiser: Politik und Herrscherauffassung des Nachfolgers Karls V*. Münster: Aschendorff, 2001.
Lendvai, Paul. *The Hungarians: A Thousand Years of Victory in Defeat*. Princeton: Princeton University Press, 2003.
Lengyelová, Tünde, ed. *Žena a právo: Právne a spoločenské postavenie žien v minulosti* [Woman and law: The legal and social status of women in history]. Bratislava: AEP, 2004.
Lengyelová, Tünde, and Géza Pálffy, eds. *Korunovácie a pohreby: Mocenské rituály a ceremónie v ranom novoveku* [Coronations and funerals: Power rituals and ceremonies in the early modern period]. Budapest: Historický ústav Filozofického výskumného centra Maďarskej akadémie vied, 2016.
———, eds. *Thurzovci a ich historický význam* [The Thurzós and their historical importance]. Bratislava: Spoločnosť Pro Historia, 2012.
Loebl, Alfred H. *Zur Geschichte des Türkenkrieges von 1593–1606*. 2 vols. Prague: Rohlíček und Sievers, 1899–1904.
Louthan, Howard. *The Quest for Compromise: Peacemakers in Counter-Reformation Vienna*. Cambridge: Cambridge University Press, 1997.

———. *A Via Media in Central Europe: Irenicism in Habsburg Vienna, 1555–1585*. PhD diss., Princeton: Princeton University Press, 1994.

Louthan, Howard, and Graeme Murdock, eds. *A Companion to the Reformation in Central Europe*. Leiden: Brill, 2015.

Lukinich, Imre. *Erdély területi változásai a török hódítás korában 1541–1711* [Territorial changes to Transylvania in the age of Ottoman expansion, 1541–1711]. Budapest: MTA, 1918.

MacHardy, Karin J. *War, Religion and Court Patronage in Habsburg Austria: The Social and Cultural Dimensions of Political Interaction, 1521–1622*. Houndmills: Palgrave-Macmillan, 2003.

Madas, Edit, and István Monok. *A könyvkultúra Magyarországon a kezdetektől 1800-ig* [Book culture in Hungary, from the origins to 1800]. 2nd revised, enlarged ed. Budapest: Balassi Kiadó, 2003.

Maksay, Ferenc. *Magyarország birtokviszonyai a 16. század közepén* [Land possession in Hungary in the mid-sixteenth century]. 2 vols. Budapest: MTA, 1990.

Malcolm, Noel. *Useful Enemies: Islam and the Ottoman Empire in Western Political Thought, 1450–1750*. Oxford: Oxford University Press, 2019.

Mannová, Elena, ed. *A Concise History of Slovakia*. Bratislava: HÚ SAV, 2000.

Márkus, Dezső, ed. *Magyar törvénytár. (Corpus Juris Hungarici) 1526–1740. törvényczikkek* [Acts of 1526–1740]. 3 vols. Budapest: Franklin-Társulat, 1899–1900.

Marosi Ernő, ed. *On the Stage of Europe: The Millennial Contribution of Hungary to the Idea of European Community*. Budapest: Research Institute for Art History of the HAS, 2009.

Martí, Tibor, and Roberto Quirós Rosado, eds. *Eagles Looking East and West: Dynasty, Ritual and Representation in Habsburg Hungary and Spain*. Turnhout: Brepols, 2021.

Maťa, Petr, and Thomas Winkelbauer, eds. *Die Habsburgermonarchie 1620 bis 1740: Leistungen und Grenzen des Absolutismusparadigmas*. Stuttgart: Franz Steiner, 2006.

Máté, Ágnes, and Teréz Oborni, eds. *Isabella Jagiellon, Queen of Hungary (1539–1559): Studies*. Budapest: RCH, 2020.

Medvedeva, K[atja] T[atjana]. *Avstrijskie Gabsburgi i soslovija v nacale XVII veka* [Austrian Habsburgs and society at the beginning of the seventeenth century]. Moscow: Rossiiskaia akademiia nauk, Institut Slavyanovegeniia, 2004.

Mihalik, Béla. *Papok, polgárok, konvertiták: Katolikus megújulás az egri egyházmegyében (1670–1699)* [Priests, burghers and converts: Catholic renewal in the diocese of Eger, 1670–1699]. Budapest: MTA BTK TTI, 2017.

Mikó, Árpád, and Katalin Sinkó, eds. *Történelem-kép: Szemelvények múlt és művészet kapcsolatáról Magyarországon. Kiállítás a Magyar Nemzeti Galériában 2000. március 17–szeptember 24* [History and image: Selections from the relationship between art and history in Hungary. Exhibition at the Hungarian National Gallery, March 17, 2000–September 24, 2000]. Budapest: MNG, 2000.

Mikó, Árpád, and Mária Verő, eds. *Mátyás király öröksége: Késő reneszánsz művészet Magyarországon (16–17. század). Kiállítás a Magyar Nemzeti Galériában 2008. március 28–2008. július 27*. [The heritage of King Matthias Corvinus: Late Renaissance art in Hungary (sixteenth to seventeenth centuries). Exhibition at the Hungarian National Gallery, March 28, 2008–July 27, 2008]. 2 vols. Budapest: MNG, 2008.

Mitev, Plamen, et al., eds. *Empires and Peninsulas: Southeastern Europe between Karlowitz and the Peace of Adrianople, 1699–1829*. Berlin: LIT, 2010.

Mód, Aladár. *400 év küzdelem az önálló Magyarországért* [400 years of struggle for an independent Hungary]. 7th enlarged and revised ed. Budapest: Szikra, 1954.

Molnár, Antal. *Confessionalization on the Frontier: The Balkan Catholics between Roman Reform and Ottoman Reality*. Rome: Viella, 2019.

———. *Eine Handelsgesellschaft aus Ragusa im osmanischen Ofen: Geschichte und Dokumente der Gesellschaft von Scipione Bona und Marino Bucchia, 1573–1595*. Budapest: BFL, 2009.

———. *Le Saint-Siège, Raguse et les missions catholiques de la Hongrie Ottomane 1572–1647*. Rome: Accademia d'Ungheria, Roma, 2007.

———. *Magyar hódoltság, horvát hódoltság: Magyar és horvát katolikus egyházi intézmények az oszmán uralom alatt* [Ottoman Hungary, Ottoman Croatia: Hungarian and Croatian church institutions under Ottoman rule]. Budapest: BTK TTI, 2019.

———. *Mezőváros és katolicizmus: Katolikus egyház az egri püspökség hódoltsági területein a 17. században* [The market town and Catholicism: The Catholic Church in the Ottoman-occupied territories of the bishopric of Eger]. Budapest: METEM, 2005.

Molnár, Miklós. *A Concise History of Hungary*. Cambridge: Cambridge University Press, 2001. Reprint ed., Cambridge: Cambridge University Press, 2005.

Monok, István. *A művelt arisztokrata: A magyarországi főnemesség olvasmányai a XVI–XVII. században* [The erudite aristocrat: What the Hungarian aristocracy read in the sixteenth and seventeenth centuries]. Budapest: Kossuth Kiadó, 2012.

———, ed. *Blue Blood, Black Ink: Book Collection of Aristocratic Families from 1500 to 1700*. Budapest: National Széchényi Library, 2005.

———, ed. *Myth and Reality: Latin Historiography in Hungary 15th–18th Centuries. Exhibition in the National Széchényi Library 7 July–3 September 2006*. Budapest: National Széchényi Library, 2006.

Murdock, Graeme. *Beyond Calvin: The Intellectual, Political and Cultural World of Europe's Reformed Churches, c. 1540–1620*. Basingstoke: Palgrave-Macmillan, 2004.

———. *Calvinism on the Frontier, 1600–1660: International Calvinism and the Reformed Church in Hungary and Transylvania*. Oxford: Clarendon, 2000.

Nagy, László. *A Bocskai szabadságharc katonai története* [The military history of the war of independence of Stephen Bocskai]. Budapest: Akadémiai Kiadó, 1961.

———. *Bethlen Gábor a független Magyarországért* [Gabriel Bethlen for an independent Hungary]. Budapest: Akadémiai Kiadó, 1969.

———. *Egy szablyás magyar úr Genfben. (A sokarcú Bocskai István)* [A sabre-bearing Hungarian nobleman in Geneva: The complexities of Stephen Bocskai]. Hajdúböszörmény: Hajdúsági Múzeum, Polgármesteri Hivatal, 2000.

———. *"Megint fölszánt magyar világ van . . .": Társadalom és hadsereg a XVII. század első felének Habsburg-ellenes küzdelmeiben* ["It is a topsy-turvy Hungarian world again . . .": Society and the military in the anti-Habsburg struggles of the first half of the seventeenth century]. Budapest: Zrínyi Katonai Kiadó, 1985.

Nehring, Karl. *Adam Freiherrn zu Herbersteins Gesandtschaftsreise nach Konstantinopel: Ein Beitrag zum Frieden von Zsitvatorok (1606)*. Munich: Oldenbourg, 1983.

Nemes, D[ezső], et al., eds. *Études historiques hongroises 1975 publiées à l'occasion de XIVe Congrès International des Sciences Historiques par la Commission Nationale des Historiens Hongrois*. Vol. 1. Budapest: Akadémiai Kiadó, 1975.

———. *Études historiques hongroises 1980 publiées à l'occasion de XVe Congrès International des Sciences Historiques par la Commission Nationale des Historiens Hongrois*. Vol. 1. Budapest: Akadémiai Kiadó, 1980.

Németh, István H. *Várospolitika és gazdaságpolitika a 16-17. századi Magyarországon (A felső-magyarországi városszövetség)* [Urban and economic policies in sixteenth- and seventeenth-century Hungary: The city alliance of Upper Hungary]. Budapest: Gondolat Könyvkiadó, 2004.

Nemeth Papo, Gizella, and Adriano Papo. *Frate Giorgio Martinuzzi: Cardinale, soldato e statista dalmata agli albori del Principato di Transilvania*. Canterano: Aracne, 2017.

———. *Ludovico Gritti: Un principe-mercante del Rinascimento tra Venezia, i turchi e la corona d'Ungheria*. Mariano del Friuli (Gorizia): Edizione della Laguna, 2002.

———, eds. *I turchi, gli Asburgo e l'Adriatico*. Duino Aurisina: Associazione culturale italoungherese Pier Paolo Vergerio, 2007.

Niederhauser, E[mil], Á[gnes] Rozsnyói, and J[enő] Szűcs, eds. *Études historiques 1970 publiées à l'occasion de XIIIe Congrès International des Sciences Historiques par la Commission Nationale des Historiens Hongrois*. Vol. 1. Budapest: Akadémiai Kiadó, 1970.

Niederkorn, Jan Paul. *Die europäischen Mächte und der "Lange Türkenkrieg" Kaiser Rudolfs II. (1593–1606)*. Vienna: VÖAW, 1993.

North, Michael, ed. *Kommunikationsrevolution: Die neuen Medien des 16. und 19. Jahrhunderts*. Cologne: Böhlau, 2001.

Oborni, Teréz. *Az ördöngős Barát. Fráter György (1482–1551)* [The devilish monk: Friar Georg, 1482–1551]. Pécs: Kronosz Kiadó, 2017.

———. *Erdély fejedelmei* [Princes of Transylvania]. Budapest: Pannonica Kiadó, 2002.

———. *Erdélyi országgyűlések a 16-17. században* [Transylvanian diets in the sixteenth and seventeenth centuries]. Budapest: Országház Könyvkiadó, 2018.

———. *Erdély pénzügyei I. Ferdinánd uralma alatt* [The finances of Transylvania during the reign of Ferdinand I]. Budapest: Szentpétery Imre Történettudományi Alapítvány, 2002.

———. *Udvar, állam és kormányzat a kora újkori Erdélyben (Tanulmányok)* [Court, state and government in the early modern Transylvania: Collected studies]. Budapest: ELTE BTK Középkori és Kora Újkori Magyar Történeti Tanszék, 2011.

Oborni, Teréz, Lilla Tompos, and Gábor Bencsik. *Bilderbuch der Völker des alten Siebenbürgens: Handschriftliches Trachtenbuch aus der Zeit der Apafis.* Budapest: Magyar Mercurius, 2009.

Opll, Ferdinand, Heike Krause, and Christoph Sonnlechner. *Wien als Festungsstadt im 16. Jahrhundert: Zum kartografischen Werk der Mailänder Familie Angielini.* Vienna: Böhlau, 2017.

Oross, András. *A Magyar Királyság törökellenes határvédelmi rendszerének felszámolása és átszervezése* [Liquidation and reorganization of the border defense system against the Ottomans in Hungary]. Budapest: Szentpétery Imre Történettudományi Alapítvány, 2013.

Pach, Zsigmond Pál. *Die ungarische Agrarentwicklung im 16–17. Jahrhundert: Abbiegung vom westeuropäischen Entwicklungsgang.* Budapest: Akadémiai Kiadó, 1964.

———. *Hungary and the European Economy in Early Modern Times.* Aldershot: Variorum, 1994.

———, ed. *Magyarország története tíz kötetben* [The history of Hungary in ten volumes]. Vols. 3/1–2, *Magyarország története 1526–1686* [The history of Hungary, 1526–1686]. Edited by Zsigmond Pál Pach and Ágnes R. Várkonyi. 2nd ed. Budapest: Akadémiai Kiadó, 1987.

Pakucs Willocks, Mária. *Sibiu—Hermannstadt: Oriental Trade in Sixteenth Century Transylvania.* Vienna: Böhlau, 2007.

Pál, Judit. *A Habsburg Monarchia története 1526–1848* [The history of the Habsburg Monarchy, 1526–1848]. Kolozsvár: Mega Könyvkiadó, 2014.

Pálffy, Géza. *A császárváros védelmében: A győri főkapitányság története 1526–1598* [Defending the imperial city: A history of the Győr captaincy general, 1526–1598]. Győr: Győr-Moson-Sopron Megye Győri Levéltára, 1999.

———. *A három részre szakadt ország 1526–1606* [The triparted country: Hungary, 1526–1606]. Budapest: Kossuth Kiadó, 2009.

———, ed. *A Szent Korona hazatér: A magyar korona tizenegy külföldi útja (1205–1978)* [The homecoming of the Holy Crown: The Hungarian crown's eleven trips abroad, 1205–1978]. Budapest: MTA BTK TTI, 2018.

———. *A tizenhatodik század története* [The history of sixteenth-century Hungary]. Budapest: Pannonica Kiadó, 2000.

———. *Die Anfänge der Militärkartographie in der Habsburgermonarchie: Die regelmäßige kartographische Tätigkeit der Burgbaumeisterfamilie Angielini an den kroatisch-slawonischen und den ungarischen Grenzen in den Jahren 1560–1570.* Budapest: Ungarisches Nationalarchiv, 2011.

———. *Die Krönungsfahnen in der Esterházy Schatzkammer auf Burg Forchtenstein: Die Geschichte der Krönungsfahnen der Länder der Stephanskrone vom Spätmittelalter bis Anfang des 20. Jahrhunderts.* Eisenstadt: Esterhazy Privatstiftung, 2018.

———, ed. *Gemeinsam gegen die Osmanen: Ausbau und Funktion der Grenzfestungen in Ungarn im 16. und 17. Jahrhundert. Katalog der Ausstellung im Österreichischen Staatsarchiv 14. März–31. Mai 2001:* Vienna: ÖStA, 2001.

———. *Győztes szabadságharc vagy egy sokféle sikert hozó felkelés? A magyar királysági rendek és Bocskai István mozgalma (1604–1608)* [Victorious war of independence or an uprising bringing a variety of achievements? The estates of the Kingdom of Hungary and the movement of Stephen Bocskai, 1604–1608]. Budapest: MTT, 2009.

———. *The Kingdom of Hungary and the Habsburg Monarchy in the Sixteenth Century.* New York: Columbia University Press, 2009.

———. *Romlás és megújulás 1606–1703* [Decay and rejuvenation, Hungary 1606–1703]. Budapest: Kossuth Kiadó, 2009.

Pálffy, Géza, Miljenko Pandžić, and Felix Tobler. *Ausgewählte Dokumente zur Migration der Burgenländischen Kroaten im 16. Jahrhundert.* Eisenstadt: Kroatisches Kultur- und Dokumentationszentrum, 1999.

Pálosfalvi, Tamás. *From Nicopolis to Mohács: A History of Ottoman-Hungarian Warfare, 1389–1526.* Leiden: Brill, 2018.

Pamlényi, Ervin, ed. *A History of Hungary.* London: Collet's, 1975.

Papp, Klára, and Judit Balogh. *Bethlen Gábor képmása* [A portrait of Gabriel Bethlen]. Debrecen: DE Történelmi Intézete, 2013.

Papp, Klára, et al., eds. *Báthory Gábor és kora* [Gabriel Báthory and his age]. Debrecen: DE Történelmi Intézete, 2009.
——. *The First Millennium of Hungary in Europe*. Debrecen: Multiplex Media, 2002.
Papp, Sándor. *Die Verleihungs-, Bekräftigungs- und Vertragsurkunden der Osmanen für Ungarn und Siebenbürgen: Eine quellenkritische Untersuchung*. Vienna: VÖAW, 2003.
——. *Török szövetség—Habsburg kiegyezés: A Bocskai-felkelés történetéhez* [Ottoman alliance—Habsburg compromise: To the history of the Bocskai uprising]. Budapest: KGRE, 2014.
Parker, Geoffrey. *The Military Revolution: Military Innovation and the Rise of the West, 1500–1800*. 2nd revised ed. Cambridge: Cambridge University Press, 1999.
Paulinyi, Oszkár. *Gazdag föld—szegény ország: Tanulmányok a magyarországi bányaművelés múltjából* [Rich land—poor country: Studies in the history of mining in Hungary]. Edited by János Buza and István Draskóczy. Budapest: Budapesti Corvinus Egyetem, 2005.
Pauser, Josef, Martin Scheutz, and Thomas Winkelbauer, eds. *Quellenkunde der Habsburgermonarchie (16.–18. Jahrhundert): Ein exemplarisches Handbuch*. Vienna: Oldenbourg, 2004.
Pavličević, Dragutin. *Povijest Hrvatske* [History of Croatia]. 3rd enlarged ed. Zagreb: Naklada Pavičić, 2002.
Perjés, Géza. *The Fall of the Medieval Kingdom of Hungary: Mohács 1526–Buda 1541*. Boulder, CO: Social Sciences Monographs, 1989.
——. *Seregszemle: Hadtörténeti és művelődéstörténeti tanulmányok* [Muster: Collected studies on military and cultural history]. Budapest: Balassi Kiadó, 1999.
Péter, Katalin. *A magyar romlásnak századában* [In the century of Hungarian decline]. Budapest: Gondolat Kiadó, 1979.
——, ed. *Beloved Children: Aristocratic Childhood in Early Modern Hungary*. Budapest: CEU Press, 2000.
——. *Házasság a régi Magyarországon. 16–17. század* [Marriage in Old Hungary (sixteenth to seventeenth centuries)]. Budapest: L'Harmattan, 2008.
——. *Magánélet a régi Magyarországon.* [Private life in Old Hungary]. Budapest: MTA BTK TTI, 2012.
——. *Papok és nemesek: Magyar művelődéstörténeti tanulmányok a reformációval kezdődő másfél évszázadból* [Priests and nobles: Studies in the Hungarian cultural history of the first century and a half of the Reformation]. Budapest: Ráday Gyűjtemény, 1995.
——. *Studies on the History of the Reformation in Hungary and Transylvania*. Edited by Gabriella Erdélyi. Göttingen: Vandenhoeck und Ruprecht, 2018.
Petrić, Hrvoje. *Pogranična društva i okoliš: Varaždinski generalat i Križevačka županija u 17. stoljeću* [Border society and environment: The Varasd/Varaždin captaincy general and Körös/Križevci county in the seventeenth century]. Samobor: Meridijani, 2012.
Pickl, Othmar, ed. *Die wirtschaftlichen Auswirkungen der Türkenkriege: Die Vorträge des 1. Internationalen Grazer Symposions zur Wirtschafts- und Sozialgeschichte Südosteuropas (5. bis 10. Oktober 1970)*. Graz: Selbstverlag der Lehrkanzel für Wirtschafts- und Sozialgeschichte der Universität Graz, 1971.
Rácz, István. *Hajdúk a XVII. században* [Haiducks in the seventeenth century]. Debrecen: KLTE, 1969.
Radvánszky, Anton. *Grundzüge der Verfassungs- und Staatsgeschichte Ungarns*. Munich: Rudolf Trofenik, 1990.
Rady, Martyn. *Customary Law in Hungary: Courts, Text, and the Tripartitum*. Oxford: Oxford University Press, 2015.
——. *Nobility, Land and Service in Medieval Hungary*. Houndmills: Palgrave, 2000.
Rauscher, Peter, ed. *Kriegführung und Staatsfinanzen: Die Habsburgermonarchie und das Heilige Römische Reich vom Dreißigjährigen Krieg bis zum Ende des habsburgischen Kaisertums 1740*. Münster: Aschendorff, 2010.
——. *Zwischen Ständen und Gläubigern: Die kaiserlichen Finanzen unter Ferdinand I. und Maximilian II. (1556–1576)*. Vienna: Oldenbourg, 2004.
Rauscher, Peter, Andrea Serles, and Thomas Winkelbauer, eds. *Das "Blut des Staatskörpers": Forschungen zur Finanzgeschichte der Frühen Neuzeit*. Munich: Oldenbourg, 2012.
Réthelyi, Orsolya, et al., eds. *Mary of Hungary: The Queen and Her Court 1521–1531. Budapest History Museum, 30 September 2005–9 January 2006. Slovenská národná galéria, 2 February–30 April 2006*. Catalogue. Budapest: BHM, 2005.
Rill, Bernd. *Kaiser Matthias: Bruderzwist und Glaubenskampf*. Graz: Styria, 1999.
Rogers, Clifford J., ed. *The Military Revolution Debate: Readings on the Military Transformation of Early Modern Europe*. Boulder, CO: Westview, 1995.

Römer, Claudia. *Osmanische Festungsbesatzungen in Ungarn zur Zeit Murāds III. Dargestellt anhand von Petitionen zur Stellenvergabe.* Vienna: VÖAW, 1995.
Romsics, Ignác, ed. *Magyarország története* [The history of Hungary]. Budapest: Akadémiai Kiadó, 2007.
———. *Magyarország története* [The history of Hungary]. Budapest: Kossuth Kiadó, 2017.
Roşu, Felicia. *Elective Monarchy in Transylvania and Poland-Lithuania, 1569–1587.* Oxford: Oxford University Press, 2017.
Rothenberg, Gunther Erich. *The Austrian Military Border in Croatia, 1522–1747.* Urbana: University of Illinois Press, 1960.
Roy, Philippe, and Ferenc Tóth. *La défaite Ottomane: La début de la reconquête hongroise (1683).* Paris: Economica, 2014.
Rózsa, György. *Magyar történetábrázolás a XVII. században* [The presentation of Hungarian history in the seventeenth century]. Budapest: Akadémiai Kiadó, 1973.
Rúzsás, Lajos, and Ferenc Szakály, eds. *Mohács: Tanulmányok a mohácsi csata 450. évfordulója alkalmából* [Mohács: Studies commemorating the 450th anniversary of the Battle of Mohács]. Budapest: Akadémiai Kiadó, 1986.
Salamon, Franz. *Ungarn im Zeitalter der Türkenherrschaft.* Leipzig: H. Haessel, 1887.
Sárosi, Edit. *Deserting Villages—Emerging Market Towns: Settlement Dynamics and Land Management in the Great Hungarian Plain, 1300–1700.* Budapest: Archaeolingua, 2016.
Scheutz, Martin, and Arno Strohmeyer, eds. *Von Lier nach Brüssel: Schlüsseljahre österreichischer Geschichte (1496–1995).* Innsbruck: Studienverlag, 2010.
Schulze, Winfried. *Landesdefension und Staatsbildung: Studien zum Kriegswesen des innerösterreichischen Territorialstaates (1564–1619).* Vienna: Böhlau, 1973.
———. *Reich und Türkengefahr im späten 16. Jahrhundert: Studien zu den politischen und gesellschaftlichen Auswirkungen einer äußeren Bedrohung.* Munich: C. H. Beck, 1978.
Seipel, Wilfried, ed. *Kaiser Ferdinand I. 1503–1564: Das Werden der Habsburgermonarchie. Eine Ausstellung des Kunsthistorischen Museums Wien. 15. April bis 31. August 2003.* Catalogue. Vienna: Skira, 2003.
———, ed. *Kaiser Karl V. (1500–1558): Macht und Ohnmacht Europas. Eine Ausstellung des Kunsthistorischen Museums Wien. 16. Juni bis 10. September 2000.* Catalogue. Vienna: Skira, 2000.
Shore, Paul. *Jesuits and the Politics of Religious Pluralism in Eighteenth Century Transylvania: Culture, Politics, and Religion, 1693–1773.* Aldershot: Ashgate, 2007.
Sienell, Stefan. *Die Geheime Konferenz unter Kaiser Leopold I.: Personelle Strukturen und Methoden zur politischen Entscheidungsfindung am Wiener Hof.* Frankfurt am Main: Peter Lang, 2001.
Simon, Éva Sz. *A hódoltságon kívüli "hódoltság": Oszmán terjeszkedés a Délnyugat-Dunántúlon a 16. század második felében* [Ottoman advance in southern Transdanubia in the second half of the sixteenth century]. Budapest: MTA BTK TTI, 2014.
Sinor, Denis. *History of Hungary.* London: George Allen and Unwin, 1959. Reprint ed., Westport, CT: Greenwood, 1976.
Soltész, Ferenc Gábor, Csaba Tóth, and Géza Pálffy. *Coronatio Hungarica in Nummis: Medals and Jetons from Hungarian Royal Coronations (1508–1916).* Budapest: HAS RCH, Institute of History, 2019.
Spannenberger, Norbert, and Szabolcs Varga, eds. *Ein Raum im Wandel: Die osmanisch-habsburgische Grenzregion vom 16. bis zum 18. Jahrhundert.* Stuttgart: Franz Steiner, 2014.
Sperl, Karin, Martin Scheutz, and Arno Strohmeyer, eds. *Die Schlacht von Mogersdorf/St. Gotthard und der Friede von Eisenburg/Vasvár: Rahmenbedingungen, Akteure, Auswirkungen und Rezeption eines europäischen Ereignisses.* Eisenstadt: Amt der Burgenländischen Landesregierung, 2016.
Spielman, John P[hilip]. *The City and the Crown: Vienna and the Imperial Court, 1600–1740.* West Lafayette, IN: Purdue University Press, 1993.
———. *Leopold I of Austria.* London: Thames and Hudson, 1977.
Štefanec, Nataša. *Država ili ne: Ustroj Vojne krajine 1578. godina i hrvatsko-slavonski staleži u regionalnoj obrani i politici* [State or not: The organization of the military border in 1578 and the Croatian-Slavonian estates in regional defense and politics]. Zagreb: Srednja Europa, 2011.
Storrs, Christopher, ed. *The Fiscal-Military State in Eighteenth-Century Europe: Essays in Honour of P. G. M. Dickson.* Burlington, VT: Ashgate, 2009.
Strohmeyer, Arno. *Konfessionskonflikt und Herrschaftsordnung: Widerstandsrecht bei den österreichischen Ständen (1550–1650).* Mainz: Philipp von Zabern, 2006.

Strohmeyer, Arno, Norbert Spannenberger, and Robert Pech, eds. *Frieden und Konfliktmanagement in interkulturellen Räumen: Das Osmanische Reich und die Habsburgermonarchie in der Frühen Neuzeit*. Stuttgart: Franz Steiner, 2013.

Sudár, Balázs. *Dzsámik és mecsetek a hódolt Magyarországon* [Djamis and mosques in Ottoman Hungary]. Budapest: MTA BTK TTI, 2014.

Sugar, Peter F., Péter Hanák, and Tibor Frank, eds. *A History of Hungary*. Bloomington: Indiana University Press, 1990.

Szabó, András, ed. *Iter Germanicum: Deutschland und die Ungarländische Reformierte Kirche im 16–17. Jahrhundert*. Budapest: Kálvin Kiadó, 1999.

———. *Respublica litteraria: Irodalom- és művelődéstörténeti tanulmányok a késő humanizmus koráról* [*Respublica litteraria*: Studies in the history of literature and culture in the age of the late humanism]. Budapest: Balassi Kiadó, 1999.

Szabó, Irén, ed. *Katolikus megújulás Északkelet-Magyarországon* [Catholic renewal in northeastern Hungary]. Sárospatak: Római Katolikus Egyházi Gyűjtemény, 2014.

Szabó, István. *Ungarisches Volk: Geschichte und Wandlungen*. Budapest: Verlaganstalt Danubia, 1944.

Szabó, János B. *Erdély tragédiája 1657–1662* [Tragedy of Transylvania, 1657–1662]. Budapest: Corvina Kiadó, 2019.

Szabó, János B., and Ferenc Tóth. *Mohács (1526): Soliman le Magnifique prend pied en Europe centrale*. Paris: Economica, 2009.

Szádeczky, Lajos. *Báthory István lengyel királlyá választása, 1574–1576* [The election of Stephen Báthory as king of Poland, 1574–1576]. Budapest: MTA, 1887.

Szakály, Ferenc. *Gazdasági és társadalmi változások a török hódítás árnyékában* [Economic and social changes in the shadow of the Ottoman conquest]. Budapest: MTA TTI, 1994.

———. *Hungaria eliberata: Die Rückeroberung von Buda im Jahr 1686 und Ungarns Befreiung von der Osmanenherrschaft (1683–1718)*. Budapest: Corvina Kiadó, 1986.

———. *Lodovico Gritti in Hungary 1529–1534: A Historical Insight into the Beginnings of Turco-Habsburgian Rivalry*. Budapest: Akadémiai Kiadó, 1995.

———. *Magyar adóztatás a török hódoltságban* [Hungarian taxation in Ottoman Hungary]. Budapest: Akadémiai Kiadó, 1981.

———. *Magyar intézmények a török hódoltságban* [Hungarian institutions in Ottoman Hungary]. Budapest: MTA TTI, 1997.

———. *Mezőváros és reformáció (Tanulmányok a korai magyar polgárosodás kérdéséhez)* [The market town and the Reformation: Studies in early Hungarian embourgeoisement]. Budapest: Balassi Kiadó, 1995.

———. *Parasztvármegyék a XVII. és XVIII. században* [Peasant counties in the seventeenth and eighteenth centuries]. Budapest: Akadémiai Kiadó, 1969.

———. *Virágkor és hanyatlás 1440–1711* [Heyday and decline, 1440–1711]. 2nd ed. Budapest: História Alapítvány, 2006.

Szalay, László. *Magyarország története* [History of Hungary]. 6 vols. Lipcse: Geibel, 1852–1859.

———. *Válogatott történeti tanulmányok* [Selected historical studies]. Edited by István Soós. Budapest: Osiris Kiadó, 2000.

Szántó, Imre. *Küzdelem a török terjeszkedés ellen Magyarországon: Az 1551–52. évi várháborúk* [The struggle against Ottoman expansion in Hungary: The fortress wars of 1551–1552]. Budapest: Akadémiai Kiadó, 1985.

Szathmári, István. *Régi nyelvtanaink és egységesülő irodalmi nyelvük* [Our Old Hungarian grammars and our unifying literary language]. Budapest: Akadémiai Kiadó, 1968.

Szathmáry, Tibor. *Descriptio Hungariae: Magyarország és Erdély nyomtatott térképei 1477–1600* [*Descriptio Hungariae*: Printed maps of Hungary and Transylvania, 1477–1600]. Fusignano: Grafiche Morandi, 1987.

Székely, György. *La Hongrie et la domination ottomane (XVe–XVIIe siècles)*. Budapest: Akadémiai Kiadó. 1975.

Székely, György, and Erik Fügedi, eds. *La Renaissance et la Réformation en Pologne et en Hongrie*. Budapest: Akadémiai Kiadó, 1963.

Szekfű, Gyula. *Magyar történet* [Hungarian History]. Vols. 3–4. 2nd ed. Budapest: Magyar Királyi Egyetemi Nyomda, 1935.

Szentpétery, József, ed. *Cross and Crescent (1526–1699): The Turkish Age in Hungary*. CD-ROM. Budapest: Enciklopédia Humana Egyesület, 1999.

Szijártó, M. István. *A diéta: A magyar rendek és az országgyűlés 1708–1792* [The diet: The Hungarian estates and the Parliament, 1708–1792]. 2nd ed. Keszthely: Balaton Akadémia, 2010.
———, ed. *Az indigenák* [The "indigenae"]. Budapest: ELTE Eötvös Kiadó, 2017.
———. *Estates and Constitution: The Parliament in Eighteenth Century-Hungary*. New York: Berghahn, 2020.
Szilágyi, Alexander. *Gabriel Bethlen und die schwedische Diplomatie*. Budapest: Kilián, 1882.
Szilágyi, Emőke Rita, ed. *Nicolaus Olahus 450: Proceedings of the International Conference on the 450th Anniversary of Nicolaus Olahus' Death*. Vienna: Institut für Ungarische Geschichtsforschung in Wien, 2019.
Szilágyi, Sándor, ed. *Monumenta comitialia regni Transylvaniae/Erdélyi Országgyűlési Emlékek* [Documents from the Transylvanian diets]. 21 vols. Budapest: MTA, 1875–1898.
Szvák, Gyula, ed. *Magyarország uralkodói* [Rulers of Hungary]. Budapest: Pannonica Kiadó, 2003.
Takáts, Sándor. *Rajzok a török világból* [Sketches from the Turkish era]. 3 vols. Budapest: MTA, 1915–1917.
Tamás, Edit. *The Glorious Era of the Rákóczis: Guide to the Permanent Exhibition of the Rákóczi Museum of the Hungarian National Museum*. Edited by János Pintér. Sárospatak: HNM, 2004.
Tapié, Victor-Lucien. *The Rise and Fall of the Habsburg Monarchy*. New York: Praeger, 1971.
Tardy, Lajos. *Beyond the Ottoman Empire: 14th–16th Century Hungarian Diplomacy in the East*. Szeged: Universitas Szegediensis de Attila József nominata, 1978.
Timon, Ákos. *Ungarische Verfassungs- und Rechtsgeschichte mit Bezug auf die Rechtsentwicklung der westlichen Staaten*. 2nd enlarged ed. Berlin: Puttkammer und Mühlbrecht, 1909.
Tóth, Endre, and Károly Szelényi. *The Holy Crown of Hungary: Kings and Coronations*. 3rd ed. Budapest: Kossuth Kiadó, 2015.
Tóth, Ferenc, ed. *Correspondance diplomatique relative à la guerre d'indépendance du prince François II Rákóczi (1703–1711)*. Paris: Champion, 2012.
———, ed. *Journal des campagnes du duc Charles V de Lorraine*. Paris: Champion, 2017.
———, ed. *Raimondo Montecuccoli: Mémoires ou Principes de l'art militaire en général 1712*. Paris: Institut de Stratégie Comparée, 2017.
———. *Saint-Gotthard, 1664: Une bataille européenne*. Panazol: Lavauzelle, 2007.
Tóth, Ferenc, and Balázs Zágorhidi Czigány, eds. *A szentgotthárdi csata és a vasvári béke: Oszmán terjeszkedés—európai összefogás* [The Battle of Szentgotthárd and the Peace Treaty of Vasvár: Ottoman advance—European collaboration]. Budapest: MTA BTK, 2017.
Tóth, Gergely, ed. *Clio inter arma: Tanulmányok a 16–18. századi magyarországi történetírásról* [*Clio inter arma*: Studies in the Hungarian historiography of the sixteenth to eighteenth centuries]. Budapest: MTA BTK TTI, 2014.
Tóth, István György, ed. *A Concise History of Hungary: The History of Hungary from the Early Middle Ages to the Present*. Budapest: Corvina Books, 2005.
———. *Három ország—egy haza* [Three states, one country]. Budapest: ADAMS Kiadó, 1992.
———. *Literacy and Written Culture in Early Modern Central Europe*. Budapest: CEU Press, 2002.
———. *Politique et religion dans la Hongrie du XVIIe siècle: Lettres des missionnaires de la Propaganda Fide*. Paris: Champion, 2004.
Tóth, Sándor László. *A mezőkeresztesi csata és a tizenöt éves háború* [The Battle of Mezőkeresztes and the Fifteen Years' War]. Szeged: Belvedere, 2000.
Tózsa-Rigó, Attila. *A dunai térség szerepe a kora újkori Közép-Európa gazdasági rendszerében: Délnémet, osztrák, (cseh-)morva és nyugat-magyarországi városok üzleti és társadalmi hálózatai* [The place of the Danube region in the economic system of Central Europe: Economic and social connections of the South-German, Austrian, Bohemian-Moravian, and West-Hungarian cities]. Miskolc: Miskolci Egyetem, 2014.
Tracy, James D. *Balkan Wars: Habsburg Croatia, Ottoman Bosnia, and Venetian Dalmatia, 1499–1617*. Lanham: Rowman and Littlefield, 2016.
Trencsényi, Balázs, and Márton Zászkaliczky, eds. *Whose Love of Which Country? Composite States, National Histories and Patriotic Discourses in Early Modern East Central Europe*. Leiden: Brill, 2010.
Trócsányi, Zsolt. *Erdély központi kormányzata 1540–1690* [The central government of Transylvania, 1540–1690]. Budapest: Akadémiai Kiadó, 1980.
Tusor, Péter. *Magyar történeti kutatások a Vatikánban* [Hungarian historical research at the Vatican]. Budapest: PPKE Egyháztörténeti Kutatócsoportja, 2004.

———. *Pázmány, a jezsuita érsek: Kinevezésének története, 1615–1616 (Mikropolitikai tanulmány)* [Pázmány, the Jesuit prelate: His appointment as primate of Hungary, 1615–1616 (a micropolitical study)]. Budapest: MTA-PPKE 'Lendület' Egyháztörténeti Kutatócsoport, 2016.

———. *Purpura Pannonica: Az esztergomi "bíborosi szék" kialakulásának előzményei a 17. században* [Purpura Pannonica: The "Cardinalitial See" of Strigonium and its antecedents in the seventeenth century]. Budapest: PPKE Egyháztörténeti Kutatócsoportja, 2005.

Újváry, Zsuzsanna J., ed. *Batthyány I. Ádám és köre* [Ádám Batthyány and his circle]. Piliscsaba: PPKE Bölcsészettudományi Kar, 2013.

Varga, J. János. *Válaszúton: Thököly Imre és Magyarország 1682–1684-ben* [At the crossroads: Imre Thököly and Hungary, 1682–1684]. Budapest: MTA TTI, 2007.

Varga, J. János, and János Kalmár, eds. *Einrichtungswerk des Königreichs Hungarn (1688–1690)*. Stuttgart: Franz Steiner, 2010.

Varga, Katalin S. *Az 1674-es gályarabper jegyzőkönyve: Textus és értelmezés* [The protocol of the galley-slave trial of 1674: Text and interpretation]. Budapest: Universitas Kiadó, 2008.

Varga, Szabolcs. *Europe's Leonidas: Miklós Zrínyi, Defender of Szigetvár (1508–1566)*. Budapest: HAS RCH, 2016.

Varga, Szabolcs, and Lázár Vértesi, eds. *Egyházi társadalom a Magyar Királyságban a 16. században* [Ecclesiastical society in the Kingdom of Hungary in the sixteenth century]. Pécs: Pécsi Püspöki Hittudományi Főiskola Pécsi Egyháztörténeti Intézet, 2017.

———, eds. *Katolikus egyházi társadalom a Magyar Királyságban a 17. században* [Catholic ecclesiastical society in the Kingdom of Hungary in the seventeenth century]. Pécs: Történészcéh Egyesület, 2018.

Varjas, Béla. *A magyar reneszánsz irodalom társadalmi gyökerei* [The social roots of Hungarian Renaissance literature]. Budapest: Akadémiai Kiadó, 1982.

Várkonyi, Ágnes R. *A Királyi Magyarország 1541–1686* [Royal Hungary, 1541–1686]. Budapest: Vince Kiadó, 1999.

———. *Europica varietas—Hungarica varietas 1526–1762: Selected studies*. Budapest: Akadémiai Kiadó, 2000.

———. *Három évszázad Magyarország történetében 1526–1790* [Three centuries in the history of Hungary, 1526–1790]. Vol. 1, *A megosztottság évszázada 1526–1606* [The century of division, 1526–1606]. Budapest: Korona Kiadó, 1999.

Várkonyi, Ágnes R., and Júlia Székely, eds. *Magyar reneszánsz udvari kultúra* [Hungarian Renaissance court culture]. Budapest: Gondolat Kiadó, 1987.

Vlachovič, Jozef. *Slovenská meď v 16.–17. storočí* [Slovak copper in the sixteenth and seventeenth centuries]. Bratislava: VSAV, 1964.

Vocelka, Karl. *Die politische Propaganda Kaiser Rudolfs II. (1576–1612)*. Vienna: VÖAW, 1981.

———. *Glanz und Untergang der höfischen Welt: Repräsentation, Reform und Reaktion im habsburgeroschen Vielvölkerstaat (1699–1815)*. Vienna: Ueberreuter, 2001.

———. *Rudolf II. und seine Zeit*. Vienna: Böhlau, 1985.

Vocelka, Karl, and Anita Traninger, eds. *Die frühneuzeitliche Residenz (16. bis 18. Jahrhundert)*. Vienna: Böhlau, 2003.

Volkmer, Gerald. *Siebenbürgen zwischen Habsburgermonarchie und Osmanischem Reich: Völkerrechtliche Stellung und Völkerrechtspraxis eines ostmitteleuropäischen Fürstentums 1541–1699*. Munich: de Gruyter, 2015.

Westermann, Ekkehard, ed. *Internationaler Ochsenhandel (1350–1750): Akten des 7th International Economic History Congress Edinburgh 1978*. Stuttgart: Klett-Cotta, 1979.

Wilson, Peter H. *Europe's Tragedy: A New History of the Thirty Years War*. London: Penguin, 2010.

Winkelbauer, Thomas. *Ständefreiheit und Fürstenmacht: Länder und Untertanen des Hauses Habsburg im konfessionellen Zeitalter (1526–1699)*. 2 vols. Vienna: Ueberreuter, 2003.

Zachar, József. *Habsburg-uralom, állandó hadsereg és magyarság 1683–1792* [Habsburg rule, standing army, and the Hungarians, 1683–1792]. Budapest: Zrínyi Kiadó, 2004.

Zimányi, Vera. *Economy and Society in Sixteenth and Seventeenth Century Hungary (1526–1650)*. Budapest: Akadémiai Kiadó, 1987.

———, ed. *La Pologne et la Hongrie aux XVIe-XVIIIe siècle: Actes de colloque polono-hongrois, Budapest 15–16 octobre 1976*. Budapest: Akadémiai Kiadó, 1981.

———, ed. *Óra, szablya, nyoszolya: Életmód és anyagi kultúra a 17–18. századi Magyarországon* [Clock, saber, bed: Everyday life and material culture in seventeenth- and eighteenth-century Hungary]. Budapest: MTA TTI, 1994.

———, ed. *Studien zur deutschen und ungarischen Wirtschaftsentwicklung (16.–20. Jahrhundert)*. Budapest: Akadémiai Kiadó, 1985.

Zombori, István, ed. *Az értelmiség Magyarországon a 16.–17. században* [The intelligentsia in Hungary in the sixteenth and seventeenth centuries]. Szeged: Csongrád Megyei Múzeumok Igazgatósága, 1988.

———, ed. *Fight against the Turk in Central-Europe in the First Half of the 16th Century*. Budapest: METEM, 2004.

Zombori István, Pál Cséfalvay, and Maria Antonietta De Angelis, eds. *A Thousand Years of Christianity in Hungary / Hungariae Christianae Millennium*. Budapest: Hungarian Catholic Episcopal Conference, 2003.

Zsilinszky, Mihály. *A magyar országgyűlések vallásügyi tárgyalásai a reformátiotól kezdve (1523–1712)* [The debates of the Hungarian diets on religious issues from the Reformation on, 1523–1712]. 4 vols. Budapest: Magyarországi Protestánsegylet, 1880–1897. Reprint ed., Budapest: Históriaantik Könyvkiadó, 2012–2013.

NAMES AND NATIONALITIES INDEX

Numbers in italics refer to illustrations. The index does not include the terms Habsburgs, Hungarians, Germans, *or* Ottomans.

Abádi, Benedek, xxiv, 107
Abbas I, the Great, shah of Persia, 125
Ahmed I, Ottoman sultan, 119, 156, 247
Ahmed II, Ottoman sultan, 247
Ahmed III, Ottoman sultan, 247
Ahmed, Kara, second vizier, xxiv
Ahmed, Köprülüzade Fazıl, grand vizier, xxix, 135, 137, 139
Ahmed, Seydi, beylerbey of Buda, xxix, 133
Alaghy family, 65, 174
　Menyhért, 146, 249
Alapy, Gáspár, 250
Albert II of Habsburg, king of Germany and Hungary, 11, 13
Alexander the Great, 15
Ali, Hadim, beylerbey of Buda, xxiv, 19
Ali, Köse, serdar in Hungary, xxix, 133, 135
Ali, Magyaroglu, beylerbey of Silistra, 156
Alsted, Johann Heinrich, 210
Alvinczi, Péter, 199, 208
Amalie Charlotte, princess of Hessen-Rheinfels, 232
Andrew II, king of Hungary, 242
Andronicus (Parthenius), Tranquillus, 45
Anjou dynasty, 1
Anna of Jagiello, empress and queen of Hungary, 11
Apafi family
　Michael I, prince of Transylvania, xxix–xxx, 135, 161–162, 164, 248
　Michael II, only elected prince of Transylvania, 164, 248
Apáczai Csere, János, 202, 207–208, 210

Apor of Altorja family, 164
　Péter, 155
Apponyi family, 174
Arany, János, 106
Aristotle, 108
Arsenije III Čarnojević, patriarch of Peć, 189

Babenberg dynasty, 11
Bakić, Pavle, 84
Balassi (Balassa) family, 34, 174
　Bálint, xxvi, *100*, 105–106, 208–209
　János, 22
Bánffy from Alsólendva family (in Hungary), 64, 174
　István, 249
　Kristóf, 250
Bánffy from Losonc family (in Transylvania), 164
Baranyai, Decsi János, 102, 108
Barcsay, Ákos (Achatius), prince of Transylvania, xxviii–xxix, 133, 135, 248
Barkóczy family, 174, 226
Basta, Giorgio, xxvi–xxvii, 116, 248
Báthory from Ecsed family, 34, 64
　András Jr., 53, 249–250
　András Sr., 250
　Anna, 94
　István, palatine of Hungary, 31–32, 248–249
　István, chief justice, 115, 249
　Miklós, 249
Báthory from Somlyó family, 159
　Andrew, prince of Transylvania, xvi, 57, 248
　Gabriel, prince of Transylvania, xxvii, 155–156, 248
　Stephen, prince of Transylvania and king of Poland, xxv, 52, 54, 57–58, 78, 97–98, 107, 110, 133, 157, 159, 189, 248

　Sigismund, prince of Transylvania, xxv–xxvi, 53, 55, 57–58, 98, 110, 115–116, 248
　Zsófia, 159
Batthyány family, 34, 64, 66, 83, 86, 103, 144, 147, 164, 169, 174, 181–182, 211, 213, 226
　Ádám I, 180
　Ádám II, 249–250
　Boldizsár, 107, 110
　Ferenc Jr., 146
　Ferenc Sr., 86, 249
Bebek family, 64
Becher, Johann Joachim, *176*, 183
Bekes, Gáspár, xxv, 54, 78
Belgiojoso, Giacomo Barbiano, xxvi, 198
Bercsényi family, 174
　Miklós, 235
Berényi family, 174
Berzeviczy, Márton, 110
Bethlen family, 164, 211
　Gabriel, prince of Transylvania, xxvii–xxviii, 118, 128, 130, 133, 146–147, *154*–159, 162, 164, 167, 174, 202–203, 212–213, 245, 248
　Miklós, historiographer, 210, 216
　Stephen, pretender to the throne, 159
Bèze, Théodore de, 94
Bisterfeld, Johann Heinrich, 210
Blandrata, Giorgio, 94
Block, Benjamin, 213
Blotius, Hugo, 96–97, 109
Bocskai, Stephen, prince of Transylvania and Hungary, xxvi–xxvii, 55, 98, *112*, 114, 116, 118–120, 126, 143–145, 155, 162, 168–170, 198, 203, 248
Bocskay, György, 72
Bogáti Fazakas, Miklós, 103
Bonfini, Antonio, 105, 109

273

Bónis, Ferenc, xxix, 151
Bornemisza (Abstemius), Pál, 108–109, 248
Bornemisza, Péter, 96, 105, 107
Bošić, Radić, 84
Bosnians, 25, 99, 190–191, 193
Bottyán, János (Vak/the Blind), 236
Bruto, Giovanni Michaele, 107
Bullinger, Heinrich, 94

Calvin, John, 94
Caraffa, Antonio, xxx, 164, 203
Carlone, Carlo, 213
Castaldo, Gianbattista, xxiv, 48
Castell family, 76
Catherine of Brandenburg, xxviii, 158, 248
Cedulini, Pietro, 99
Charles I of Anjou, king of Hungary, 242
Charles II of Habsburg, king of Spain, 232
Charles V of Habsburg, emperor, xvii, xxiii, 7, 11, 17–18, 29, 48, 247
Charles VI of Habsburg, emperor, III as king of Hungary, xxxi, 247
Charles X Gustav, king of Sweden, 245
Charles of Lorraine, xxx, 164, *218*, 221
Charles the Brave (the Bold), duke of Burgundy, 11
Choron family, 64
Christian IV, king of Denmark, 128
Christian August of Saxe-Zeitz, archbishop of Esztergom, 251
Clusius, Carolus, 109–110
Comenius (Komenský), Johannes Amos, 210–211
Comuleo, Alessandro, 99
Corvinus, Elias, 109
Croats, 62, 66, 86–88, 96, 136, 146, 169, 190–193, 209, 241–242. *See also Croatia in Place Index*
Csáky family, 147, 174, 213, 226, 235
 István, 249–250
 László, 249
 Mihály, 56
 Zsigmond, 250
Császár, Péter, xxviii
Czibak, Imre, xxiii

Cziráky family, 174
 Mózes, 63
Czobor family, 174, 226

Dávid, Ferenc, 94, 96
Deák family, 226
Dessewffy, János, 250
Dévai Bíró, Mátyás, 93, 102
Dietrichstein, Adam von, 65
Dobó family, 34, 78, 174
 Ferenc, 115
 István, xxiv, 64, 78
Dobokay, Sándor, 98
Dóczy family, 34, 174
 András, 65
Doroshenko, Petro, Cossack ataman (hetman), 137
Dózsa, György, 68, 243
Drágffy family, 64
 Gáspár, 94
Draskovics/Drašković family, 34, 64–65, 147, 174, 213
 György/Juraj, 98, 198, 248, 250
 János /Ivan Jr., palatine, 248–250
 János/Ivan Sr., ban, 250
 Miklós/Nikola, 249
Drugeth de Homonna family, 34, 64, 78, 174
 Bálint, 155, 249
 György, 97, 156, 199, 249
 János, 249
Dudith, András, 97, 107

Elias (Ilie Rareș) II, voivode of Moldavia, 48
Ellebodius, Nicasius, 108, 110
Engel, Pál, 3
Enyedi, György, 94
Erasmus of Rotterdam, 103, 108
Erdődy family, 34, 64–65, 78, 86, 147, 164, 174, 213
 György Jr., 249
 György Sr., 250
 Imre, 250
 Kristóf, 251
 Miklós, 152, 250
 Péter, 250
 Sándor, 251
 Tamás, 250
 Zsigmond, 250
Ernest of Habsburg, archduke, 35, 54
Ernst family, 177

Ernuszt family, 64
Esterházy family, 147, 164, 174, 182, 211, 213
 Antal, 235
 Dániel, 235
 Miklós, xxviii, 97, *142*, 144, 188–189, 212, 248–249
 Pál, xxx, 152, 162, 174, 181, 209, 213, 215, 223, 225, 232, 249
Eugene of Savoy, xxxi, 223
Evliya Çelebi, Ottoman traveler, 191

Fejérkövy, István, 248, 251
Ferdinand I of Habsburg, emperor and king of Hungary, xxiii–xxv, 7, 9, 11, 13, 15, 17–19, 28–29, 31–35, 43–46, 48, 64, 84, 92–93, 97, 109, 247
Ferdinand II of Aragon, king of Castile and Aragon, 11
Ferdinand II of Habsburg, emperor and king of Hungary, xxvii–xxviii, 128, 146, 157, 168, 247
Ferdinand III of Habsburg, emperor and king of Hungary, xxviii, 128, 147, 159, 247
Ferdinand IV of Habsburg, only elected and crowned king of Hungary, xxviii
Ferdinand of Tyrol, archduke, xxiv, 19
Ferenczffy, Lőrinc, 211
Festetics family, 175
Fodor, Pál, 15
Fördős family, 184
Forgách family, 34, 78, 147, 174, 213
 Ádám, 135, 249–250
 Ferenc I, bishop of Várad, 97, 110
 Ferenc II, archbishop of Esztergom, 97, 198–199, 248, 251
 Imre, 96
 Mihály, 97
 Simon I, 35, 64–65, 96
 Simon II, 235
 Zsigmond I, 96
 Zsigmond II, 156, 248–250
Forró, György, 98
Francis I, king of France, 43
Frankopan/Frangepán family, 64, 174
 Franjo/Ferenc, 250

Franjo Krsto/Ferenc Kristóf, xxix, 151
Nikola/Miklós, 250
Frankovith, Gergely, 107
Frederick III of Habsburg, emperor, 11
Frederick V, elector of the Palatinate, king of Bohemia, 128
Fugger family, 76
    Maria, 64

Gálffy, János, 55
Gálszécsi, András, 93
Geizkofler, Zacharias, 188
Geleji Katona, István, 202, 207
Gergei, Albert, 106
Gerendi, Miklós, 250
Ghiczy, András, 155
Ghillány family, 175
Gindly family, 184
Grassalkovich family, 175
Greeks, 181, 183
Gregory XIII, pope, 99
Gritti, Lodovico, xxiii, 45
Guallandro, Matthia, 183
Gustav Adolph, king of Sweden, 128
Gutenberg, Johannes, 92, 106
Gyalui Torda, Zsigmond. *See* Torda, Zsigmond (Gyalui)
Gyöngyösi, István, 208–209, 216
Gyulay, Pál, 53, 55, 110

Haller family, 164
Hardegg, Ferdinand Count of, 198
Harrach, Leonhard IV von, 65
Hasan, Abaza, beylerbey of Aleppo, 133
Hasan, beylerbey of Bosnia, xxv–xxvi, 113
Heltai, Gáspár (German Helth, Kaspar), 102, 105, 107
Henckel family, 177–178
    Lazarus Sr., 76
Henry VIII, king of England, 43
Herbst family, 76
Hierschel, Lazarus, 184
Hocher, Johann Paul, 151
Hoffgreff, Georg, 107
Hoffhalter family
    Raphael, 107
    Rudolf, 107

Hohenlohe, Julius Wolfgang Count of, xxix, 136
Homonnai Drugeth. *See* Drugeth de Homonna
Honterus, Johannes, 93
Hörnigk, Philipp Wilhelm, 183
Horváth of Veglia family, 174
    Gáspár, 251
Horváth-Kissevics family, 174
Hunyadi, Demeter, 94
Huszár, Gál, 93, 96, 107

Ibrahim, Ottoman sultan, 247
Ibrahim, Peçevi, Ottoman historiographer, 121
Ibrahim, Uzun, beylerbey of Buda, 162
Illésházy family, 65, 174
    István, xxvii, 118–119, 144, 248–249
Ilosvai Selymes, Péter, 106
Innocent XI, pope, xxx, 219
Isabella of Castile, queen of Castile, 11
Isabella of Jagiello, queen of Hungary, xxiii–xxv, 45–46, 48, 56
Iskender, beylerbey of Temesvár, 156
Istvánffy family, 65
    Miklós, 64, 109

Jagiello dynasty, 1, 45, 64. *See also individual family member names*
Jews, 74, 181, 183–184, 245
Joanelli family, 177–178
Johanna (Juana) of Spain, the Mad, 11
John (János) I, Szapolyai, king of Hungary, xxiii–xxiv, 17–18, 29, 31, 34, 42–46, 50, 55–57, 64, 84, 92, 115, 118, 150, 234–237, 247
John III, Sobieski, king of Poland, xxx, 137, 139, 219
John George II, elector of Saxony, xxx
John Sigismund (János Zsigmond) II, Szapolyai, only elected king of Hungary, xxiv–xxv, 17–19, 45–46, 48, 53–55, 57, 94, 98, 247–248

Joseph I of Habsburg, emperor and king of Hungary, xxxi, 224, 235, 247
Joseph II of Habsburg, emperor and king of Hungary, 83
Jósika, István, 55
Jurisics, Miklós (Jurišić, Nikola), xxiii

Káldi, György, 200, 208
Kálmáncsehi Sánta, Márton, 94
Kanizsai family, 64
    László, 70
    Orsolya, 64, 70
Karlović, Ivan, 249
Károli, Gáspár, xxv, 102, 208
Károlyi family, 174
    Sándor, 235, 239
Kasim, beylerbey of Buda, 48
Katzianer, Hans, xxiii, 44
Keglevics/Keglević family, 86, 174
    Péter/Petar, 250
Kemény, John (János), prince of Transylvania, xxix, 135, 157–158, 210, 248
Kendeffy family, 189
Kendi, István, 156
Kéry family, 174, 226
    Ferenc, 181
Khevenhüller, Franz Christoph, 204
Kielman, Andreas, 96
Koháry family, 174
    István, 209
Kollonitsch (Kollonich), Leopold, 224–225, 251
Komáromi Csipkés, György, 207–208
Komjáti, Benedek, xxiii, 103, 107
Konsky family, 174
Korlátkövy family, 64
Kovacsóczy, Farkas, 55, 110
Kutassy, János, 248, 251

Łaski, Hieronim(us), 44–45
Lazarus secretarius, 109
Lazius, Wolfgang, *xxii*
Leopold I of Habsburg, emperor and king of Hungary, xxix–xxxi, 133, 135, 137, 139, 148–*149*, 152, 161, 164, 189, 219, 223, 226, 235, 242, 245, 247
Lescalopier, Pierre, 56

Lippay family, 174
    Gáspár, 251
    György, 145, 147, 150, 201, 203, 248, 251
Lipsius, Justus, 97
Liszthy (Listhius) family, 34, 147, 174
    István, 65
    János Jr., 65
    János Sr., 65
Lobkovic, Ladislav Popel z, 65
Lorántffy, Zsuzsanna, 158
Losonczy family, 64
Lósy, Imre, 201, 210, 251
Louis I of Anjou, king of Hungary and Poland, 7
Louis II of Jagiello, king of Hungary and Bohemia, xxiii, 6, 9, 11, 247
Louis XIV (the Great; Sun King), king of France, xxx, 128, 219, 232, 234, 245
Louis of Baden, xxxi, 221
Luther, Martin, 91, 101
Luxembourg dynasty, 1

Macskássi family, 189
Mágochy family, 64, 78, 174
Magyari, István, 68, 208
Majláth family
    Gábor, 65
    István, 65
Manlich family, 76
Manlius, Joannes (Johann), 107
Mantskovit, Bálint, 107
Marsigli (Marsili), Luigi Ferdinando, 223
Mary of Burgundy, 11
Mary of Habsburg/Hungary, queen of Hungary, 11, 108, 248
Martinuzzi, George, Friar, xxiv, 18–19, 45–46, 48, 251
Matthias I Corvinus (Hunyadi), king of Hungary, 31, 105, 108, 157, 209, 241
Matthias I of Habsburg, emperor, II as king of Hungary, xxvi–xxvii, 35, 119, *124*, 126, 128, 143–144, 156, 247
Maximilian I of Habsburg, emperor, 11, 13, 243, 247
Maximilian II Emanuel, elector of Bavaria, 221, 234

Maximilian II of Habsburg, emperor and king of Hungary, xxv, 22, 54, *67*, 87, 98, 247
Maximilian of Habsburg, archduke, xxvi
Medgyesi, Pál, 202, 208
Mednyánszky family, 175
Mehmed III, Ottoman sultan, xxvi, 115, 247
Mehmed IV, Ottoman sultan, 247
Mehmed, Kara, beylerbey of Buda, 139
Mehmed, Köprülü, grand vizier, xxviii, 125, 133
Mehmed, Küçük, beylerbey of Temesvár and Jenő, xxix, 135
Mehmed, Lala, grand vizier, xxvii, 118
Mehmed, Sokollu, beylerbey of Rumelia, 18
Melanchthon, Philipp, 93, 108
Melith family, 174
    Péter, 146
Melius Juhász, Péter, 94, 107
Memi, sanjak-bey of Esztergom, 77
Mérey family, 34
    Mihály, 64
Michael the Brave (Mihai Viteazul), voivode of Wallachia, xxvi, 116, 248
Michael, Simon, 184
Miller, Hans Rudolf, 212
Mircea IV (the Shepherd), voivode of Wallachia, 48
Montecuccoli, Raimondo, xxix, 135, 155
Mossóczy, Zakariás, 109
Murad III, Ottoman sultan, 54, 247
Murad IV, Ottoman sultan, 247
Mustafa I, Ottoman sultan, 247
Mustafa II, Ottoman sultan, xxxi, 223, 247
Mustafa, Kara, grand vizier, xxx, *132*, 139, 219
Mustafa, Köprülüzade Fazıl, grand vizier, 221
Mustafa, Sokollu, beylerbey of Buda, 78

Nádasdy family, 64–66, 78, 86, 103, 147, 174, 182, 211–213
    Ferenc I, 115

Ferenc II, xxix, 145, 149, 150–151, 153, 181, 213–215, 249
Tamás, xxiv, 19, 31, 38, 64, 87, 93, 102–103, 105–106, 212, 248–250
Náprágyi, Demeter, 107
Negroni family, 177
Németh, Jakab, 211
Nenad, Jovan, 84
Nyáry family, 34, 64–65, 174
    István, 146

Oláh, Miklós, xxv, 39, 74, 97, 107–109, 198, 248, 251
Oppenheimer, Samuel, 184
Országh family, 64
    Kristóf, 249
Osman I, Ottoman sultan, 7
Osman II, Ottoman sultan, 247
Österreicher family, 177
Osztrosics (Slovak Ostrošić) family, 63
Ozorai, Imre, 93

Paar family, 146
Palaeologus, Jacob(us), 95
Paler family, 76, 178
Pálffy family, 65, 147, 164, 174, 213, 226
    János, 239, 250
    Miklós, chief justice, 249
    Miklós, general, xxvi, 33–34, 64–65, 77, 116, 120
    Pál, xxviii, 145, 248–249, 251
Pallavicini, Sforza, xxiv, 19
Pálóczy family, 64
Pannonius, Janus, 109
Paradeiser, Georg, 198
Pázmány, Péter, xxvii–xxviii, 58, 97–98, 145, *196*, 199, 201, 208–210, 251
Péchi, Simon, 245
Pekry family, 174
    Lajos, 249
Pemfflinger, Stefan, 250
Pereghy, Albert, 250
Perényi family, 34, 64, 78, 103
    Ferenc, 146
    Gábor, 249–250
    Péter, 45, 48, 93, 107
Pereszlényi, Pál, 208
Pestaluzzi family, 177
Pesti, Gábor, 102–103

Peter the Great, Russian tsar, xxxi, 235
Pétervárady, Balázs, 250
Pethe family
  Márton, 198, 248
  László, 251
Pethő family, 34, 174
  János, 65
Petrőczi (Petrőczy), Kata Szidónia, 216
Petrovics (Petrović), Péter, 18, 48, 93
Philip the Fair (the Handsome), king of Castile, 11
Pietsch family, 177
Pilgram family, 177
Pinelli, Gian Vincenzo, 110
Piscator, Ludwig Philipp, 210
Podmaniczky family, 63
  István, xxiii
Prágai, András, 208
Probst family, 177
Pruskovský, Jiří, 65
Puchheim, Wolfgang von, 78
Purkircher, Georg, 109

Rabutin, Jean Louis, 235
Ráday family, 211
Radéczy, István, 109, 248, 251
Radu X, Şerban, voivode of Wallachia, xxvi, 156
Ragusa, Bonifacio di, 99
Rákóczi family (dynasty), 55, 65, 146, 169, 174, 182, 202, 210–211, 213
  Francis (Ferenc) I, only elected prince of Transylvania, 151, 231, 248
  Francis II, prince of Hungary and Transylvania, xxxi, 2, 167, 170, 174, 204, 215–216, 225, 227, 230–237, 239–240, 248
  George I, prince of Transylvania, xxviii, 128, 130, 133, 146–147, 155, 158–159, 202–203, 208, 212, 231, 248
  George II, prince of Transylvania, xxviii–xxix, 125, 133, 135, 148, 155, 159, 161, 212, 231, 248
  László, Hungarian aristocrat, 153
  Pál, chief justice of Hungary, 249

Sigismund, prince of Transylvania, xxvii, 155, 248
Rascians. See Serbs
Ráttkay (Croatian Rattkay) family, 174
  Juraj, 193
Rauch, Dániel, 180–181
Raveni, Mihály, 86–87
Rehlinger family, 178
Révay family, 34, 211
  Ferenc, 64
  Péter, 145
Rhédey, Francis, prince of Transylvania, 248
Rimay, János, 106, 208
Romanians, 63, 83–84, 96, 107, 120, 186, 188–189, 193, 241, 246
Rota, Martino, 110
Rudolf II of Habsburg, emperor and I as king of Hungary, xxv–xxvii, 35, 115, 118–119, 126, 144, 247
Rueber, Hans, 65, 96
Ruthenians, 84, 193
Ruyter, Michiel de, xxx

Salm und Neuburg family, 64
  Eck, 65
  Julius, 65
  Niklas III, 65
Sambucus, Johannes (Hungarian Zsámboky, János), 60, 62, 67, 105, 109
Saxons (in Hungary and Transylvania), 56–57, 81, 83, 93–94, 105, 107, 156, 181, 189, 235, 245–246
Schönborn, Johann Philipp von, archbishop-elector of Mainz, 245
Schröder, Wilhelm von, 183
Schwarzenberg, Adolf von, xxvi
Schwendi, Lazarus von, 53, 66–67
Selim I, Ottoman sultan, 9, 247
Selim II, Ottoman sultan, xxv, 22, 247
Serbs, 25, 63, 66, 74, 84–85, 87–88, 96, 99, 120, 181, 183, 188–191, 193, 226–227. See also Serbia in Place Index
Serédy family, 64
Serényi family, 147, 174
Sidney, Philip, Sir, 109

Sigismund I of Jagiello, the Old, king of Poland, xxiii, 43
Sigismund III, Wasa, king of Poland, xxv
Sigismund of Luxemburg, emperor and king of Hungary, 7, 31
Sinan, Koca, grand vizier, xxvi, 115, 188
Sinzendorf, Elisabeth von, 65
Slovaks, 63, 84, 94, 96, 193
Souches, Jean Louis Raduit Count de, 136
St. Stephen I, king of Hungary, 3, 22, 56, 241, 243
Statileo, Giovanni, 45
Stöckel, Leonhard, 93
Süleyman I (the Magnificent), Ottoman sultan, xxiii, xxv, 7, 9, *14–15*, 17–19, 22, 29, 43–46, 48, 50, 54, 74, 120, 133, 135, 139, 247
Süleyman II, Ottoman sultan, 247
Süleyman, Sari, grand vizier, xxx
Sully, duke of, Maximilien de Béthune, 148
Svetkovics (Švetković), Katalin, 86
Sylvester, János, xxiv, 102–*104*, 107
Szabó, Máté, 77
Szakmárdy, János (Croatian Zakmardi, Ivan), 191
Szaláházy, Tamás, 31, 248
Szalárdi, János, 210, 213
Szántó Arator, István, 98
Szapáry family, 175
Széchényi family, 175
  György, 251
Széchy family, 174
  György, 146
Szegedi Kis, István, *90*, 94
Szeklers (Székelys), xxvii, 56–57, 83, 96, 157, 189, 245–246
Székely, István, 102
Székely, Moses, only elected prince of Transylvania, xxvi, 55, 99, 248
Szelepchény (Szelepcsényi), György, 152, 203, 249, 251
Szenci Kertész, Ábrahám, 211
Szenci Molnár, Albert, 102–103, 207
Szentgyörgyi-Bazini family, 64
Szentiványi (Szvatojánszky) family, 63
Szikszai Fabricius, Balázs, 102, 108

Szirmay family, 175
Szkhárosi Horvát, András, 93
Sztankováchky, Gáspár, 250
Sztárai, Mihály, 93, 105
Szuhay, István, 198, 251
Szunyogh family, 174

Tardi, György, 103
Telegdy family
    Kata, 106
    Miklós, 105, 107
Teleky family, 211
Teufel family
    Andreas, 96
    Erasmus, 65
Teuffenbach, Christoph von, xxvi
Thököly family, 65, 174, 182
    Imre, prince of Hungary, xxx, 2, 139, 152, 161–162, 164, 166–167, 170, 203–204, 209, 215, 219, 221, 223, 227, 232, 234–235
    Sebestyén, 72, 77
Thomas, Jan, 213, 215
Thuróczy, Benedek, 250
Thury, György, 67
Thurzó family, 34, 64, 76, 78, 174
    Ádám, 201
    Bernát/Bernhard, 65
    Elek, 31–32, 93, 248–250
    Ferenc, 33, 35, 250
    György, 34, 145, 156, 212, 248–249
    Szaniszló, 146, 248–249
Tinódi, Sebestyén, 103, 106
Toldi, Miklós, 106
Tolnai, Máté, 92

Tolnai Dali, János, 202
Torda, Zsigmond (Gyalui/from Gyalu), 108
Tornallyai, Jakab, 45
Torstensson, Lennart, 159
Toygun, beylerbey of Buda, 19
Török family, 174
    Bálint, 45, 48
Tótfalusi Kis, Miklós, 211
Trauttmansdorff, Maximilian von, 204
Trombitás, János, 77–78, 96
Turós, Miklós, 180

Újfalvi, Imre, 201
Újlaky family
    Ferenc, 248
    János, 250
Ungnad von Sonnegg family
    Christoph, 250
    David, 96
Uskoks, 85–86, 88, 168, 246

Várday, Pál, xxiv, 31–32, 248, 251
Vehe-Glirius, Matthias, 96
Verancsics (Croatian Vrančič) family
    Antal/Antun, 109–110, 248, 251
    Faustus, 102
Veterani, Friedrich, xxxi, 223
Viczay family, 174
Vitezović Ritter, Pavao, 193
Vízkelethy family, 174
    Tamás, 251
Vlachs, 25, 85–88, 99, 120, 168, 189–191, 193, 246

Volkra, Otto Christoph, 251
Vörösmarty, Mihály, 106

Wagner family, 76
Wallenstein, Albrecht von, xxviii
Wathay, Ferenc, 106
Weiß family, 76
Werbőczy, István, 45, 62, 107, 246
Wertheimer, Samson, 184
Wesselényi family, 174, 182
    Ferenc, xxix, 145, 149–151, 161, 209, 231, 248–249
Władysław (Vladislav) II of Jagiello, king of Hungary and Bohemia, 11
Wolfart family, 177
Wortley Montague, Lady Mary, 240

Zay, Ferenc, 78
Zichy family, 174, 226
    István Jr., 224
    István Sr., 152, 250–251
Zollikofer family, 177
Zrínyi/Zrinski family, 34, 64–66, 78, 86, 147, 169, 174, 181–182, 211, 213, 244
    György/Juraj Jr., 201, 250
    György/Juraj Sr., 34, 250
    Ilona/Jelena, 232
    Miklós/Nikola, general and poet, xxix, 35, 130, 135–137, 145, 149, 169, 206, 208–209, 250
    Miklós/Nikola, hero of Szigetvár, xxv, 22, 64, 82, 209, 250
    Péter/Petar, ban, xxix, 150–151, 250
Zwingli, Ulrich, 94

PLACE INDEX

Numbers in italics refer to illustrations. The index does not include the terms Asia, Austria, Central Europe, Europe, Habsburg Empire, Habsburg Monarchy, Hungary, *or* Ottoman Empire. *Present locations are indicated by the following abbreviations.*

A = Austria
BG = Bulgaria
BiH = Bosnia and Herzegovina
CH = Switzerland
CZ = Czech Republic
D = Germany
H = Hungary
HR = Croatia
I = Italy
NL = Netherlands
PL = Poland
RO = Romania
RUS = Russia
SK = Slovakia
SLO = Slovenia
SRB = Serbia
TR = Turkey
UA = Ukraine

Aargau (CH), 9
Abaúj county, xxiii, xxviii, 44, 62–63, 157
Abrudbánya (Abrud RO), 57
Adrianople. See Edirne
Adriatic Sea, 22, 38–39, 86, 181, 209, 246
Aegean Sea, 223
Ajnácskő (Hajnáčka SK), xxvi
Aleppo, 133
Álmosd (H), xxvi, 118
Alvinc (Vințu de Jos RO), 212–213
Amsterdam, 178, 211
Anatolia, 22, 125
Andrusovo (RUS), 137
Antwerp, 76, 85, 109
Arad (RO), 235
Aragon, 11
Árva county, 63
Asia Minor, 7, 15
Augsburg (D), 73, 76, 93, 145, 177–178, 211, 213
Auspitz (Hustopeče CZ), 74

Austrian hereditary lands/provinces, xxvii, 36, 221, 246. See also names of individual lands
Azerbaijan, 22
Azov (RUS), 223

Babócsa (H), xxiv, 19
Bačka. See Bácska region
Bács (Bač SRB), 190–191
Bácska region, 190, 235, 241
Baja (H), 190
Bajmóc (Bojnice SK), 216
Bakabánya (Pukanec SK), 78
Balaton lake, xxv, 19
Balázsfalva (Blaj RO), xxx, 164, 213
Balkans, Balkan Peninsula, 7, 9, 15, 17, 22, 25, 44, 85, 99, 136, 168, 190–191, 246
Banat (Hungarian Temesköz), xxxi, 18–19, 25, 48, 84–85, 219, 223, 241, 245
Baranya county, 62, 74, 85, 96, 99, 120, 186, 188, 245
Barcaság (German Burzenland), 161, 164
Barsszentkereszt (Žiar nad Hronom SK), xxx
Bártfa (Bardejov SK), 68, 78, 93, 107, 211
Basel (CH), 109, 210
Bavaria, 74, 139, 180, 234
Bazin (Pezinok SK), 172
Becse (Novi Bečej SRB), 19
Becskerek (Zrenjanin SRB), 19
Bélabánya (Banská Belá SK), 78
Belgrade (Beograd SRB), xxx–xxxi, 9, 26, 74, 189, 191, 221. See also Nándorfehérvár
Bereg county, 63, 119, 157, 193, 227, 232
Berethalom (Biertan RO), 94
Beszterce (Bistrița RO), 74

Besztercebánya (Banská Bystrica SK), xxvii, 76, 78, 158, 178, 210
Bethlenszentmiklós (Sânmiclăuș RO), 212
Bihać (BiH), xxv, 39, 113
Bihar county, xxvi, 119, 156, 169, 189
Black Sea, 223
Blenheim (Höchstädt D), 234
Bohemia, xxiii, xxv, xxvii, 6, 9, 19, 28–29, 31–32, 35–36, 38, 65–66, 73–74, 83–84, 126, 128, 130, 143, 148, 157, 174, 178, 210, 213, 221, 232, 242
Bohemian lands/provinces, 31, 65, 83–84, 178, 221. See also names of individual lands
Borsod county, xxviii, 63, 157
Bosnia, xxv–xxvi, 9, 15, 24–25, 31, 85, 99, 113, 190–191, 193, 245
Böszörmény (Hajdúböszörmény H), 119
Brassó (Brașov RO), xxvi, 57, 74, 93, 108, 181, 211
Bratislava (present SK), xvii, 37, 241. See also Pozsony
Brezan (Berezsani UA), xxxi, 232
Breznóbánya (Brezno SK), 172
Britain, 187, 202, 210, 234
Brünn (Brno CZ), xxviii, 159
Buccari (Bakar HR), xxx, 181
Buda (part of Budapest H), xvii, xxiii–xxiv, xxix–xxx, 13, 15, 17–19, 22, 24–26, 31–33, 36, 44–48, 50, 62, 67, 78–79, 84, 92–93, 103, 107, 115–116, 120, 133, 139, 152, 159, 162, 168, 172, 181, 189–192, 204, 210, 221–222, 225–226, 235, 241–242, 246
Budakalász (H), 189
Budapest (after 1873), xvii, 162, 199
Buják (H), xxvi, 19
Bulgaria, 7, 181, 189, 221
Burgenland, 88

279

Place Index

Burgundy, 11
Bursa (TR), 7
Byzantium (Byzantine Empire), 7

Cambridge, 108, 210
Candia, 137
Carinthia, 11, 38, 85
Carniola, 9, 11, 38, 85–86, 107, 181
Carpathian Basin, 3, 7, 75, 84, 88, 93, 107, 113, 115, 119, 137, 187–188, 224
Castile, 11
Cegléd (H), 79
Černomelj. *See* Tschernembl
Cetin (HR), 86
Cisdanubia (Cis-Danubian area/region), 39, 118, 241
Cluj-Napoca (present), xvii. *See also* Kolozsvár
Cologne (Köln D), 242, 245
Constantinople, 9, 106, 242. *See also* Istanbul
Cracow. *See* Krakow
Crete, 125, 137
Croatia, xvii, xxv–xxvi, xxix, 9, 15, 22, 31–33, 36, 39, 62–64, 74, 85–88, 92, 113, 116, 136, 145–146, 151, 158, 167–169, 174, 190–191, 193, 201, 209, 221, 223, 226, 241, 244–247, 249
Csáktornya (Čakovec HR), 213
Csallóköz region, 76
Csanád
 bishopric, 92
 fortress (Cenad SRB), 19, 92
Csíksomlyó (Şumuleu RO), 92
Csíkszereda (Miercurea Ciuc), 212
Cyprus, 22

Dalmatia, 85, 110, 181, 191, 241, 245
Danube River, xxvi, xxix, 7, 15, 18, 22, 25, 31, 39, 44, 55, 74, 76–77, 84–85, 94, 96, 99, 115, 119–120, 125–126, 135–137, 139, 188–190, 219, 224–226, 234, 239–241, 244
Danzig. *See* Gdańsk
Dardanelles, 133
Debrecen (H), 68, 74, 77, 79, 94, 107–108, 172, 177, 201, 210–211
Denmark, 178
Dés (Dej RO), 57, 202
Detrekő (Plávecké Podhradie SK), 107
Déva (Deva RO), 55, 96

Divény (Divín SK), xxv–xxvi, 116
Dnieper River, 137
Dorog (Hajdúdorog H), 119
Drava River, xxiii, xxix, 15, 19, 85–86, 96, 136, 168, 190–191, 193, 235, 244–245
Drégely (H), xxvi, 19
Dürnkrut (in the Marchfeld, A), 11

Ecsed (Nagyecsed H), 31, 34, 159, 248–250
Edelény (H), xxvii
Edirne (TR), xxiv–xxv, 7, 18, 22, 77, 93, 115, 125, 177
Eger
 bishopric, 109, 248
 fortress (H), xxiv, xxvi, xxx, 19, 24, 64, 78, 115–116, 188, 191, 204, 221, 227
Egypt, 9
Eisenstadt. *See* Kismarton
England, 43, 242
Eperjes (Prešov SK), xxx, 68, 78, 93, 108, 203, 215
Erdőd (Ardud RO), 94
Érsekújvár (Nové Zámky SK), xxvii, xxix–xxx, 39, 77, 135–137, 180, 201, 215, 221
Eszék (Osijek HR), xxiii, xxix, 74, 85, 136
Esztergom (H, German Gran)
 archbishopric, xvii, xxiv–xxv, xxvii–xxviii, 18, 31, 39, 58, 62, 74, 79, 92, 97, 103, 108, 145, 148, 150, 152, 196, 199, 203, 208, 248–249, 251
 fortress (H), xxiv, xxvi, xxx, 18, 22, 77, 79, 115–116, 120, 139, 204, 210, 219

Fehér county, xxvi
Fejér county, 85, 190
Fiume (Rijeka HR), 74
Flanders, 108
Fogaras (Făgăraș RO), xxx, 164, 212–213
Fogarasföld / Fogaras land (Germam Fogaraschland), 161, 188
Fonyód (H), xxv
Forchtenstein. *See* Frakno
Frakno (Forchtenstein A), 213, 215
France, 43, 128, 139, 148, 161, 232, 234–235

Franeker (NL), 210
Frankfurt (am Main), xxiv, 128
Friuli, 11
Fülek (Fiľakovo SK), xxiv, xxvi, xxx, 19, 22, 116, 162

Galgóc (Hlohovec SK), 159
Gálszécs (Sečovce SK), 118
Gara. *See* Gorjani
Garam River, 76, 78, 94, 178
Gdańsk, 76
Germany. *See* Holy Roman Empire
Giurgiu (RO), xxvi, 115
Gorjani (HR), xxiii
Gorizia, 11
Goroszló (Guruslău RO), xxvi
Gömör county, xxviii, 39
Gönc (H), xxv
Grábóc (H), 85
Graz (A), 39, 108, 168, 199, 210
Great (Hungarian) Plain (Hungarian Alföld, Nagy Alföld), 31, 77, 180, 193, 221, 237, 241–243
Grodno (PL), xxv
Güns, xxiii, 7, 17. *See also* Kőszeg
Gyalu (Gilău RO), xxiv, 46
Gyarmat (Balassagyarmat H), 19, 125
Gyergyószárhegy (Lăzarea RO), 212
Gyöngyös (H), 92, 99
Győr
 bisphopric, 199, 248
 city/fortress (H, German Raab), xxvi, 24, 39, 54, 65, 67–68, 74, 79–80, 96, 98, 115–116, 120, 146, 180–181, 183–184, 190, 198–199, 201, 210, 212, 215, 235
Gyula (H), xxv, 19, 24, 62, 221, 224
Gyulafehérvár (Alba Iulia RO), xxv, xxviii, xxxi, 1, 55, 58, 92, 94, 98, 108, 110, 156, 159, 161, 202, 210–213

Habichtsburg (CH), 9
Hadház (Hajdúhadház H), 119
Hajdú county, 119
Halle (D), 210
Hamburg (D), 178
Hátszeg area, 188
Hatvan (H), xxiv, 18, 22
Hegyalja, xxxi, 74, 167, 180, 182, 227
Heidelberg (D), 108, 210
Herborn (D), 210

Hermannstadt. *See* Nagyszeben
Hernád River, 169
Herzegovina, 85, 190, 245
Heves county, 25
Hollókő (H), xxvi, 19
Holy Roman Empire (Old Empire), xvii, xxiv, 7, 11, 18, 28–29, 33, 38, 64, 74, 78, 83, 91, *124*, 126, 128, 178, 183–184, 212–213, 246–247
Homonna (Humenné SK), 199, 202, 210
Hont county, 19
Horvátnádalja (part of Körmend H), 87
Höchstädt. *See* Blenheim
Hunyad county, 189
Hustopeče. *See* Auspitz

Inner Austria, 33, 36, 39
Istanbul, xxiii, xxv, xxvii, 1, 9, 15, 17–18, 43–44, 48, 50, 54–55, 85, 109, 113, 115, 125–126, 135, 147, 150, 155, 157, 159, 162, 213. *See also* Constantinople
Istria, 181
Italy, 29, 31, 38, 43, 73–74, 76, 79, 83, 94, 105, 107–108, 110, 174, 177–178, 180, 182–183, 212
Ivanics (Ivanić-Grad HR), 168
Izbég (part of Szentendre H), 189
Izmit (TR), 164

Jánoshalma (H), 188, 190
Jászberény (H), 92, 99
Jászság, 226, 243
Jena (D), 108, 210
Jenő (Ineu RO), xxix, 22, 116, 135
Jindřichův Hradec (CZ, German Neuhaus), 232

Kahlenberg (near Vienna A), xxx, 139, 219
Kakat (Štúrovo SK), 77
Kálmáncsehi (Kálmáncsa H), 79
Kalocsa (H), 92, 98, 224, 248
Kanizsa (Nagykanizsa H), xxvi, xxix, xxxi, 24, 39, 64, 74, 113, 116–*117*, 136, 144, 198, 221, 224, 227
Kápolna (Căpîlna RO), 56
Kaposvár (H), 19
Kapronca (Koprivnica HR), 168
Kapuvár (H), 64

Karánsebes (Caransebeş RO), 19
Karlobag (HR), 86
Karlóca (Sremski Karlovci SRB), xxxi, 165, 223, 231–232. *See also* Karlowitz
Karlovac. *See* Karlstadt
Karlowitz, xxxi, 165, 223, 231. *See also* Karlóca
Karlstadt (Karlovac HR), 39, 86
Kassa (Košice SK), xxv–xxviii, xxx, 36, 39, 65, 67–68, 74, 77–78, 93, 96, 118, 146, 157–159, 180, 198–199, 202, 210–212
Kecskemét (H), 25, 79
Kékcd (H), 212
Kékkő (Modrý Kameň SK), xxv, 150
Kerelőszentpál (Sânpaul RO), xxv, 54
Késmárk (Kežmarok SK), 172
Királyhágó, 246
Kiskomárom (Zalakomár H), 113, 136, 180
Kiskunhalas (H), 25, 188
Kismarton (Eisenstadt A), 87, 172, 182, 201, 213, 215
Kisszeben (Sabinov SK), 68, 78, 93
Kolozs
  city (Cojocna RO), 57
  county, xxix, 46
Kolozsmonostor (part of Cluj-Napoca RO), 98
Kolozsvár (Cluj-Napoca RO), xvii, xxiv, xxvii, 57, 67, 74, 77, 94, 98, 107–108, 135, *160*–161, 177, 211, 213
Komárom (Komárno SK), 67, 77, 79, 85, 115, 125, 181, 190, 199, 210, 235
Koprivnica. *See* Kapronca
Korotna (Nagybajom H), 19
Korpona (Krupina SK), 172
Kosovo, 96, 189
Kostajnica (Hrvatska Kostajnica HR), *87*
Körmend (H), 87
Körmöcbánya (Kremnica SK), 78, 201
Körös River(s), 96, 169
Körös
  city (Križevci HR), 168
  county, 86, 191, 245
Körösbánya (Baia de Criş RO), 57
Kőszeg (H, German Güns), xxiii, 7, 17, 172, 210, 212

Kővár (Berchezoaia RO), 55, 135
Krakow (PL), xxiii, xxv, 74, 76, 107–108, 210
Kraszna county, xxvi
Križevci. *See* Körös
Kronstadt. *See* Brassó
Kulpa River, 85
Kunság, 226, 242
Küküllő county, xxv, 54
Külső-Szolnok county, 25

Laibach (Ljubljana SLO), 74
Lands of the Bohemian Crown. *See* Bohemian lands/provinces
Légrád (Legrad HR), 74
Leiden (NL), 97, 210
Leitha (Hungarian Lajta) River, 9
Léka (Lockenhaus A), 64, *179*, 213
Lepanto, 22
Léva (Levice SK), 77, 136
Levant, 74, 99, 181
Libeň (part of Prague CZ), xxvii, 126
Libetbánya (Ľubietová SK), 78
Libya, 19
Linz (A), xxviii, 147, 159, 203
Lipótvár (German Leopoldstadt, Leopoldov SK), 235
Lippa (Lipova RO), xxiv, xxvii, 19, 22, 116, 156
Liptó county, 63, 241
Ljubljana. *See* Laibach
Lorettom (Loretto A), 213
Lower Austria, 32–33, 36, 38, 65, 87, 91, 120, 130, 143, 177, 181, 198, 212
Lőcse (Levoča SK), 68, 78, 93, 210, 211, 215
Lugos (Lugoj RO), xxxi, 19, 223

Macedonia, 190
Mád (H), 182
Madrid, 29
Magyarnádalja (H), 87
Magyaróvár (Mosonmagyaróvár H), 74, 115, 180
Mainz (D), 245
Malta, 19
Máramaros county, 63, 188–189, 193
Marchfeld, 11, 87
Maria Ellend (A), 177
Márkusfalva (Markušovce SK), 212
Maros River, xxiv, 62, 96, 189, 226, 241, 244

Marosszereda (Miercurea Nirajului RO), xxvii, 116
Marosvásárhely (Târgu Mureş RO), xxix, xxxi, 102, 108, 161, 237
Medgyes (Mediaş RO), xxiii, xxvii
Medimurje. *See* Muraköz region
Mediterranean, 9, 17, 29, 54, 125
Metlika. *See* Möttling
Mezőkeresztes (H), xxvi, 115
Mezőség, 120, 188
Mezőtúr (H), 79
Mihályi (H), 212
Miriszló (Mirăslău RO), xxvi
Modor (Modra SK), 172
Modrus (Modruš HR), 74
Mogersdorf (A), xxix, 136, 219
Mohács (H), xxiii–xxiv, xxx, 1–3, 5, 9, *10*, 11, 15, 17, 26, 32–33, 35, 44–45, 64–65, 85, 92, 188, 190, 221, 225
Moldavia, Voivodship of, 48, 55, 74, 115, 156–157, 159, 161, 188
Moravia, xxx, 38, 62, 74, 87, 126, 130, 135–136, 143, 174, 182
Morgarten, 11
Möttling (Metlika SLO), 85
Mura River, 135, 169, 244
Muraköz region, 66, 74, 87, 169, 181, 244
Murány (Muráň SK), xxix, 150
Mühlberg (D), 48
Münster (D), 128

Nádalja (Magyarnádalja H), 87
Nagybánya (Baia Mare RO), 57
Nagyenyed (Aiud RO), 79, 94, 161
Nagyharsány (H), xxx, 221
Nagykőrös (H), 25, 79
Nagymaros (H), 79, 96
Nagyszeben (Szeben, Sibiu RO), 57, 74, 164, 181, 211, 213
Nagyszombat (Trnava SK), xxiv, xxviii, 62, 67–68, 77–79, 92, 96–98, 103, 108–109, 120, 156, 198–199, 208, 210–212, 235–236
Nagyszőlős (Seleuş RO), xxix, 135
Nánás (Hajdúnánás H), 119
Nándorfehérvár (Beograd SRB), 9. *See also* Belgrade
Naples, xxx, 11, 221
Nedelic (Nedelišće HR), 74, 107
Németújvár (Güssing A), 87, 103, 110

Netherlands, xxx, 11, 34, 76, 108, 210, 234–235
New Zrínyi Castle (Hungarian Zrínyi-Újvár), xxix, 135–136
Nikolsburg (Mikulov CZ), xxviii, 146, 157, 203
Niš (SRB), 221
Nógrád
 county, 62
 fortress (H), xxiv, xxvi, 18
Novi Sad (SRB), 241
Novo mesto (SLO), 85
Nuremberg (Nürnberg D), xvii, xxix, 73–74, 76, 102, 177, 211, *213–214*
Nyitra
 bishopric, xxiii, 97, 108, 248
 county, 159, 201
 fortress/city (Nitra SK), 97
Nyírbátor (H), xxiv, 19, 48, 79

Offenbánya (Baia de Arieş RO), 57
Ogulin (HR), 86
Olmütz (Olomouc CZ), 43, 210
Olomouc. *See* Olmütz
Ónod (H), xxxi, 234, 237
Oppeln, 48
Osgyán (Ožďany SK), xxvii
Osnabrück (D), 128
Oxford, 108, 210
Ozora (H), 18
Ödenburg. *See* Sopron

Padua (Padova I), 97, 108–110, 210
Pákozd (H), xxvi
Palást (Plášťovce SK), 19
Pannonhalma. *See* Szentmárton
Pápa (H), 24, 79, 108, 115–116, 130, 210, 245
Papacy (Papal State, Holy See), 25, 97, 99, 219, 234
Paris, 109
Párkány (Štúrovo SK), xxix, 77, 135, 139
Partium, xxix, 46, 48, 54–55, 62, 83, 119, 151, 169, 181, 188–189, 235, 241, 244
Passau (D), 145
Peć (present Peja, Kosovo), 96, 189
Pécs
 bishopric, 18, 92, 105
 city, fortress (H), xxiv, 25, 78, 190–191, 204, 210, 221
Peja. *See* Peć

Peloponnesian Peninsula, 223
Persia, 17–19, 22, 54, 113, 116, 125, 191
Pest
 city (part of Budapest H), xxiv, xxvii, 22, 67, 78, 116, 221, 223, 235
 county, 25
Pétervárad (Petrovaradin SRB), 235
Pettau (Ptuj SLO), 74
Podolia, 139, 223
Podolin (Podolínec SK), 201
Poland, xxiii–xxv, xxviii, xxx, 43–44, *52*, 54, 73–74, 83, 98, 118, 125, 133, 137, 139, 170, 180, 223, 232
Polgár (H), 119
Pomáz (H), 189
Porte. *See* Istanbul
Pottendorf (A), 153, 213
Pozsega county, 190, 193, 245
Pozsony (German Pressburg, Bratislava SK)
 castle, xxvii, *37*, 136, 144, *149*, 157, 243
 city, xvii, xxiii–xxv, xxvii–xxxi, 11, 29, 36, *37*, 67–68, 74, 77–79, 87, 92, 96, 98, 103, 108–109, 118, 120, 136, 144, 147, *149*, 152, 170, 182, 198–199, 203–204, 210–211, 224–226, 235, 241
 county, 39, 63, 107, 241
Prague (Praha CZ), xxv, xxvii, 25, 32, 33–36, 61, 74, 77, 110, 115, 118–119, 126, 128, 144, 198, 211, 232, 242–243
Pressburg. *See* Pozsony
Privigye (Prievidza SK), 201, 215
Prussia, 234
Ptuj. *See* Pettau

Raab. *See* Győr
Rába River, 68, 136, 169
Ráckeve (H), 79
Radnót (Iernut RO), 212–213
Ragusa (Dubrovnik HR), 25, 74, 99, 191
Rákos (part of Budapest H)
 brook, 116
 field, xxiv, xxvii, 116
Ratibor, 48
Regéc (H), 159
Regensburg (D), 73, 130, 219, 221
Rhine River, xxx, 74, 137, 219, 221, 245

Rijeka. *See* Fiume
Rinya River, 19
Rohonc (Rechnitz A), 83, 87, 213
Rome (Roma I), 108, 210. *See also* Papacy
Romhány (H), xxvi
Russia, xxx–xxxi, 103, 137, 139, 219, 223, 235
Ruszt (Rust A), 172, 182

Ság (Šahy SK), 19
Sajó River, 169
Sankt Gallen (CH), 177
Sardinia, 11
Sáros county, 193
Sárospatak (H), xxxi, 79, 103, 108, 182, 202, 210–213, 215, 237
Sárvár (H), xxiv, 64, 102–104, 106, 212–213
Sátoraljaújhely (H), 182
Sava (Save) River, 15, 19, 31, 74, 84–85, 189–190, 193, 226, 235, 244–245
Saxon Lands (in Transylvania), 56–57, 81, 83, 93–94, 105, 156, 181, 189, 235, 245–246
Saxonia, xxx, 139
Scandinavia, 96, 187
Schleswig-Holstein, 178
Scotland, 96
Séd River, 201
Sellenberk (German Schellenberg, Şelimbăr RO), xxvi
Selmecbánya (Banská Štiavnica SK), 78, 215
Senj. *See* Zengg
Serbia, xxxi, 7, 9, 15, 24–25, 63, 74, 85, 168, 181, 188–191, 193, 221, 223, 226, 241, 244
Sichelberg (Croatian Žumberak), 85–86
Sicily, 11
Siklós (H), xxiv, 221
Silesia, 48, 74, 182
Silistra (BG), 156
Simánd (Şimand RO), 79
Simontornya (H), 18
Sisak. *See* Sziszek
Slavonia, xxv, xxix, 9, 15, 25, 31, 33, 39, 61, 63, 85–86, 92, 113, 118, 146, 168–169, 180, 189, 191, 193, 199, 201, 221, 223, 241–242, 244–245, 249
Slovakia, xxiv, 37, 76, 241, 245

Slovenia, 85
Slunj (HR), 86
Smolensk (RUS), 137
Solymos (Şoimoş RO), 116
Somlyó (Şimleu Silvaniei RO), xxv, 54–55, 159, 248
Somogy county, 19, 62, 74, 85, 136, 188, 190
Somoskő (Hrad Šomoška SK), xxv–xxvi
Sopron
  city (H, German Ödenburg), xxviii, xxx, 68, 78, 87, 144, 146–147, 151–152, 162, 182, 199, 203, 210, 215, 225, 231, 235, 241–242
  county, 62–63, 215
Sopronkeresztúr (Deutschkreutz A), 213
South Arabia, 17
Spain, 11, 29, 34, 38, 76, 105, 178, 221, 232, 234
Speyer (D), xxv, 54, 66
Strasbourg, 97, 108
Styria, 9, 11, 35, 38, 85–87, 120, 130, 136, 181
Syria, 9, 125
Syrmium (Hungarian Szerém[ség])
  county, 193, 223, 245
  region, 15, 25, 74, 85, 235
Swabia, 74, 245
Sweden, xxv, xxviii, 128, 130, 159, 178, 234–235, 245
Switzerland, 9, 11, 187, 210
Szabadka (Subotica SRB), 190
Szabolcs county, xxvii, 63, 157–158, 169
Szakolca (Skalica SK), 68
Szalánkemén (Stari Slankamen SRB), xxxi, 221
Szalónak (Stadtschlaining A), 83, 87
Szamosújvár (Gherla RO), 55, 135
Szászfenes (Floreşti RO), xxix, 133
Szászrégen (Reghin RO), xxix
Szatmár
  county, 63, 94, 119, 157, 159
  fortress (Satu Mare RO), xxxi, 2, 53, 207, 215, 236, 239
Szeben. *See* Nagyszeben
Szécsény (H), xxvi, xxxi, 19, 237
Szeged (H), 74, 78, 92, 99, 188, 221, 235
Szék (Sic RO), 57
Székelyhíd (Săcueni RO), 135, 137

Székesfehérvár (H, German Stuhlweißenburg), xxiii–xxiv, xxvi, xxx, 11, 18, 22, 29, 219, 221, 242
Szekler Land (Transylvania), 56–57, 83, 96, 157, 189, 245–246
Szekszárd (H), 85, 188
Szentendre (H), 189–190
Szentgotthárd (H), xxix, 136–137, 150, 219
Szentgyörgy (Svätý Jur SK), 172
Szentmárton (Pannonhalma H), 92, 201
Szepes county, 93
Szepesség (Szepes region, German Zips, present Spiš SK), xxxi, 46, 93–94, 107, 201, 245
Szerém(ség). *See* Syrmium
Szerencs (H), xxvii, 116, 182
Szigetvár (H), xxiv–xxv, 19, 21–22, 24, 62, 64, 209, 221, 224
Szikszó (H), 103
Szina (Seňa SK), xxiii, 44
Sziszek (Sisak HR), xxvi, 113
Szoboszló (Hajdúszoboszló H), 119
Szolnok (H), xxiv, 19, 48, 221
Szombathely (H), 201
Szőny (part of Komárom H), 125

Tamási (H), 18
Tarcal (H), 159, 182
Tarnów (PL), xxiii, 44
Tata (H), xxiv, xxvi, 74
Tállya (H), 93, 182
Temes county, 18. *See also* Banat
Temes River, xxiv
Temesköz. *See* Banat
Temesvár (Timişoara RO), xxiv, xxix, 19, 22, 24–25, 74, 135, 156, 191
Thuringia, 182
Tisza River, xxiv, 18, 25, 46, 48, 62, 94, 168, 188–190, 221, 226, 241, 244
Tiszahát, xxxi
Titel (SRB), 188
Tokaj
  district, 74, 76, 182. *See also* Hegyalja
  market town and fortress (H), 43, 159, 182
Tolcsva (H), 182
Toledo, 29

Place Index

Tolna
 market town (H), 79
 county, 74, 85, 120, 190, 224
Torda
 market town (Turda RO), 46, 57, 161
 county, 156
Torna county, xxviii
Trencsén
 city (Trenčín SK), xxxi, 68, 199, 210, 212, 215, 234–237
 county, 63
Transdanubia, xxv–xxvi, xxxi, 18–19, 24–25, 39, 62, 64, 66, 74, 85, 87, 94, 96, 113, 115–116, 118, 136, 146, 152, 169, 188, 190, 199, 210, 212, 236, 245
Transylvania, xvii, xxiii–xxxi, 1–2, 18–19, 38–39, 45–46, 48–50, 52–59, 61, 65, 67, 74, 77–79, 81, 83, 92–94, 96–98, 101–103, 105, 107–108, 110, *112*, 115–116, 118–120, 125–126, 128–130, 133–135, 137, 144–148, 150–151, *154*–162, 164–165, 167, 169–170, 174, 177–178, 180–181, 184, 188–189, 193, 197, 202–204, 207, 210–213, 215, 221, 223, 227, 231–232, 234–237, 239, 241–242, 244–246, 248
Trent (Trento I), 92, 97, 99, 197, 199
Trier (D), 245
Trieste (I), 74
Trnava. See Nagyszombat
Tschernembl (Črnomelj SLO), 85
Tunis, 22
Turkey, 7
Turóc county, 63, 98
Tübingen (D), 108
Tyrol, xxiv, 11, 19

Ugocsa county, 119, 157, 193
Újbánya (Nová Baňa SK), 78
Ukraine, 137, 139
Una River, 87
Ung county, 63, 193
Ungvár (Uzshorod UA), 199, 210, 215

Upper Hungary, xxv–xxvi, xxviii–xxx, 19, 39, 46, 53–54, 66, 78, 93–94, 96–97, 103, 118–119, 135, 144, 146, 151, 156, 158, 162, 167, 169, 172, 177, 198–199, 202, 210, 212, 227, 236, 241
Utrecht (NL), 210

Vác (H), xxiv, 92, 221
Vág River, xxviii, xxx
Vágsellye (Šaľa SK), 98, 198
Valkó county, 190, 193, 245
Vámospércs (H), 119
Várad
 bishopric, 18, 92
 city, fortress (Nagyvárad, Oradea RO), xxiii, xxvii, xxix–xxx, 17, 45–46, 53, 55, 57, 67, 74, 77–78, 96, 98, 108, 133, 137, 155, 159, 164, 177, 180, 211–213, 221, 224, 235
Varasd
 city/fortress (Varaždin HR), 39, 210
 county, 191, 245
Varaždin. See Varasd
Várpalota (H), xxvi, 19, 115
Vas county, xxix, 83, 102, 181
Vasvár (H, German Eisenburg), xxix, 137, 149–150, 152, 231
Venice (Venezia I), xxiii, xxx, 45, 74, 76, 85–86, 125, 133, 159, 168, 181, 209, 213, 219, 223
Veszprém
 bishopric, 92, 97, 108, 201
 county, 245
 fortress/city (H), xxvi, 19, 92, 115, 130
Vidin (BG), 221
Vienna (Wien A), xvii, xxiii–xxv, xxvii–xxxi, 1, 11, 15, 17–19, 22, 25, 29, 31–36, 39, 44, 48, 53–54, 57, 61–62, 64–65, 67, 72–74, 76–77, 79, 85–87, 97, 102–103, 105, 108–110, 115–116, 118–120, 125–126, 128, 135–139, 143–148, 150–152, 155–156, 158, 161–162, 164–165, 168, 177–178, 180–184, 190, 198–200, 203, 208–211, 213, 219, 223–227, 231–232, 235, 237, 239, 242–243, 246
Visegrád (H), xxiv, 18, 96, 221, 243
Vizsoly (H), xxv, 95, 102, 107, 208
Vízakna (Ocna Sibiului RO), 57
Vojvodina (Hungarian Vajdaság), 241
Vöröskő (Červený Kameň SK), 213

Wallachia, Voivodship of, xxvi, 48, 55, 74, 115–116, 155–157, 159, 161, 164, 188, 221
Warsaw (PL), xxxi, 235
Westphalia, 128
White Mountain (Hill), 128
Wiener Neustadt (A), xxiii, xxix, 7, 182, 232
Wittenberg (D), 91–93, 97, 102, 108–109, 208, 210

Yemen, 18

Zagreb
 bishopric, 193, 199
 city (HR), 36, 74, 210
 county, 191, 245
Zala county, 63, 244
Zalatna (Zlatna RO), 57
Zemplén county, 63, 118, 157, 193, 199
Zengg (Senj HR), 74, 86
Zenta (Senta SRB), xxxi, 223
Zernyest (Zărnești RO), 164
Zips. See Szepes region
Znióváralja (Kláštor pod Znievom SK), 98
Zólyom
 city (Zvolen SK), 172
 county, 63
Zombor (Sombor SRB), 190
Zrínyi-Újvár. See New Zrínyi Castle
Zsámbék (H), 62
Zsitva River, xxvii, 119, 125, 155, 177
Zsolna (Žilina SK), 94
Žumberak. See Sichelberg
Zurawno (UA), 139

www.ingramcontent.com/pod-product-compliance
Lightning Source LLC
Chambersburg PA
CBHW041243240426

43668CB00026B/2465